OTHER A TO Z GUIDES FROM
THE SCARECROW PRESS, INC.

205. *The A to Z of Australia* by James C. Docherty, 2010.
206. *The A to Z of Burma (Myanmar)* by Donald M. Seekins, 2010.
207. *The A to Z of the Gulf Arab States* by Malcolm C. Peck, 2010.
208. *The A to Z of India* by Surjit Mansingh, 2010.
209. *The A to Z of Iran* by John H. Lorentz, 2010.
210. *The A to Z of Israel* by Bernard Reich and David H. Goldberg, 2010.
211. *The A to Z of Laos* by Martin Stuart-Fox, 2010.
212. *The A to Z of Malaysia* by Ooi Keat Gin, 2010.
213. *The A to Z of Modern China (1800–1949)* by James Z. Gao, 2010.
214. *The A to Z of the Philippines* by Artemio R. Guillermo and May Kyi Win, 2010.
215. *The A to Z of Taiwan (Republic of China)* by John F. Copper, 2010.
216. *The A to Z of the People's Republic of China* by Lawrence R. Sullivan, 2010.
217. *The A to Z of Vietnam* by Bruce M. Lockhart and William J. Duiker, 2010.
218. *The A to Z of Bosnia and Herzegovina* by Ante Cuvalo, 2010.
219. *The A to Z of Modern Greece* by Dimitris Keridis, 2010.
220. *The A to Z of Austria* by Paula Sutter Fichtner, 2010.
221. *The A to Z of Belarus* by Vitali Silitski and Jan Zaprudnik, 2010.
222. *The A to Z of Belgium* by Robert Stallaerts, 2010.
223. *The A to Z of Bulgaria* by Raymond Detrez, 2010.
224. *The A to Z of Contemporary Germany* by Derek Lewis with Ulrike Zitzlsperger, 2010.
225. *The A to Z of the Contemporary United Kingdom* by Kenneth J. Panton and Keith A. Cowlard, 2010.
226. *The A to Z of Denmark* by Alastair H. Thomas, 2010.
227. *The A to Z of France* by Gino Raymond, 2010.
228. *The A to Z of Georgia* by Alexander Mikaberidze, 2010.
229. *The A to Z of Iceland* by Gudmundur Halfdanarson, 2010.
230. *The A to Z of Latvia* by Andrejs Plakans, 2010.
231. *The A to Z of Modern Italy* by Mark F. Gilbert and K. Robert Nilsson, 2010.
232. *The A to Z of Moldova* by Andrei Brezianu and Vlad Spânu, 2010.
233. *The A to Z of the Netherlands* by Joop W. Koopmans and Arend H. Huussen Jr., 2010.
234. *The A to Z of Norway* by Jan Sjåvik, 2010.
235. *The A to Z of the Republic of Macedonia* by Dimitar Bechev, 2010.
236. *The A to Z of Slovakia* by Stanislav J. Kirschbaum, 2010.
237. *The A to Z of Slovenia* by Leopoldina Plut-Pregelj and Carole Rogel, 2010.
238. *The A to Z of Spain* by Angel Smith, 2010.
239. *The A to Z of Sweden* by Irene Scobbie, 2010.
240. *The A to Z of Turkey* by Metin Heper and Nur Bilge Criss, 2010.
241. *The A to Z of Ukraine* by Zenon E. Kohut, Bohdan Y. Nebesio, and Myroslav Yurkevich, 2010.
242. *The A to Z of Mexico* by Marvin Alisky, 2010.
243. *The A to Z of U.S. Diplomacy from World War I through World War II* by Martin Folly and Niall Palmer, 2010.
244. *The A to Z of Spanish Cinema* by Alberto Mira, 2010.
245. *The A to Z of the Reformation and Counter-Reformation* by Michael Mullett, 2010.

The A to Z of Descartes and Cartesian Philosophy

Roger Ariew
Dennis Des Chene
Douglas M. Jesseph
Tad M. Schmaltz
Theo Verbeek

The A to Z Guide Series, No. 155

THE SCARECROW PRESS, INC.
Lanham • Toronto • Plymouth, UK
2010

Published by Scarecrow Press, Inc.
A wholly owned subsidiary of
The Rowman & Littlefield Publishing Group, Inc.
4501 Forbes Boulevard, Suite 200, Lanham, Maryland 20706
http://www.scarecrowpress.com

Estover Road, Plymouth PL6 7PY, United Kingdom

British Library Cataloguing in Publication Information Available

Library of Congress Cataloging-in-Publication Data

The hardback version of this book was cataloged by the Library of Congress as
follows:

Historical dictionary of Descartes and Cartesian philosophy / Roger Ariew ...
[et al.].
    p. cm. — (Historical dictionaries of religions, philosophies, and movements
; no. 46)
    Includes bibliographical references.
    1. Descartes, Renâe, 1596–1650—Dictionaries. I. Ariew, Roger. II. Series.
B1831.H57 2003
194—dc21   2003012223

ISBN 978-0-8108-7582-1 (pbk.: : alk. paper)

Portrait of Descartes by Frans van Schooten

Contents

Editor's Foreword

Philosophers and philosophies come and go; few have the staying power of René Descartes and Cartesianism. Active, and also path-breaking, during the 17th century, some of this heritage is still useful for the 21st. Admittedly, Descartes's work on mathematics, physics, and other scientific subjects has been largely superceded, although that was once his main claim to fame. But the thought on the human condition, his approach to science and reasoning in general, his meditations on the mind and soul, and even God, remain valid for some and challenging for others. In this more intellectual sphere we are still searching, nearly four centuries later, and if we are closer to the truth than before it is because Descartes and the Cartesians pointed us in the right direction. Moreover, in certain ways most of us, at least indirectly, are their heirs, doubtlessly more so on the European continent than in the Anglo-Saxon countries, let alone further afield, and if we search for traces some are bound to be found.

This *Historical Dictionary of Descartes and Cartesian Philosophy*, as befits a dictionary, includes many entries on Descartes's writings, concepts, and findings. Since it is historical, there are other entries on those who supported him, those who criticized him, those who corrected him, and those who together formed one of the major movements in philosophy: Cartesianism. To better understand the period, there is a brief chronology, and to see how Descartes and Cartesianism fit into the general picture, there is a helpful introduction and a biography. Since everything cannot be summed up in one volume, there is an ample bibliography that directs readers to numerous other sources on issues of particular interest.

This volume was written by five eminent scholars, specialists on Descartes and Cartesianism, whose collective knowledge is very extensive (and is detailed at the end of the book). They are Roger Ariew, who organized and coordinated the project, Dennis Des Chene, Douglas M. Jesseph, Tad M. Schmaltz, and Theo Verbeek. Between them, they have produced an impressive number of books and articles while teaching at notable universities in the United States and Europe. Most important, they cover a wide array of specializations, which is essential to compose a valid picture of a philosopher with so many varied concerns.

Jon Woronoff
Series Editor

Portrait of Descartes by Sébastien Bourdon,
painted in Stockholm a few years after Descartes's death

Preface

We usually divide the history of the philosophical world into periods—Ancient, Medieval, and Modern—and teach Modern Philosophy beginning with René Descartes and ending with Immanuel Kant. The reason for this typically involves a view of Modern Philosophy consisting of two distinct camps: Continental Rationalists (Descartes, Baruch Spinoza, and Gottfried Wilhelm Leibniz), who it is said emphasize reason at the expense of the senses, and British Empiricists (John Locke, George Berkeley, and David Hume), who accentuate the senses after rejecting innate ideas. As we teach him, Descartes, "the father of modern philosophy," breaks with scholasticism and Medieval Philosophy by calling all beliefs into doubt (especially those based on the senses); he seeks to ground all knowledge on the innate ideas he discovers within himself and then reflects upon, beginning with the one he has of himself as a thinking thing (in the *cogito*). The other rationalists follow, trying to come to a clear and distinct conception of their own ideas and to establish knowledge about the world with the same kind of absolute certainty and necessity attainable in mathematics. Locke and the empiricists, in turn, break with the rationalists by rejecting innate ideas, claiming instead that the content of all of our mental states stems from experience, whether through sensation or reflection. The proper task of philosophy becomes the one of analyzing the meaning of the ideas we receive from sensation and reflection and determining what we can come to know about the world on that basis. Given this picture, Kant is then presented as the culminating figure of modern philosophy because of his attempt to synthesize the rationalist and empiricist traditions.

While there is some truth in the simple schema we teach, its greatest deficiency is that it misses too much of the real Descartes. In the 17th century Descartes was known as well, if not more, for his achievements in mathematics, physics, cosmology, physiology, philosophical psychology, and so forth. It would be difficult to overstate the influence of Descartes over practically every aspect of 17th-century thought, even over such far-flung subjects as geology and medicine. Moreover, the followers of Descartes were extraordinarily committed to their master's thought; and anti-Cartesians were just as determined to condemn Cartesianism, to refute it, to be rid of it in any way possible. This strain between the new generation of Cartesian students and the scholastic old-timers is clearly palpable in the description of the Cartesians' behavior, in one of the entries from François Babin's *Journal*, written at the College of Angers in the 1670s and taking the point of view of the anti-Cartesians:

> Young people are no longer taught anything other than to rid themselves of their childhood prejudices and to doubt all things —including whether they themselves exist in the world. They are taught that the soul is a substance whose essence is always to think something; that children think from the time they are in their mothers' bellies, and that when they grow up they have less need of instructors who would teach them what they have never known than of coaches who would have them recall in their minds the ancient ideas of all things, which were created with them. It is no longer fashionable to believe that fire is hot, that marble is hard, that animate bodies sense pain. These truths are too ancient for those who love novelty. . . . They tell us that something does not stop being true in philosophy even though faith and the Catholic religion teach us the contrary—as if the Christian and the philosopher could have been two distinct things. Their boldness is so criminal that it attacks God's power, enclosing him within the limits and the sphere of things he has made, as if creating from nothing would have exhausted his omnipotence. Their doctrine is yet more harmful to sovereigns and monarchs, and tends toward the reversal of the political and civil state.

The tension broke into open intellectual warfare. Cartesians lost many battles: some Cartesian priests were corrected and disciplined by their superior; a few Cartesian professors were expelled from their teaching positions. But they ultimately won the war. Perhaps because of the intense struggle, however, the 17th century was a period rich in debate and remarkable in philosophical doctrine. We hope to be able to impart the flavor of these debates, that is, to say something about the people taking part in them and the doctrines they supported or opposed.

Chronology

1596   René Descartes is born at La Haye in Touraine on March 31.

1597   His mother dies on May 13. His maternal grandmother raises him with his older brother and sister.

1607   He begins his studies at the Jesuit College of La Flèche in Anjou.

1610   Henry IV, King of France and patron of La Flèche, is assassinated. Galileo publishes the *Starry Messenger*, announcing the discovery of Jupiter's satellites.

1611   A commemorative celebration is held at La Flèche on June 4 in honor of Henry IV; students read poems they have written, including one praising Galileo's astronomical discoveries.

1615   Descartes leaves La Flèche, having completed the curriculum, including three years of philosophy and mathematics.

1616   He receives a *license* in canon and civil law from the University of Poitiers in November.

1618   He enlists in the Netherlands in the army of Prince Maurice of Nassau and has a chance encounter with Isaac Beeckman at Breda; he composes his first work, on musical theory, which he dedicates to Beeckman.

1618–48 The Thirty Years' War rages in the German states, with France siding with Protestant forces against Catholic forces supported by Spain.

1619   Descartes travels in Germany and has a series of strange dreams on November 10. He writes in his notebook that the dreams have "set him on the right course of life"; he begins *Rules for the Direction of the Mind*, which he leaves unfinished in 1628.

1620   Descartes seeks out Rosicrucians, including the mathematician Johannes Faulhaber. He writes that he "began to understand the foundations of a wonderful discovery."

1621   Descartes returns to Paris but also takes an extended trip to Italy the next few years (1623-1625).

1624   Trial of the libertine poet Théophile de Viau and condemnation of anti-Aristotelian theses posted by the alchemists and atomists Etienne de Clave, Jean Bitaud, and Antoine Villon.

1627   Descartes meets the founder of the Oratory, Pierre de Bérulle, at the residence of the Papal ambassador during the lecture of an alchemist with whom he openly disputes, giving Descartes the opportunity to display his method.

1628   He leaves for the Netherlands.

1629   He begins a small treatise in metaphysics (now lost) and starts to work on the essays *Meteors* and *Dioptrics* and the treatise *The World*.

1632   Galileo is condemned for defending the motion of the earth.

1633   Descartes stops the publication of *The World* upon hearing of Galileo's condemnation.

1635   He prepares final drafts of the *Meteors* and *Dioptrics* and starts to work on a preface to them. His daughter Francine is born in July and baptized August 7.

1637   Descartes publishes *Discourse on the Method* with *Dioptrics*, *Meteors*, and *Geometry*. He considers publishing objections and replies to the work.

1640   He writes *Meditations on First Philosophy*, which he sends out for objections, and reads scholastic philosophy to be prepared for the onslaught of criticism. Francine dies in September 1640.

1641   He publishes *Meditations on First Philosophy* with sets of *Objections* by Johann de Kater (Caterus), Thomas Hobbes, Antoine Arnauld, Pierre Gassendi, two sets collected by Marin Mersenne, and his *Replies*. He begins work on an exposition of the whole of his philosophy in textbook form.

1642   Descartes publishes the second edition of the *Meditations* with a new set of *Objections* by the Jesuit Pierre Bourdin and his *Replies*, plus the *Letter to Father Dinet.*

1643   The University of Utrecht prohibits the teaching of the new philosophy (reaffirmed in 1645); Descartes starts a correspondence with Princess Elisabeth of Bohemia.

1644   Descartes briefly returns to France for the first time; he publishes *Principles of Philosophy,* which he dedicates to Princess Elisabeth.

1647   He publishes French translations of the *Meditations* and *Principles*, plus *Notes Against a Program*, a critique of a broadsheet written by Henricus Regius, his former disciple. He travels to France for a second time, meeting Pierre Gassendi and Blaise Pascal, among others.

1648   The University of Leyden prohibits the teaching of his works. Descartes's principal correspondent, Marin Mersenne, dies.

1649   At the invitation of Queen Christina, Descartes leaves for Sweden in the autumn. He publishes *Passions of the Soul.*

1650   Descartes dies at Stockholm on February 11. His manuscripts and correspondence are sent to his literary executor Claude Clerselier in Paris.

1659   Jacques Rohault begins his popular conferences on Cartesian natural philosophy in Paris. The conferences continue until his death in 1672.

1663   An edition of Descartes's writings is placed on the *Index of Prohibited Books* in Rome with the note "until corrected."

1667   Descartes's remains are reburied in Paris with great ceremony; the funeral oration of Pierre Lallement is prohibited at the last moment by royal decree.

1671   Louis XIV issues a decree prohibiting the teaching of anti-Aristotelian views at the University of Paris. This decree provides the basis for a decade-long campaign against Cartesianism in French universities and religious orders.

1674–75 The *Search After Truth* of the Oratorian Nicolas Malebranche is published and becomes a major Cartesian text.

1677 Spinoza's *Opera Posthuma*, which includes his *Ethics*, is published.

1680 The *Sentimens de M. Descartes* of Louis La Ville (the Caen Jesuit Le Valois) is published. It charges that Cartesianism supports the Calvinist rejection of transubstantiation. The Cartesian Pierre-Sylvain Régis returns to Paris to publish his *Système de philosophie* and to revive Jacques Rohault's conferences, but the conferences are banned and permission to publish is refused, due to the controversy over transubstantiation.

1689 The critique of Descartes in Pierre-Daniel Huet's *Censura philosophiæ cartesianæ* is published. It draws an immediate response from Cartesians in France, the Netherlands, and the German states.

1691 Adrien Baillet's two-volume biography *Vie de Descartes* is published. The philosophy faculty at the University of Paris is required to sign a formulary condemning a set of Cartesian and Jansenist propositions. The formulary is in place until the end of Louis XIV's reign in 1715.

1699 The Cartesians Nicolas Malebranche and Pierre-Sylvain Régis are admitted to the Paris Académie des sciences. Cartesian natural philosophy begins to predominate in the Académie and in the French universities.

1720 Descartes's writings are officially incorporated into the curriculum at the University of Paris.

Introduction

Descartes: Life and Times

René Descartes, son of Joachim Descartes and Jeanne Brochard, was born in Touraine at La Haye (now known as Descartes) on March 31, 1596. Descartes observed in 1645 that having been "born of a mother who died a few days after my birth of a lung illness caused by some distress, I inherited from her a dry cough and a pale color . . . so that the doctors condemned me to an early death" (AT, vol. IV, pp. 220–21). In fact, his mother died a year after his birth, on May 13, as a result of the birth of another son who lived only a few days (whom Descartes never mentioned). His father, a lawyer and magistrate, remarried around 1600 and had two more children with his second wife. René spent his childhood together with his older siblings, Pierre and Jeanne, at the home of his maternal grandmother, Jeanne Sain. Pierre left home in 1604 to study at the Jesuit institution, the Collège Henri IV, newly established at La Flèche, in Anjou, and René later followed him there, probably in 1607, at Easter. As he reported later in his letter on his birth, René was a sickly child, and his entrance into La Flèche was delayed due to illness. His delicate constitution perhaps explains the report of his biographer Adrien Baillet that, while he was in school, he was regularly allowed to stay in bed until late in the morning. The story is no doubt apocryphal; it is difficult to believe that his Jesuit teachers would have indulged him to this extent. In any event, the evidence indicates that Descartes spent about eight years at La Flèche, until approximately 1615.

The sponsors of La Flèche, the Society of Jesus, was a relatively new Catholic order, founded by Ignatius Loyola in 1540, and dedicated to education. The order had installed themselves in Paris under royal protection in 1561, despite the opposition of the Parlement and the University. However, the Jesuits were expelled from France in 1595, after a Jesuit theology student attempted to assassinate King Henry IV of France. La Flèche was established in 1604 to mark the readmission of the Jesuits into France and their reconciliation with King Henry. After the assassination of Henry in 1610, his heart was taken to La Flèche, where it was interred with great ceremony.

The education at La Flèche reflected the standard Jesuit course of study, consisting of four or five years of French and Latin grammar and a year of rhetoric from Greek and Roman authors, culminating in three years of the philosophy curriculum: logic and ethics; natural philosophy and mathematics; and metaphysics. Philosophical studies at La Flèche followed the model of textbooks written by the Jesuits of the University of Coimbra (for example, Peter Fonseca and the Conimbricenses) or those of the Collegio Romano (for example, Franciscus Toletus). They involved lectures and commentaries on the works of Aristotle, often interpreted in a Thomist fashion, reflecting an eclectic Thomism that had weathered three centuries of commentary and criticism. In 1640 Descartes recalled that 20 years before, in his school days, he had read the textbooks of the Coimbrans, Toletus, and Antonio Rubio, a Jesuit missionary to Mexico (AT, vol. III, p. 185).

Descartes's education at La Flèche can be characterized as progressive. The emphasis of mathematics in their collegiate curriculum was an important innovation. Descartes is even reported to have said in 1646 that he had no other instruction in algebra than his reading of Clavius more than 30 years before—that is, before 1616, when he was a student at La Flèche (AT, vol. IV, pp. 730–31). The Jesuits also seemed to be at the forefront of scientific investigations. For example, a commemorative celebration was held at La Flèche on June 4, 1611, in honor of King Henry, patron of La Flèche. The same year as Henry's assassination, in 1610, Galileo Galilei published in Venice the *Starry Messenger*, announcing the discovery of Jupiter's satellites and suggesting that Nicolas Copernicus was right in placing the sun at the center of the universe and moving the earth around it. For the occasion of the memorial celebration, the students of La Flèche composed and performed verses. One of the poems had the unlikely title "Concerning the Death of King Henry the Great and the Discovery of Some New Planets or Wandering Stars around Jupiter Noted the Previous Year by Galileo, Famous Mathematician of the Grand-Duc of Florence." In the sonnet the reader is treated to the image of the sun taking pity on the sorrow of the French people for the loss of their king, and offering them a new torch, the new stars around Jupiter. The young poet residing in the French Jesuit college was obviously taught about Galileo's experiences in Venice within a year of their dissemination.

After La Flèche, René Descartes, like his father, his older brother, and his younger half brother, studied law and received an advanced degree in canon and civil law from the University of Poitiers in November 1616.

At the age of 21, having gained some independence from his father, Descartes enlisted at Breda, in the Netherlands, as a gentleman soldier in the army of Maurice of Nassau, Prince of Orange, a Protestant ally of France during the war between the Netherlands and Spain. At the time there was a truce in the war, so Descartes did not participate in any military action. The precise nature of Descartes's military duties is unknown; his biographer Baillet suggests that he was attracted by Prince Maurice's ability in the art of fortifications and siege. Prince Maurice liked mathematicians and engineers; he understood fortifications and was known to have invented several mechanisms for fording streams and laying siege to cities. In any case, the army provided Descartes with the opportunity to travel and to study the differences in human societies and values.

While at Breda, on November 10, 1618, Descartes had a chance encounter with Isaac Beeckman, who translated for him into Latin a mathematical problem posted in Dutch. A warm friendship ensued, Descartes demonstrating his mathematical abilities to Beeckman and Beeckman teaching him the application of mathematics to problems of physics: "you alone have roused me from my state of indifference and reawakened the learning that had almost disappeared by then from my memory," he later told Beeckman (AT, vol. X, p. 162). On New Year's eve, Descartes offered him as a gift his first work, a mathematical treatise on musical theory called *Compendium musicae*. He also began writing his thoughts down in a notebook. Beeckman returned to his home in Middelburg, however, and in March 1619, Descartes set off to Germany at the start of the Thirty Years' War, to enlist in the Catholic army of Maximilian of Bavaria, in search of military action.

Descartes seems not to have found any armed combat, but he witnessed the coronation of Emperor Ferdinand II at Frankfurt in the process and met the Rosicrucian mathematician Joannes Faulhaber at Ulm. He spent the winter in the Catholic principality of Neuberg, on the shores of the Danube, in a "stove-heated room," as he described it (AT, vol. VI, p. 11). That winter, "full of enthusiasm," he perceived "the foundations of a wonderful science" (AT, vol. X, p. 189). He recorded that, on the night of November 10, 1619, he had three strange dreams that set him on the right course of life. Baillet re-created the details of these dreams on the basis of documents now lost. In the third and most symbolic of the dreams, Descartes happens upon a dictionary and a book of verse. Opening the latter, he reads the words *quod vitae sectabor iter* (what course of life shall I follow?). According to Baillet, Descartes took these words to indicate that it was time for him to choose what sort of life he would lead, and took the presence of the dictionary to show that "the Spirit of Truth . . . wanted to open to him through this dream the treasurehouse of all of the branches of knowledge" (AT, vol. X, p. 186).

Descartes's own work during this time reflects his concern to explore the treasurehouse of knowledge. He worked, for instance, on the *Mathematical Treasury* of Polybius the Cosmopolitan (a pseudonym he considered adopting) about universal mathematics. Moreover, this seems to be the time that he started his own *Rules for the Direction of the Mind*, a treatise on method in the sciences that he composed in various stages over the course of a decade but abandoned unfinished around 1628.

Descartes wrote most of the *Rules* in Paris, to which he returned sometime in 1621 after having definitively abandoned his military career. There he acquainted himself with Marin Mersenne, an older student from

La Flèche who had joined the Minim order and had established a circle of physicists, mathematicians, and technicians meeting in his cell at the Minims' convent near the Place Royale. Descartes worked with two members of that circle, the mathematician Claude Mydorge and the technician Jean Ferrier, on optics and the construction of lenses. He also took the opportunity to sell the inheritance left to him from his mother's estate, providing himself with a modest income through most of his life, but also losing the title "Seigneur du Perron," which he had adopted in his monogram RSP. Other financial matters required him to take a lengthy trip through Italy (though, apparently, he did not seek out or meet Galileo during his stay). While he was away, Parisians were discussing the trial of the libertine poet Théophile de Viau and the condemnation of 14 anti-Aristotelian theses posted by Etienne de Clave, Jean Bitaud, and Antoine Villon, who were sympathetic to atomism and alchemy. De Viau died shortly after being released from jail, and de Clave and the others were prohibited from defending their theses and exiled from Paris. On his return to Paris in April 1625, Descartes continued his association with the Mersenne circle, including exchanges with the chemist and engineer Etienne de Villebressieur and the mathematician-astrologer Jean-Baptiste Morin. He also frequented literary and theological circles and became friends with the religious apologist Jean de Silhon, the essayist Guez de Balzac, and the Oratorian theologian Guillaume Gibieuf, among others. Together with Mersenne, these became some of his principal correspondents.

Around this same time, Descartes attended a meeting at the residence of the papal ambassador in which a M. de Chandoux, an alchemist, talked about his own new philosophy. Descartes wrote that he used the occasion to correct Chandoux: "I made the whole company acknowledge what the art of reasoning well can do for the mind of those who are only barely clever and how my principles are better established, more true, and more natural than any of the others received up to now by the learned world" (AT, vol. I, p. 213). The large and distinguished audience included Cardinal Pierre de Bérulle, founder of the Oratorians. Following the meeting, according to Descartes, Bérulle granted him a private audience and encouraged him to develop his philosophy as an antidote to atheism. But Paris was not allowing Descartes sufficient uninterrupted time to work on his various projects and even the French countryside did not provide enough peace and quiet. Descartes left for the Netherlands near the end of 1628 and, although he moved frequently, he stayed there for most of the next 20 years (until his disastrous trip to Sweden in 1649), returning for the first time to Paris for a short visit in 1644. In a letter to Balzac, he described the charms of Amsterdam, contrasting it with Paris and the French countryside:

> However accomplished a country home may be . . . the very solitude you hope for is never altogether perfect. . . . It can happen that you

will have a quantity of little neighbors who will bother you at times, and whose visits will be even more bothersome than those you get in Paris. Instead, in this large city where I live, everyone but me is engaged in a trade, and as a result is so attentive to his own profit that I could live my whole life without ever being noticed by anyone. I walk each day amid the bustle of the crowd with as much freedom and tranquility as you could obtain in your country walks, and I pay no more attention to the people I meet than I would to the trees in your woods. (AT, vol. I, p. 203)

As soon as he arrived in the Netherlands, Descartes began a small treatise in metaphysics, now lost; as he said, "the first nine months I was in this country I worked at nothing else." He revealed, in one of the famous letters he wrote to Mersenne on the creation of the eternal truths, that he thought he "found out how one can demonstrate the truths of metaphysics in a way that is more evident than the demonstrations of Geometry"; he claimed that he tried to begin his studies in this way and that he "would never have known how to discover the foundations of physics, if [he] had not sought them by that path"—a path consisting in attempting to know God and the self (AT, vol. I, p. 144).

However, by summer 1629, Descartes became intrigued with the reported phenomenon of multiple suns, and began working on meteorology, optics, and physics. The essays called *Meteors* and *Dioptrics* date from this period, as do the beginnings of *The World* with its lengthy chapter on man (published posthumously as two treatises, that is, *The World or Treatise on Light* and *Treatise on Man*). In 1633, Descartes was preparing *The World* for publication when he heard that the Catholic Church had condemned Galileo for defending the motion of the earth. Descartes stopped the publication of his own treatise that contained the proposition deemed heretical, because, as he said, all the things he explained in his treatise "were so completely dependent on one another, that the knowledge that one of them is false is sufficient for the recognition that all the arguments [he] made use of are worthless." And Descartes added, he "would not for anything in the world maintain [these propositions] against the authority of the Church" (AT, vol. I, p. 285).

Instead, he prepared drafts of the *Dioptrics* and *Meteors*, that is, scientific treatises on less controversial topics, and began to work on a preface linking them together, the successor to something he once called "the history of my mind" (AT, vol. I, p. 570), which became the *Discourse on Method*. At the start of 1636 he added the *Geometry*, as another of the essays appended to the *Discourse* to demonstrate the soundness of his method. The printing of Descartes's first publication was completed in June 1637 and issued anonymously at Leyden; it was entitled *Discourse on the Method for Conducting One's Reason well and for Seeking the Truth in the Sciences, with Dioptrics, Meteors, and Geometry, which are*

Essays of this Method. Also dating from this period is something called the "Treatise on Mechanics," which essentially consists of a few pages appended to one of Descartes's letters to Constantijn Huygens (AT, vol. I, pp. 431–47). These pages might have been part of the larger project of *The World.* Huygens kept asking for "a piece of your *World*" (AT, vol. I, p. 604) and ultimately requested just "three pages of mechanics," saying he was jealous of the gentleman for whom Descartes had written the *Treatise on Music* (AT, vol. I, p. 642). The gentleman, of course, was Beeckman, and the treatise, the *Compendium musicae.*

During his time in the Netherlands, Descartes became reacquainted with Beeckman. However, the two had a serious falling out in 1630, most likely because Descartes was worried that Beeckman would publish his own writings on mathematical physics before he had the chance to publish his own views on natural philosophy. There was a nasty exchange of letters, in which Descartes ridiculed the mild-mannered Beeckman and claimed to have learned nothing from him. By 1634, Descartes and Beeckman had had some sort of reconciliation, but Descartes reacted rather coldly to the news of Beeckman's death in 1637, and continued to belittle his accomplishments. In this whole Beeckman episode, we see Descartes perhaps at his worst.

Even so, Descartes's accomplishments were such that he developed a following in Dutch intellectual circles; among these were the physicians Henricus Reneri and Henricus Regius, the logician Adriaan Heereboord, and the statesman Huygens (father of the polymath Christiaan Huygens). Descartes's relation to Regius was particularly tempestuous. He initially looked upon Regius as the favored disciple, and in 1641 he offered Regius advice for handling a dispute at Utrecht with the orthodox Calvinist theologian Gisbertius Voetius. However, Descartes broke openly with Regius after the latter published his *Fundamenta Physices.* Descartes (unjustly) charged that Regius had plagiarized his own work, but more fundamentally Descartes was disturbed that Regius denied the certainty of particular metaphysical claims, such as the distinction between mind and body, that Descartes himself took to provide the proper foundations for physics. Descartes expressed his reservations in a preface to the 1647 French edition of the *Principles.* Regius responded with a broadsheet that spells out his differences with Descartes, to which Descartes responded at the beginning of 1648 in the *Comments on a Certain Broadsheet.*

In more personal matters, Descartes conceived a daughter, Francine, from a union with a servant named Helene Jans. Francine was born in June or July 1635 and baptized August 7, 1635, as the daughter of "René, son of Joachim." In August 1637 Descartes arranged to have Francine join him as "his niece," and employed her mother Helene as a servant. In 1640 Descartes planned a trip to France with Francine, in order to leave her and her education in the charge of a relative. However, Francine caught scarlet fever and died in September of that year. Descartes learned the next month of the death of his father, about whom it was reported that, because of the publication of the *Discourse*, he had talked about being disappointed in having a son who was ridiculous enough to have himself bound up in calf leather. Descartes's sister Jeanne also died shortly thereafter. When Descartes tried to console a friend for the death of his brother, he told him that he shared his pain and that he was not one of those who thought that tears and sadness were not appropriate for men: "Not long ago I suffered the loss of two people who were very close to me, and I found out that those who wanted to prevent me from being sad only made things worse, whereas I was consoled by the kindness of those whom I saw to be touched by my grief" (AT, vol. III, pp. 278–79). Descartes did not specify which two of the three recent deaths made him sad, but it could be conjectured that he was thinking of his daughter and sister.

Although Descartes published the *Discourse on Method* anonymously, he also insisted on receiving many author's copies as part of the publishing contract; these he sent to people far and wide: close friends, the nobility, Jesuits, and other intellectuals. For example, he indicated in a letter that, of the three copies of the *Discourse* enclosed, one was for the recipient of the letter, another for Cardinal Richelieu, and the third for the king himself (AT, vol. I, p. 387). He even sent the volume to one of his old teachers as a fruit belonging to him, since it was the recipient who sowed its first seeds in his mind (AT, vol. I, p. 383). When Descartes published the *Meditations*, he also published a series of *Objections* and *Replies* to the work. He had hoped to do the same thing previously. In part 6 of the *Discourse*, Descartes had announced: "I shall be very happy if [my writings] are examined, and, in order to have more of an opportunity to do this, I am imploring all who have any objections to make against them to take the trouble to send them to my publisher and, on being advised about them by him, I shall try at the same time to append my reply to the objections; and by this means, seeing both of them together, readers will judge the truth all the more easily" (AT, vol. VI, p. 75). However, his request for objections (and sending out copies) did not succeed as well as he wished. He wrote to Huygens: "As for my book, I do not know what opinion the worldly people will have of it; as for the people of the schools, I understand that they are keeping quiet, and that, displeased with not finding anything in it to grasp in order to exercise their arguments, they are content in saying that, if what is contained in it were true, all their philosophy would have to be false" (AT, vol. II, p. 48). Ultimately, Descartes received a number of responses to the *Discourse*; among them was a critique by Libertius Fromondus, an anti-atomist, and several sets of objections by Plempius, a student of Fromondus, and Jean-Baptiste Morin. Mersenne asked Descartes whether foreigners formulated better objections than the French. He replied that he did not count any of those received as French other than Morin's, and referred to a dispute with Pierre Petit, saying that he did not take Petit seriously but simply mocked him in return. Descartes then listed the objections of the foreigners: Fromondus from Louvain, Plempius, an anonymous Jesuit from Louvain, and someone from The Hague (AT, vol. II, pp. 191–92). Descartes also reported the more hopeful response from someone at his old school: "I have just received a letter from one of the Jesuits at La Flèche; in it I find as much approbation as I would desire from anyone. Thus far he does not find difficulty with anything I wanted to explain, but only with what I did not want to write; as a result, he takes the occasion to request my physics and my metaphysics with great insistence" (AT, vol. II, p. 50). So, to satisfy this and other such demands, Descartes produced his metaphysics. In 1640, he expanded Part IV of the *Discourse* into the *Meditations on First Philosophy* (first published in 1641).

Descartes first sent the manuscript of the *Meditations* to some Dutch friends, who transmitted it to Johan de Kater (or Caterus), a Dutch Catholic theologian. He then appended Caterus's objections and his replies to the manuscript and had Mersenne circulate the whole set to various intellectuals. Mersenne collected objections from Thomas Hobbes, Antoine Arnauld, and Pierre Gassendi and put together two sets out of the objections of various philosophers and theologians. Separately, Descartes became embroiled in a controversy with the Jesuit mathematician Pierre Bourdin. Bourdin sent a set of objections, and Descartes published it with the second edition of the *Meditations* (in 1642). As an appendix to this work, Descartes also published a long letter to Jacques Dinet, Bourdin's superior, complaining about Bourdin's objections. The *Objections* and *Replies* enable one to see genuine philosophical debate conducted on the spot. This is true for the confrontation between Descartes and Caterus's scholasticism. It is also true for Descartes's battle with Hobbesian materialism. Hobbes accepted none of Descartes's arguments and the exchange looks increasingly heated. The best set of objections was, arguably, the one written by Arnauld, at the time a theology doctoral candidate at the University of Paris. In the critical but sympathetic exchange one can see Arnauld's keen analytical mind at work, from his criticism of Descartes's notion of material falsity, to his comments on God as positive cause of himself, to his questioning whether the *Meditations* are circular.

In 1644, Descartes further revised his philosophy into textbook form and disseminated it with his physics as *Principles of Philosophy*. Descartes dedicated the *Principles* to Princess Elisabeth of Bohemia, one of his more important correspondents from their first meeting in 1643 until his death. Interestingly, he wrote the bulk of Part I of the *Principles* at the same time as he was writing his replies to the various objections to the *Meditations*. On December 31, 1640, he said in a letter to Mersenne: "I have resolved to use this year for writing my philosophy in such an order that it can easily be taught. And the first part, which I am now working on, contains almost the same things as the *Meditations* that you have, except that it is in an entirely different style, and that what is said at length in the one is more abridged in the other, and vice versa" (AT, vol. III, p. 276). One of Descartes's more colorful ways of describing the *Principles* is that it would make his *World* speak Latin, that is, with it he would be able to teach his physics to an educated 17th-century international audience: "Perhaps these scholastic wars will cause my *World* to be brought into the world. I believe it would be out already, were it not that I would want first to teach it to speak Latin. I would call it *Summa Philosophiae*, so that it would be more easily introduced into the conversation of the people of the schools, ministers as well as Jesuits, who are now persecuting it and trying to smother it before its birth" (AT, vol. III, p. 523). In keeping with this intent, the *Principles* was often published with the Latin translation of the *Discourse on Method (Specimina philosophiae seu dissertatio de methodo, dioptrice et meteora*, 1644). Together these treatises were responsible for Descartes's considerable international scientific reputation.

Descartes became embroiled in several controversies during the period after the publication of the *Meditations*. In 1643, the academic senate of the University of Utrecht, following the recommendation of its rector, the previously mentioned Gisbertus Voetius, prohibited the teaching of the new philosophy. Here is a portion of the Utrecht edict, as quoted by Descartes himself:

> The professors reject this new philosophy for three reasons. First, it is contrary to the ancient philosophy that universities throughout the world have taught thus far with the greatest success, and it undermines its foundations. Second, it turns away the young from this sound and ancient philosophy and prevents them from reaching the heights of erudition; once they have begun to rely on this so-called philosophy, they are unable to understand the technical terms used in the books of traditional authors and in the lectures and debates of their professors. And, finally, various false and absurd opinions either follow from the new philosophy or can be imprudently deduced from it by the young, opinions that are in conflict with other disciplines and faculties and, above all, with orthodox theology. (AT, vol. VII, p. 592; Descartes replies in AT, vol. VII, pp. 596–98)

The prohibition clearly ran the gamut from pragmatic to pedagogical to doctrinal concerns. Descartes wrote a vehement response to Voetius in 1643, but the city council of Utrecht regarded the letter as defamatory and issued a warrant against Descartes. Descartes sought the protection of the French ambassador against the warrant and the affair abated somewhat. The University of Utrecht reaffirmed its prohibition against the works of Descartes in 1645. Similar troubles arose at the University of Leyden in 1647, which resulted in a prohibition against the teaching of Descartes's works in 1648.

During this same period, Descartes made a few trips to France (1644, 1647, and 1648), the first since his departure to the Netherlands in 1628. During the first two trips he resided with the abbé Claude Picot, who was a member of Mersenne's circle and the future translator of the *Principles*. Descartes was able to review some of Picot's translation as early as 1644 and, in 1646–1647, he made significant corrections to it, including the addition of replies to some objections. Thus, the French translation of the *Principles* ought to be seen as a separate revised edition of the work. Descartes's trips to France allowed him to be reconciled with such critics as Bourdin and Gassendi. They also provided the occasion for him to meet Claude Clerselier, the future translator of the *Objections and Replies* and executor of his literary estate, and Hector-Pierre Chanut, Clerselier's brother-in-law and future French ambassador to Sweden and to the Netherlands.

Descartes began a correspondence with Queen Christina of Sweden through the intermediary of Chanut. Queen Christina invited Descartes to spend the summer of 1649 at Stockholm, but Descartes delayed the visit. He even refused to board the ship the Queen sent for him. Descartes finally departed for Sweden in the fall, after a personal visit from Chanut. During this period Descartes published his final major work on philosophical psychology, the *Passions of the Soul*. In December 1649, Descartes began discussing philosophy with Queen Christina in her palace, at her bidding during the early hours of the morning, around five o'clock. He did not last the winter, catching pneumonia at the beginning of February and dying about a week later.

Descartes was buried in Stockholm; his body was transferred to Paris in 1667 and reburied at the Abbey of Sainte Geneviève with great ceremony. However, the funeral oration by Pierre Lallement was prohibited at the last minute. Descartes's skull was separately sent to Paris and displayed in the Musée de l'Homme (where it still resides, though no longer on display). In 1793, the Revolution had passed an edict transferring his remains to the newly erected Pantheon, but the edict was never carried through. However, Descartes was reburied once more around 1817 in a chapel of the church of Saint-Germain-des-Prés, where he still rests.

Chanut transferred Descartes's literary estate to France. Clerselier received the manuscripts and proceeded to produce various posthumous publications: the *Rules*, *The World*, a three-volume set of *Correspondence*, and various collections and translations of Descartes's works. He also became an advocate of Cartesian philosophy. The larger group around Clerselier wrote various commentaries on Descartes's works. In 1659, Clerselier's son-in-law, Jacques Rohault, began his popular Paris conferences on Cartesian natural philosophy (they continued until his death in 1672). In 1671, Rohault published his *Traité de physique*, a Cartesian physics text that was later translated into English and became part of the English collegiate curriculum. It was the main Cartesian text until Pierre-

Sylvain Régis's *Système de philosophie* (1690) in four volumes. Other Cartesians published important treatises during the 1660s and 1670s: Baruch Spinoza printed a commentary on the first two parts of Descartes's *Principles of Philosophy* in 1663 and Nicolas Malebranche issued a major philosophical treatise, *Search after Truth*, in 1674–75.

Though Cartesianism gained a following during the second half of the 17th century, it also produced a severe backlash. As already indicated, Descartes's philosophy had been condemned in the Netherlands during his own lifetime. However, in the decades following his death it was censured in other parts of Europe. In 1662, Catholics at Louvain condemned various propositions from Descartes concerning the nature of corporeal substance and its qualities. At one point there was the particular charge that Descartes's denial of real accidents conflicts with Catholic teachings concerning the Eucharist. This controversy over Descartes led to an edition of his works being placed on the *Index of Prohibited Books*, albeit only *donec corrigantur* ("until corrected"), by the censors of Rome in 1663. In France, Louis XIV issued an edict against the new philosophy in 1671, and there were renewed condemnations at Angers and Caen during 1675–78. Here again, a main issue was the compatibility of Cartesianism with Church teachings concerning the Eucharist. Another issue, however, was the purported alliance between Cartesianism and Jansenism, the theological movement triggered by the publication of Cornelius Jansenius's *Augustinus* in 1640. Louis came to see both movements as a threat to the stability of the state, and thus in 1678 had the Oratorians condemn "the teaching of Descartes in philosophy and of Jansenius in theology."

The war over Cartesianism intensified with numerous attacks in print, such as Louis de la Ville's *Sentiments de M. Descartes* (1680) and Pierre-Daniel Huet's *Censura philosophiae cartesianae* (1689). Huet's work drew responses from Cartesians across Europe, the most prominent of whom was Régis. The anti-Cartesians also attacked Cartesianism with satire, the most notorious being Gabriel Daniel's *Voyage to the World of Cartesius*.

There was a renewed effort against Cartesianism at the University of Paris in 1691, which lasted until the end of Louis XIV's reign. In 1720, however, Descartes's writings were officially accepted into the curriculum of the University of Paris, due in large part to the efforts of Edmond Pourchot, who was one of the first to introduce Cartesianism into the universities. For a time, Cartesian mechanism even provided a primary source of opposition on the Continent to the appeal to gravitational forces in the work of Sir Isaac Newton. By the middle of the 18th century, however, Newtonianism had for the most part won out over Cartesianism. A widespread view of Descartes during this time was that he had succumbed to the spirit of system.

But even Descartes's opponents could not prevent themselves from showing their admiration in the midst of their criticism. For example, the

Jesuit René Rapin wrote in *Réflexions sur la philosophie* that Descartes "is one of the most extraordinary geniuses of these times. . . . In truth, he teaches one to doubt too much, and that is not a good model for minds who are naturally credulous; however, in the end, he is more original than the others" (p. 366). Perhaps Descartes's legacy can be best encapsulated by a comment from the often critical G. W. Leibniz: "When I think of everything Descartes has said that is beautiful and original, I am more astonished with what he has accomplished than with what he has failed to accomplish" ("Letter to Foucher," in *Leibniz: Philosophical Essays*, p. 2).

The Dictionary

– A –

ABSTRACTION. A common thesis in scholastic theories of the mind was that the intellectual faculty (often called the agent **intellect**) was capable of separating out or abstracting certain contents from perception, thereby framing general notions. Scholastic authors distinguished two kinds of abstraction—*abstractio totius* ("abstraction of the whole") and *abstractio formae* ("abstraction of a form"). The first of these involves abstraction of commonalities from particulars to form general concepts. Thus, by abstracting from individual men, the intellect can frame the general concept "man," abstract further to form the concept "animal," and continue abstracting to arrive at "body," and so forth. The abstraction of a form involves the separation of a **quality** or **quantity** from a body, such as when the three-dimensional figure is mentally separated from the matter of a perceived billiard ball to generate the abstract idea of a mathematical sphere. Descartes accepted the general outlines of this doctrine, and he illustrates it in the Second Meditation when the sensible qualities of the piece of wax are mentally separated to reveal the abstract idea of **extension** as the fundamental concept of body. Descartes's epistemology identifies abstract ideas generated by *abstractio totius* with the "true and immutable **natures**" of things, which he illustrates in the Fifth Meditation by the abstract idea of a triangle which is found innately in the mind and forms the basis for a **demonstration** of its properties (AT, vol. VII, p. 64).

ACCIDENT. *See* SUBSTANCE.

ACQUAVIVA, CLAUDIO (1543–1615). General of the Society of Jesus (1581–1615) at a time when Descartes was a student in a **Jesuit** college. Acquaviva's rule was marked by rapid growth in the Society and in the number of its colleges. Since Ignatius Loyola, founder of the Jesuits, had produced only an outline of the order's intended system of education, Acquaviva resolved to draw up a precise code. As a result, Jesuits undertook extraordinary pedagogical discussions, leading to the publication of their *Ratio studiorum* (principle of studies). As early as 1586 Acquaviva summarized what Jesuits needed to teach and issued a directive that they must ordinarily follow **Aristotle** in philosophy and Thomas Aquinas in theology (see **Thomism**). According to Acquaviva, the primary goal in Jesuit teaching was strengthening the faith. Hence, members of the order were required to teach only what was in conformity with the Catholic Church and received traditions. Jesuits were asked to avoid creating something new or to teach any new doctrine, not to defend any opinion against what most would judge was the common thinking of the theological schools, and not to adopt new opinions or to introduce new questions in matters related to religion.

AIR. *See* ELEMENT.

ALCHEMY. Alchemists were interested in the transmutation of metals, especially that of lead into gold. Some of them claimed that the matter they sought, the "Philosopher's Stone," could heal illness, extend life, and purify and redeem **souls**. They are commonly considered to be an alternative to **Aristotelian** philosophy, but early modern chemists often blended Peripatetic and Paracelsian attitudes together with other older alchemical traditions in unusual ways. Some alchemists explicitly interpreted alchemical texts in **atomistic** fashion; others rejected atoms as ultimate particles or preferred to remain agnostic about them.

Daniel Sennert (1572–1637), a prolific author of works in **natural philosophy**, chemistry, and medicine, provides a good example of a corpuscularian alchemist. In his mature work, he developed the notion that the matter constituting bodies is composed of particles that can be divided again into their original minimal form. Like other chemists, he used alchemical operations to argue that there are "atoms" in **nature**. According to Sennert, if gold and silver are melted together, the atoms of the gold and silver become so intermingled that they cannot be discerned from one another, yet they retain their forms. The experimental evidence he gave for this is the fact that if you put *aqua fortis* on the mass of molten gold and silver, the silver turns into a liquid, but the gold remains in the form of a powder. Sennert's "atoms" were of two kinds: first are the smallest things in nature from which all things are made, that is, the four Aristotelian **elements** of fire, air, water, and earth. He claimed that the particles of fire are the smallest atoms not because there is a limit to their **quantity**, but because there is a limit to their **form**, and argued that this is consistent with the division of the continuum to infinity. The second atoms, which he identified with the principles of the alchemists, are the first mixtures, that is, the second-order corpuscles composed out of the atomic elements. These are rarely divided, but other compound bodies normally resolve into them. Sennert's hierarchy of corpuscles enabled him to recover the alchemical tradition as a middle level theory within an Aristotelian framework of the four elements differentiated at the basic level by their forms.

In *Discourse on Method*, Descartes disparaged alchemy as a false doctrine whose worth he knew well enough not to be deceived by its promises, that is, by "the ruses and boasts of those who profess to know more than they do" (AT, vol. VI, p. 10). However, Descartes studied chemistry as early as 1630 and developed his own views about the entities to which alchemical principles referred. In *Principles of Philosophy* IV, art. 63, he related his three kinds of corpuscles to the three alchemical principles of salt, sulfur, and mercury, and devoted much of that part of the work to his explanations of chemical processes, such as distillation and calcination. *See also* BOYLE, ROBERT; CLAVE, ÉTIENNE DE; NEWTON, ISAAC.

ALGEBRA. The fundamental concept in algebra is the generalization of arithmetical identities to state relationships that hold among all kinds of quantities. The arithmetical fact that $6 \times (5 + 3) = (6 \times 5) + (6 \times 3)$ is an instance of the more general fact that, given any quantities a, b, and c, $a(b + c) = ab + ac$, a result that holds for all numbers or any quantities whatever. The third-century Greek mathematician Diophantus of Alexandria studied general numerical or arithmetical equations and is often credited with being the "father of algebra," but the most important early advances in the subject are due to the ninth-century Arab mathematician Al Khwarizmi. His treatise entitled *Compendium on Calculation by Completion and Balancing* studied the properties of equations and developed solution methods for several forms of quadratic equations (i.e., equations with terms in the second power x^2). Indeed, the term algebra derives from the Arabic *al-jabr*, or "completion," which was a method used by Al Khwarizmi to remove negative terms from an equation.

In the early 12th century the Persian mathematician Omar Khayyam wrote a treatise on algebra based on Euclid's methods in which he identified 25 types of equations and made the first formal distinction between arithmetic (which deals with the properties of integers and fractions) and algebra (whose equations apply to any measurable quantity, commensurable or incommensurable). In the later 12th century Al Khwarizmi's works were translated and became available to Western scholars, principally in Italy. Methods for solving cubic (third degree) equations were discovered about 1515 by the Italian mathematicians Scipione del Ferro, Niccolò Tartaglia, and Gerolamo Cardano, and for the quartic (fourth degree) equation by Ludovico Ferrari about 1545.

By the late 16th century algebra was recognized as an essential branch of **mathematics**. In 1591 **François Viète** published his influential *In artem analyticem isagoge* ("Introduction to the Analytic Art"), which remained the standard work on the subject for decades. Viète conceived of algebra as part of a general method of **analysis**, where the solution to a problem arises by first stating the conditions of solution in the form of an equation, then resolving the equation into more elementary forms or fundamental identities, and finally reversing the course of reasoning to show how the solution can be constructed by **synthesis** from these elementary identities. Viète's successes led some to identify algebra or the "analytic art" with **mathesis universalis**, or the universal method that enables the solution of any mathematical problem, arithmetical or geometrical.

Descartes was highly skilled in algebra, although he was reticent about the sources of his knowledge and admitted only studying the 1608 *Algebra* of **Christopher Clavius**. The fundamental insight in his *Geometry* is that geometric problems can be represented algebraically by first interpreting algebraic operations as geometric constructions and then identifying a curve with an indeterminate equation in two unknowns, represented by the coordinate axes x and y. The third book of the *Geometry* also contains purely algebraic results in the theory of equations, including his so-called rule of signs for determining the number of what Descartes called the "true" (positive) and "false" (negative) roots of an equation. The rule asserts that the number of positive real roots of a polynomial is bounded by the number of "changes of sign" in its coefficients; more specifically, it is equal to the number of changes of sign or is less than this number by a multiple of two (AT, vol. VI, p. 446).

ANALYSIS. A distinction between analytic and synthetic methods has a history in methodology dating back to ancient Greece. **Pappus of Alexandria** defined analysis as "the path from what one is seeking, as if it were established, by way of its consequences, to something that is established by synthesis" (*Mathematical Collection* VII; Pappus, vol. II, p. 635). The basic idea is that analysis starts by assuming the **truth** of the proposition to be demonstrated and "works backward" to find first principles that suffice for its **demonstration**, where synthesis begins with these first principles and derives the desired result. It was also common to mark the distinction in epistemological terms—analysis is the "order of discovery" which indicates how a result is obtained, while synthesis is the "order of demonstration" that shows how it is to be established in a way that proceeds from clearly grasped first **principles**.

In the 16th and 17th centuries the distinction between analytic and synthetic methods became a commonplace and was thought to extend beyond mathematics to encompass all areas of inquiry. In its specifically mathematical usage, analysis came to be identified with **algebra,** largely through the work of **François Viète,** whose *In artem analyticem isagoge* ("Introduction to the Analytic Art," 1591) presented algebraic methods as a method of analysis that could be applied to the solution of any mathematical problem.

Descartes's account of analysis and synthesis is set out most fully in the "Geometrical Appendix" to his reply to the second set of *Objections,* when he complied with the request to present his argument in the style of traditional **geometry,** with the full apparatus of **common notions,** definitions, and postulates. In his prefatory remarks to this appendix, Descartes distinguishes between analysis and synthesis by describing analysis as the kind of reasoning which shows "the true way by means of which the thing in question was discovered methodically, and as it were *a priori*" (AT, vol. VII, p. 155). Synthesis, in contrast, "clearly demonstrates its conclusion in an opposite way, proceeding, as it were, *a posteriori.* . . . It demonstrates the conclusion clearly and employs a long series of definitions, postulates, axioms, theorems, and problems, so that if anyone denies one of the conclusions it can be shown at once that it is contained in what has gone before" (AT, vol. VII, p. 156).

This usage reverses the traditional terminology of *a priori* and *a posteriori* in relation to analysis and synthesis: *a priori* reasoning was usually thought to be synthetic, while analytic reasoning starts with what is sought and works backward in a manner that was traditionally considered *a posteriori.* The point of Descartes's usage here is that, as he conceives of it, analytic reasoning starts "from scratch" by rejecting **preconceived opinions** and seeking out an unshakable foundation upon which to construct a system of knowledge, while synthesis assumes an array of first principles and derives conclusions from them, without calling the principles in question. Analysis is therefore *a priori* in the sense that it must precede a synthetic demonstration and it reveals the steps by which proper first principles are discovered. As Descartes explains, the *Meditations* were presented in an analytic form because "I wanted to make it clear that I would have nothing to do with anyone who was not willing to join me in meditating, and giving the subject matter attentive consideration" (AT, vol. VII, p. 157).

ANGEL. On the traditional **scholastic** position, angels are intellectual substances that are entirely separate from matter, and thus that lack sensory faculties, which depend on the **mind-body union.** In a 1642 letter to **Henricus Regius,** Descartes endorsed the position that any angel in a human body "would not have sensations as we do, but would simply perceive the motions that are caused by external objects" (AT, vol. III,

p. 493), whereas in a 1649 letter to **Henry More**, he claimed that rea-son cannot decide "whether angels are created like minds distinct from bodies, or like minds united to bodies" (AT, vol. V, p. 402). Though he may not have had a settled view on this issue, however, Descartes's re-mark to More reflected his reluctance to follow the scholastics in ad-dressing in detail questions concerning the angelic **nature**.

Some of Descartes's successors did not share in his reluctance. For instance, **Robert Desgabets** and **Pierre-Sylvain Régis** appealed to **Thomistic** angelology in arguing for the conclusion that all of our **thoughts** derive from the **soul**-body union. In particular, they empha-sized the view in Thomas and his followers that human thoughts differ from the purely intellectual thoughts of angels insofar as the former, but not the latter, are governed by a **time** that is tied to **motion**. The ulti-mate target here was the view in Descartes, which other Cartesians such as **Nicolas Malebranche** staunchly defended, that we have a pure **in-tellect** that operates independently of the body.

ANGER. *See* HATE.

ANGERS, COLLEGE OF. An **Oratorian** college founded in 1624 in the town of Angers, on the foundations of the dilapidated Collège d'Anjou. The most noted early Oratorian professors, such as William Chalmers, Jacques Fournenc, and **Jean-Baptiste Duhamel**, taught there. Angers gained notoriety as a hotbed of Cartesian philosophy. In the 1670s four Oratorian professors, including **Bernard Lamy**, were expelled from Angers for teaching Cartesian doctrines. Censors examined the lectures of the Angers Oratorians and objected to a number of propositions they called Cartesian (and that were thus prohibited from being taught in colleges, by royal decree). For example, the censors disapproved of propositions they specifically identified as Cartesian that **real accidents** are not to be distinguished from **substances** and that **transubstantia-tion** can be explained without having recourse to real accidents. Moreover, they objected to the Cartesian doctrine of the **indefiniteness** of the universe and to Cartesian **doubt**.

ANIMAL SPIRITS. In the fourth part of the *Dioptrique*, "on the senses in general" (mostly written before 1629), Descartes makes some points with respect to the relation between **body** and **mind**: 1) awareness be-longs to the **soul**, not to the body, for if the soul is rapt away by a pro-found meditation there is no feeling, even if the body is in a normal condition; 2) the soul is not situated in the organs of perception but in the brain, because if the brain is damaged all feeling disappears even if the other organs remained intact; 3) sensations are transmitted to the brain by the nerves, for if a nerve is damaged, all bodily parts that depend on it are without feeling. In the nerves, however, three different things must be distinguished: 1) their skin, which takes its origin from the membranes enveloping the brain; 2) their "internal substance," which consists of threads running loosely in the nerves, forming a network through the body; 3) the animal spirits "which are like a very subtle air or wind which, coming from the chambers or cavities of the brain, flows into the muscles." Descartes admits that these views are not new, except that others have imagined that there are two types of nerves (one for sensation, the other for motion), which, according to Descartes, is "utterly repugnant to both experience and **reason**," because there is no nerve that does not serve both motion and sensation. His proposal is to explain motion by the spirits, which, "flowing through the nerves and inflating them more or less according as the brain distributes them differently through the body," and feeling by "the small threads that compose the inner substance of the nerves" (AT, vol. VI, p. 110).

All this is also found, in a more elaborate form, in the *Treatise on Man*, where Descartes explains not only the precise **mechanism** of motion, but also the origin of the animal spirits. They are **particles** of the blood so small, subtle, and quick that they have the power to reach the brain, where they serve not only to maintain its substance, but also to produce "a very subtle wind or rather a very lively and pure flame, which is called animal spirits" (AT, vol. XI, p. 129). These are filtered by "a small gland, situated more or less in the middle of the cerebral substance, where the cavities begin" (*ibid.*), that is, by the pineal gland (see **common sense**). They permeate the "pores" of the brain and from there penetrate into the nerves, where they have the power to change the shape of the muscle to which each nerve belongs.

Without the nerves and the animal spirits, all animal motion is impossible and, inversely, no bodily part that can move (muscles but also organs, like the heart, the spleen, and the liver) fails to have a nerve attached to it. According to Descartes, all muscles come in pairs, being connected with each other by some sort of valves. They are completely filled with animal spirits, which is also the reason why they are hard. If one of the muscles is inflated only a little bit more by the influx of new spirits, the other immediately empties itself into the first, without making it possible for the animal spirits to flow back. Swelling shortens the first muscle, which in turn makes the member to which it is attached move. To illustrate the idea that whatever the animal spirits do is the effect of the form and structure of the nervous system, Descartes's model is hydraulic: "Just as in the gardens of our kings, in their grottos and fountains, you may have observed that all you need to move various machines is the power of water" (AT, vol. XI, p. 130). Elsewhere Descartes compares the nervous system with a church organ.

Although there seems to be a clear division of labor between animal spirits and the nervous thread or inner substance of the nerves, animal spirits prove to be indispensable for the explanation of any psychological phenomenon, including **sensation, memory, imagination,** and **passion.** Given the fact that animal spirits completely fill the brain they transmit the stimuli from the end of the nerves to the **pineal gland.** The fact that by their movement animal spirits leave a trace in the cerebral substance explains memory and imagination as well as action and movement insofar as they depend on memory and imagination, such as instinctive behavior, learned behavior, and what we call reflexes. Sleeping and waking are explained by the fact that the animal spirits are respectively "strong" or "weak." Dreams, finally, are the result of the autonomous movement of the spirits, which, given the fact that they are not corrected either by reason or by actual experience, is of course very confused.

The essential thing about animal spirits, generally, is that they are purely corporeal. They are blood, even if they do not have the form of blood. As a result their quality reflects the quality of the blood. In an indirect way, therefore, the spirits are also affected by the quality of the food, the air, the disposition of the various organs, and so forth. This explains much of the passions. If spirits are abundant, they excite the movements of goodness and love; if big and strong, of confidence and courage; if equal in shape, form, and size, of constancy; if quick and mobile, of promptness, diligence, and desire; if equal in movement, of tranquility of mind. Inversely there may be viciousness, inconstancy, timidity, unrest, laziness, if the spirits have the opposite qualities. It is no doubt against this background that we must understand Descartes's remark in the *Discourse* that "even the mind depends so much from the temperament and from the disposition of the bodily organs that if it is at all possible to find something by which to make men more wise and more intelligent than they were until now, it must be sought in medicine" (AT, vol. VI, p. 62).

The general explanation of the *Treatise on Man* was repeated, without substantial change, in the *Discourse*, **Principles, Passions of the Soul,** and **Description of the Human Body.** Descartes's theory of spirits is summarized, systematically presented, and compared to the traditional view in a letter to the Leiden professor of medicine Adolph Vorstius of 19 June 1643. The correspondence does not add very much to this except that in a letter to **Marin Mersenne** of November 13, 1639, Descartes suggests that "the **force** that moves the animal spirits" is in fact subtle matter or ether, that is, the first **element,** which is found everywhere in the material universe. But Descartes rejects the association with Neo-Platonic and Paracelsian ideas.

ANIMALS. Among the more notorious and widely opposed doctrines attributed to Descartes is the denial of animal **souls**. An animal is a machine, an **automaton**. If by soul one means the "principle of life," then, says Descartes, animals can be said to have a soul: namely, the blood or the heat of the **heart**. But an animal has no immaterial soul; nor does it have a soul in the **Aristotelian** sense—no **substantial form** to serve as the principle of vital powers and to give the body its unity as an individual substance. Instead all the movements of animals can be explained by reference to the same principles we use to explain the movements of nonliving things. In the *Treatise on Man* and the *Description of the Human Body*, Descartes sets out to vindicate that claim, and to explain mechanistically all the actions that others had ascribed to souls, excepting only those that indicate the use of **reason**. He opposes himself not only to the Schools but also to authors like **Michel de Montaigne** and **Pierre Charron** who had argued that animals exhibit reason. Gomez Pereira, in a work that received rather little notice in its own time, had argued a similar view in his *Antoniana maragarita* (1554); Descartes, however, denies having read that work.

Descartes's claim about animals comprises two notions: 1) Animals are part of **nature** and have no initiative of their own; 2) given the fact that the essence of the soul, or the **mind**, is to think, the fact that an animal has no soul seems to entail that, although it reacts to stimuli, it has no consciousness and therefore no feelings (like **pain**), bodily sensations (like hunger), or emotions (like **joy** and sadness). Both aspects of this issue are equally represented in Descartes's first discussion of this problem in the *Discourse*. Animals are part of nature, that is, all their behavior can be explained mechanically. Given the fact that the laws of **mechanics** derive from the laws of nature, this means that to explain their behavior there is no need to postulate the intervention of an animal soul. The fact that some of the actions of animals display a certain amount of perfection is, according to Descartes, not an argument against his view, "for whereas **reason** is a universal instrument, which can be used in all sorts of circumstances, those organs (of an animal) for each particular action require a particular disposition" (*Discourse* V, AT, vol. VI, p. 57). So even if a particular action is perfect, the range of actions an animal has at its disposal is severely limited. Or, as Descartes puts it in one of his earliest notes: "The fact that some of the actions displayed by animals are perfect suggests that they do not have a **free will**" (AT, vol. X, p. 219). Inversely the fact that we are unable to produce an animal as we can a clock is not an argument against

Descartes's views either. An animal may be a machine but it is a highly complicated machine such as can be actually constructed only by **God**. The methodological justification of the idea that animals are machines is that a phenomenon is sufficiently explained if we show how it can be produced. So if all animal functions can be simulated by mechanical devices, even if these can only be imagined, the animal can be treated as if it were a machine or automaton.

Descartes's denial of feelings to animals has a different foundation. According to Descartes awareness is a form of thinking. So if the essence of the human soul, or mind, is to think, the attribution of feelings and awareness to animals would entail that they have a human, that is, an immortal, soul. That animals have feelings is, according to him, an idea of Epicurus. And although Descartes verbally endorses the words of Scripture that the soul of animals is (in) their blood, he rejects the metaphorical use of words such as "vegetative soul" and "animal soul" because they could lead people to believe that human beings have three souls—vegetative, sensitive, and rational—an idea which is not only forbidden by the Roman Catholic Church, but is also illogical. In fact, the idea that animals have awareness and feelings is simply the effect of prejudice. This also affects the theory of man for, to the extent that there is a mechanical equivalent for human actions, men are also machines and can be explained "mechanically."

The human body is not essentially different from the body of an animal. Still, according to Descartes, there will always be two signs by which we recognize that a man is not just a machine but an animated being: his use of articulated **language** and the flexibility of his behavior. Animals may use sounds but the "words" they utter do not express any **thoughts**, whereas humans even if they do not have the use of their voice, manage to invent some signs to express their ideas. And although animals may be more effective in their instinctive behavior they are unable to adapt themselves to a changing environment, whereas the gift of reason allows humans to survive in many different circumstances.

The denial of feelings to animals may have been less categorical, however, in Descartes's thought. Descartes speaks of animals having "**passions**" (AT, vol IV, pp. 574–75), by which he means movements of the **animal spirits** that in humans cause and are caused by love, hate, anger, and so forth. Regardless, later authors, whether they agreed with him or not, interpreted his doctrine to be a through-and-through denial of feeling to animals, on the previously discussed grounds that all feeling is thought and thus would entail the existence of an immaterial soul in animals. **Nicolas Malebranche** argues that if animals were capable of suffering, then God would be unjustly punishing creatures who had committed no sin. **Antoine Arnauld** likewise supported the doctrine. Moreover, not only the enemies of Cartesianism but some of its friends refused to deny souls to animals. Gabriel Daniel (who notes that the doctrine is a "touchstone" among Cartesians), Pierre-Sylvain Régis (otherwise quite orthodox), Jacques Bossuet, and Bernard de Fontenelle all rejected the Cartesian view. The celebrated entry on *Rorarius* (a 16th-century defender of animals whose *Quod animalia bruta ratione utantur melius homine,* written in the mid-1540s, was not published until 1648) in Pierre Bayle's *Dictionnaire historique et critique* (1696) presents a thorough, incisive summary of the debate to that point; Bayle himself tends to agree with those who attribute reason to animals.

ARISTOTLE (384–322 B.C.E.) AND ARISTOTELIANISM. Aristotle was one of the dominant figures in ancient Greek philosophy; his thought was central to the development of Western philosophy well into the 17th century. Aristotle's fundamental contributions to all branches of philosophy, including logic, metaphysics, natural philosophy, ethics, and political theory earned him the sobriquet "master of those who know" or simply "the philosopher." In the context of Descartes's philosophy, the most important Aristotelian doctrines concern metaphysics and natural philosophy.

Aristotle's metaphysics takes its fundamental point of departure from a theory of substance that characterizes substances as a combination of underlying matter to which a form has been added. To use one of Aristotle's examples, in a bronze statue we can distinguish the material component (i.e., the bronze) from its shape or form. The same bronze could have had a different form, by being cast as a big ball or turned into a bunch of coins. Similarly, if the statue is of Poseidon, the same form could have existed in different matter, say by being carved out of a block of marble. Natural objects like trees and humans can also be understood in terms of form and matter: the material particles that make up an oak tree are organized according to the form of oak, and it is plausible that the same particles (had they been arranged in another form) could have constituted something very different. In the case of humans, the body is the material constituent and the soul is the form.

Aristotelian natural philosophy stresses the importance of seeking knowledge of nature through investigating the causes of things. Aristotle distinguished four different kinds of causes: formal, material, efficient, and final. Thus, the explanation of what produced a statue of Poseidon can make reference to the statue's form or shape (it is a statue of Poseidon and not Zeus), in part by the matter which makes it up (it is a bronze and not a marble statue), in part by the activity of casting (the efficient or productive cause), and in part by the end or purpose for which it was created, i.e., the fact that it was set up to honor the sea deity. The model of Aristotelian natural philosophy is the **geometry** of Euclid, where definitions, **common notions**, and postulates are stated at the outset and theorems are shown to follow by strict logical deduction. As Aristotle defines it, scientific knowledge must be based on **demonstrations** from first principles that are true, primary, better known than the conclusion, and explanatory of the conclusion. In the end, this results in the doctrine that what is known scientifically cannot be otherwise, so that (for example) if we have a scientific account of the planets, we can be sure that we have shown that the planets must be a certain way and they could not possibly be otherwise. The principal task for an Aristotelian natural philosopher is to uncover causal principles that can generate knowledge, which are typically derived by investigating the form of the object investigated. Thus, to have scientific knowledge of the nature of the horse, one must first understand the form of the horse, since it is from this form that the active powers and manifest properties of the horse derive.

The transmission of Aristotelian thought into Western Europe was through Arabic philosophers, who translated the Greek texts into Arabic, and whose works were then translated into Latin. Avicenna (980–1037) and Averroes (1126–98) were most important in this regard; Averroes's extensive commentary on Aristotle led to him being referred to simply as "the commentator." The philosophy of St. Thomas Aquinas (ca. 1225–74) incorporated a great deal of Aristotelian doctrine, as mediated by Avicenna and Averroes. Aristoteliansim was controversial enough in the 13th century that it was condemned on several occasions, culminating with the massive condemnation of 219 propositions issued by the bishop of Paris in 1277. Nevertheless, by the 16th century, Aristotelianism had become the more or less received view in philosophy: it was widely taught in the universities and was central to both philosophy and theology. Descartes consciously rejected Aristotelian metaphysics and natural philosophy, and he saw his own system as a worthy replacement for it. *See also* ATOMISM, ARISTOTELIAN; SCHOLASTICISM; SCOTISM; SUBSTANTIAL FORM; THOMISM.

ARNAULD, ANTOINE (1612–94). A French theologian associated with the convent of Port-Royal who was a prominent advocate both of **Jansenist theology** and of the new Cartesian philosophy. He followed other Jansenists in calling for a theology that depended on tradition rather than philosophical reasoning, and even criticized Descartes's views when they encroached on theological territory. However, Arnauld also insisted that Descartes's proofs of the immateriality of **mind**

and the **existence of God** were more conducive to piety than what is found in the established **scholastic philosophy**.

Arnauld was a licentiate in theology at the **Sorbonne** when he composed the *Fourth Set of Objections* to Descartes's *Meditations* (see also *Objections and Replies*). Though this text drew attention to problems with the **Cartesian circle** and the implications of Cartesian physics for the Eucharist, it also emphasized the affinities of Descartes's views to those of **Augustine**. Soon after composing this work, Arnauld published *De la fréquente communion* (1643), a defense of the views of his spiritual counselor Saint Cyran (Jean Duvergier Hauranne) against **Jesuit** critics. Descartes reacted to the controversy over this work by claiming in a 1644 letter that his own writings "touch neither near nor far on theology" (AT, vol. IV, p. 103f).

After Descartes's death, in 1656, Arnauld was expelled from the Sorbonne for his defense of the theological views of **Cornelius Jansenius**. In 1662, Arnauld published with Pierre Nicole *La Logique, ou l'art de penser*, which became the main Cartesian text in **logic**. During a brief respite in the official French campaign against Jansenism in the 1670s, Arnauld and Nicole composed a series of works defending the Catholic doctrine of **transubstantiation** against **Calvinist** critics. It was due in part to Arnauld's concern to distance Cartesianism from Calvinism that he vigorously opposed a Cartesian account of transubstantiation in **Robert Desgabets** that critics took to resemble the heretical Calvinist view on this issue. Arnauld also seems to have written *Plusieurs raisons pour empecher la censure ou la condamnation de la philosophie de Descartes* (1671), an (unsuccessful) plea to the Sorbonne to refrain from condemning Cartesian philosophy.

In 1679, at the request of **Louis XIV**, Arnauld joined other Jansenist sympathizers who went into exile in the Spanish Netherlands (Belgium). The following year he published *Examen d'un écrit*, a defense of the compatibility of Descartes's philosophy with **truths** of the Catholic faith. In 1683, he published *Des vraies et des fausses idées*, a critique of **Nicolas Malebranche**. This triggered a protracted debate between the two Cartesians over the **nature** of ideas and the doctrine of grace and divine providence. During 1686 to 1690, Arnauld engaged in a correspondence with **Gottfried Wilhelm Leibniz** concerning the latter's *Discours de la métaphysique*. Arnauld's last years were preoccupied with his dispute with Malebranche and with debates among his fellow Jansenists over the nature of grace and **freedom**.

ATHEISM. In the 17th century the term atheism covers a variety of meanings, which have no more in common than that an idea is thought to weaken and undermine religion, even if it does not imply that there is no **God** at all. Accordingly, the term atheist is applied not only to those who explicitly and directly deny the existence of God but also to libertines, blasphemers, satirists, deists, pantheists, and so forth. **Gysbertus Voetius**, for example, calls atheist anyone "who, directly or indirectly, takes away either from himself or from others knowledge of, belief in, or service to, God" (*Disputationes theologicae selectae*, I, p. 416), a definition he wants to apply to heterodox Christians (Socinians), people who endorse the worldly use of ecclesiastical goods or make bad jokes about ministers or the Church (Lucianists or Rabelaisians), as well as philosophers who stress the political significance of religion and would like to subject the Church to the authority of the magistrate (Machiavellians or politico-theologians).

On the other hand **Marin Mersenne**, who had a lifelong preoccupation with all forms of atheism and deism, seems to restrict the use of the term to an explicit denial of the existence of God, deism being no more than a wrong conception of God (primarily that God is not the creator of the world). This much is clear: there was a widespread belief in the 17th century that if it is possible at all for someone sincerely and explicitly to deny the existence of God (which, for reasons founded on Romans 1:20, not everyone took for granted), his aim is to do as he pleases. The main ingredients of atheism therefore were thought to be the denial, not only of God's legislative **will**, but also of the **immortality** of the soul. This practical interpretation of the notion of atheism makes it possible that, although all agreed that "real" atheists (people who are sincere in their denial of the existence of a God) are very rare, atheism in the broad sense of the word (impiety, libertinism, etc.) was generally believed to be widespread, especially in the larger cities.

The first mention of atheism in Descartes's correspondence, in 1630, concerns a "bad book" (or "méchant livre," which may be either dialogues by La Mothe le Vayer or, more likely, a Socinian book claiming that God's power is subject to the laws of **reason**). Having worked on a "small treatise on **metaphysics**" during the first months of his stay in the Low Countries (Fall 1629), Descartes already claims that the best argument against atheism is that metaphysical **truths** (more particularly the existence of God and the immateriality of the soul) are better known than geometrical truths. This was to remain his main line of attack, especially in the *Meditations*. His second argument is that the human soul is essentially different from that of **animals**, which are no more than unconscious machines, because that means that, unlike the supposed soul of an animal, the human soul does not die with the **body**.

The fact that Descartes found his own philosophy extremely useful against the atheists may explain his indignation when he was himself associated with atheist ideas. Voetius and **Martinus Schoock** in particular compared Descartes with the famous atheist **Lucilio Vanini** (burned at the stake in 1619), not because Descartes denies the existence of God but because he destroys the traditional arguments for God's existence and replaces them with an argument based on our having an **idea** of God; indeed, according to Schoock and Voetius, this meant that all the atheist had to do was to deny that he had ever had such an idea. After Descartes's death the discussion concentrated on the interpretation of Scripture, the contentious issue being heliocentrism. The Calvino-Cartesian solution (developed particularly by Christoph Wittich) was to separate **theology** (interpretation of Scripture) and philosophy, and to claim that, reading Scripture carefully, the conclusion must be that Scripture does not mean to teach anything on **nature** or that the language in which Scripture is written is that of the common people, whose prejudices it necessarily reflects. In the last quarter of the 17th century the discussion became dominated by the question whether or not Descartes had prepared to ground for **Baruch Spinoza**, who came to replace Vanini as the most famous atheist of the century.

ATOMISM. It is generally conceded that one of the more important changes in early modern philosophy is the movement from **scholasticism** to atomism. However, significant variations in both **Aristotelianism** and atomism make such seemingly true generalizations difficult to defend. Descartes is sometimes thought to be an atomist, but in *Principles of Philosophy*, Part IV, art. 202, entitled "The philosophy of Democritus differs from my own just as much as it does from the standard view of Aristotle and others," Descartes carefully delineated his philosophy from Democritus's atomism and from Aristotle's anti atomism. There he enumerated three principal reasons often given for the rejection of classical atomism: Democritus supposed his corpuscles to be indivisible; he imagined a **vacuum** around them; and he attributed **gravity** to his corpuscles. Descartes accepted these arguments, since he himself rejected the indivisibility of corpuscles, claimed to demonstrate the impossibility of vacuum, and argued that there is no such thing as gravity in any body by itself. Descartes ended his article by denying "all of Democritus's suppositions" (with only one exception) together with "practically all the suppositions of the other philosophers."

It was clear to Descartes that his philosophizing had no more affinity with the Democritean method than with any other. The only relation that held between his philosophy and that of Democritus was the exception he called "the consideration of shapes, sizes and motions": There are particles in each body so small they cannot be perceived by the senses and all bodies perceivable by the senses arise from the conglomeration and mutual interaction of such corpuscles. Descartes asserted that he shared this consideration with Aristotle and all other philosophers. According to him, "no one can doubt that there are in fact many such particles." Descartes, therefore, considered himself a kind of corpuscularian, but not an atomist. *See also* ALCHEMY; ATOMISM, ARISTOTELIAN; BASSO, SEBASTIAN; CORDEMOY, GÉRAULD DE; GASSENDI, PIERRE.

ATOMISM, ARISTOTELIAN. There was a surprising development in **Aristotelian** matter theory during the early modern period. Aristotle as a rule was strongly anti-atomist, but he also uttered the obscure statement that "neither flesh, bone, nor any such thing can be of indefinite size in the direction either of the greater or of the less" (*Physics*, I, chap. 4). By the 17th century, the resulting doctrine entailed that there are intrinsic limits of greatness and smallness for every sort of living thing.

Since, for a **scholastic**, every natural **body** has an actually determined **form**, every natural body must have determinate accidents and a limited **quantity**. An exception to this rule would be the **elements** or simple homogeneous bodies, which have no determinate magnitude of themselves and intrinsically. However, the elements would have an extrinsic limitation in respect to the limitation of prime matter: there may not be enough prime matter to sustain a form and the amount of prime matter is finite. They cannot, therefore, be augmented **indefinitely** and their division cannot be continued indefinitely. The elements also cannot be condensed or rarefied—they cannot have their quantity changed indefinitely—without being corrupted. For example, earth cannot become as rarefied as fire and fire as condensed as earth; when air is condensed too much, it is turned into water, and water overly rarefied is turned into air. In this way, **rarefaction and condensation**, that is, augmentation and diminution in quantity, can result in generation and corruption, under appropriate circumstances. There is, then, a natural minimum of any given element. Late scholasticism could therefore countenance a kind of corpuscularianism, something not usually associated with Aristotelianism. This doctrine of a natural minimum was used to bridge the Aristotelian and alchemical theories of matter. *See also* ATOMISM.

ATTRIBUTE. *See* SUBSTANCE.

AUGUSTINE (353–430). Augustine, bishop of Hippo, was a major force in the early Christian Church. He appealed to a Platonism that emphasizes the transcendence and unity of the source of creation in arguing against a Manichean dualism that posits good and evil forces in **nature**.

Augustine also emphasized the gratuitous nature of salvation in his campaign against a **Pelagianism** that holds that salvation depends on merit deriving from the exercise of **free will.**

Marin Mersenne was one of the first to draw Descartes's attention to the anticipations of his views on **doubt,** the *cogito,* and **dualism** in the work of Augustine. While Descartes himself was not particularly impressed by these connections, **Antoine Arnauld** and others were drawn to his system primarily because they saw in it an Augustinian alternative to the sort of **Aristotelianism** that was dominant in **scholastic philosophy.** After Descartes's death, the association with Augustine was prominent in the campaign to promote the new Cartesian philosophy in the face of the charge that it conflicts with theological orthodoxy. There were two different approaches here, which Henri Gouhier has captured in distinguishing between "Cartesianism Augustinized" and "Augustinianism Cartesianized." **Claude Clerselier** is an example of an Augustinized Cartesian who was interested primarily in promoting Cartesian **natural philosophy** by invoking the name of Augustine. In contrast, Arnauld is an example of a Cartesianized Augustinian who was concerned to use Cartesian natural philosophy as a shield to protect Augustinian theology against the incursions of scholasticism. The fact that Cartesianized Augustinians tended to be sympathetic to the interpretation in **Cornelius Jansenius** of Augustine's views on grace and free will helps to explain the common (though misleading) perception that Jansenism and Cartesianism are naturally allied.

AUGUSTINIANISM. *See* AUGUSTINE (353–430).

AUTOMATON. From his early days Descartes seems to have been fascinated by automata, that is, **mechanical** devices that, in a seemingly spontaneous manner, imitate the behavior of living beings, whereas actually they are moved by springs. In one of his earliest notes he not only comments on the pigeon of Archytas (a mechanical device much referred to in **scholastic** literature), but also gives (or records) the plan of an automaton, which, with the help of a magnet and a few springs, moves and reacts to stimuli. The general point about these machines is methodological. According to Descartes a phenomenon is explained if we indicate the way in which it *can* be produced. So if a vegetative or animal function can be simulated mechanically, its explanation is also mechanical. But, also, the rejection of **substantial forms** entails that there is no reason to make a distinction between natural things and artifacts. Automata are as much products of **nature** as living beings.

Inversely, there is no fact or reason why we should not see **animals** as machines. Someone who has never seen anything but automata would naturally see animals as machines or automata. That we do not see an animal as a machine is the effect of a prejudice caused by our judging animals by analogy to ourselves. Instead Descartes uses mechanical devices like organs and the complicated machinery found in the royal parks to clarify the workings of animals. Still, we should make a distinction between automata and other artifacts, like swords and keys, which relate to each other as a living animal and a dead body. Both are part of nature but, whereas an automaton or a living body has its own principle of motion, an ordinary device or a dead material body depends on external forces for its movement. That the body works as an automaton is mainly the result of the circulation of the blood, which is the underlying process of all biological functions. The animal adapts and survives by an "institution of nature" (*Passions of the Soul* I, art. 50, AT, vol. XI, p. 369; II, art. 137, AT, vol. XI, p. 430), which owes nothing to the soul. Inversely, death is never the result of the soul leaving the body; on the contrary, if the soul leaves the body that is the effect of the fact that the heart or the brain is severely damaged.

AXIOM. *See* COMMON NOTION.

– B –

BACON, SIR FRANCIS (1561–1626). English lawyer, politician, essayist, and natural philosopher, the first Baron Verulam and Viscount St. Albans. Born in London, Bacon was the younger of two sons of Sir Nicholas Bacon, lord keeper of the great seal under Queen Elizabeth I and Anne Cooke, sister to the wife of the queen's chief minister, Lord Burghley. Bacon studied at Trinity College, Cambridge from 1573–75 but left without taking a degree. In 1576 he was admitted as a senior governor of Gray's Inn (an institution for legal education) and also traveled to Paris with the English ambassador, Sir Amyas Paulet. He was admitted to the bar in 1582 and elected to Parliament in 1584 for the first of several constituencies he was to represent. His connections to court through his uncle, Lord Burghley, eased his career path and in 1591 he became close associate of the Earl of Essex, an influential advisor to the queen. Bacon's connection to Essex secured him a prominent place as a lawyer. He used this position to great effect in 1601 when he vigorously assisted in the prosecution of Essex for treason, an affair that ended in the conviction and execution of Essex and a knighthood for Bacon in 1602.

After Elizabeth's death in 1603, Bacon advanced rapidly through a series of high offices: he was appointed solicitor general in 1607, attorney general in 1613, lord keeper of the seal (the office his father had held) in 1617, and lord chancellor in 1618, the same year he was made Lord Verulam. Only months after being created Viscount St. Albans in 1621, Bacon was charged in the House of Commons with taking bribes as a judge. He admitted his guilt and was sentenced by the House of Lords to a huge fine, imprisonment in the Tower of London, disqualification from Parliament, and exclusion from the court. The fine was remitted and he spent only a couple of days in the Tower, but the affair ended his life in politics and at court. His remaining years were occupied with energetic study and writing, a project in which **Thomas Hobbes** assisted him as a secretary.

Even from his earliest days at Cambridge Bacon had a strong interest in methodology and he dreamed of developing a scientific **method** that would provide a decisive break with the **Aristotelian and scholastic natural philosophy**. Bacon emphasized the limitations of three prevailing ways of seeking to gain knowledge: the abstract disputation of the scholastics, the elegant but insubstantial writings of the humanists, and the preoccupation with marvels and monstrosities of the Renaissance occultists. In their stead Bacon proposed that **nature's** secrets should be unlocked by a process of induction, making a gradual ascent from the level of observed particulars to ever more general laws that would reveal the true causes of things.

Bacon was a prolific author, addressing subjects from law to morals to natural philosophy in forms ranging from short essays to extensive treatises. His more significant philosophical works are *The Advancement of Learning* (1605; in an expanded Latin version as *De dignitate et augmentis scientiarum*, 1623), *Instauratio magna* ("The Great Instauration," 1620), which includes the very influential part entitled *Novum organon* ("New Organon"), *Sylva sylvarum* (1626), and *New Atlantis* (1627). Descartes held Bacon in high esteem, and his own grand methodological project of the *Regulae* has important similarities with Bacon's. According to Descartes's biographer **Adrien Baillet**, Descartes was among those who were "deeply touched" by the news of Bacon's death in 1626, seeing in him one whose methods held out the promise of an entirely new scheme for the acquisition and organization of knowledge (Baillet, *La Vie de M. Descartes*, vol. I, p. 146).

BAILLET, ADRIEN (1649–1706). Adrien Baillet was born June 13, 1649, at Neuville (hence the pseudonym "M. de Neuville"), a small town between Beauvais and Clermont. His parents were from Picardy and of modest means. Baillet was educated at the Collège de Beauvais, where he later became a teacher of humanities. In 1670 he entered the Seminary and in 1676 was ordained priest of the Diocese of Beauvais. He moved to Paris in 1680 to become a librarian. Although he is now known mainly for his biography of Descartes (1692), he was a prolific writer, who published not only erudite compilations and bibliographies, such as *Jugements des savants sur les principaux auteurs* (1685) and *Des auteurs déguisés* (1690), but also historical works, such as *Histoire de Hollande* (1690) and *Histoire des démêlés du Pape Boniface VIII avec Philippe le Bel* (published posthumously in 1718), and books on devotion and piety, such as *Dévotion à la Vierge et le culte qui lui est dû* (Paris 1694) and *Les vies des saints* (Paris 1701). These last works came under criticism from the Church because Baillet was thought to be playing into the hands of the anti-Catholics. His **Jansenist** sympathies, which cannot be denied, were frequently blamed for this. He died in Paris January 21, 1706.

According to Baillet's biographer it was the Abbé Le Grand (see **Correspondence**) who persuaded him, sometime in 1690, to "put some order to the various reports he had collected on the Life and Philosophy of the famous Philosopher M. Descartes." Hence, Baillet worked on material already collected by Le Grand. This could explain the comparatively short time needed by Baillet to complete his biography, which was published in February 1691. In any case, Le Grand, to whom Clerselier had given all the material he still possessed of Descartes, gave Baillet access to Descartes's letters to **Claude Clerselier, Claude Picot,** Tobias Andreae, and **Henricus Regius**, as well as the letters to his family, for all of which Baillet is our only source. Above all, Le Grand and Baillet actively tried to collect evidence from the Netherlands, where they approached people who had known Descartes or could possess information on his life and letters.

The result of these efforts is a work in two volumes of 500 pages each: *La Vie de M. Des-Cartes* ("The Life of Mr. Des-Cartes," 1691). As a source it is indispensable, but it should be used with some caution, not only because Baillet is excessively concerned with depicting Descartes as a pious Roman Catholic and in a general way as a hero of irreproachable manners (which sometimes results in an unjust treatment of Descartes's adversaries), but also because his presentation of the facts is sometimes confused. More particularly, it is not always clear whether he is using an independent (and reliable) source or is making up his own interpretation. In any case, his information should be checked whenever possible and in any case critically assessed. When the book was sold out Baillet was persuaded to make a shortened edition, which was published in 1692.

BALZAC, JEAN-LOUIS GUEZ DE (1597–1654). French writer and friend and correspondent of Descartes. Balzac's chosen literary form was the letter. His first publication, *Lettres du Sieur de Balzac* (1624), was criticized because of its neoclassical style of writing, but defended by Descartes and **Jean de Silhon**. Balzac was pleased with Descartes's long open letter of support and dedicated to him three short essays, "Trois discovrs envoyez à M. Descartes," subsequently published in *Le Socrate Chrestien* (1657).

BASSO, SEBASTIAN (ca. 1577–post-1625). French physician and natural philosopher. Basso (or Basson) was educated at the **Jesuit** Academy at Pont-à-Mousson (founded in 1572) and taught humanities at the Protestant Academy at Die-en-Dauphiné, in the Bernese territories of Lausanne, from 1611 to 1625. His main work, *Philosophiae naturalis adversus Aristotelem, Libri XII* (1621), was an early attempt to revive the **atomist** doctrines of Democritus (and others) and an attack on the **natural philosophy** of Aristotle. Rejecting **scholastic** debates about form and matter, Basso proposed that matter makes up its own natural *minima* with arrangements of homogeneous and incorruptible atoms; these retain their differences when conjoined. He maintained the four kinds of elementary atoms coinciding with the four traditional elements, but unlike typical atomists, he posited in addition a *pneuma*, ether, world soul, or "spirit of the universe."

For Basso, all natural change is explained in terms of the arrangement of atoms in the ether: generation and augmentation in **quantity** result from the clustering of atoms; corruption and diminution from their dispersal. Alteration in quantity is a consequence of the changing ratios of the kinds of atoms in a cluster. Basso's fifth element, the ether, allowed him to explain **rarefaction and condensation**. Atoms compose the ether, but ethereal atoms permeate the pores and gaps of all objects, causing the motion of the other atoms. Since the ether fills all space, an object becomes more rarefied because the ether interposes itself to a greater degree in its pores, increasing its size and decreasing its density. By appealing to the ether, Basso could agree with Aristotle that **"nature** abhors a **vacuum."** Moreover, for Basso, all **motions** of objects occur as a result of the ether's motion directing the motion of the elementary atoms according to their aptitude.

Basso's views were well-known and controversial both because of their atomism and their anti-Aristotelianism. For example, Descartes's principal correspondent, **Marin Mersenne**, classified him as an **atheist** for his atomism. In *L'impiété des Déistes* (1624), after having discussed such "despicable" authors as **Pierre Charron, Giordano Bruno**, the "accursed" **Lucilio Vanini**, Basso, "and similar rogues," Mersenne complained specifically about their adherence to the principle that "inside bodies there are atoms with quantity and figure" (pp. 237–38). In *La vérité des sciences* (1625), Mersenne placed Basso in the same bad company, but this time described them as authors "who raise monuments to Aristotle's fame through their writing, since they are not able to strive high enough to bring down the flight and glory of the Peripatetic Philosopher, for he transcends everything of the senses and imagination, and they grovel on the ground like little worms" (pp. 109–10).

Descartes's intellectual relations with Basso were mixed. He seems to have been influenced by him, but he also kept a safe intellectual distance. Descartes said that he agreed with Basso about rarefaction but that perhaps he did not explain the ether in the same way (AT, vol. I, p. 25). He also ranked Basso among innovators who could not really have influenced him: "Plato says one thing, Aristotle another, Epicurus another, Telesio, Campanella, Bruno, Basso, Vanini, and all the innovators all say something different. Of all these people, I ask you, who is it who has anything to teach me, or indeed anyone who loves wisdom?" (AT, vol. I, p. 158). In another negative, but typically Cartesian remark, Descartes said that Basso's book was only good for destroying Aristotle's opinions, but that he, Descartes, sought only "to establish something, so simple and manifest, that the opinions of all others would agree with it" (AT, vol. I, pp. 602–3).

BAYLE, FRANÇOIS (1622–1709). A physician and, for most of his life, a member of the Faculty of Medicine at the University of Toulouse (from 1666 on). Bayle was associated with the Société des Lanternistes, a forum for discussing current ideas and reporting on new experiments; he was an active participant in the society's meetings, teaching alongside **Pierre-Sylvain Régis**, Emmanuel Maignan, and others. His Cartesian sources included Régis and through him, **Robert Desgabets**. The luminaries and Cartesians of his era, such as **Nicolas Malebranche**, knew him. His main philosophical work, *The General Systeme of the Cartesian Philosophy* (1670), which survived only in English translation, was a synopsis of the Cartesian system, constructed out of Descartes's whole corpus. In the *General Systeme*, Bayle went through the system in an order somewhat reminiscent of the *Principles*: he detailed the *cogito*, the consequence that the **soul** knows itself better than it knows any other thing, both proofs for the **existence of God**, God's guarantee that we cannot err in what we clearly and distinctly know, the certainty of the existence of **bodies**, that errors proceed from the ill-use of our **freedom**, and so forth. However, he ended his part I, Metaphysics, by asserting that "when we say that the certainty of our Understanding is greater than that of our Senses, we mean nothing else, than that the **judgments** we form in a riper age, by reason of some new Observations we have made, are more certain than those, we have formed from infancy, without having reflected on them." Thus, Bayle was an "empirical" Cartesian. For him the corrective for the prejudices of childhood was not **reason**, but experience. His empiricism became even more marked in his later works.

BAYLE, PIERRE (1647–1706). Pierre Bayle was a **Calvinist** and a skeptic. He became professor of philosophy at the Protestant Academy of Sedan and then at the Ecole Illustre, Rotterdam. A religious thinker, he edited a volume of essays dealing with the Cartesian explanation for the sacrament of the Eucharist, *Recueil de quelques pièces curieuses concernant la philosophie de M. Descartes* (1684). (See **transubstantiation.**) He is best known for his multivolume philosophical dictionary. He first published *Projet et fragmens d'un Dictionnaire critique* (1692) then the *Dictionnaire historique et critique* itself (1697, with numerous subsequent editions).

BEATITUDE. *See* HAPPINESS.

BEAUGRAND, JEAN DE (1595–1640). French mathematician and critic of Descartes. Beaugrand studied under **François Viète** and in 1630 was appointed court mathematician to Gaston d'Orleans, third son of Henri IV. In 1631, he published an edition of Viète's *Isagoge in artem analyticam*, and in 1635, was appointed by Cardinal Richelieu (along with Etienne Pascal, **Claude Mydorge**, and Pierre Hérigone) to a committee charged with evaluating **Jean-Baptiste Morin**'s claimed solution to the problem of determining longitude by lunar observation. He was named *sécretaire du Roi* in the same year, a post he held until his death.

Beaugrand had close ties to **Pierre de Fermat**, and from the mid-1630s was his principal correspondent in Paris, serving as the link between him and Parisian mathematicians (notably those in the circle around **Marin Mersenne**). Beaugrand's *Geostatice* (1635) proposed and defended the principle that the weight of a **body** varied with its distance from the center of the earth. Descartes poured scorn on this opinion, expressing astonishment that anyone would deem the book worth reading and characterizing its author as displaying "as much impudence and effrontery as ignorance" (AT, vol. II, p. 188). Beaugrand responded by publishing anonymous pamphlets attacking Descartes and accusing him of having plagiarized his **geometry** from Viète. He also engaged in a series of polemics with his erstwhile friend **Girard Desargues** over the solution to various geometric problems, and it was his unauthorized provision of a prepublication copy of Descartes *Dis-*

course and *Essays* to Fermat that led to their dispute. On the whole, the Parisian mathematical community had little cause to mourn his death in 1640.

BEAUNE, DE. *See* **DEBEAUNE.**

BEECKMAN, ISAAC (1588–1637). Beeckman studied in Leiden, where he matriculated in 1607 and 1609, after which he took up the same trade as his father, who owned a factory of pipes and candlesticks. In the meanwhile, he studied medicine privately and took a degree from Caen (1618). He never became a medical practitioner. After a short interval as deputy headmaster of the Latin School (a preparatory school) of Utrecht in 1620, he took the same position in Rotterdam, also in 1620, and in 1626, he became headmaster of the Latin School of Dordrecht, where he remained until his death. Apart from his M.D. thesis, of which only the title page and corollaries survive, he did not publish during his lifetime. However, he carefully recorded his reflections on problems of natural science in what he called his *loci communes* (commonplace book). When he died, **Marin Mersenne**, who heard of his death one year later (and not from Descartes), was particularly concerned about this "big volume in which he wrote down everything that came to his mind." He apparently had seen it when he visited Beeckman in Dordrecht. A selection from it was printed as *Mathematicophysicarum meditationum, quaestionum, solutionum centuria* (1644). The original manuscript resurfaced in the 19th century, when the Provincial Library of Zeeland bought it. Cornelis de Waard, who published it in its entirety as *Journal tenu par Isaac Beeckman de 1604 à 1634*, discovered it there. It shows that Beeckman was well ahead of his time. The significance of his work is now universally recognized, though it still awaits critical assessment.

According to Daniel Lipstorp, Beeckman and Descartes met each other in Breda while studying a broadsheet proposing a mathematical problem. Allegedly, Descartes asked someone to translate the text for him from Dutch to Latin or French and Beeckman volunteered a translation on the condition that Descartes provided him the solution. This at least is clear: the first meeting with Descartes recorded by Beeckman was on November 10, 1618. A few weeks later he proudly noted that *Renatus Picto* (René from Poitou), who frequented "many **Jesuits** and other students and learned men," told him that he, Beeckman, was the only person he ever met who studies **nature** by joining together physics and **mathematics** (AT, vol. X, p. 52).

Other entries in the notebook concerned music and harmony; it is on that subject that Descartes wrote his first work, *Compendium of Music*, which he offered Beeckman as a New Year's gift for 1619. But many other issues, such as the law of falling bodies, retained the attention of the two friends. In several letters to him, Descartes testified to his loving friendship and glorified Beeckman for having rekindled his interest in science. After a long interval, during which apparently there were no contacts at all, Descartes returned to Beeckman on October 8, 1628, to tell him of the progress he had made, especially in mathematics. Indeed, one of the reasons why he paid a short visit to the Netherlands was that he wanted Beeckman's help in preparing the publication of his "Algebra," which he promised to send him as soon as he would be back in Paris. Afterwards Beeckman jotted down several notes on problems treated in the *Dioptrics* and *Geometry*, which apparently he had discussed with Descartes.

Relations with Beeckman remained cordial until the end of 1629, but Descartes interpreted an unfortunate remark reported by Mersenne as a claim that he, Descartes, had learned everything from Beeckman. In a letter to Mersenne Descartes spoke of the "ingratitude" of his friend, attributed to "the honor you [Mersenne] have done him to write him a letter," which made him imagine "that he [Beeckman] has been my teacher ten years ago" (AT, vol. I, p. 24). Descartes asked for the *Compendium* back and broke with Beeckman in a nasty letter. A reconciliation followed, possibly in the summer of 1631 when, according to **Adrien Baillet**, Descartes visited Beeckman in Dordrecht, because "old age and illness threatened him with death" (Baillet I, p. 260). Beeckman in turn visited Descartes in Amsterdam several times—at least in October 1631 and in August 1634. On the last occasion he brought with him **Galileo Galilei's** *Dialogue*; this allowed Descartes to examine the book quickly and give his reaction to Mersenne. But apparently the relations between the two men never became as cordial as they had been. When Beeckman died, Descartes wrote a short letter of condolence to Andreas Colvius, minister of the Walloon Church in Dordrecht, telling him that he regretted Beeckman's death but that "the time we live in this world is so short as compared with eternity that we must not worry if we are taken away some years earlier or later" (AT, vol. I, pp. 379–80).

BEKKER, BALTHASAR (1634–98). Balthasar Bekker was born 20 March 1634 in Metslawier (Friesland), where his father, Henricus, was a minister of the Dutch Reformed Church. Balthasar studied theology in Groningen and Franeker and was admitted to the ministry in 1655. In 1657 he was appointed in Oosterlittens (Friesland), where he wrote his first work, a rhymed catechism for children, *Gerymde Kinderleer* (1661). In 1665, he obtained the degree of Doctor in Divinity at the University of Franeker. Before long, Bekker became involved in a number of conflicts, some of them personal (he never was an easy man) or liturgical (he was attacked for delivering a funeral sermon at the occasion of the death of his first wife), others doctrinal. According to some, his Catechism for adults, *De vaste spyse der volmaakten* (1670), was Cartesian and Socinian and, after unfavorable interventions of the Theological Faculty of Franeker University and the Frisian Synod the book was forbidden by the States of Friesland. So Bekker gladly accepted a call to Holland, where he became minister in Loenen (1674), Weesp (1676), and finally Amsterdam (1679). Meanwhile he also worked as an army preacher (1678). In the summer of 1683 he visited England and France. In 1683 Bekker published a small work on comets, *Onderzoek van de beteekeninge der Kometen* ("An Investigation into the meaning of Comets"), in which he denounced the superstitious beliefs connected with their appearance.

It was the prelude to a much larger book, *De betoverde Weerelt* ("The World Bewitched," 1691, reprinted several times and translated in most European languages), a voluminous work in which Bekker uses Cartesian philosophy to refute the belief in devils and evil spirits. According to Bekker "a spirit is a thinking **substance** and a **body** an extended substance." All we know about spirits apart from Revelation rests on the knowledge we have of our own **mind** or **soul**. This teaches us that if **God** is a spirit he must be one, which in turn means that there can be no demons or demigods. Moreover, we know by experience that minds (souls, spirits) can only work upon a single body, namely, the one with which they are intimately connected. According to Scripture, on the other hand, there are **angels** (messengers) and also fallen angels, who are led by Satan and are all chained in Hell (II Peter 2:4; Jude 6). But most of what Scripture tells us on devils and angels should be interpreted metaphorically. Although Bekker fits into a tradition of Protestant fight against superstition, his book caused a storm of protests, which ultimately led to his dismissal in 1692. He died June 11, 1698.

BERNIER, FRANÇOIS (1620–88). French philosopher, physician, and traveler. Bernier received a medical degree from Montpellier in 1652. He became a proponent of **Pierre Gassendi**'s philosophy. His principal work was the *Abregé de la philosophie de Gassendi* (1678), consisting of a multivolume abridgment, French translation, and interpretation of Gassendi's main work, the *Syntagma*. Yet he diverged from Gassendi's views on several points in his *Doutes sur quelques uns des principaux chapitres de son Abrégé de Gassendi* (1682). For example, he rejected Gassendi's doctrine of an absolute, incorporeal, penetrable, immobile **space**, in order to identify space and **body**, as Descartes did, although, against Descartes, he defended the possibility of the **void**. Bernier's own characterization of his *Doubtes* should be kept in mind, however. According to him, they are not about the foundation of Gassendi's philosophy, for one cannot philosophize reasonably using any system other than **atoms** and the void. As he said, Gassendi's philosophy is the simplest and most rational of all; it has the advantage that it allows a great number of **truths** to be discovered, which, without its assistance would remain hidden. Bernier also published some polemics against Cartesian philosophy in **Pierre Bayle's** *Recueil de quelques pieces curieuses concernant la philosophie de M. Descartes* (1684). For example, he criticized Descartes's view on **animals** as machines, his **proofs for the existence of God**, and the Cartesian theory of **occasional causes**.

BÉRULLE, PIERRE DE (1575–1629). A French cardinal interested in Church reform who founded the Congregation of the **Oratory** in 1611 as an alternative to the **Jesuit** Order. Bérulle was present with Descartes at a lecture given in 1627/28 by an **alchemist**, M. de Chandoux, at the Paris home of the papal nuncio. Descartes reported that he proclaimed the "new philosophy" of Chandoux as less certain than his own, whereupon Bérulle urged him to commit his views to writing. The fact that Bérulle was almost exclusively a **theologian** makes it unlikely that he was deeply interested in Descartes's reforms in the sciences. However, the prevalence in the Oratory of Platonic **Augustinianism** helps to explain how Descartes's anti-**Aristotelian** views in **natural philosophy** were able to gain a foothold there through the influence of Oratorians such as **Nicolas Malebranche**.

BEVERWIJCK, JOANNES VAN (1594–1647). Joannes van Beverwijck (Beverovicius) was born in Dordrecht on November 17, 1594. He studied medicine in **Leiden**, Caen, Paris, Montpellier, Padua, and Bologna. He settled in practice in Dordrecht around 1618. In 1627, he became a member of the Vroedschap (municipal government). He wrote many popular works on medicine but also literary and historical works. He died in 1647. The first recorded contact between Van Beverwijck and Descartes is a letter of Van Beverwijck of June 10, 1643, in which he asks Descartes to send him his explanation of the **circulation of the blood**. Presumably the Dutch minister Andreas Colvius (1596–1676) had introduced Descartes to him. Descartes reacted on July 5, 1643, not by sending Van Beverwijck a Latin translation of the relevant part of the *Discourse*, but by completing that presentation with a more accurate explanation of the movement of the **heart**. In the same letter Descartes offers the text of his **correspondence** with **Vopiscus Plemp**, who, according to Descartes, had provided an incomplete and mutilated version of it in his *Fundamenta Medicinae*. Although Van Beverwijck's relations with Descartes seem to have been cordial and friendly—according to **Adrien Baillet**, Descartes visited Beverwijck whenever he passed Dordrecht on his way to and from Rotterdam—there is no trace of Descartes's influence in his work, which is practical rather than theoretical.

BLOOD, CIRCULATION OF. Although Descartes's first detailed explanation of the circulation of the blood was given only in the *Discourse*, the fact that the blood circulates through the body is constantly taken for granted in the *Treatise on Man*. We must assume therefore that Descartes became convinced of it shortly after its discovery by **William Harvey**, who published his views in 1628. Descartes invariably gives credit to Harvey for this discovery but is also at pains to point out their differences. According to Descartes, Harvey is right only about circulation but wrong about its cause. Whereas according to Harvey the heart works like a pump and expulses the blood during the diastole (that is, when the heart contracts), Descartes believes that the blood leaves the heart by its own force during the systole (when the heart expands). For Harvey, the diastole is the active phase, but for Descartes it is the phase in which the heart relaxes. According to Descartes there is in the heart a "fire without light," analogous to the heat developed by fermentation, which he sometimes claims is entertained by the blood that comes from the veins. As a result the heart is warmer than the rest of the body. The blood that enters the heart is immediately heated; it expands and breaks its way out of the heart to the lungs, where it cools down, so as to be able to return to the heart, where it is heated again and acquires so much force that it can enter the arteries and start its way through the body.

The texts of both the *Discourse* and especially the *Description of the Human Body* show that Descartes conducted numerous observations, not only to show that there is circulation, but also to defend his explanation of the movement of the heart against Harvey. The significance of the circulation of the blood goes far beyond the strictly medical sphere, given the fact that, according to Descartes, all vegetative functions and animal functions can be explained if we assume that the **animal spirits** are a product of the blood. The circulation of the blood, therefore, is the only **principle** of all biological phenomena. As such it replaces vegetative and animal **souls** or more generally **substantial forms**. But circulation is also important to Descartes because it is the one process by which the living body can be seen as a self-regulatory machine. The more the blood circulates, the more homogeneous it becomes. Accordingly, it is ultimately by means of the circulation of the blood that the blood purifies itself, that the body gets rid of toxic substances, and that equilibrium with the environment is achieved. Since on the other hand the main bodily effect of the **passions** is, either the disturbance (in the case of passions like sadness and **hatred**), or the facilitation (in the case of passions like **joy** and **love**) of the circulation, it also explains why control of the passions is necessary for health.

BODY. Body (Latin *corpus*, French *corps*) is best discussed under three headings: 1) body in general; 2) individual bodies; 3) *the* body, i.e. the human body considered in its **union** with the **soul**.

Body in general. Body in general is the entirety of physical space or "**indefinite extension**," considered as the homogeneous Ur-substance from which individual bodies arise by virtue of **motion**. Body in general serves in Cartesian physics some of the functions served by prime matter in **Aristotelian natural philosophy**: it is the ultimate substrate of all natural change; insofar as the shapes of bodies are akin to what an Aristotelian would call form, body in general, like prime matter, "gives being" to form. Hence Descartes sometimes uses "matter" as if it were synonymous with "body in general."

Individual bodies. An individual body is a region of space whose boundaries are determined by its motion relative to its immediate neighbors. Descartes therefore sometimes speaks of individual bodies as "parts of matter." An individual body is a **substance** insofar as it is capable of existing apart from all other actual or possible individual substances save God; but the same can be said even of those regions of space which are not now individual bodies. On the strictest definition, only a connected region of space is an individual body. Spatially separated regions are bodies only in one or another extended sense—for example, if they "move together" with respect to surrounding bodies, or if they are all joined with a single soul.

The body. The human body, uniquely among individual bodies, is joined with an immaterial substance—the human soul. We can speak of it as one thing with respect to that relation. More precisely, *the* body of a human being at any moment is simply all the individual bodies that happen to be joined with it at that moment, as Descartes puts it in a letter to **Denis Mesland** (AT, vol. IV, p. 166). That collection of individual bodies (in the strict sense) is changing all the time. The body "through time," which is what we ordinarily refer to as "the body," is the sequence of bodies-at-a-moment.

Animal bodies have no principle of unity comparable to the human soul. Aristotelian philosophers, who did attribute souls to animals and plants, could extend to them the criterion employed by Descartes to define the human body. An animal body is not an individual body in the strict sense: Descartes, in likening animal bodies to machines, in fact emphasizes the enormous number of parts in animal bodies. Like a machine, it has at most a sort of functional unity insofar as the movements of its parts can be seen to tend toward a single end. The functional unity of machines can be defined only in relation to the ends of their makers; it corresponds to nothing in **nature**. God is the maker of animal-machines, but since we cannot with any certainty determine the ends for which God has made the creatures of this world, the unity of the animal-machine remains a mere *as-if* unity.

BOURDIN, PIERRE (1595–1653). French Jesuit and teacher of **mathematics**. From 1618 to 1623, Bourdin taught humanities at the Jesuit Collège de **La Flèche**, which Descartes had attended. He returned to La Flèche in 1633, teaching rhetoric (and mathematics the next year). In 1635, he was transferred to the Jesuits' main educational institution in France, the Collège de Clermont (later Collège Louis-le-Grand) in Paris, where he remained as professor of mathematics until his death. He published several practical textbooks in mathematics, taken broadly. Among other topics, his *Cours de mathématique* (3rd ed., 1661) contained discussions of military architecture, fortification, terrain, and sections on cosmography and the use of the terrestrial globe. In his cosmology, as represented by two small treatises, *Sol flamma* and *Aphorismi analogici* (published together in 1646; *Sol flamma* might have been written by **Etienne Noël**), Bourdin followed the modified geocentric system of Tycho Brahe. He argued a position he knew was inconsistent with the **Aristotelian** theory of the heavens, and supported by such innovators as Descartes, that the sun is a blazing fire. According to Bourdin, the sun is a body on which there are sunspots and small torches, as the telescope rendered evident. Thus, the sun is corruptible matter and not incorruptible ether as Aristotle had it.

Bourdin is best known for the highly critical set of objections he wrote against Descartes's *Meditations,* published in the second edition of the *Meditations* (1642). His strategy in the objections was to show that Descartes's **method of doubt** failed, either because it was untrue to itself and smuggled in various principles, or, if it did not smuggle anything in, it led nowhere. He argued that Descartes's **principles** are not as certain as the common principles denied by the method of doubt. He also argued that the method ultimately could not have produced anything since it cut itself off from traditional means of argumentation and rejected any major premise whatever. The exchange was not successful; Descartes treated Bourdin's objections as silly or misguided, and publicly complained about them in a letter he addressed to Jacques Dinet, head of the French Jesuits. *See also OBJECTIONS AND REPLIES.*

BOYLE, ROBERT (1627–91). Boyle was one of the foremost experimental and **mechanical** philosophers of his day, a subscriber to the philosophical reforms of **Francis Bacon.** He cultivated an interest in **alchemy** and taught himself anatomy. He settled in Oxford around 1656 and became a leading member of the circle of experimental **natural philosophers** who were to form the core of the Royal Society of London. In 1660 he published the results of his experiments with an air pump: *New Experiments Physico-Mechanicall, Touching the Spring of the Air*; subsequently he had controversies with **Thomas Hobbes** and Francis Linus, over the existence of the **vacuum** and the **nature** of the "spring" of the air, and with **Baruch Spinoza,** over the interpretation of experiments. He rejected the **Aristotelian** and Paracelsian conception of the **elements** in *The Sceptical Chymist* (1661). He articulated his mechanical and corpuscularian philosophy in *Certain Physiological Essays* (1661), the *Origine of Formes and Qualities* (1666), and *Experiments, Notes etc. about the Mechanical Origine or Production of Divers Particular Qualities* (1675). Many of his other publications were concerned with natural **theology.**

BRASSET, HENRI (1591–?). Henri Brasset became secretary of the French Embassy in The Hague in 1627. In 1634 he became resident (permanent representative), a post he retained until 1654. Brasset was a loyal friend of Descartes and intervened on his behalf in his quarrels with **Gysbertus Voetius** and **Martinus Schoock** and with **Leiden University.** More particularly he represented Descartes's cause to the French ambassador, Gaspard Coignet de la Thuillerie (1594–1653), and to the stadtholder, Frederick-Henry of Orange (1584–1647). Although his main role was to forward letters of Descartes to **Pierre-Hector Chanut** and vice versa, there are also a few personal letters, particularly one in which he thanks Descartes for sending him the *Passions of the Soul.* It shows that Descartes did not see Brasset and his family only on official business. Old and blind, Brasset left the Netherlands in 1654. It is not known when he died.

BRUNO, GIORDANO (1548–1600). Italian philosopher famous for defending the thesis of the **infinity** of the world, one of several heterodox opinions that led to his being burned at the stake as a heretic. Bruno's education was in the traditional **scholastic** model, and he entered the Dominican order in 1665, giving up his given name Filippo and taking that of Giordano. He was ordained in 1572, but his criticism of traditional **theological** doctrines led to allegations of heresy in 1576. He left the Dominican order in the same year and became an itinerant scholar, taking up residence in Geneva, Toulouse, Lyons, Paris, Oxford, Frankfurt, and Venice. He published a number of works, the most important of which are *Cena de le Ceneri* ("The Ash Wednesday Supper") and *De l'Infinito, Universo e Mondi* ("On the Infinite, the Universe and Worlds"), both published in 1584. In the former work, he satirized the intellectual failings of the professors at Oxford (who had denied him a license to lecture) and defended Copernicanism. The latter work argued that the universe is infinite and contains an infinity of worlds inhabited by intelligent beings. Although there was never a question of Bruno's intellectual gifts, his dogged and vitriolic defense of controversial opinions alienated the authorities wherever he went. He was arrested by the Inquisition in 1591 after offending his Venetian patron, and was forced to abjure his erroneous opinions. This failed to satisfy the Inquisition in Rome, which obtained his extradition and kept him imprisoned until trying him on charges of heresy in 1599.

Bruno espoused a materialistic pantheism that does not distinguish between God and the world or between matter and spirit. According to this scheme, our world is but one of an infinity of worlds, and each and every part of it (mineral as well as plant and animal) is animated. Intermixed with these speculations, which find echoes in the teachings of **Baruch Spinoza** and **Gottfried Wilhelm Leibniz**, are mystical pronouncements on natural magic and allegorical disquisitions on the logic of Raymond Lull or Neoplatonic numerology. This farrago of speculative and scientific teachings led **Pierre Bayle** to dub Bruno "the knight errant of Philosophy." Descartes shared Bruno's dislike for much of traditional **natural philosophy**, and his execution as a heretic certainly gave Descartes a vivid example of the dangers involved in differing with traditional views about God and the world. He nevertheless found nothing of substance in Bruno's philosophy. Writing to **Isaac Beeckman** in October of 1630, Descartes lumps Bruno together with other "innovators" whose opinions merit little attention: "Telesio, Campanella, Bruno, Basso, **Vanini**, and all the innovators all say something different. Of all these people, I ask you, who is it who has anything to teach me, or indeed anyone who loves wisdom?" (AT, vol. I, p. 158).

BURMAN, FRANS (1628–79). Frans (François or Franciscus) Burman (Burmannus) was born in Frankenthal and Emmerich (Germany), the son of the Calvinist minister Caspar Burman. In 1643 he matriculated at **Leiden University** as a student in theology, apparently without obtaining a degree. From 1650 to 1661 he was minister in Hanau (Germany). He then received a call to Leiden to be deputy dean of the Statencollege (a theological college for bursars of the States of Holland). In 1663 Leiden University conferred upon him a doctorate in theology *honoris causa*. He was appointed to the chair of divinity of **Utrecht University**, as a counterbalance for **Gysbertus Voetius**. In Utrecht he founded a Cartesian club (the "College der Sçavanten"), which adversaries saw as a rallying point of theological and political dissidence. His general position was orthodox (in the sense that he subscribed to the confessional basis of the Dutch Reformed Churches), but his theology was Coccejan (named after the Franeker/Leiden theologian Joannes Coccejus), which, as compared to Voetian orthodoxy, implies a stronger emphasis on the idea of a covenant, a marked aversion from **scholastic** formalism, and a certain relativism in the interpretation of divine law, each law or set of laws being part of a particular covenant. Burman's main work, *Synopsis theologiae* (1671), even became a classic for this school of theology. He became involved in a controversy on the sanctification of the Sabbath, which according to him was based on a ceremonial command, thus valid only for the Jews; his criticism of **miracles** almost inevitably led to the accusation of **Spinozism**. On April 16, 1648, Burman, then still a student, was given permission to submit several questions to Descartes concerning his works. He carefully recorded Descartes's answers, which are interesting as clarifications on metaphysical and methodological issues, and a few days later (on 20 April) allowed **Johannes Clauberg** to make a copy. All modern editions of the conversation are based on the copy in the University Library of Göttingen. *See also* SPINOZA, BARUCH.

– C –

CALVIN, JOHN (1509–64), AND CALVINISM. Calvin was one of the great Reformers and the leader of the Reformed Church in Geneva. Calvinism was dominant in the United Provinces during the period when Descartes resided there. In the early 17th century there were heated **theological** disputes in the Provinces between Orthodox Calvinists, who insisted on the irresistibility of divine grace and the gratuitous **nature** of divine election, and the Remonstrants who, following Jacobus Armenius (1560–1609), wanted to allow some room for human **freedom** and merit. For the Orthodox, the Remonstrant position on freedom smacked of a heretical **Pelagianism**. The Orthodox won the political battle, and also became the main defenders in the universities of the **Aristotelian** status quo against the incursions of the new Cartesian philosophy. Members of this faction, such as **Gysbertus Voetius** of Utrecht, associated Cartesianism with the heterodox theological views of the Remonstrants. There is some irony in this association given that Cartesianism was later associated by its critics in France with the **Jansenists,** who were accused by their **Jesuit** opponents of advocating views on grace and **free will** similar to those of orthodox Calvinists.

Another aspect of Calvinism that is germane to an understanding of Cartesianism is its rejection of the Catholic doctrine of **transubstantiation.** This rejection was one source of the religious wars in late-16th-century France between the Catholic majority and the Calvinist Huguenot minority. Though the 1598 Edict of Nantes brought about an uneasy truce, the issue of transubstantiation continued to be controversial throughout the 17th century in France. Descartes entered into this controversy when he offered an account of transubstantiation in correspondence with **Denis Mesland.** After Descartes's death, **Claude Clerselier** refrained from publishing this correspondence in his editions of Descartes's writings out of fear that critics would associate this account with the heretical views of the Cartesians. However, the publication in 1671 of **Robert Desgabets**'s defense of the account in this correspondence helped to bring about an official campaign against Cartesianism in France, one which continued, with varying degrees of effectiveness, until the end of the reign of **Louis XIV.**

CARTESIAN CIRCLE. *See* CIRCLE, CARTESIAN.

CATEGORY. In the **Aristotelian** corpus of **logical** writings known collectively as the *Organon*, the first work concerns what Aristotle calls the "ways that being is said." This work, the *Categories*, establishes a list of 10. In Medieval philosophy that list tended to be reduced to just five: **substance, quantity, quality,** place, and relation. The primary division is between substance and the rest of the categories, which are called *accidents.* Substance is divided into "first" substances or concrete individuals and "second" substances, commonly identified by Medieval philosophers with genus and species. Socrates the individual man is a first substance; Socrates' humanness, or Socrates *qua* human, is a second substance. The first three categories of accident just mentioned are those in which change or **motion** can occur, and are thus the most significant for **natural philosophy.**

Descartes, like many of his contemporaries, regarded Aristotelian logic as of little use—at best a rhetorical device by which to "**demonstrate**" what is in fact already known by other means. Nevertheless in the *Principles*, a work at first meant to be a Cartesian counterpoint to the textbooks of the Schools, he includes a brief treatment of some standard terms like *universal, genus,* and *species,* and—more importantly—a revision of the basic substance-accident distinction. Descartes's new list of categories is reduced, as far as its logic goes, to just two: substance and **mode**. The role of second substances is played by what Descartes calls the "principal attributes" of created things—**thought** and **extension**. The principal attribute of a thing determines all its other modes. A thinking thing can be angry or resolute, an extended thing cannot; an extended thing can have **shape**, but no thinking thing can.

Descartes's revision of the categories, and in particular his subsumption of second substances under modes, which in Aristotelian terms reduces them to accidents, was taken up by **Antoine Arnauld** and Pierre Nicole in the Port Royal *Logic*. That work became the basis for philosophical logic until well into the 19th century; even now, the first-order logic most commonly used by philosophers continues to treat all predication on an equal footing.

CATERUS, JOHANNES (ca. 1590–1655). Presumably, Caterus (Kater or de Kater) was born in Antwerp, where his family had fled the Reformation. He obtained a master's degree in **Louvain** and became a licentiate in **theology**. After his ordination he went to Amsterdam and later Alkmaar, where his family originally came from, to live the semiclandestine life of a Roman Catholic priest. He seems to have been effective as well as courageous in the performance of his ecclesiastical duties. In any case he was appointed arch-priest (corresponding to deacon) and member of the Haarlem Chapter, which in the absence of a bishop governed the diocese of Holland and Zeeland. Caterus was "the learned theologian" who, in 1640, wrote the first objections to Descartes's *Meditations*, something for which he had been asked allegedly by their common friends, the Haarlem priests Jan Albert Bannius (1597/8–1644) and Augustinus Alstenius Blommert or Bloemaert (1585–1659), to whom, allegedly, they are also addressed. These objections concentrate on Descartes's **idea of God**, more particularly the idea that God is *causa sui* (cause of himself), something Descartes implicitly relies on in his second proof of the existence of God. Caterus asked Descartes to clarify his thought and explain in what sense this was meant: "positively" in the sense that God literally is the cause of his own being; or "negatively" in the sense that God's being is not caused by something else. Although in his reply Descartes tries to avoid the idea that God is his own efficient cause he insists that he means it in a positive sense. Since this exchange was part of the text as Descartes sent it to Paris, it could also be read by the authors of the other objections, **Antoine Arnauld** particularly, who further elaborated this theme.

CAUSE, EFFICIENT. In late **Aristotelian metaphysics**, the efficient cause is that which "gives being" to a thing by virtue of bringing it into existence. The efficient cause of a newborn animal is the seed from which it springs, or the formative power of that seed; the **final cause** is the perfected form of the organism; the formal cause is its specific form—say, human—and the material cause is the mixture of elements from which it is made. Like the final cause, the efficient cause is extrinsic: it is an individual distinct from the individual it affects, or if identical then identical only *per accidens*, as when an **animal** moves itself or a doctor cures himself.

Descartes not only rejects all but the efficient cause, he also reduces efficient causation to collisions of **particles**, the effect of which is change in the direction and speed of local **motion** (see, for example, *Principles* IV, art. 200, AT, vol. VIIIA, p. 325). Efficient causation can therefore be, in principle, analyzed into interactions to which the laws of motion can be directly applied. In fact Descartes rarely does so, depending instead either on models suggestive of the results one *would* arrive at by **geometry** and the **laws of nature**, or else on lemmas concerning the aggregate behavior of particles each of which is supposed to move in a lawlike fashion (see, for example, the lemmas on fluid motion at the end of *Principles* II, AT vol. VIIIA, pp. 71–77).

In **theology**, too, the only causality of **God** with respect to the world that Descartes is willing to consider is efficient causation, in its traditional three aspects of creation, **conservation**, and concurrence. Here Descartes's chief innovations are 1) to subsume the **eternal truths** under created things, and thus subordinate the divine knowledge of those truths to the divine **will**; 2) to identify—in this differing little from predecessors like **Francisco Suárez**—conservation with continued creation, as one and the same act enduring so long as its object endures, even though Descartes also emphasizes the logical independence of each instant of continued creation from all the rest; 3) to hint, at least, at an **occasionalist** treatment of the efficient causation of motion by bodies impinging upon one another—to transfer, in other words, the active power or **force** by which, according to common sense and the Schools, change is affected by bodies from bodies themselves to God. Later philosophers, notably **Nicolas Malebranche**, took up the hint, and held that no created thing can ever properly be said to act on another.

CAUSE, FINAL. The final cause of a thing is its end or the goal for the sake of which it has been produced, considered as (like other causes) "giving being" to that thing. Already in Medieval works on **metaphysics** and **natural philosophy** the status of the final cause was called into question; in the actions of inanimate things, the final cause tended to be identified with divine purpose, and in the actions of animate, especially rational, it tended to be identified with the conception of the form in the mind of the agent; in both cases, the final cause could be identified as a particular sort of **efficient cause**, namely, the end as represented in the agent. Thus the end of seed-formation in birds was identified with the idea of their offspring, or more remotely with that of the preservation of the species, residing in the divine mind. **Francisco Suárez**, following **Thomas Aquinas**, argues at some length, however, that the causality of the end is distinct from the efficient causality of its idea in the mind of the agent, on the grounds that the attraction exerted by the end on the will of the agent is distinct from the efficient-causal action of the idea on the will.

Descartes, and with him many Cartesians (but not **Robert Boyle**, for example) argued not only against natural ends but against any appeal to divine ends in **natural philosophy**. Among his arguments are that it would be presumptuous for us to suppose we had any access to the reasons **God** chose to act as he did (*Principles* III, art. 2, AT, vol. VIIIA, pp. 80–81); that ends explain nothing that cannot be explained better by efficient causes; and that to impute intrinsic ends to stones and the like is tantamount to imputing cognition of those ends, and thus to imputing **minds** to them. The doctrine of the creation of **eternal truths** can be taken to imply that not only would it be presumptuous to inquire into God's purposes, but that it is would be idle to do so: *ante factum* God can have no end in creating the world, since "we can come up with nothing good, nor bad, nor anything to be believed, or done, or omitted whose idea was in the divine intellect before his will determined itself to bring it about that it should be such" (*Sixth Replies*, AT, vol. VII, p. 432). If, moreover, the world passes through, as Descartes suggests in the *Principles*, all physically possible states in such a way that *any* such state could be the state of the world at creation, then providence, as **Gottfried Wilhelm Leibniz** unhappily noted, insofar as it presupposes a particular temporal ordering of those states, with a designated beginning and end, has no place in a Cartesian history of nature.

CAUSE OF ITSELF (*CAUSA SUI*). See CATERUS, JOHANNES (ca. 1590–1655).

CAVENDISH, SIR CHARLES (1595?–1654). English nobleman and mathematician, younger brother of **William Cavendish**. Educated by private tutors rather than at a university, he was created a knight by King James in 1619. Described by John Aubrey as "a weake, crooked man," who was suited "neither for the court nor camp," Cavendish devoted himself to pure and applied **mathematics** and maintained correspondence with many of the leading mathematicians and philosophers of his day, including Descartes, François Derand, Thomas Harriot, **Thomas Hobbes, Marin Mersenne, Claude Mydorge,** William Oughtred, **John Pell,** and Walter Warner. Cavendish was a member of the Short Parliament of 1640, although he played only a limited role in the political struggles that led to the English Civil War. He served in the Royalist army, but left for the Continent with his brother William after the defeat at the battle of Marston Moor in 1644. Cavendish remained in exile until 1651, and during this period he spent much time in Paris where he met frequently with Mersenne and Hobbes, as well as keeping up a correspondence with mathematicians elsewhere in Europe. He served in 1645 as an intermediary between Descartes and **Gilles Personne de Roberval** in their dispute over the centers of percussion, and he assisted Pell in gathering demonstrations and opinions from various mathematicians as part of Pell's controversy with Christian Severin Longborg over the quadrature of the circle. Cavendish published nothing during his lifetime and established his reputation purely through correspondence; although he achieved no great results of his own, he was a respected and important contributor to the development of the mathematics of his day.

CAVENDISH, WILLIAM, DUKE OF NEWCASTLE (1593?–1696). English aristocrat and notable patron of science, literature, and philosophy. Educated at St. John's College, Cambridge he was created Viscount Mansfield by King James in 1620, and in 1628 Earl of Newcastle. He hosted two famous (and hugely expensive) entertainments for Charles I in 1633 and 1634 at the family estate of Welbeck, which included masques by the poet and dramatist Ben Jonson. These established Cavendish's reputation as a patron of learning and the arts, and Welbeck became a center of learned discussion that regularly included **Sir Charles Cavendish** (brother of William), **Thomas Hobbes, Sir Kenelm Digby,** and Robert Payne, among others. In 1638 he was appointed governor of the Prince of Wales (the future Charles II) and made a member of the king's Privy Council. In 1640, Cavendish sided with the Royalist cause in the English Civil War, raising money and troops for King Charles I and leading an army, for which service he was created Marquess of Newcastle in 1643. In the aftermath of the severe Royalist defeat at the battle of Marston Moor (1644), he left England for Paris.

During his exile in Paris Newcastle married Margaret Lucas in 1645 (his first wife having died in 1643). Margaret Cavendish went on to become a notable figure in English letters: as one of the first women in England to write principally for publication she produced poetry, works of fiction, and philosophical tracts. Newcastle remained on the Continent until the restoration of the English monarchy in 1660 and was active in expatriate literary and intellectual circles in Paris and Rotterdam. He was created Duke of Newcastle in 1665. He authored numerous literary pieces and two treatises on horsemanship, as well as corresponding with *savants* and hosting numerous literary, philosophical, and scientific gatherings at his various residences. He and Sir Charles Cavendish invited Descartes to relocate to England in 1640 (presumably to reside at Welbeck), but the offer was declined.

CERTAINTY. Descartes distinguishes between two kinds or grades of certainty, one he calls moral or physical, and another he calls absolute, mathematical, or more than moral. At the end of the *Principles,* Descartes uses an analogy with a clock to talk about the explanations of phenomena that make use of corpuscles which our senses do not perceive. Two clocks identical on the outside may indicate the time equally well but use different operating mechanisms. So also **God** could have produced the phenomena we perceive in innumerably different ways. As a result, the causes postulated by Descartes to explain some effects may correspond to the phenomena manifested by **nature,** but may not be the ones by which God produced those effects. These explanations, according to Descartes, are morally certain, that is, they suffice for the conduct of life, although, given the absolute power of God, they can be doubted. Descartes uses another example to explain moral certainty. He refers to a code breaker who has decoded a message and who is certain of his solution, but who understands that another solution might be possible. The situation is different with absolute certainty, which, according to Descartes, we possess for "mathematical demonstrations, the knowledge that material things exist, and the evidence of all clear reasoning that is carried on about them" (*Principles* IV, art. 206). An important instance in which Descartes claims to have reached moral, not absolute certainty is the case of **animals** and **machines.** We have moral certainty that an entity using **language** or acting through knowledge will be human, and not animal or machine: "for it is morally impossible for there to be enough different organs in a machine to make it act in all the contingencies of life in the same way as our **reason** makes us act" (*Discourse* V, AT, vol. VI, p. 57).

CHANUT, PIERRE-HECTOR (1601–62). Chanut was a diplomat, the French ambassador to Sweden and then to the Netherlands. He was brother-in-law to **Claude Clerselier** and came to know Descartes through him. Chanut moved to Sweden in 1645 to take up a diplomatic post (becoming ambassador in 1649). He acted as an intermediary in a correspondence between Queen **Christina** of Sweden and Descartes, ultimately convincing Descartes to move to Sweden.

CHARLET, ÉTIENNE (1570–1652). Charlet entered the **Jesuits** in 1589, became professor of theology at **La Flèche** in 1606 and rector there from 1608 to 1616 (during Descartes's stay at the college). He subsequently held various significant administrative offices in the order. He was distantly related to Descartes and seemed to have looked after him during his school years. As Descartes said to him in correspondence: "you have acted like a father to me throughout my youth" (AT, vol. IV, p. 156).

CHARLETON, WALTER (1620–1707). English natural philosopher and physician. Charleton received a degree of M.D. from Oxford in 1643 and became physician to Charles I. He left for France during the English Civil War. There he met **Thomas Hobbes** and assimilated the **natural philosophy** of Descartes and **Pierre Gassendi.** He was one of the original members of the Royal Society of London and later became president of the Royal College of Physicians (1689–91).

In 1652 Charleton published *The Darknes of Atheism Dispelled by the Light of Nature,* a work on natural **theology,** in which he made use of Descartes's proofs for the **existence of God,** from the *Meditations.* But Charleton's sympathies for Descartes's project also extended to his **mechanist** philosophy. Like Descartes, he dismissed **scholastic** real **qualities** and accidental **forms** and accepted corporeal **substance** as magnitude or **quantity** extended in three dimensions. His principal work, *Physiologia-Epicuro-Gassendo-Charltoniana* (1654), consisted of translation and paraphrase of parts of Gassendi's late work, *Animadversiones,* with additions from the then-unpublished *Syntagma.* As claimed by its title, the book was an attempt to resurrect "a fabrick of science natural upon the hypothesis of atoms" as "founded by Epicurus, repaired by Petrus Gassendus and augmented by Walter Charleton." It became a major vehicle for the dissemination of the new philosophy in England. But, by his admission, Charleton was not fully a Gassendist. In *Physiologia,* he classified himself as one "electing" among a variety of opinions and not belonging either to the class of "assertors of philosophical liberty" or "renovators" of ancient philosophies, to which he claimed Descartes and Gassendi respectively belonged. *Physiologia* incorporated a healthy dose of Cartesian thought and of Charleton's own interpretations into Gassendi's **atomism.**

CHARRON, PIERRE (1541–1603). French lawyer who became a theologian and skeptic. Charron studied Greek and Latin in Paris and juris-

prudence at Orléans and Bourges. After his doctorate in 1571, he practiced law without much success. In 1576 he studied **theology** and was
ordained; he served as Canon of Bordeaux (1576–93). Charron came
into contact with **Michel de Montaigne** in 1589 and conversed with
him during the final three years of his life. In 1594 he published his
great theological work, *Les Trois Véritez*, an attack against **atheists**,
pagans, Jews, Muslims, and, above all, the Calvinists. He published his
most important philosophical work, *De la sagesse*, in 1601, and died
during the publication of the second edition.

There are significant parallels between Charron's *De la sagesse* and
Descartes's various writings. Descartes even owned a copy of the work.
For Charron, the true knowledge and true study of man is man; understanding of man leads to knowledge of **God**. Part of this type of self-
knowledge comes from an examination of our human capacities, that is,
the senses and **reason**. But the senses are defective. We may not have
all the senses requisite for knowledge. Our senses vary with different
conditions in us and in the external world. Therefore, we have no way
of obtaining any certain knowledge by means of the senses. Moreover,
our rational faculties are defective as well. They are also unreliable; if
reason uses the senses, it is bound to be unreliable. Even rational persons disagree about everything. In fact, there is no judgment that cannot
be opposed by good reasons. We have no standards that enable us to
distinguish **truth** from falsehood. We believe mainly by the **passion** or
force of majority pressure. There are no **principles** for us unless divinity has revealed them: everything else is but smoke and dream.

Charron's solution to the weakness of our capacities for avoiding
error and finding truth is that we should examine all questions freely
and dispassionately. We should keep all prejudice and emotion out of
decisions, develop a universality of **mind**, and reject any and all solutions that are at all dubious. We should remain to ourselves free, universal, open, and ready for anything. By applying systematic **doubt**, we
can thoroughly cleanse the mind of all dubious opinions and present
ourselves naked and ready before God, to receive the stamp of wisdom.

CHRISTINA, QUEEN OF SWEDEN (1626–89). Christina inherited the
throne of Sweden upon the death of her father, Gustavus Adolphus.
Unlike most women in the 17th century, she knew Latin and Greek and
read treatises on astronomy, **alchemy**, and medicine. She corresponded
and met with many prominent scholars, such as **Antoine Arnauld, Pierre Gassendi**, and **Blaise Pascal**. She studied the ancients and such
moderns as Descartes. Christina invited Descartes to spend the summer
of 1649 at Stockholm, but Descartes delayed the visit. He finally departed for Sweden that autumn. At Christina's bidding, Descartes began

discussing philosophy with her during the early hours of the morning, around five o'clock. Descartes did not last the winter; he caught pneumonia at the beginning of February and died about a week later. In 1655, Christina publicly converted to Catholicism and abdicated her throne. In her later years, she was a patron of artists and musicians. The academies she sponsored focused on skepticism, cosmology, and **natural philosophy**.

CIRCLE, CARTESIAN. The standard label for a structural problem with Cartesian epistemology. This problem was introduced most directly by **Antoine Arnauld** in his *Fourth Set of Objections* to Descartes's *Meditations*. As Arnauld expressed it, the difficulty is that "we can be certain that **God** exists only because we clearly and distinctly perceive this," but that we cannot rely on our clear and distinct perceptions to prove the existence of God given Descartes's claim at the beginning of the *Third Meditation* that we can be "certain that what we clearly and distinctly perceive is true only because God exists" (AT, vol. VII, p. 214). In reply to this objection, Descartes drew attention to the difference between clear and distinct perceptions to which one is actually attending and clear and distinct perceptions that one merely remembers having considered in the past. His claim is that the former sort of perceptions are beyond doubt, but that the latter sort of perceptions cannot be trusted until it is established that a nondeceptive God exists (AT, vol. VII, pp. 140–41, 144–46). There is controversy among Descartes scholars about whether he took the fact that we cannot doubt our present clear and distinct perceptions to indicate merely a psychological fact about us, or rather to justify the claim that such perceptions are true. A related controversy is over whether Descartes was interested mainly in providing a psychologically stable system of beliefs, or whether he wanted to establish that these beliefs in fact correspond to reality. *See also* CLARITY AND DISTINCTNESS; MEMORY.

CLARITY AND DISTINCTNESS. Descartes made it a central principle of his system that all our clear and distinct perceptions are true. However, early modern critics such as **Pierre-Daniel Huet** and **Gottfried Wilhelm Leibniz** objected that Descartes did not offer a sufficiently clear account of what the clarity and distinctness of a perception consists. In the *Principles*, Descartes did explain that a clear perception is one "present and accessible to the attentive **mind**," whereas a distinct perception is one that "is so sharply separated from all other perceptions that it contains in itself only what is clear" (AT, vol. VIII-1, p. 22). Here he provided as an example of the former a perception of an intense pain that is clear insofar as it is present to the attentive mind, but that is not distinct insofar as the perception is contaminated by the false judgment that the pain resembles something in the body. The implication here, made explicit elsewhere in the *Principles*, is that even our **sensations** can be clear and distinct insofar as they are considered only as **thoughts** (AT, vol. VIII-1, p. 33). However, elsewhere Descartes spoke of the sensory states of the **union of mind and body** as being, in contrast to purely intellectual states of mind, intrinsically confused and obscure. At one point he even attempted to explain this obscurity and confusion by claiming that our sensations involve a certain kind of prejudgmental **material falsity**.

When Descartes speaks of clear and distinct perception, he often has in mind the perception not of a particular state or object but of propositional **truths** concerning objects. This is so, for instance, in his emphasis on the fact that clear and distinct perception is involved in our apprehension of the truth of *cogito ergo sum*. However, this particular case broaches a problem for Descartes's account of clarity and distinctness that is connected to the objection of **Baruch Spinoza** that the **judgment** that an **idea** has certain features does not differ from the perception of that idea. On Descartes's official view, judgment involves an act of **will**, and so is distinct from perception, which involves the **intellect** alone. Yet it is difficult to see how he can distinguish the clear and distinct perception of the *cogito* from the assent to the truth of the *cogito*. One possibility is that clear and distinct perception amounts in this case to the perception of the inconceivability of the falsity of the *cogito*. But it might be that this account cannot be extended to other cases of clear and distinct perception, and thus that a more general account of clarity and distinctness is still required.

CLAUBERG, JOHANNES (1622–65). Johannes Clauberg (Claubergius) was born February 24, 1622, in Solingen (Germany) and studied in Cologne and Bremen. There he met Tobias Andreae (1604–76), whom he joined in Groningen in 1644 after Andreae was appointed professor of Greek (1635). Descartes's philosophy does not seem to have made any impact on his mind before Andreae sent him (after travels to France and England) to **Johannes de Raey** in Leiden in 1648. Meanwhile Andreae had published Clauberg's first book, *Ontosophia* (1647), which if anything betrays the influence of Comenius (1592–1670) and is based on material collected by Clauberg during his years in Bremen (the work was rewritten in a Cartesian sense for later editions). That by 1648 Clauberg had become interested in Descartes's philosophy is shown however by the fact that on April 20, 1648, he made a copy of **Frans Burman's** report (or helped Burman to make a report) of his conversation with Descartes. In that period Clauberg was sounded about a professorship in Herborn (Germany), which he accepted the following year. Clauberg's duties were in philosophy and (to a lessser extent) in **theology**. Apart from the fact that this meant that he had a heavy teaching load he also resented this combination, insisting, like all Cartesians, on the separation of theology and philosophy. Before long a conflict with more conservative colleagues became inevitable. On November 1, 1651, it was officially decided that the only philosophy allowed in Herborn was "Aristotelico-Ramist philosophy, either separately or mixed." Clauberg and his friend Christoph Wittich, who had been appointed junior professor of **mathematics**, left Herborn in December 1651 and accepted posts in Duisburg. For the rest of his years Clauberg led the busy life of a professor in a small German town. He attracted many students, several of whom became professors themselves.

Possibly when still in Leiden Clauberg had already started on his second book, the *Defensio cartesiana*, which however was published only in 1652. It is a reply to *Consideratio theologica* (1648) by **Jacobus Revius** (1586–1658). His most influential book probably was *Logica vetus nova*, first published by Elzevier in 1654. In it Clauberg reduces Descartes's methodological precepts to a number of easily remembered rules, thus creating a Cartesian **logic**, which would remain standard until the *Logique de Port-Royal* (1662). Most of Clauberg's other works are dedicated to the explanation of Descartes's physics and **metaphysics**. In Germany, where the first edition of Descartes's *Opera* would be published only in 1692, his name became almost synonymous with that of Descartes. He died 31 January 1665. The Amsterdam professor of philosophy Johann Theodor Schallbruch (1655–1723) provided a posthumous edition of Clauberg's works, *Opera omnia philosophica* (1691), which was partly based on unpublished material in the possession of Clauberg's son.

CLAVE, ÉTIENNE DE (fl. 1624–ca. 1635). A French **alchemist**. De Clave became notorious when he, Jean Bitault, and Antoine Villon announced a disputation for August 24 and 25, 1624, by posting 14 anti-**Aristotelian** theses on the streets of Paris. The disputation did not take place. The president of Parlement saw copies of the theses and prohibited the disputants from sustaining them on pain of death. Parlement then sent the theses to the **Sorbonne** to be examined. A few days later, the Sorbonne replied with a censure of some of the theses and Parlement ordered Villon, de Clave, and Bitault to leave Paris, never to teach again within their jurisdiction, on pain of corporal punishment. Among the prohibited theses were propositions claiming that the prime matter of the Peripatetics is utterly fictitious and denying **substantial forms**, except for rational **soul**. The official condemnation said that the theses were "overly bold, erroneous, and close to heresy." The faculty also objected to the proposition that physical alterations happen through the introduction or destruction of an accidental entity, because, they said, it attacked the "holy sacrament of the **Eucharist**."

The condemnation of the anti-Aristotelians in 1624 became the precedent for the condemnation of Cartesianism in the second half of the 17th century. In 1671 the archbishop of Paris published a verbal decree from King Louis XIV requiring that "no other doctrine be taught in the universities other than the one set forth by the rules and statutes of the university, and that nothing of these other doctrines be put into theses." The king thus prohibited "certain opinions that the faculty of theology has once censured and whose teaching or publication was prohibited by the Parlement," which, as he put it, "could bring some confusion into the explanation of our mysteries." The reference in the decree to "opinions the faculty of theology once censored" was an allusion to the condemnation of 1624. The king's exhortation recalled the subsequent *arret* issued by the Court du Parlement. That legal document prohibited "all persons, under pain of death, from either holding or teaching any maxims against the ancient authors which were not approved by the doctors of the Faculty of Theology." Although Louis did not directly mention Cartesianism, it was clearly the "other doctrine" against which the decree was directed. In any case, he clarified his intent in 1675 by specifically naming those who "taught the opinions and thoughts of Descartes" as ones who "might bring disorder to our Kingdom." Louis ordered that "they be prevented from continuing their lessons in any way whatsoever."

CLAVIUS, CHRISTOPHER (1537–1612). German-born mathematician and astronomer, foremost mathematician at the **Collegio Romano** and influential contributor to pure and applied **mathematics**. Almost nothing is known of his early life, aside from the fact that he was born near Bamberg in Franconia. Even his name is uncertain—the Latinized "Clavius" has been suggested to derive from the German words "Schlüssel" (key) or "Klau" (claw). He was admitted to the **Jesuit** Order in Rome in 1555 and was educated at the University of Coimbra in Portugal. His mathematical abilities were soon manifest, and his observation of the total solar eclipse of 1560 inspired him to pursue astronomy. In 1560 he returned to Rome and began his study of **theology** at the Collegio Romano. He was ordained in 1564 while still pursuing his theological studies and admitted as a full member of the Society of Jesus in 1575. He began teaching mathematics at the college, as early as 1564 and, aside from a two-year stay in Naples in 1595–97, he remained professor of mathematics at the Collegio Romano until his death.

Astronomy was the field in which Clavius was best known during his lifetime. His influential *Commentarius in Sphaeram Joannis de Sacro Bosco* (first published in 1570) was the standard textbook on astronomy for generations, introducing such luminaries as Tycho Brahe, **Johannes Kepler**, and **Galileo Galilei** to the subject. Calvius was also instrumental in the 1582 reform of the Julian calendar. The Julian leap-year rule (one additional day every fourth year) added three excess days every period of 385 years. As a result, by the 16th century the actual occurrence of the equinoxes and solstices had departed noticeably from their calendar dates, and Pope Gregory XIII determined to reform the calendar. Clavius proposed that Wednesday, October 4, 1582 (Julian) should be followed by Thursday, October 15, 1582 (Gregorian) and that leap years occur in years exactly divisible by four, except that years ending in 00 must be divisible by 400 to be leap years. This rule is accurate enough that it is still used today and will not require revision for several centuries. **François Viète** attacked the accuracy of the new calendar, and Clavius's *Novi calendarii romani apologia* (1595) justified the calendar reforms, defending them against the criticisms of Viète and others.

Clavius's contributions to pure mathematics occurred principally in the context of his editions and commentaries on classical authors. His 1574 edition of Euclid's *Elements* (with extensive commentary) was used very widely, and it was an integral part of his attempts to promote the study of mathematics within the Society of Jesus. His 1608 *Algebra* was also an important textbook. Descartes's mathematical education at **La Flèche** exposed him to the works of Clavius, but in keeping with his reticence about any sources of his mathematical ideas, Descartes makes almost no mention of him. In a letter to **Mersenne** in November 1629 he mentions Clavius's treatment of the curve known as the quadratrix in his commentary on Euclid (AT, vol. I, pp. 70–71), and in a letter to **Charles Cavendish** from August of 1644, **John Pell** reports that Descartes "says he had no other instructor for Algebra than the reading of Clavy algebra above 30 yeares agoe" (AT, vol. IV, pp. 730–31).

CLEAR AND DISTINCT IDEAS. *See* CLARITY AND DISTINCT-NESS.

CLERSELIER, CLAUDE (1614–84). Clerselier was born 21 March 1614, the son of a *conseiller du Roi*. In 1630 he married Anne de Virlo-rieux, with whom he had fourteen children. His sister, Marguerite, was married to **Pierre-Hector Chanut** (1601–62), who presumably brought him into contact with the circle of **Marin Mersenne** and so with Descartes. The first documented contact between Clerselier and Descartes is a letter of Descartes to Clerselier, which according to the "Exemplaire de l'Institut" is dated February 17, 1645, and was written in answer presumably to a query by Clerselier on Descartes's laws of collision. The letter shows that Clerselier is defending Descartes's metaphysical argument as well, more particularly against the objection that "the Gentiles had the idea of several Gods" (AT, vol. IV, p. 188). Apparently Descartes agrees with Clerselier's solution that the fact that the **idea of God** is innate does not entail that everybody automatically forms a correct idea of God.

Another letter shows that Clerselier also volunteered to receive for Descartes the letters of his younger sister Anne. Apparently he did the same for other members of Descartes's family as well. He was also an intermediary between Descartes and others. Clerselier's illness, which first manifested itself in 1646 by epileptic fits and some sort of arthritis or gout, was an ongoing concern for Descartes and became a serious handicap for Clerselier himself, of which he complains in the prefaces to his edition of Descartes's *Correspondence*. He died 13 April 1684.

Clerselier was perhaps more important as a mediator between Descartes and the French public than as a correspondent and friend. His plan to make a French translation of the *Meditations* dates from 1644, or perhaps even earlier, but in any case without Descartes's knowledge. When Descartes heard of it during his journey to France in the summer of 1644, he encouraged Clerselier to continue with it, despite the fact that a translation of the *Meditations* had already been made by the **Duc de Luynes**, because Clerselier intended to complete his translation of the *Meditations* with a translation of the *Objections and Replies*. Clerselier was also responsible for seeing the translation through the press. After Descartes's death Clerselier became the main editor of his *Correspondence*, which he published in three volumes, in 1657, 1659, and 1667. He also published a new edition of *The World* and a French text (after a Latin translation had been published by Schuyl) of the *Treatise on Man*. By allowing **Gottfried Wilhelm Leibniz** and Walter von Tschirnhaus access to his collection of Descartes's autographs he ensured the survival of the *Rules for the Direction of the Mind* and the *Search for Truth* (both first published in Dutch, on the basis of a copy provided by Tschirnhaus). Realizing the inadequacy of his work, caused by his ill health, Clerselier signed a contract with a Dutch publisher to provide a definitive edition. That plan however was superseded by his death in 1684. In his will he designated a considerable sum of money to be spent on a new edition of the correspondence.

COGITO ERGO SUM. Perhaps the most familiar of Descartes's claims, this phrase, "I think therefore I am," is not found in his 1641 *Meditations*, but first appeared in his 1644 *Principles of Philosophy* (though a French version, *Je pense donc je suis*, is found in his 1637 *Discourse on Method*). Several of Descartes's contemporaries pointed out that his *cogito* (as it is often called for short) was anticipated in the work of **Augustine.**

In the Second Meditation, the *cogito* is expressed as the claim that "'I am, I exist,' is necessarily true whenever it is put forward by me or conceived in my mind" (AT, vol. VII, p. 25). This claim adds to the more familiar formulation of the *cogito* the point that it is the **truth** of a conception that is in question, and that one can accept the truth of the conception only at the time it is conceived. Both additions are relevant to the "truth rule," namely, the rule that all **clear and distinct** perceptions are true, which Descartes explicitly linked to the *cogito* at the beginning of the *Third Meditation.* Significantly, Descartes responded to the problem of the **Cartesian circle** by claiming that prior to proving the existence of a nondeceptive **God**, we can accept the truth of our clear and distinct perceptions only when we are actually attending to them.

Descartes's contemporaries questioned whether the *cogito* is a **syllogism** that relies on knowledge of the major premise, everything that thinks, exists. Descartes's most complete response, indicated in a record of conversations he had with **Frans Burman**, is that though there is implicit knowledge of this premise in the *cogito*, explicitly we recognize only the particular application of the premise in our own case.

Descartes's successors, both critics and sympathizers, raised further questions about the *cogito*. There is an extended critique of this argument, for instance, in the 1690 *Censura philosophiae cartesianae* of the anti-Cartesian **Pierre-Daniel Huet.** Huet brought to the foreground the objection, familiar from the later work of **Gottfried Wilhelm Leibniz** and Immanuel Kant, that the *cogito* involves a *petitio principii* insofar as the *I think* already includes *I exist.* Huet also offered the novel claim that *I think* and *I exist* are distinct **thoughts** that cannot occur at the same time. Thus, Descartes can argue not *I think therefore I am*, but only *I think therefore I will be*, or *I thought therefore I am.* According to Huet, however, the fact that Descartes held that we can affirm our existence only at the time we derive it from our thought shows that these arguments could not be acceptable to him.

Some of Descartes's later followers objected not so much to the *cogito* itself but to his claim that this argument supports the thesis that "the **nature of mind** is better known than **body.**" Thus, **Nicolas Malebranche** claimed that though the *cogito* reveals the existence of our mind as a thinking thing is better known than the existence of body, it cannot reveal that we have a clearer knowledge of the nature of mind than we have of the nature of body. Indeed, Malebranche claimed that it is the other way around since our knowledge of the nature of our thought is far inferior to the sort of knowledge of the nature of body that derives from the idea of **extension**. However, there was a challenge in the work of the French Cartesian **Robert Desgabets** even to Descartes's claim that it follows from the *cogito* that the existence of our mind is better known than the existence of body. Desgabets objected in particular that the fact that the thoughts involved in the *cogito* have a temporal duration that matches the temporal duration of body shows that they are united with such motion. For Desgabets, then, the *cogito* reveals as clearly the existence of bodies in motion as it does the existence of mind as a thing with particular thoughts. *See also* TIME.

COLLEGIO ROMANO. The most important of the many **Jesuit** educational institutions, the Collegio Romano was founded in 1551 by Ignatius Loyola with a bequest from Francisco Borgia, duke of Gandia. The fact that the college was founded only 11 years after the Society of Jesus received papal recognition indicates the significance the order attached to its educational mission. The college was given the right to grant doctorates in philosophy and **theology** by papal bulls of 1552 and 1556, also receiving the various privileges enjoyed by the Catholic universities of Paris, Louvain, Salamanca, and Alcalá. By 1567 the Collegio Romano had over a thousand students, and in 1582 a large building was erected at the order of Pope Gregory XIII to house the growing institution. The course of education at the Collegio Romano was governed by the *Ratio atque institutio studiorum societatis Iesu* ("The Plan and Order of Studies of the Society of Jesus"), first elaborated in 1586. A revised version of the *ratio studiorum* was officially adopted in 1599 by the Superior General Claudio Acquaviva as the definitive statement of the course of study for the whole Jesuit educational network. In the 16th and 17th centuries education at the Collegio Romano emphasized traditional **scholastic** philosophy, but it also included many "humanistic" elements typical of Italian Renaissance education, as well as required study in **mathematics** and **natural philosophy**. The relatively elevated status of mathematics in the college was secured by the efforts of **Christopher Clavius**, who campaigned tirelessly to keep mathematics and astronomy central to the educational mission of the college. His efforts were so successful that nearly all of the Jesuits who distinguished themselves in science or mathematics in the 17th century either studied or taught at the college. The institution continues to occupy a prominent role in Catholic education. Among the university's graduates are 19 canonized saints, 16 popes, and 24 persons who have been beatified.

COLOR. In **Aristotelian** physics, color is a primitive quality of material **substances.** It may be determined by, but is not reducible to, other qualities like the **elemental** qualities hot, cold, wet, and dry. Color is a "proper sensible" of vision: that is, only the visual organ is affected by color *per se.* According to the predominant Aristotelian theory of color perception, a colored thing produces *species* in the medium (air or water) which are instantaneously conveyed to the organ of sight, there to become "intentional" species. These, by virtue of their causal history, represent colors to the **soul.** Intentional species, though "material" in the sense of being qualities of material things, were not full-fledged physical qualities. A thing cannot have contrary colors in the same spot at the same time, but the medium or the sense organ can receive the intentional species of contrary colors simultaneously.

Cartesian physics jettisons all this machinery. Color, considered as a property of **light,** is reducible to **motion** (it is the ratio of angular to rectilinear motion in light particles). Considered as a property of the surfaces of bodies, it is something like texture. Instead of species, the organ of vision receives impulses of motion from the light particles that impinge on it; those impulses are transmitted by the nerves to the brain, where, by means of motions of the **animal spirits,** they affect the **pineal gland,** and therefore the **mind.** Color here stands for all sensible qualities: each is reducible to motions and configurations of particles of matter which affect the sense organs in characteristic ways.

When the mind senses color, it acquires, by way of certain motions of or impressions on the pineal gland, a certain **mode**—an "idea" of color. A term like red, if it does not denote some (perhaps complex) mode of **extension,** must, according to Descartes, denote a mode of **thought.** The obscurity of ideas of color consists in their presenting themselves to us *as if* they were qualities of bodies distinct from any mode of extension; hence our **preconceived opinion** that bodies really do have such qualities (*Principles* I, art. 66, 68).

The elimination of color and other sensible qualities (if considered to be distinct from all modes of extension) was essential to the mechanistic program. **Mechanism** circumscribes the list of genuinely physical properties, and then tries to explain all natural phenomena on the basis of that circumscribed list. This part of Descartes's program enjoyed an enduring success. Even John Locke and **Gottfried Wilhelm Leibniz,** who opposed Descartes on many other points, took for granted the Cartesian program of reduction and elimination.

COMMON NOTION. In Euclid's *Elements*, a common notion (often called an axiom) is a general principle that applies to any science and is therefore common, not in the sense of being generally accepted, but rather as being generally applicable. Thus, the first common notion of the *Elements* asserts that "Things which are equal to the same thing are equal to each other," and is a principle that applies outside the realm of geometry as well as within it. Descartes understood common notions as eternal truths grasped by the mind: "when we apprehend that it is impossible that something come from nothing, this proposition *nothing comes from nothing* is not to be considered as an existing thing, nor as the mode of a thing, but as a certain eternal truth which located in our mind and is called a common notion, or an axiom" (*Principles* I, art. 49; AT, vol. VII, p. 23). The clarity and distinctness with which common notions are apprehended guarantees the mind's assent and renders them self-justifying. It might seem that such principles must garner universal assent, but Descartes held that in some cases "because these common notions are opposed to the preconceived opinions of some people" their prejudices would hinder their clear apprehension of them (*Principles* I, art. 50; AT, vol. VII, p. 24).

COMMON SENSE (*SENSUS COMMUNIS, SENS COMMUN, BON SENS, BONA MENS*). In Descartes common sense means, first a psychological faculty (generally identified as the imagination) and correspondingly a part of the brain, and second only a way of judging things (sound judgment, good sense). Descartes develops a theory of common understanding and common experience, which is actually a theory of prejudice. Traditionally the common sense or common *sensorium* is that part of the brain where all nerves come together and where all the impressions of the external senses are received and processed. That is also the way more or less in which this inner organ is conceived by Descartes, except that, according to him the nerves do not come together in one single point. They end at the edge of the brain substance, where they form a complicated pattern and are separated from the common sense by the brain cavity. The fact, however, that this is completely filled with animal spirits allows the common sense to register any change in the complex patterns the nerves form on the surface of the brain. Although Descartes admits that in humans the pineal gland is hardly visible, he makes that organ the seat of the common sense, mainly because, apart from the brain as a whole, it is the only part that is not divided into symmetric parts. Since, on the other hand, all our sensations are one (even those that reach us through two different organs, like vision and sound), there is no other part of the brain that can fulfill the role of common sense. Moreover the pineal gland (or *con-*

arion) is situated right in the middle of the brain between all its cavities, so is perfectly equipped to register what is going on. Descartes makes this the seat of the faculty of the imagination, that is, of the general faculty of receiving and processing the impressions of the senses. As such it is common to man and beast, except that in beasts it is not accompanied by awareness (see **animals**). A complication is that the same organ is also the principal seat of the human **soul**, but this must not be understood as if all the functions of the human **mind** are exercised in the *conarion*; indeed, for purely intellectual **thoughts** the soul does not need any bodily organ at all.

Descartes also frequently speaks of common sense (*sens commun*) as the capacity to make sound judgments. In principle, this capacity, which he also calls good sense (*bon sens*) or **reason** (*raison*), is present in everybody, whether cultivated or not. Since it is the basis of all moral and practical improvement, it is also the only thing that is really good. Although innate, good sense can be corrupted by the frequent confrontation with false and uncertain opinions, by the habit of disputations, and generally by the use of **scholastic** methods. But also the ordinary prejudices of the senses and of education usually prevent us from being aware even of the clearest **ideas**, in particular those of **God** and matter. Sometimes Descartes puts this in a historical perspective, claiming that in ancient times people were wiser than we are now because our **intellect** has become blunt by the daily confrontation with error. The fact that Descartes restores good sense and reason by critically examining his thoughts, which eventually also takes the form of a systematic **doubt**, makes it possible for him to claim that his principles are nothing new but on the contrary are those of **Aristotle** and, in fact, of everybody whenever he may have lived.

COMPENDIUM OF MUSIC (*COMPENDIUM MUSICAE, ABRÉGÉ DE LA MUSIQUE*). Descartes wrote the *Compendium of Music* at the end of 1618, in Breda, where he had joined the army of Maurice of Nassau. It was Descartes's first original work after his dissertation in law, presented at the University of Poitiers in December 1616. Descartes offered the monograph to his friend **Isaac Beeckman**, as a New Year's present, to honor his interest in music. Apparently, it was also the first time that Descartes, until then known as "Seigneur du Perron," used the name "Descartes," as Beeckman noted with some astonishment (AT, vol. X, p. 56). Descartes asked for the work back in November 1629, allegedly because Beeckman had spoken of it as something of his own. Descartes had interpreted an unfortunate remark by Beeckman, reported to him by **Marin Mersenne**, as a claim that he, Descartes, had learned everything from Beeckman. In the meanwhile, however, Beeckman had a copy made of the work, which ultimately found its way to his *Journal*. Other copies were made for **Constantijn Huygens** and **Frans van Schooten** around 1640. The text was first published in 1650 in Utrecht and on the basis of the copy of an unknown Cartesian. The Oratorian **Nicolas-Joseph Poisson** made a French translation, after a copy given to him by **Claude Clerselier**, and first published it in 1668.

CONCEPT. *See* IDEAS.

CONCURRENCE. *See* GOD.

CONIMBRICENSES. A group of Jesuits at the University of Coimbra, Portugal, who published a set of commentaries on the works of Aristotle (*Physica*, 1592; *De anima*, 1598, and so forth). The project was initiated by **Pedro da Fonseca** and carried out by Emmanuel de Goes. Descartes remembered having read the textbooks of the Coimbrans in his youth, along with those of **Antonio Rubio** and **Franciscus Toletus**.

CONSERVATION, PRINCIPLE OF. Fundamental physical laws often take the form of conservation principles which assert that the total amount of a certain quantity (mass, energy, momentum, etc.) remains constant or conserved even as a physical system undergoes changes. Descartes held that the total "quantity of motion" in the universe is conserved, deriving this principle from the immutability of **God**: "it is most in accord with **reason** to conclude from God's immutability that he moved the parts of matter in different ways when he first created them, and that he now conserves the whole of that matter in the same way and according to the same **principle** by which he originally created it; and this also makes it reasonable to think that God likewise always preserves the same quantity of motion in matter" (AT, vol. VIIIA, pp 61–62). Thus stated, the principle of the conservation of quantity of motion is related to the thesis in the Third Meditation that God's power is necessary to preserve things in existence, and that there is only a conceptual distinction between creation and preservation (AT, vol. VII, p. 49). Descartes identified the quantity of motion in a body with the product of its size and the speed of its motion. Because speed is not a directed quantity (unlike velocity, which arises from speed and direction), Descartes's conservation principle led him to propose seriously flawed laws of impact in the *Principles of Philosophy* (AT, vol. VIIIA, pp. 68–70). These were criticized by, among others, **Gottfried Wilhelm Leibniz**, who proposed the principle of the conservation of the product of mass and the square of the velocity (mv^2), which he called *vis viva* or "living force." Whatever its shortcomings, Descartes's conservation principle was an important advance in the development of physics and it was particularly significant for its influence on the work of **Isaac Newton**. *See also* FORCE.

CONTINUITY. The objects of **mathematical** investigation were traditionally distinguished into two classes—the continuous magnitudes studied by **geometry** and the discrete multitudes numbered by arithmetic. The hallmark of continuous magnitudes is **infinite divisibility**, which means that they cannot be composed of least elements. While every division of a line or angle yields two lines or two angles, numbers (understood in accordance with the first definition of Book V of Euclid's *Elements*) are "collections of units" that cannot be infinitely divided. The issue of continuity is of significance in three different contexts in Descartes's thought. The first is the principle that the essence of **body** is continuous **extension** in three dimensions. At the beginning of the Fifth Meditation Descartes remarks, "I distinctly imagine that **quantity** which philosophers commonly call continuous, that is the extension of quantity (or rather of the thing with quantity) in length, breadth, and depth" (AT, vol. VII, p. 63). The source of the **clear and distinct idea** of continuous extension is not, however, the **imagination** but the **intellect**, since the intellect grasps that a body can be continuously transformed through an infinite number of possible shapes while the imagination can only grasp a finite number of them (AT, vol. VII, pp. 30–31).

A second important context for Descartes's views on continuity concerns the **nature** of geometric curves. Classical sources distinguished properly geometric from nongeometric curves on the basis of whether they could be generated by appropriate means, such as rule and compass constructions or sections of a cone. Descartes, however, found this too restrictive and declared that "we have no more right to exclude more complex curves than the more simple ones, provided that they can be conceived of as described by a continuous **motion** or by several successive motions, each of which is entirely determined by those which precede it" (AT, vol. VI, pp. 389-90). The foundation of Descartes's program for analytic geometry is the assumption that any curve that can be represented algebraically in terms of an equation can be traced by such continuous motion, and likewise that each such curve can be expressed by an algebraic equation in two unknowns.

A third issue in which questions of continuity arise in Descartes's philosophy is the question of whether his principle that **God** sustains the world through continual re-creation implies a temporal **atomism**, in which **time** is not continuous but composed of a discrete collection of instants. Martial Gueroult held that the doctrine of God's continual re-creation implied that God must create successive discrete atemporal in-stants, each independent of the other and related like the frames of a motion picture. Jean-Marie Beyssade has argued that Descartes held quite the opposite view, according to which God's creation is a con-tinuous process taking place in time, while time itself (as grasped by the **mind's** experience of passage) is continuous and not composed of instants.

COPERNICAN ASTRONOMY/COPERNICANISM. *See* COPERNI-CUS, NICHOLAUS (1473–1543); EARTH, MOTION OF.

COPERNICUS, NICOLAUS (1473–1543). Copernicus was born in a portion of Prussia that is now part of Poland. He took courses in **mathematics**, astronomy, and astrology at the University of Cracow (1491–95), studied canon and civil law at the University of Bologna (1406–1501) and medicine at the University of Padua (1501–03), and received a degree in canon law at the University of Ferrara (1503). He then returned home to Warmia, serving as physician to his uncle, the Bishop of Warmia, and as canon to its Cathedral Chapter. In 1510 he moved to Frauenburg, the headquarters of the Cathedral Chapter, where he spent the remainder of his life working on various administrative matters. His main work is the treatise *De revolutionibus orbium caeles-tium* ("On the Revolutions of the Heavenly Spheres"), which he worked on the last 30 years of his life and which was published in 1543; tradi-tion has it that he was given a copy of it at his deathbed.

Copernicus is known for his espousal of the heliocentric theory: the sun is stationary near the center of the universe, with the earth revolv-ing around the sun yearly and rotating around its own axis daily. This view contradicted the predominant geocentric theory of **Aristotle**, Ptolemy, and **scholastics**, who believed the Earth immobile at the cen-ter of the world, and it was thought to be inconsistent with the authority of the Sacred Scriptures. Philosophers also claimed that it was incon-sistent with physics for a simple body to have anything other than a single and simple motion; Copernicus's opinion, of course, would en-dow a simple body—the Earth—with two motions. Moreover, given the Copernican opinion, the Earth would get closer and farther to the fixed stars in the course of a year and thus we should be able to see changes in the brightness of these stars—something that had not been observed.

Still, Copernicus's theory gained important defenders, especially **Johannes Kepler** and **Galileo Galilei**. In 1633 Descartes was preparing *The World* for publication when he heard that the Catholic Church had condemned Galileo for defending the motion of the earth. As a result, Descartes stopped the publication of his own treatise that contained the proposition deemed heretical. However, a decade later, Descartes was able to publish the *Principles of Philosophy*, containing his cosmology, by satisfying himself that he could reject the Ptolemaic system and at the same time deny the **motion** of the earth. Cartesians did not exactly follow Descartes in this; accepting his arguments against the Ptolemaic geocentric theory, they took him to be supporting Copernicus. For example, in *Le Système du monde selon les trois hypothèses* (1675), **Claude Gadroys** discussed the three main cosmological hypotheses, Ptolemaic, Copernican, and Tychonic. He discarded the Ptolemaic as the least simple of them, with its excess of eccentrics and epicycles, and as contrary to the appearances, given the phases of Venus and Mercury (pp. 124–25). He granted that the Tychonic does not have the difficulties of the Ptolemaic, but rejected it anyway, following Descartes, for the reason that "although Tycho invented his system simply to attribute no motion to the earth, still, he attributes more motion to it than does Copernicus" (p. 129). Gadroys accepted the Copernican hypothesis and argued for it, in the remainder of his work, by demonstrating its compatibility with Cartesian cosmology, something he expounded upon in great detail.

CORDEMOY, GÉRAULD DE (1626–84). Cordemoy was one of the more important French followers of Descartes. While "Cartesian" provides a convenient means of classifying some **mechanist** philosophers of the latter half of the 17th century, the latitude of the doctrines exhibited by them is remarkable. For instance, Cordemoy was an active participant in several Cartesian academies and salons. His quite popular *Le Discernement du Corps et de l'Ame* (1666) expounded a physics that looked very much like Descartes's, though, like others at the time, it gave an **occasionalist** answer to Descartes's notorious **mind-body** problem. Cordemoy followed Descartes by defining body as "extended **substance**," but claimed that body is indivisible. He accomplished this by distinguishing between body (as a substance) and matter as an aggregate of bodies. Thus body is indivisible, yet **matter** is divisible. He also accepted the possibility of **void space**. In this way Cordemoy was able to advocate **atoms** and the void and yet consider himself a staunch supporter of Cartesian philosophy.

CORPUSCULARIANISM. *See* ATOMISM; ATOMISM, ARISTOTELIAN; PARTICLES.

CORRESPONDENCE. Although there are some early letters to and from Descartes (his correspondence with **Isaac Beeckman** in particular), the bulk of Descartes's correspondence, as we know it, dates from after 1628, when Descartes definitively settled in the Netherlands. His correspondence with **Marin Mersenne** started in the summer (August or September) of 1629 and before long almost all letters to and from France (except presumably those to and from **Claude Clerselier** and **Claude Picot**) passed through Mersenne's hands. Descartes encouraged the learned Minim to submit questions, suggesting that Mersenne keep him informed of what is going on in Paris. Mersenne wrote Descartes regularly, sometimes twice a week; Descartes replied, somewhat less regularly, either because Mersenne's letters got lost or because he was too busy with other work, but with an average of once every fortnight.

Descartes also started correspondences with several Dutch personalities: **Constantijn Huygens**, David le Leu de Wilhem, Jacob Golius, **Alphonse Pollot**, and **Henricus Regius**. The correspondence with Huygens, one of the few that is more or less completely preserved in autograph, dated and all, and which, quite exceptionally, also includes the letters Huygens wrote to Descartes, deals with all sorts of subjects, from problems of lens grinding (in which Huygens was particularly interested) and details concerning the publication of the *Discourse* and the *Meditations*, to more or less personal letters on the death of Huygens's wife, complimentary letters on books written by Huygens and by Descartes, and demands for advice and intervention during the crisis that divided the **University of Utrecht**. Huygens also played an important logistic role generally because his position as secretary of the stadtholder allowed him to use the diplomatic bag or to give a letter to a special messenger—very important in an age when ordinary mail could be unreliable and letters could be opened or stolen. The correspondence with Regius, which started in 1638, is certainly one of the most tumultuous. It started with a humble letter from Regius in which he thanks Descartes for the indirect role he played in his appointment as professor of medicine in Utrecht. Descartes, naturally proud, advised Regius on his lectures and disputations, supported him during the Utrecht crisis, advised him on the steps he should take, and provided much of the text of Regius's reply to **Gysbertus Voetius**. But over the years Regius became more and more independent and started to develop views Descartes could not possibly share.

A particular place is taken by the correspondence with Princess **Elisabeth**, which began in 1643 and lasted till the end of Descartes's life. Started as a request for clarification of a point of metaphysics, it developed into an intensely personal and moving dialogue, culminating with the publication of Descartes's *Passions of the Soul*. But what is true of this particular correspondence is also true of Descartes's correspondence in general: It is an essential part of his work, not only in terms of quantity, but also because it provides the fullest picture of the variety of Descartes's interests, ranging from **mathematics, optics, mechanics,** physics, and medicine to moral philosophy, **metaphysics,** and **theology.**

The history of the correspondence after Descartes's death is complex and frustrating. **Pierre-Hector Chanut** planned a separate edition of Descartes's correspondence with Elisabeth, **Queen Christina,** and himself (an idea which to a certain extent was also entertained by Descartes himself; see to Elisabeth, 31 March 1649, AT, vol. V, pp. 330–31), but the plan had to be canceled because of Elisabeth's veto. For several years he carried Descartes's letters and papers with him on his various embassies to Lübeck (Germany) and The Hague. Early in 1654 he sent the collection to Clerselier. What Clerselier obtained from Chanut, however, were not the letters as they were actually sent but copies, draft letters ("minutes") and sometimes edited letters, that is, letters Descartes prepared for publication (for example, the exchanges concerning the *Discourse*). Clerselier published a first selection of all of these categories in 1657. His collection contains letters to Queen Christina, Princess Elisabeth, the Marquess of Newcastle, Jean Ciermans, **Jean-Baptiste Morin, Joannes van Beverwijck, Plemp, Henry More,** Regius, **Jean-Louis Guez de Balzac,** Mersenne, Huygens, Clerselier himself, and various other personalities. Other volumes followed in 1659 and 1667.

Although very successful, this publication is problematic for several reasons: 1) the date and the addressee are often lacking; 2) the order of the letters is more or less arbitrary and in any case not chronological; 3) more often than not Clerselier had to do with the draft letter; 4) he sometimes puts together fragments of different letters. Part of this can be remedied with the help of the so-called "exemplaire de l'Institut," a copy of the three volumes published by Clerselier that contains handwritten corrections, based on a comparison with autograph letters, especially those to Mersenne. Another additional instrument is **Adrien Baillet's** biography of Descartes, in which Baillet sometimes quotes from letters that are now lost (for example, letters of Regius to Descartes and of Descartes to Picot). Finally, although all the material used by Clerselier seems to be lost definitively after 1704, many of the autographs have been retrieved (for example, the correspondence with Huygens, which turned up for auction in the early 19th century and was published in the 1920s).

The first modern edition of the correspondence was that of Charles Adam and Paul Tannery (1897–1913), as part of their complete edition of Descartes's works. But before long it became clear that many of the dates they assigned to the letters were wrong. Accordingly, Charles Adam, together with Gérard Milhaud, published a new, though not a critical, edition (1936–63). The latest reprint of the edition of Adam and Tannery incorporates materials found since 1913 but is difficult to use, given the many "additions" and "new additions." Thus a completely new edition, based on fresh research, would be desirable.

COSMOLOGICAL ARGUMENT. Following Immanuel Kant, we refer to an argument for the existence of **God** as cosmological when it is derived from experience. Descartes calls such arguments *a posteriori* and gives two of them (or two variations of the same argument) in Meditation III. The first argument is that the idea of an **infinite** substance, which I possess, requires a cause that must itself be infinite, and the second that I, who possesses this idea, must have been created by an infinite substance or God. Descartes's *a posteriori* arguments resemble somewhat Thomas Aquinas's proofs for the existence of God, with the principal difference being that, because of hyperbolic **doubt**, they do not utilize the existence of the world, but are based simply on the existence of the self, which has an idea of God.

These arguments make use of a principle of causality which requires that every effect have a cause and that the cause be at least as perfect as its effect: "there must be at least as much reality in the efficient and total cause as there is in the effect of that same cause. For where, I ask, could an effect get its reality, if not from its cause? And how could the cause give that reality to the effect, unless it also possessed that reality? Hence it follows that something cannot come into being out of nothing, and also that what is more perfect (that is, what contains in itself more reality) cannot come into being from what is less perfect" (AT, vol. VII, pp. 40–41).

Descartes's causal principle is then extended to **ideas**: "But this is manifestly true not merely for those effects whose reality is actual or formal, but also for ideas in which only objective reality is considered" (AT, vol. VII, p. 41). An idea can be considered from the point of view of its formal reality, that is, the actual existence it derives by being a **mode** of my **mind**, and its objective reality, that is, its representational content, or, as Descartes defined it, "the being of a thing represented by an idea, insofar as this exists in the idea" (AT, vol. VII, p. 161). We can be the cause of the formal reality of our ideas; the question is whether we have enough perfection to be the cause of their objective reality, that is, of their representational content: "the very **nature** of an idea is such that of itself it needs no formal reality other than what it borrows from my **thought**, of which it is a mode. But that a particular idea contains this as opposed to that objective reality is surely owing to some cause in which there is at least as much formal reality as there is objective reality contained in the idea. For if we assume that something is found in the idea that was not in its cause, then the idea gets that something from nothing" (AT, vol. VII, p. 41).

In *Principles of Philosophy*, Descartes defends his causal principle applied to ideas with the example of a complex machine: "in the case of someone said to have the idea of a machine in which there is much skill displayed in its construction, we have reason to ask how he obtained the idea, e.g. whether he saw somewhere a similar machine made by another, or whether he had a thorough knowledge of the science of mechanics, or whether he were endowed with such force of mind that he was able of himself to invent the machine without having seen anything similar anywhere else. For the whole of the ingenuity involved in the idea which is possessed by this man objectively, as in a picture, must exist in its first and principal cause whatever that may be, not only objectively or representatively, but also formally or eminently" (*Principles* I, art. 17). Given his causal **principles**, Descartes's first *a posteriori* argument simply amounts to the realization that he does not have enough formal reality to account for the infinite objective reality of his idea of infinitely perfect substance: "For although the idea of substance is in me by virtue of the fact that I am a substance, that fact is not sufficient to explain my having the idea of an infinite substance, since I am finite, unless this idea proceeded from some substance which really was infinite" (AT, vol. VII, p. 45). *See also* CAUSE, EFFICIENT; ONTOLOGICAL ARGUMENT; THOMISM.

COURAGE/COWARDICE. According to Descartes, courage (as a **passion**, not as a habit or natural inclination) is a warmth or agitation disposing the **soul** to commit itself powerfully to the execution of the things it wants to do, whatever these may be. Boldness and emulation are subspecies of courage, which in fact can be divided in as many species as there are objects on which it is directed. All these passions are variants of desire and related to **anger**. An important cause of courage is **love**, which sends to the heart pure venous blood, which in turn produces the most abundant **animal spirits**. Whether courage is a good or an evil depends on the actions to which it gives rise. So much is clear: to the extent that courage gives us the experience of our **freedom** and is an expression of the control we exercise over our **will**, it is a reason for self-esteem and the basis for generosity. Cowardice, on the other hand, which is "directly opposed to courage," consists in a slowness (*langueur*) and coldness of the body that prevents the soul from committing itself to an act (*Passions* III, art. 174, AT, vol. XI, p. 462) and makes us lose the rights **God** has given us over ourselves (*Passions* III, art. 152, AT, vol. XI, p. 445). Indeed, cowardice and fear are the only passions that make Descartes doubt his general **principle** that, being part of **nature**, passions are "good." Their only good seems to be that, by preventing us from taking a course of action based on probable arguments, they protect the soul against troubles. But most of the time cowardice is not good "because it turns the will away from useful actions." Given the fact that it is based on lack of hope and desire, the only remedy is to try and intensify those emotions in us.

CREATION. *See* GOD.

CUREAU DE LA CHAMBRE, MARIN (1596–1669). Cureau de la Chambre was counselor and physician to the king and a member of both the Académie française and Académie des Sciences. His main work was *Caractères des Passions* (1640). In its second edition (1645), volume two, he appended a small treatise called "de la connaissance des bestes," arguing that **animals** not only have **imagination** and **memory**, but also a kind of **reason**. The latter point was contested by Pierre Chanet in *De l'instinct et de la connaissance des animaux, avec l'examen de ce que M. de la Chambre a escrit sur cette matière* (1646). De la Chambre replied to Chanet by his *Traité de la connaissance des animaux* (1648, with various other editions). As a contemporary of Descartes writing on similar subjects in a non-**scholastic** fashion, de la Chambre allows one to understand and assess the novelty of Cartesian philosophy and science.

CURIOSITY. Descartes uses curiosity (and related words) in two senses: 1) scientific accurateness; 2) the **desire** to know or to learn, which, like all desires, depends on the agitation of the **animal spirits**. Although there seems to be nothing wrong with curiosity in either sense, Descartes is ambivalent about curiosity in the second sense. Indeed, it should be corrected, if not replaced, by his **method** because it leads people to waste their time and efforts. To find something by curiosity is a matter of luck rather than method. Inversely, if in the course of methodically conducted research we come across something of which we can have no clear **intuition**, it is better not to be too curious, that is, not to rush to a solution. Accordingly one must make a distinction between the curiosity of "well-tempered **souls**" (*âmes réglées*), which realize that not all **truths** can be found at the same time and are satisfied with the comparatively few truths they can know, and insatiable curiosity, which is a disease and should in no case be confused with true knowledge or science. This also explains Descartes's reservations about experiments, to which he prefers the observations everybody can make, and about his own education, which can be seen as a conflict between his curiosity, or desire to learn, and his desire to distinguish truth and falsehood.

– D –

DANIEL, GABRIEL (1649–1728). A French Jesuit who taught rhetoric, philosophy, and **theology** at Rennes, and eventually became librarian of the Jesuits in Paris. Daniel was a critic of Cartesianism who attacked Descartes's philosophy in *Voiage du Monde de Descartes* (1690), and also in a sequel to this work, *Nouvelles difficultés proposées par un péripaticien* (1693). In both works, Daniel imagines travelling as a disembodied Cartesian **soul** through the Cartesian heavens, discussing issues in Cartesian **natural philosophy** with various of its proponents, including Descartes himself. The texts were an enormous success, appearing in several editions and translations. **Pierre-Daniel Huet** reported that his reading of the *Voiage* prompted him to write his own satirical account of Descartes's life in *Nouveaux mémoires* (1692).

DEATH. According to Descartes, death never occurs through the fault of the **soul** but because one of the main parts of the **body** (the brain, the **heart**) is no longer working, or more precisely because the "fire without light" which is in the heart ceases to "burn" (*Passions* II, art. 122, AT, vol. XI, p. 418). At that point there is no longer any means of reviving it. Still, the only difference between a dead body and a living body is the one that holds between a clock that works and a broken clock—both are part of **nature** and subject to the laws of nature. Undoubtedly the fact that the **animal machine** is self-regulating (see **automata**) and adapts itself to a changing environment led Descartes to believe that life can be prolonged almost indefinitely, provided nothing interferes with it. Thus he writes to **Constantijn Huygens** in 1637 that he is quite confident that one day he will be a hundred years old: "For it seems evident to me that if only we abstain from certain mistakes we make in our way of life, we could live longer and happier" (December 4, 1637, AT, vol. I, p. 649; cf. June 6, 1639, AT, vol. II, p. 682).

The complexity of vital phenomena and the impossibility to control disease, however, were the reasons why eventually Descartes found more satisfaction in moral philosophy, which teaches us not to be afraid of death, than in medicine. Fear of death can be eliminated by knowing the nature of the soul as it can subsist without the body, but also by understanding that the soul is capable of many joys not found in this life and that we are part of a greater whole (family, society, state) for which we must be prepared to die. This does not mean that we should seek death; on the contrary, "one of the points of my moral philosophy is to love life without being afraid of death" (to **Mersenne**, January 1639, AT, vol. II, p. 480). Therefore, although we must be prepared to die, we must act as if we could reach an extremely old age. *See also* IMMORTALITY.

DEBEAUNE, FLORIMOND (1601–52). Florimond Debeaune (or, less correctly, de Beaune) was born on 7 October 1601 in Blois and was educated in Paris, where he also studied law. Like other mathematicians of his day he was not a professional, and became a councilor to the court in Blois. He proved that $(xy + bx)$, $(-dy + bx)$, and $(bx - x)$ can be represented by hyperbolas, parabolas, and ellipses respectively.

It is not known how and when Descartes knew Debeaune, but from 1638 on he figures more or less frequently in the **correspondence** as someone interested in optics who shares Descartes's interest in hyperbolic lenses. Indeed, Descartes hoped that Debeaune would succeed where he had failed, namely, in constructing a machine for grinding them. Descartes also thought highly of his mathematical expertise and his work in music theory and took the trouble of answering many of Debeaune's questions; but he was less satisfied with his achievements in **mechanics** and **natural philosophy**, which in his view were vitiated by the fact that Debeaune followed **Galileo Galilei**. In a general way Descartes was glad for Debeaune's support, if only because it contrasted favorably with the hostile reactions of "greater geometers," such as **Pierre de Fermat, Jean de Beaugrand,** and **Gilles Personne de Roberval**. Inversely, he was disappointed when Debeaune proved to think as highly of **Thomas Hobbes** as did **Marin Mersenne** and was unable to understand his *Meditations*. Although Descartes did not meet Debeaune before 1644, he developed warm feelings for him and was very disturbed when Mersenne told him that Debeaune was seriously ill and possibly dead. Apart from the "Notes brièves" which Debeaune contributed to the Latin translation of Descartes's *Geometry*, he did not publish anything else.

DEDUCTION. According to Descartes, deduction is one of the two fundamental ways of knowing things, the other one being **intuition** or also experience. The general theory of deduction has been the object of philosophical investigation since classical times. **Aristotle's** theory of the syllogism codified an important class of deductive forms, and the study of **logic** in Descartes's day was strongly influenced by Aristotle's writings. Descartes's general epistemology founds all knowledge on direct and immediate intuition of primary **truths** such as "nothing comes from nothing." In addition to these primary truths, Descartes recognized that deductively valid inferences from such truths would also provide secure knowledge. In Descartes's favored metaphor, a deductive inference is like a chain, and he speaks in the second part of the *Discourse on Method* of "those long chains of completely simple and easy reasoning that geometers commonly use to arrive at their most difficult demonstrations" (AT, vol. VI, p. 19).

For Descartes, the aim of the method is to teach how to use intuition and how to find deductions. Descartes defines deduction as "an inference of something following necessarily from some other things known with certainty" (*Rules* III, AT, vol. X, p. 369). In opposition to experience, which can be deceptive, "the deduction or pure inference of one thing from another can never be performed wrongly by an **intellect** which is in the least degree rational, though we may fail to make the inference if we do not see it" (*Rules* II, AT, vol. X, p. 365). So either a deduction is made, and then it is right, or it is not made at all. This shows that Descartes is not thinking of deduction as the application of the laws of logic; on the contrary, "those chains with which dialecticians suppose they regulate human **reason** seem to me to be of little use here, though I do not deny that they are very useful for other purposes" (*Rules* II, AT, vol. X, p. 365). In fact, what he has in mind is the type of deduction used in **mathematics**, when we "see" how different propositions relate to each other and how an unknown truth follows from one or two truths already known, or in music, where we can "deduce" a table of consonants once we know the principle. Thus, deduction is nothing but an attentive comparison of two or more things and seeing the relations between them. All we need therefore to deduce things in the right way is "sagacity."

Although intuition and deduction are different in the sense that deduction involves more than one element, they both rely on a form of seeing the truth: "very many facts which are not self-evident are known with certainty, provided they are inferred from true and known **principles** through a continuous and uninterrupted movement of **thought** in which each individual thing is clearly intuited" (*Rules* III, AT, vol. X, p. 369). While deduction is reliable, Descartes consistently ranks it as less worthy than immediate intuition. The reason for this relative priority of intuition over deduction lies in the fact that intuition is instantaneous and requires no recourse to **memory** or other potentially faulty cognitive processes—to intuit the truth of a first principle is to see its truth in a way that rules out any possibility of error. Deduction, on the other hand, requires a kind of "movement" from accepted premises to inferred conclusion, and this means it must have at least some recourse to memory, especially in the case where a very long **demonstration** depends on establishing intermediate results. As Descartes put the matter in the *Rules*, "we distinguish the intuition of the **mind** from certain deduction by the fact that we are aware of a movement or some sort of succession in the latter, but not in the former, and furthermore because immediate self-evidence is not necessary for deduction, as it is for intuition; rather, deduction in some sense gets its certainty from memory" (*Rule* 3; AT, vol. X, p. 370). Given the fact therefore that memory may be uncertain, deduction should be frequently confirmed by an **enumeration**. In later works the term seems to lose its specific meaning and is applied even to the type of deduction Descartes usually rejects, namely, **syllogistic** inference.

DEMON, EVIL. *See* DOUBT.

DEMONSTRATION. In the tradition of **logic** following **Aristotle's** *Posterior Analytics*, a demonstration is a special kind of **syllogism**, namely one whose premises are true, better known than the conclusion, and related to the conclusion as cause to effect. In the "Geometrical Appendix" to his reply to the second set of *Objections* Descartes distinguished between two modes of demonstration—**analysis and synthesis** (AT, vol. VII, pp. 156–57). A synthetic demonstration satisfies the traditional definition, while an analytic demonstration begins with what is known or sought and works "backward" to uncover the **clear and distinct ideas** that form the basis of all real knowledge. It is the **intuition** of such ideas that must form the basis for any demonstration, and these are obtained by focusing the **mind** on the clear ideas of the **intellect** rather than those provided by the **sensation**. As Descartes explained to **Marin Mersenne**, his **proofs for the existence of God** are "more clear in themselves than any demonstrations of the geometers; in my view they only seem obscure to those who don't know how to withdraw the mind from the senses" (AT, vol. I, pp. 350–51).

DESARGUES, GIRARD (1591–1661). French mathematician, credited with founding projective **geometry**, although his contributions were largely ignored until the 19th century. Born to a wealthy and influential aristocratic family in Lyon, Desargues came to Paris in 1626 and became active in the circle of **mathematicians** around **Marin Mersenne**, which included Descartes, **Gilles Personne de Roberval, Claude Mydorge, Jean de Beaugrand,** and **Blaise Pascal.** Desargues had a lifelong interest in applied mathematics, especially in the use of perspective by architects and stonemasons, and in 1636 he published a treatise on perspective, *Exemple de l'une des manières universelles . . . touchant la practique de la perspective.* He developed ideas taken from the theory of perspective into a geometric theory he applied to conic sections in his *Brouillon projet d'une attainte aux événemens des rencontres d'un cone avec un plan* (1639). Desargues's treatise took as its point of departure **Johannes Kepler's** principle of continuity, according to which the conic sections are members of the same closely related family of curves; a circle, for instance, can be transformed into an ellipse by continuous motion, and the ellipse into a parabola by removing one focus to infinity. Using techniques from the theory of perspective, Desargues considered geometric figures as "projected" into a plane in the same way that painters represent three-dimensional objects as two-dimensional projections on a canvas. He then showed that although shapes and sizes of geometric figures changed according to the plane of incidence in which they are projected, certain essential properties remain invariant under projection, and these became the object of his study.

Desargues maintained a cordial relationship with Descartes, supporting him in his disputes with **Pierre de Fermat** and Beaugrand (with whom he quarreled independently). He offered to enlist the aid of Cardinal Richelieu in having lenses ground in accord with Descartes's optical theories, but the project came to nothing after Descartes expressed reservations, complaining that "if someone should work on this without my direction, I suspect that he would not succeed on the first try, and would perhaps attribute the mistake to me in order to excuse himself" (AT, vol. I, p. 501). The significance of his own geometric work was shrouded both by his penchant for a convoluted and eccentric language that made the full generality of his results difficult to appreciate, as well as his failure to exploit the algebraic methods which had made Descartes's analytic techniques so powerful. Desargues did not publish his works for a wide readership; he was content to print a small number of copies to be distributed to other mathematicians. As a result, his work in projective geometry fell into obscurity. Only with the reinvention of the subject by Gaspard Monge and his pupils in the 19th century did Desargues's contributions become widely known.

DESCRIPTION OF THE HUMAN BODY (*DESCRIPTION DU CORPS HUMAIN*). After Descartes put into order a neat copy of what was later known as the *Treatise on Man* ("Traité de l'homme") in 1640–41, he seems to have neglected human biology. The reason was that he needed more experiments than he could do, which was also the reason why neither animal nor human biology was treated in the *Principles*. In the winter of 1647–48, however, Descartes started writing a new work containing "a description of the functions of **animal** and man" which would also contain an explanation of "the way an animal is formed from the beginning" (to **Elisabeth**, 25 January 1648, AT, vol. V, p. 112). This is confirmed by a remark in the so-called "Conversation with **Burman**" of 1648, where a "Treatise on Animals" is mentioned, on which Descartes had still worked "last winter" (AT, vol. V, p. 170). The occasion of rethinking animal biology may be provided by the work on the *Passions of the Soul*, by which however the *Description* was presumably also superceded—indeed, the physiological part of the *Passions* is by far the most complete that was published during Descartes's lifetime. In any case Descartes never finished the work. The program spelled out at the beginning of the text announces not only discussions on the movement of the **heart** and on nutrition, but also on **animal spirits**, perception, **imagination**, and **memory**, but it is not carried out beyond nutrition. After a long "digression" (consisting of two chapters) on embryology the text abruptly ends. The part on embryology is also its main interest, given the fact that that subject is not treated in any other work, although Descartes was already interested in it in 1632 (to **Mersenne**, June 1632, AT, vol. I, p. 254).

The *Description* was among the papers left by Descartes when he died in Stockholm. Claude Clerselier posthumously published it in 1664 as a sequel to the *Treatise on Man*. Although it was given the title "Description du corps humain" (which may or may not be Descartes's but vaguely corresponds to the formula used in the letter to Elisabeth), the title page announces it as *Treatise on the Formation of the Fetus* ("Traitté de la formation du foetus"), which is also the running title at the head of the pages. In it Descartes defends an epigenetic view of the formation of the embryo, claiming that it is initially produced by the coming together of male and female seed, which being heterogeneous, cause some sort of fermentation out of which grows the heart. In that view Descartes was practically alone, not only in the 17th century, but also in the Cartesian school, who adopted a preformationist view (the idea that the embryo is preformed in the male or the female "seed").

DESGABETS, ROBERT (1610–78). A Lorraine Benedictine who was a partisan both of the new Cartesian philosophy and of **Jansenist theology**. Desgabets held various academic and administrative posts in his order. During a brief stay in Paris toward the end of the 1650s, Desgabets joined in the discussions of Cartesian physics in the private academies there, and even composed his own treatise on a technique for blood transfusion. Earlier in this decade, Descartes's literary editor **Claude Clerselier** had drawn him into disputes concerning Descartes's claim in correspondence with **Denis Mesland** concerning **transubstan-**

tiation. Desgabets defended this account in an anonymous pamphlet, *Considérations sur l'état présent,* that was published in 1671 and was promptly condemned by the French royal confessor **Jean Ferrier** as "heretical and very pernicious." Even the fellow Jansenist and Cartesian **Antoine Arnauld** criticized this pamphlet, and Desgabets's order was prompted by the controversy to prohibit him from speaking out publicly on theological matters. Ferrier's condemnation of the pamphlet also coincided with a decree from **Louis XIV** that requested the suppression of anti-**Aristotelianism** at the University of Paris. This decree marks the start of an official campaign against the teaching of Descartes in the French schools and religious orders that continued until the end of Louis's reign.

In his pamphlet, Desgabets defended Descartes's account of transubstantiation by appealing to his own doctrine of the "indefectibility" or indestructibility of matter. In an early, unpublished work on this doctrine, the "Traité de l'indéfectibilité des créatures" (ca. 1654), Desgabets defended it by appealing to Descartes's claim that **God** is the free cause of **eternal truths.** Desgabets argued that such truths are grounded in created substances that have an atemporal and therefore immutable existence.

Desgabets only published philosophical text was his *Critique de la critique de la recherche de la vérité* (1675), a response to the critique of **Nicolas Malebranche's** *Recherche* by the French skeptic **Simon Foucher.** Malebranche professed himself to be displeased by this response, which offered an argument for the existence of the external world that conflicts with his own claim that we see bodies through ideas in God. Desgabets's most systematic exposition of his philosophical views occurs not in his *Critique,* however, but in the "Supplément de la philosophie de M. Descartes" (1675), his unpublished commentary on the *Meditations.* In addition to further developing his version of Descartes's account of the eternal truths there, he further defended two controversial claims that he took to undermine the Cartesian **method** of beginning philosophical investigation with hyperbolic **doubt** of the existence of the external world. The first claim is that all of our **ideas** of substances correspond to objects that exist external to those ideas. Here Desgabets took himself to be developing Descartes's "**truth rule,**" according to which all of our **clear and distinct** perceptions are true. The second claim is that the **nature** of **time** reveals that our temporal **thoughts** depend essentially on the **mind-body union,** and in particular with the union of our thought with bodily motion. Desgabets appealed to this claim in rejecting the implication of Descartes's discussion of the *cogito* that we have knowledge of our existence as thinking things that does not presuppose any knowledge of body.

These controversial features of Desgabets's version of Cartesianism were the primary topic of discussion at a series of conferences held at the Commercy chateau of Cardinal de Retz, a former leader of a rebellion against the monarchy in the late 1640s (the Fronde). This version of Cartesianism also gained a following in the Lorraine Benedictine monasteries, though the publication of an official edition of Desgabets's works was thwarted by officials due to concerns over the suspect nature of his theological views. Outside of the Benedictine order, Desgabets's most prominent admirer was the French Cartesian **Pierre-Sylvain Régis**, who called him "one of the greatest metaphysicians of our century." This compliment is reflected in the fact that Régis took over Desgabets's views on the eternal truths, the correspondence of ideas to external objects, and the essential nature of the union of temporal thought with motion.

DESIRE. Together with admiration, love and hatred, joy and sadness, desire is one of the six primitive **passions** for Descartes. It is distinguished from those other passions by the fact that its object is in the future and that it has no opposite. Descartes defines it as "an agitation of the soul, caused by the spirits, which causes the soul to will the things it represents to itself as suitable" (*Passions* II, art. 86, AT, vol. XI, p. 392). There is no contrary passion because aversion also springs from desire. There are as many forms of desire as it can have different objects. It is also an ingredient in other passions, like hope, despair, jealousy, etc. It is based on a violent motion of the heart, causing an abundant flow of animal spirits to the brain, which in turn sharpens the senses and makes all parts of the body more mobile. However, this happens only if the desired object is imagined as being obtainable. Otherwise the agitation remains limited to the brain, where it engenders a kind of indolence or languor. As long as desire is based on true knowledge and is not excessive, it is always good. If it is based on a passion it can also be bad. It is indispensable in the economy of the passions because without it no passion could ever lead to an action.

DIGBY, SIR KENELM (1603–65). English natural philosopher, naval commander, and diplomat. Born to a wealthy aristocratic family, Digby attended Gloucester Hall, Oxford from 1618–20, but left without taking a degree. He toured throughout continental Europe in 1620–23, ending in Madrid where his uncle was the English ambassador. The Prince of Wales (later Charles I) came to Madrid in 1623 on a matrimonial mission and Digby became a member of his household. He accompanied the prince on his return to England after the failure of that mission, was knighted later in the year and became a member of the prince's privy council. In 1627–28 Digby led a successful privateering expedition against French ships in the Mediterranean, an exploit that earned him an appointment as naval commissioner from 1629 to 1635. The death of his wife Venitia in 1633 affected Digby greatly; he withdrew from public life and spent two years at Gresham College in London studying various topics in **natural philosophy**, including magnetism, optics, and physiology. In 1636–37 Digby was in France, where he met **Thomas Hobbes** and **Marin Mersenne** and became an active participant in the "Mersenne circle." By 1639 Digby had returned to England, but in the political climate of the time his Catholicism (which had not previously hindered his career) made him a target of Protestant radicals, who were concerned that his close relationship with Charles I might assist a reconciliation between the Church of England and the Roman Church. In 1641 he was summoned to face charges in Parliament and was imprisoned in 1642. He was discharged after a few months, on the condition that he accept exile in France.

Digby left England for Paris, where in 1644 he brought out his most important work, the *Two Treatises*, one of which dealt with the **nature of body** and the other with the nature of the human **soul**. Paris remained Digby's principal residence for a decade, but between 1645 and 1648 he undertook two diplomatic missions to Rome in the company of **Thomas White** to negotiate on behalf of the exiled queen, but these missions delivered no concrete results. After his return to England in 1654 he was a confidant of Cromwell, who employed his diplomatic skills in several foreign diplomatic affairs. Notwithstanding his service to Cromwell, Digby was well received by Charles II at the Restoration in 1660. Digby's remaining years were devoted primarily to the study of natural philosophy. He joined the Royal Society in 1660 as one of its earliest members and served on its council in 1662–63.

Digby's natural philosophy combines **Aristotelian, atomist,** and Cartesian themes. It is best characterized as an attempt to retain certain Aristotelian categories (such as the theory of four **elements**) while embracing a broadly **mechanistic** account of the world in which local **motion** and impact are fundamental explanatory principles. Digby's insistence in the *Two Treatises* on an essential distinction between soul and body, in which the soul's "operations are such, as cannot proceed from those principles [of body]," met with Descartes's approval, although he had no great enthusiasm for Digby's Aristotelian leanings.

Descartes first mentions Digby in a letter to Mersenne in June of 1638, remarking that he "is much obliged to M. Digby for what he says so favorably of me," and in another letter from August of the same year he tells Mersenne that he has "received the writing against me that M. Digby addressed" (AT, vol. II, p. 192, p. 336). Just what hostile work

Descartes is referring to here remains obscure, as does the nature of Digby's response, but the two men were clearly on good terms. This is made more evident in Descartes's description of himself as "extremely concerned" at the news of Digby's imprisonment in 1642 and "relieved" to hear that he had been released (AT, vol. III, p. 582, p. 590). According to **Adrien Baillet**, Digby "had long and frequent talks [*conférences*] with Descartes at the College of Boncourt," during Descartes's 1644 stay in Paris, which apparently dealt with Digby's account of mind and body as it was worked out in his *Two Treatises* (Baillet, *Vie de M. Descartes*, vol. II, p. 244).

DIOPTRICS (DIOPTRIQUE). Although the *Dioptrics* (a treatise on refraction) was published in 1637 as one of the *"essais"* belonging to the *Discourse*, it is one of Descartes's earliest works, presumably started in his Parisian period (1625–28), when he worked with **Claude Mydorge**. The work is first mentioned by name in a letter to **Marin Mersenne** of November 25, 1630. Toward the end of the letter it becomes clear that it is the first work Descartes intended to publish: "My Dioptrics will teach me whether I am capable of explaining my ideas and convincing others of a **truth** of which I have convinced myself—that which I do not believe" (AT, vol. I, p. 182). The indications are that most of it was ready when Descartes came to the Low Countries. What Descartes lacked as yet was a machine for grinding hyperbolic lenses in a controlled way, which he hoped to realize there. Descartes did not work on *Dioptrics* as he had planned in Franeker, not only because Jean Ferrier, a Parisian artisan he invited to work with him, but possibly also because Adriaan Metius (1571–1635), Franeker professor of astronomy (to whose brother Jacobus Descartes attributed the invention of the telescope) did not meet his expectations. Back in Amsterdam, Descartes's thoughts were soon occupied by his plan to write a general physics (see *The World*). Still, a treatise on refraction is sometimes mentioned in his correspondence.

In 1632 Descartes sent Jacob Golius, professor of oriental languages and mathematics in Leiden, a copy of his "Analyse" (presumably an early version of the *Geometry*) and *Dioptrics*, apparently because Golius wanted to do some experiments. In April 1632, Golius told **Constantijn Huygens** that the *Dioptrics* was almost ready and, in a letter of June 1632, Descartes told Mersenne that he would not leave Deventer (where he had settled the previous May) before he had finished the *Dioptrics*. In the first week of April 1635, Descartes finally read parts of his work in Amsterdam to a party that included Huygens, who received the text from him two weeks later. In fact, Descartes's problem was the same as when he came to the Low Countries: although he had the design of a machine for grinding hyperbolic lenses (the same presumably he submitted to Ferrier) it proved unpractical. In any case, no lens cutter seemed ready to try it out, since they were used to the traditional "tour," or spinning top, the use of which Descartes forbid because it caused an irregular surface. Even so, Huygens urged Descartes to publish his work—to which Descartes finally consented. This is the start of the project of the *Discourse*, ultimately published almost two years later, in the summer of 1637. In March 1636 Descartes had already decided that the work would consist of four treatises in French: *Dioptrics*, *Meteors*, and *Geometry*, preceded by "the plan of a universal science by which our nature can be elevated to the highest level of perfection" (AT, vol. I, p. 339).

Of the works composing the *Discourse*, the *Dioptrics* was printed first, starting presumably in May 1636. The engraver worked on it in June, at any rate, and it was finished at the end of October. On January 1, 1637, Descartes had the printed text sent to Huygens to forward it by diplomatic mail to Paris, where it was needed in connection with the French printing license. As the result of an indiscretion of the censor, **Jean de Beaugrand**, the work was shown to others, particularly **Pierre Fermat** and **Gilles Personne de Roberval**. The news that Descartes was publishing a book began to spread in Paris. *See also* OPTICS.

DISCOURSE ON METHOD (*DISCOURS DE LA MÉTHODE, DISSERTATIO DE METHODO*). The *Discourse on the Method of Rightly Conducting one's Reason and Seeking the Truth in the Sciences* was Descartes's first publication (1637), which in its original form also comprised "dioptrics, meteorology, and **geometry** which are applications of that **method**." The whole was meant as a kind of prospectus of the new philosophy, a presentation of its main achievements so far, preceded by an introduction on the method used, which in turn would be not only the reason for its success, but also its main distinction. When, at the end of 1633, the condemnation of **Galileo Galilei** caused Descartes to decide that he would never publish anything, he did not stop working. For one thing he carried on with the second part of the original *Treatise on Light*, on human biology, and he also continued to work on the *Dioptrics* and the *Meteors*. From 1635 on Descartes was much encouraged in these efforts by **Constantijn Huygens** and Jacob Golius (1596–1667, a Leiden professor of oriental languages and mathematics), both of whom had a keen interest in optics. It is they, together presumably with **Henricus Reneri**, who pressed Descartes to revisit his decision and to publish, if not a work on the whole of physics, some samples of "subjects which, without being highly controversial and without obliging me to reveal more of my principles than I wished, would nonetheless show quite clearly what I can, and what I cannot, achieve in the sciences" (*Discourse* VI, AT, vol. VI, p. 75). The evolution of this project can be followed closely in the correspondence with Huygens and **Marin Mersenne**. In September or October 1635 Descartes decided to publish his *Dioptrics* with the Leiden Elzeviers, but the plague prevented him from going to Leiden and to supervise the printing. In November he added the *Meteors* and decided that the whole would be preceded by a short introduction, which corresponds presumably to the actual Sixth Part of the *Discourse*. When in January 1636 Descartes finally did move to Leiden, Elzeviers no longer showed any interest and Descartes sought another publisher and even considered the possibility of having his book printed in France. But the delay also allowed him to revise his plans and include some other work as well. At that point Descartes thought of a book of 50 to 60 leaves (that is, 200 to 280 pages), which would consist of four parts: a first part in which he presents his method and proves the existence of **God** and the incorporeality of the **soul**; a second containing his thoughts on **light** and vision; a third on meteorology; and a fourth on geometry. A few months later he decided to publish his book with the Leiden publisher Jean Maire (or Le Maire), with whom Descartes signed a contract on December 2, 1636. The drawings for the engravings were made by **Frans van Schooten**.

Since it was Descartes's intention to obtain not only a Dutch privilege (which was granted on December 20, 1636), but also a French *privilège* (to protect the publisher's interests in France and to be safe in case of future publications in France), Descartes had to submit to the censor either the entire manuscript or an important part of it. This was the reason that the *Dioptrics* was already printed in the last months of 1636 and could be sent to France in the first week of 1637, together perhaps with a small part of the *Discourse*. The unexpected result was that the *Dioptrics* started to circulate among French mathematicians, especially **Pierre de Fermat**, to whom the censor, **Jean de Beaugrand**, had passed a copy, and later **Gilles Personne de Roberval**. Although at first Descartes humored Mersenne on his attempts to organize this discussion, he became annoyed when Fermat and Roberval remained unconvinced and reacted in ways he did not like. He was also increasingly irritated by the fact the *privilège* did not come. There were several complications: 1) Descartes wanted a *privilège* not only for this particular book but for any book he would publish later; 2) Descartes wished that the *privilège* be given in such a way that his name would not be revealed to the public; 3) the *privilège* could be granted only on the basis of a complete text. Since printing had been going on after the *Dioptrics* was sent to Paris, this condition could be fulfilled in March

1637. The privilege was granted finally on May 4, 1637. Descartes was informed of it by Huygens in a letter of June 2, after he had again complained about its failure to appear in a letter of May 20. Apparently, it was sent directly to the printer, as Descartes had asked Mersenne to do. For the publisher this was the signal to have the title page and the pages containing the privileges printed (the *achevé d'imprimer* is from June 8). In June Descartes started the distribution, sending copies to the stadtholder, the French ambassador, the king of France, and others.

As already pointed out the discussion about the *Discourse* started even before the book was published. And although Descartes did not particularly like the reactions of Fermat and others to his *Dioptrics* and in a general way was skeptical about the use of discussion, he encouraged his readers "to take the trouble to send [their objections] to the publisher," so that they could be published in a second edition, with his replies "so that readers can see both sides together and decide the **truth** all the more easily" (*Discourse* VI, AT, vol. VI, p. 75). But only a few people cared to react. Apart from three professors from Louvain, **Libertus Fromondus, Vopiscus Fortunatus Plemp,** and the Jesuit mathematician Jean Ciermans, Descartes obtained objections only from **Jean-Baptiste Morin** and from a group of Dutch friends, organized possibly by **Alphonse Pollot.** Although Descartes was only half satisfied with that result he took the trouble of having all texts copied, possibly to include them in a Latin translation. But although eventually a Latin translation was published, the plan to include objections was shelved definitively on the advice of Huygens.

Plans for a translation on the other hand seem to have been formed as early as 1637. A letter shows not only that a translation of the *Essays* (and presumably also of the *Discourse*) was made somewhere in 1639 or even earlier, but also that it was extensively revised by Descartes. Presented as a companion volume to the *Principles* (1644) the translation of the *Discourse*, the *Dioptrics*, and the *Meteors* (the *Geometry* was left out) was finally published under the title: *Specimina philosophiae* (1644). The translation is generally attributed to the Remonstrant minister Étienne de Courcelles or Curcellaeus (1586–1659), who also worked as a reader and corrector for Elzevier. An examination of the variants with respect to the French version make it more than likely that it was revised by Descartes.

DISTINCTION, REAL, MODAL, AND RATIONAL. The word *distinctio* appears in the title of the second edition of the *Meditations* (1642), in effect correcting the title of the first, which promised but did not deliver a **demonstration** of the **immortality of the soul.** Instead Descartes (responding in effect to a point raised by the *Second*

Objections) promises only to show that they are *distinct*; from this, one may conclude that the alteration of the body, or even its destruction, is not a sufficient cause for the destruction of the soul (*Second Replies*, AT, vol. VII, p. 153). In the *Fourth Objections*, **Antoine Arnauld** introduces the **Scotist** terminology of formal and real distinctions, holding that Descartes has not managed to prove that **mind** and body are really distinct.

The terminology of distinctions is inherited from medieval **logic.** The first and most fundamental division is between those distinctions that have some foundation in things, and those that do not, but are entirely creatures of our conception. A distinction of **reason** is a distinction between ways of conceiving the same thing: for Descartes, a body and its **quantity** or **extension** are one and the same thing conceived in two ways. The primary instance of a distinction of reason is the distinction between a **substance** and its essence or **nature,** which Descartes calls its "principal attribute" (*Principles* I, art. 62, AT, vol. VIIIA, p. 30). Among those distinctions that have some foundation in things, Descartes recognizes a real and a modal distinction. A real distinction in the primary sense holds between two substances—more precisely, between two things each of which is self-subsistent; from that it follows that each can subsist without the other. A modal distinction holds between two things such that the first can subsist without the second, but not the second without the first. The primary instance is the distinction between a substance (or the principal attribute from which it is distinct only in reason) and any of its nonprincipal modes; the figure of a cube cannot subsist if the substance or quantity of the cube is annihilated, but that quantity can certainly subsist with a new figure.

Descartes distinguishes between the ontological basis of distinctions and their epistemology: we *recognize* that mind and body are really distinct by virtue of having a "complete idea" of each, an idea by virtue of which we understand that a thinking thing (that is, a thing to which we attribute only thought and its modes) can subsist independently of all things save **God,** and likewise an idea of body by virtue of which we understand that an extended thing can subsist independently of all things save God; and, finally by virtue of understanding that in the **idea** of mind there is nothing that pertains to body and in that of body nothing that pertains to mind. Similarly we recognize that a mere distinction of reason exists between a body and its duration by virtue of noting that we cannot clearly and distinctly perceive either without the other (*Principles* I, art. 62, AT, VIIIA, p. 30).

Divine power is invoked as the **cause,** in a certain sense, of a real distinction rather than as its basis in things: God, it is said, can bring about whatever we clearly and distinctly perceive, or—in Descartes's most careful formulation—whatever we conceive "as complete" (*Fourth Replies*, AT, vol. VII, p. 221). In other words, we can be certain that such-and-such a situation is within God's power to realize if (and only if) we clearly and distinctly perceive the things in that situation: mind existing while the body is annihilated, for example. Modal **truths** ("it is possible that my mind should exist without my body") are grounded in the creative act of God; our thought cannot set limits to divine power, but our **clear and distinct ideas** can, by virtue of the warrant provided by God's veracity for our faculties when they are used correctly, enable us to discover some of those truths once they and we have been created.

DIVISIBILITY. According to Descartes, the essence of **body** is **extension**. This carries the consequence, clearly indicated in the Sixth Meditation, that every body is divisible: "there is no corporeal or extended thing I can think of which I cannot easily divide into parts in my **thought**; and this very fact makes me understand that it is divisible" (AT, vol. VII, p. 86). The divisibility of extension is part of the basis of the **real distinction** between **mind** and **body**—the mind is by **nature** a thinking, unextended thing, while nature of body entails that it is extended and divisible. A further consequence of the fact that every body is divisible is that there can be no **atoms** or indivisible least parts of extension. This consequence is drawn in the *Principles of Philosophy*: "if indeed there were [atoms], they would necessarily be extended, no matter how small we might imagine them to be, and hence we could divide each of them in our thought into two or more smaller parts, and thus know that they are divisible" (*Principles* II, art. 20). This denial of atoms makes the structure of the physical bodies mirror that of **geometric** magnitudes; just as the lines, angles, or surfaces of pure geometry are always divisible into smaller magnitudes of the same kind, every Cartesian body is divisible into smaller extended bodies.

This raises some conceptual puzzles in the foundation of Descartes's physics. In particular, it seems to make traditional paradoxes of the **infinite** divisibility of geometric continua apply to the minute particles that constitute Cartesian matter. Such paradoxes reason that, if every part of a geometric magnitude contains an infinity of lesser parts, then every magnitude is infinitely large or contains a half which is equal to its whole. Descartes emphasized that it was only the **indefinite** division of matter that was an issue, but he admitted that "the mind does not comprehend . . . the division of any particle of matter infinitely or indefinitely, and in so many parts that however small we make a particle in our thought, we always understand that it is in fact divided into still smaller particles" (*Principles* II, art. 34). This inability is merely a consequence of our minds' being finite, however, and takes nothing away from the clarity and distinctness of the principle that every body is divisible into smaller bodies.

DOUBT. According to the *Rules for the Direction of the Mind* doubt is the opposite of *science* (or knowledge): "All knowledge is certain and evident cognition. Someone who has doubts about many things is no wiser than one who has never given them a thought; indeed he appears less wise if he has formed a false opinion about any of them. Hence it is better never to study at all than to occupy ourselves with objects which are so difficult that we are unable to distinguish what is true from what is false and are forced to take the doubtful as certain" (*Rules* II, AT, vol. X, p. 362). That is also the point of the first rule of the method: "never to accept anything as true if I did not have evident knowledge of its truth: that is, carefully to avoid precipitate conclusions and preconceptions, and to include no more in my judgments than what presented itself to my mind so clearly and so distinctly that I had no occasion to doubt it" (*Discourse* II, AT, vol. VI, p. 18). Meanwhile the reason why something is doubtful has changed or at least has got a different accent.

In the *Rules* doubt is the result of a lack of method and order (some things are too difficult not to be doubtful if they are not approached in the right order), whereas in the *Discourse* doubt is the result of prejudice and hasty reasoning. In any case we should try and become free from doubt, even if Descartes makes it clear frequently that in practical matters we should not expect the certainty we are entitled to ask for in the domain of theoretical science. This field, where we are dealing with probability, pertains to the will and is ruled by authority and obedience, the senses, the bodily sensations (hunger, thirst), and the passions. Inversely if we use the rule of doubt to achieve certainty we should set apart whatever pertains to practical life and to the public sphere (religion in particular) and decide not to doubt it.

The rule of doubt is applied to theoretical truth in the *Discourse*, the First Meditation, and the *Principles*, where Descartes systematically tests his beliefs according to this criterion, after having divided them into two or three different classes: beliefs based on the senses and the imagination (including memory) and beliefs based on the intellect (see enumeration). But the senses are sometimes deceptive; the imagination also produces dreams; and we know of people who are mad and as a result completely mistaken about their own condition. Descartes concludes that the senses and the imagination are doubtful and accordingly that beliefs based on the senses and the imagination (among other things the belief that there is an external world and that we have a material body) may as well be rejected as false. In the *Meditations* and the

Principles doubt also extends to **mathematical** demonstrations. This particular doubt, which Descartes calls "hyperbolic" or "metaphysical," is inspired by the idea that we were created by **God** who, given his infinite power, could have made us in such a way that we are continually deceived. Of course, one could deny the existence of God, but that makes things worse, given the fact that in that case I would be dependent of something that is even less perfect than God. As an alternative Descartes suggests the hypothesis of what he calls an evil genius (*genius aliquis malignus, malin génie*) who is powerful enough to deceive me whenever I am irresistibly inclined to affirm something as true.

In the *Principles* a similar argument returns, but formulated in a somewhat different way: we have heard that there is a God, who is powerful enough to deceive us and who, given the fact that in **judgments** based on the senses we are actually deceived is, apparently, able to deceive us. Accordingly, we should not trust ourselves even in those judgments we believe to be the most certain of all, namely, mathematical **demonstrations**. As a result, this exercise in doubt, which was meant to separate what is clear from what is unclear, seems to leave us with nothing at all. However, someone who doubts knows at least that he doubts, a point Descartes already makes in the *Rules for the Direction of the Mind* but which from the *Discourse* will take the form of the *cogito*. Accordingly, if systematic doubt is part of a skeptical argument, radical doubt shows that it is self-defeating—that the more I doubt, the more certain it becomes that I think. The main problem of this argument is that, if we do seriously doubt whatever we believe to know, there should be nothing left to remove doubt. For even if I grant that I think and therefore exist I need certain general **principles** (such as the notion that an effect cannot have more reality than its **cause**) to go beyond that and to prove that God exists. So either I doubt those principles and am no longer able to prove that God exists or I do not doubt them but then my doubt is not really radical. Descartes solves this problem by relying on what he calls "natural light" (see **intuition**) but, according to many critics, an appeal to the natural light could be justified only after I know that God cannot deceive me. *See also* CARTESIAN CIRCLE.

DUALISM. In the 17th century dualists are those, like Zoroastrians or Manichaeans, who believe in a dual ontology of principles of good and evil. That is how **Pierre Bayle** employs the term in his *Historical Dictionary* and how **Gottfried Wilhelm Leibniz** in turn uses it in his *Theodicy*. In contemporary philosophy, the term refers generally to the view that reality consists of two disparate elements, that there is an unbridgeable gap between two orders of being. Descartes's real distinction between extended and thinking **substance**, between passive **body** and active **mind**, thus qualifies as substance dualism. Given the gap between Descartes's two kinds of substances, the problem becomes one of reconciliation: how can those essentially different substances causally interact? How can the mind influence the body, the body influence the mind? **Baruch Spinoza's** property dualism of mutually exclusive but parallel attributes, **Nicolas Malebranche's occasionalism**, and Leibniz's preestablished harmony are all taken to be solutions proposed to the problem of interactive dualism. *See also* UNION OF MIND AND BODY.

DUHAMEL, JEAN († ca. 1734). Not to be confused with **Jean-Baptiste Duhamel**, this Duhamel was a professor of philosophy at the Collège du Sorbonne-Plessis from 1668 to about 1690 and a confirmed **scholastic** critic of the new Cartesian philosophy. He was the author of the *Réflexions critiques sur le système cartésien de la philosophie de M. Régis* (1692), which beyond responding to the particular version of Cartesian **metaphysics** and physics in **Pierre-Sylvain Régis's** *Système* also repeats criticisms of Descartes's views on the **method** of **doubt** and the *cogito* in **Pierre-Daniel Huet's** *Censura* (1690). Régis had this latter feature in mind when he protested in a *Réponse* to Duhamel's *Réflexions* that his critic merely repeats old objections that have already been refuted. Duhamel responded to Régis in a further *Lettre . . . pour servir de réplique à M. Régis* (1699), but this drew no reply from his Cartesian opponent. Duhamel subsequently published his *Philosophia universalis* (1705), one of the last defenses of traditional **Aristotelianism** against the new Cartesian philosophy. This text includes an appendix that records various censures that go back to the Condemnation of 1277 of positions found in Descartes.

DUHAMEL, JEAN-BAPTISTE (1623–1706). Duhamel entered the **Oratorians** in 1643 and left in 1653 to become the curé of Neuilly-sur-Marne, near Paris. He held further prominent church and academic positions, such as royal almoner, prior of Saint-Lambert, and chair of Greek and Latin Philosophy at the Collège Royal (1682–1704). Duhamel was the first secretary of the Académie Royale des Sciences. He is best known for his attempt to reconcile ancient and modern philosophy. For example, he wrote *Astronomia physica* and *De meteoris et fossilibus* (both 1660) as conversations among three persons—Theophilus, the advocate of ancient philosophy, Menander, a passionate Cartesian, and Simplicius, a philosopher indifferent between ancients and moderns, who takes what is best from each (representing Duhamel's own position). Duhamel also wrote *De consensu veteris et novae philoso-*

phiae (1663) and *Philosophia vetus et nova ad usum scholae accomo-data* (1678) in this same vein.

DURATION. *See* CONSERVATION; TIME.

DU ROURE, JACQUES (fl. 1654–83). One of the first followers of Descartes, belonging to the group centering on his literary executor **Claude Clerselier.** Du Roure is the first to have published a complete textbook of Cartesian philosophy, *La Philosophie divisée en toutes ses parties* (1654), and subsequently *Abrégé de la vraye philosophie* (1665), before the more famous ones of **Antoine Le Grand** and **Pierre-Sylvain Régis.** In Du Roure's case, the parts of philosophy include the usual parts of the curriculum—**metaphysics, logic,** ethics, and physics—plus natural **theology.** Thus, Du Roure is the first to have written a Cartesian logic or ethics. He also published popular essays, some about Latin language and grammar. Of particular interest is his *Dessein d'une institution universelle,* inspired by **Francis Bacon's** *Advancement of Learning.* In the section on philosophy as a whole, Du Roure recommends reading **scholastics** such as **Eustachius a Sancto Paulo,** but says that he "could set aside some of these, as he has set aside others, because they have given us only trifles" and because he "has never or almost never noticed any demonstrations or experiments in their works, only interminable disputes and a confusion of speech beyond anything that can be imagined" (p. 5). He adds, "whoever wants to become attached to **truth** in philosophy, rather than to sects, must read the works of Descartes, **Gassendi, Hobbes, Kepler, Galileo,** Bacon," among others (p. 6).

– E –

EARTH. *See* ELEMENT.

EARTH, MOTION OF. Nicolaus Copernicus's astronomy revived the Pythagorean view that the sun is the center of the world, with all the fixed stars, planets, and four **elements** revolving around it. A consequence of this heliocentric system is that earth is given a double **motion,** a diurnal rotation around its axis and an annual motion around the sun. However, such a double motion would be inconsistent with **Aristotelian** physics, for which a simple body cannot have anything other than a single and simple motion. And for Aristotelians, the simple motion of the element earth would have the center of the universe as end.

Moreover, the immobility of the sun and motion of the earth would seem to contradict such well-known biblical passages as "The Lord laid the foundations of the Earth, that it should not be removed for ever," and "Then spoke Joshua to the Lord . . . 'Sun, stand thou still upon Gibeon.' And the Sun stood still." As a result, the Catholic Church condemned the Copernican system in 1616 and subsequently condemned **Galileo Galilei** for defending it in 1633.

Descartes was preparing *The World* for publication in 1633 when he heard that the Catholic Church had condemned Galileo for defending the motion of the earth. He stopped the publication of his own treatise containing the proposition deemed heretical, because, as he said, all the things he explained in his treatise "were so completely dependent on one another, that the knowledge that one of them is false is sufficient for the recognition that all the arguments [he] made use of are worthless." He added that he "would not for anything in the world maintain [these propositions] against the authority of the Church" (AT, vol. I, p. 285). Instead, he prepared drafts of the *Dioptrics* and *Meteors*, scientific treatises on less controversial topics. Descartes later returned to the issue; he came to define motion as "the transference of one part of matter or one body from the vicinity of those bodies that are in immediate contact with it, and which we consider at rest, into the vicinity of others" (*Principles* II, art. 25). This relativistic definition has the advantage of allowing him to claim that the earth can be conceived as a fixed locus around which the surrounding world moves. He therefore could technically deny the motion of the earth (*Principles* III, art. 19). Descartes thus avoided Galileo's difficulty that had prevented him from publishing *The World*.

ELEMENT. In *Generation and Corruption*, **Aristotle** defines four elements in terms of the elemental qualities hot, cold, dry, and wet. The element earth is cold and dry, water is cold and wet, air is hot and wet, and fire is hot and dry. Elements in their pure forms are said to have those qualities *in extremis*. Pure fire is as hot as anything can be, and so on. The elements in pure form never occur terrestrially. All terrestrial substances are mixtures of elements in various proportions. Aristotle's account was adopted by virtually every medieval philosopher, though some, like Paracelsus, who were influenced by **alchemical** theories, offered competing proposals.

Descartes replaces the four Aristotelian elements with three elements defined, as they had to be, solely in terms of the modes of **extension**. There is, first of all, the coarse-grained stuff we see and feel; and a finer stuff consisting of spherical particles fitting between particles of the first sort; and a yet finer, irregular stuff that fills the remaining space. These three sorts Descartes calls elements; the finest is the first element or *fire*; the next finest is the second element, *air*; the coarsest is the third element, *earth*.

The **vortices** that surround heavenly bodies are composed primarily of the second element, whose movement is invoked to explain light. Stars emit streams of first-element particles, including the "channeled" particles that Descartes supposes in order to explain magnetism. Third-element particles can be of various sizes and **shapes**; the differences among them account for such physical properties as density, viscosity, and transparency (all topics discussed in *Principles* IV). Descartes's explanations here resemble those of the **atomists**.

ELISABETH, PRINCESS OF BOHEMIA, COUNTESS OF THE PALATINATE (1618–80). Elisabeth was born in 1618, the eldest daughter of Frederick of Bohemia and Elisabeth Stuart, a daughter of Charles I, king of England. After Frederick (the Winterking) lost his throne in 1620, the family went into exile in The Hague, where they lived in relative poverty, financially supported by the States General, the States of Holland, and the stadtholder. Elisabeth had a keen interest in philosophy and **mathematics** and was tutored in those disciplines (as well as in Scripture, history, and the humanities) by professors of **Leiden University**. She left the country after her brother Philip killed a French officer for spreading the rumor that their unmarried sister, Louise Hollandine (so called because the States of Holland stood as her godfather), was pregnant (Elisabeth was suspected to have incited her brother to defend the family's honor). She spent the rest of her life with her German relations (Berlin, Heidelberg, Kassel) and in 1667 became abbess of a Lutheran convent in Herford (Westphalia). **Alphonse Pollot**, who presumably also taught Elisabeth the fundamentals of Descartes's philosophy and mathematics, mediated her contacts with Descartes.

Elisabeth's first letter to Descartes shows that she knew Cartesian philosophy well; there are also a few letters in which she deals with mathematical problems. Over the years the **correspondence** between Elisabeth and Descartes took a more personal tone, especially on behalf of Elisabeth, who not only was weak and ailing, but also, as eldest daughter, was particularly affected by the ill fortunes that beset her house. Given the fact that Descartes ascribes Elisabeth's illnesses to an emotional disturbance, many letters concentrate on the theory of the **passions** and the **union** of **body** and **mind**. Indeed, it is for her that Descartes wrote the *Passions of the Soul* (1649). Descartes also proposes a study by correspondence of Seneca's *De vita beata*, which however does not provide her much pleasure. Descartes's *Principles* (1644) were dedicated to Elisabeth. After Descartes died Elisabeth did

not allow **Pierre-Hector Chanut** to publish her part of the correspondence. Still, copies of her letters were apparently made and were published by Foucher de Careil in the 19th century.

EMOTIONS. Descartes still uses the word *émotion* (Latin: *commotio*) to
indicate the agitation and unrest of the blood when the **soul** is violently
affected, but also more generally as a perturbation of the **body**, or a
movement in the soul, or as what he also calls **passions**. Emotions therefore can be defined as "those perceptions, or feelings . . . the soul
particularly refers to itself, which are caused, entertained and reinforced
by some movement of the spirits" (*Passions* I, art. 27, AT, vol. XI, p.
349). They are perceptions in the generic sense only, that is, to the extent that they are "**thoughts** which are not actions of the soul" but not
because they are evident knowledge or **clear and distinct ideas**; indeed, they are obscure and confused (*Passions* I, art. 28, AT, vol. XI,
pp. 349–50). They are said to be particularly referred to the soul because Descartes wants to distinguish them from other feelings, which relate
to external objects (like smells, sounds, **colors**) or to our own body (like
hunger, thirst, pain). Finally, they are said to be caused, entertained, and
reinforced by the **animal spirits** to distinguish them from acts of the
will, "which one could equally call 'emotions of the soul which the soul
refers to itself' but which are caused by itself" (*Passions* I, art. 29, AT,
vol. XI, p. 350).

ENUMERATION (*ENUMERATIO, DÉNOMBREMENT*). Enumera-
tion, generally speaking, is a technique for making the results of an argument general. As such it can be compared to induction, with which it
is sometimes identified by Descartes. Descartes defines it as a close and
accurate examination of whatever pertains to the question proposed
such that we can conclude certainly and evidently that we have not for-
gotten anything. There are no strict rules of enumeration, which may be
the reason why it is sometimes difficult. It can be complete (if all items
can be actually counted), or distinct (if we manage to reduce the items
to a few classes and order those classes hierarchically), but sometimes it
is neither. All one can say is that it has to be sufficient and systematic.
An enumeration can be required before solving a problem, more or less
in the way **Francis Bacon** requires a "history." For example, we should
make an enumeration of the properties of magnets before starting to explain magnetism. Or we make an enumeration of our simple notions to
see to what extent they are clear or obscure; of our faculties to see of
what use they are in the pursuit of knowledge; of the **passions**. A classical enumeration at the beginning of a project is also the way Descartes
reduces all his opinions to a few classes in the First Meditation (see

doubt), so as not to have to examine each of them separately. Enumeration may also be situated halfway through a project. Thus, for example, if we have fully examined the **mechanism** of vision it becomes easy to make an enumeration of the ways it can be improved. And enumeration may be necessary at the end to ensure that we have explained everything we wanted or to show that a solution is the most simple and the most general that can be had.

ERROR (*ERROR, ERREUR*). In Descartes's earlier work error is a problem only insofar as it is not always easy to avoid—but we can avoid it by proceeding cautiously and methodically and by relying exclusively on our **clear and distinct ideas.** In the Fourth Meditation, however, after Descartes has proved that, given the fact that **God** cannot deceive us, it is impossible for us to be mistaken in our clear and distinct ideas, error as such becomes problematic because, if God cannot deceive us, error seems not to be possible at all. An explanation could be that I am somewhere between God and nothingness and participating in both, but upon further reflection Descartes does not find that a satisfactory solution. Error is not just a negation, but a privation: by making an error we are deprived from knowledge we should and could have. Moreover, God could have made us such that we are free from error. Finally, to be free from error is a greater perfection than to be subject to error.

Descartes solves this problem by making an analysis of **judgment.** This consists of two elements: an **idea** or set of ideas and an act of the **will**, by which I affirm those ideas to be true. Accordingly, an error must be the result of a defect, either in the contents of my judgment (an idea or set of ideas) or in the act by which I affirm those contents to be true. As long as I restrict my judgments to contents that are clearly and distinctly given and understood, there should be no risk of error. The problem therefore seems to be that, even if I am confronted with contents that are not clearly and distinctly given nor understood, I have the power to affirm those contents as true. In other words, error is possible only because I am free. Now this still does not settle the question with respect to God, for two reasons: 1) God could have created me in such a way that I would never affirm something that is not clearly and distinctly given and understood to be true; 2) God could have made me so that I would only have clear and distinct ideas. So God could still be held responsible for my errors.

Descartes's answer is, as far as the first point is concerned, that God could have solved that problem only by not giving me a **free will.** But since it is undoubtedly a greater perfection to have a free will than to be a **machine**, God cannot be blamed. The second problem is solved in the Sixth Meditation, where Descartes argues that, given the intimate **union of body and mind**, obscure and confused perceptions (sense perceptions, bodily sensations, **passions**) are not only inevitable but useful because they allow us to judge a given thing or situation in terms of its use for ourselves as a psychophysical unity. Therefore, as long as we use obscure and confused perceptions in this way and do not base any theoretical conclusions upon them we remain comparatively free from error.

ETERNAL TRUTHS. Descartes took eternal truths to include **common notions** or axioms, such as the proposition that nothing comes from nothing, as well as truths concerning essences, such as that the radii of a circle are all equal. He claimed in the *Principles of Philosophy* that these eternal truths do not presuppose the existence of any object and that they "reside only within our **mind**" (AT, vol. VIII-1, p. 23f).

Descartes's most distinctive claim concerning the eternal truths, however, is that they depend entirely on the **free and indifferent will** of **God.** He introduced this claim in a 1630 correspondence with **Marin Mersenne** in which he announced a work on the metaphysical foundations of physics (never published) that included a defense of the thesis that God is the **efficient cause** of the eternal truths. Descartes understood such a thesis to imply that God was free both to refrain from creating these truths and to create different truths. For him, one must embrace these results in order to do full justice to the incomprehensible power of God.

Among Descartes's successors, one of the most enthusiastic supporters of his doctrine of the creation of the eternal truths was the French Cartesian **Robert Desgabets**. Desgabets understood this doctrine to complement the emphasis in **Augustine** on the omnipotence of God. However, Desgabets developed the doctrine in ways that go beyond anything found in Descartes. Desgabets held, for instance, that God creates the eternal truths by creating **substances** that have an "indefectible" or indestructible existence that is outside of **time.** He was motivated here to find some aspect of created reality that could ensure the stability of the eternal truths. Desgabets's version of the doctrine was adopted by the French Cartesian **Pierre-Sylvain Régis.**

Nevertheless, there were also followers of Descartes who rejected his doctrine of created eternal truths. Principal among these was the French Cartesian **Nicolas Malebranche.** In direct opposition to Desgabets, Malebranche urged that an Augustinian view of the sort found in the work of Thomas Aquinas (see **Thomism**) supports the conclusion that the eternal truths depend not on God's will but rather on uncreated ideas in God's **intellect.** Malebranche added to this his distinctive position that we see the material world by means of these **ideas** in God. This position was disputed by the French Cartesian **Antoine Arnauld.** In his polemic with Malebranche over the **nature** of ideas, however, Arnauld did not take up the defense of Descartes's doctrine of created eternal truths.

ETERNITY. On a traditional view expressed in the work of Thomas Aquinas (see **Thomism**), there are three different measures of existence. **Time** measures the existence of beings that are essentially subject to **motion.** In contrast, the "aevum" measures the existence of beings, such as **angels**, that are not essentially connected to motion. Finally, eternity measures the existence of **God**, which is completely simultaneous or *tota simul.*

In keeping with his reticence on the status of angels, Descartes had little to say about the category of aeviternal existence. In correspondence with **Antoine Arnauld,** however, he did endorse the distinction between successive time and nonsuccessive eternity when he claimed that the duration of our **mind** cannot be compared to God's duration since "our **thoughts** display a successiveness that in no way can be admitted in divine thoughts" (AT, vol. V, p. 193).

EUCHARIST. *See* TRANSUBSTANTIATION.

EUSTACHIUS A SANCTO PAULO (1573–1640). French **scholastic** philosopher and theologian. Eustachius (Eustache Asseline) studied **theology** at the **Sorbonne** (at the same time as **Pierre de Bérulle**) and received a doctorate in 1604. The next year he entered the Parisian Cistercian monastery of the Feuillants, where he held a number of prominent offices. He was influential in French Catholic circles and familiar with the leading religious figures of the time, such as François de Sales, Mme Acarie, and de Bérulle. Eustachius published two important textbooks, *Summa philosophiae quadripartita de rebus dialecticis, moralibus, physicis, et metaphysicis* (1609), and *Summa theologiae tripartita* (1613–16). Descartes called his *Summa philosophiae* the best work ever written in that genre, a primer in late scholastic philosophy.

Like many other school texts written at the time, Eustachius's *Summa* consisted of a blend of **Thomist,** Scotist, and Humanist doctrines. At one time Descartes conceived a project of writing his own textbook "in an order, where without superfluous discourse, I will only put down all my conclusions, with the true reasons from which I derive them." He also intended in the same book "to publish an ordinary philosophy course, such as perhaps the one of brother Eustachius," with notes at the end of each question, where he would "add the various opinions of others and what one should think of them all," and at the end "make a comparison between these two philosophies" (AT, vol. III, p. 233). However, he abandoned the publication of the "ordinary philosophy" and the comparison of the two philosophies, using the death of Eustachius as a pretext; instead, he concentrated on the positive part of the project, which eventually resulted in the publication of his *Principles of Philosophy*.

EXISTENCE OF GOD, PROOFS FOR THE. *See* COSMOLOGICAL ARGUMENT; ONTOLOGICAL ARGUMENT.

EXTENSION. Descartes defines matter or **body** as *res extensa*, an "extended thing," a portion of space. Extension is, like **thought**, a "primitive" **idea** not admitting of definition. Unlike his **scholastic** predecessors, Descartes does not try to define it in terms of "parts outside of parts" (*partes extra partes*), though he does assume that actual extension, or space, has "distinguishable parts" of "determinate magnitude and figure" (AT, vol. V, pp. 270–71; AT, vol. VII, p. 86). Extension has three dimensions. But to think of it as really decomposable into three distinct entities, length, breadth, and depth, is to perform an illegitimate **abstraction**. Even **God** cannot create a Flatland. Surfaces, lines, and points are not really **distinct** from the extended things they are modes of.

Individual **bodies** are portions of space, distinguishable by their **motions**. Their only properties, aside from duration and the like which are common to all substances, are what Descartes calls the **modes** of extension: figure, size, and motion. The figure or shape of a body cannot exist apart from that body itself, not even by the absolute power of God. Extension is what in the *Principles* Descartes calls a "principal attribute," that is, a property of a **substance** on which all its other properties depend. It is therefore said to "constitute the **nature**" of body (*Principles* I, art. 48, II, art. 1). **Divisibility**, for example, follows simply from being extended; likewise "figurability"—the capacity of acquiring one or another shape. Extension here plays something of the role occupied by **substantial form** in **Aristotelian natural philosophy**.

There is, then, nothing more to bodies than extension and its modes. In particular, bodies do not have **colors**, tastes, or other sensible qualities if by that one means qualities that are not modes of extension. Nor do they have "solidity" or "impenetrability." Descartes held that whatever is extended will by virtue of that alone exclude all other extended things from the volume it occupies. His position proved to be controversial. **Henry More** argued against it at length, both in his correspondence with Descartes and in his *Enchiridion metaphysicum*

(1679); extension is so far from being the nature of body that immaterial things, including God, can be extended too (but are not divisible). **Robert Boyle**, though sympathetic toward Descartes's view, doubted that solidity could be eliminated from the list of basic properties of body. Experiments like those performed by Evangelista Torricelli and **Blaise Pascal** with inverted tubes of mercury in the 1640s and by Boyle with his air pump in the 1660s yielded persuasive evidence for the existence of vacua. The identification of extension and body became less and less tenable. By the first decade of the 18th century, despite the efforts of Cartesians like **Pierre-Sylvain Régis**, virtually all natural philosophers rejected his view.

– F –

FABRI, HONORÉ (1607–88). A French **Jesuit** who was a professor of philosophy and **mathematics** in Lyon from 1640 to 1646 and who later became a high curial official in Rome. The perception that he was sympathetic to the new Cartesian philosophy led to his transfer to Rome in 1647. Indeed, in his 1671 *Entretiens sur la philosophie*, the Cartesian **Jacques Rohault** noted that Fabri had anticipated his conclusion that human **souls** are the only **substantial forms** separable from matter. While he praised the "singular genius" of Descartes, however, Fabri also noted that he offers many opinions that are "false" and "not acceptable." After Descartes's death, a copy of his correspondence with **Denis Mesland** on **transubstantiation** found its way to Fabri through a Jesuit correspondent of **Claude Clerselier**, and in 1660 Fabri composed a "Censura" of views found in this text. He also was rumored to have played a major role in placing an edition of Descartes's works on the Catholic *Index librorum prohibitorum* in 1663.

In 1670 Fabri wrote a text defending moral probabilism, which he defended against the Jansenist charge of being overly "laxist." Since criticism of **Jansenism** was prohibited at this time, Fabri's own text was placed on the Church's *Index of Prohibited Books*, and he suffered a brief period of imprisonment. Though he was restored to his old position in Rome with the help of friends in high places, the condemnation of his book was never lifted.

FAITH. Descartes distinguished at one point among questions that can be answered by faith alone (e.g., concerning the Incarnation), those that concern faith but can be answered by natural **reason** (e.g., concerning the existence of **God** and the **distinction** of **mind** from **body**), and those that can be answered by natural reason alone (e.g., concerning the making of gold by **alchemy**) (AT, vol. VIIIA, p. 353). He often emphasized that the first class of questions is properly **theological**, and so outside of his jurisdiction as a **natural philosopher**. However, there were two issues on which Descartes was drawn into theological battles. The first is that of **freedom**, where he was forced to side at times in the disputes between **Jesuits** and their **Jansenist** opponents. The second issue is that of **transubstantiation**, which Descartes attempted to show is consistent with his philosophical **principles**. While this attempt drew support from followers such as **Robert Desgabets**, other Cartesians such as **Antoine Arnauld** and **Pierre-Sylvain Régis** argued that it violated the separation between faith and reason.

FAULHABER, JOHANNES (1580–1635). A mathematician who, around 1613, became interested in Hermeticism, biblical prophecy, and the cabala by reading some tracts by the **Rosicrucians**. Faulhaber dedicated his 1615 work, *Mysterium Arithmeticum*, to the brotherhood. He had hoped to join the Rosicrucians but, as late as 1618, had failed to meet any of its members. According to Daniel Listorp, Descartes visited Faulhaber in Ulm in early 1620. Although Descartes did not mention him by name in any extant writing, it seems that Faulhaber did influence his early mathematical work.

FERMAT, PIERRE DE (1601–65). French mathematician who made fundamental contributions to nearly all areas of 17th-century **mathematics**. Little is known of his early life and education, aside from the fact that he was born to a prosperous merchant family in Beaumont-de-Lomagne and was educated for a legal career, probably at the Universities of Toulouse and Orléans, and perhaps at Bordeaux. In 1631 Fermat became *conseiller au Parlement* at Toulouse, a position he retained until his death. Although he was a lawyer by profession, his main interest was mathematics. His serious mathematical investigations seem to have begun in the late 1620s, when he spent time in Bordeaux before taking his law degree. He was in contact with **Jean de Beaugrand** during the late 1620s; Beaugrand later served as a principal intermediary between Fermat and the Parisian mathematical community. In 1636 fellow *conseiller* at Toulouse, Pierre de Carcavi, also helped introduce Fermat's work to Parisian mathematicians, principally those connected with **Marin Mersenne** and including **Gilles Personne de Roberval, Claude Mydorge, Blaise Pascal,** and **Girard Desargues.**

Fermat's mathematical work took its primary orientation from the analytic program of **François Viète**, but the fundamental improvements he introduced make Fermat's methods vastly more powerful. Like many mathematicians of his day, he undertook speculative "restorations" of lost works of ancient **geometry**, and by the late 1620s he had begun a restoration of the lost treatise *Plane Loci* of Apollonius of Perga using methods derived from Viète. His study of loci (sets of points satisfying a specific geometric condition) led him to the insight that **algebraic** principles could be applied to the study of geometric curves. In particular, when equations in two unknowns were applied to a set of coordinate axes, the equations define a geometric curve. Thus, he could characterize the ordinary parabola as a locus satisfying the algebraic condition $ay = x^2$, which could then be generalized to an equation for a general parabola of the form $x^{(n-1)} = x^n$.

Descartes had pursued the same basic line of reasoning in his *Geometry*. In 1637 he learned from Mersenne of Fermat's investigations (though without seeing Fermat's results in their full generality). He then showed himself keen to establish both his priority in discovery and preeminence as a geometer in a condescending letter to Mersenne, reporting that one of Fermat's propositions on plane loci "is quite easily solved by what I have written in my *Geometry*," and expressing the hope that "if this *conseiller* is an open honest man, he will be one of those to make the most of my work" (AT, vol. I, p. 377).

In 1638 Fermat offered some criticisms of the *Dioptrics*, a copy of which Beaugrand had sent to him without authorization and apparently with the suggestion that the author would welcome criticisms. Fermat replied with a letter to Mersenne, objecting among other things that the sine law of **refraction** (the sines of angles of incidence and refraction of light passing through media of different densities are in a constant ratio) could not be validly deduced from the definition of **light** as an inclination to move rather than movement itself. Descartes had sought to justify the sine law for refraction by the principle that light travels more rapidly in denser media, but Fermat appealed to the "principle of least time" and offered to assist Descartes in finding a true demonstration of the law.

Descartes did not react kindly to criticisms from one he regarded as his obvious intellectual inferior. When Fermat then forwarded a copy of his treatise on the determination of geometric maxima, minima, and tangents, Descartes replied with a scorching denunciation of Fermat's methods, which he prefaced with the remark to Mersenne that "I would prefer to say nothing about the paper you sent me, because I could not say anything that would be to the advantage of the person who wrote it. But, because I recognize it is the same person who earlier tried to refute my *Dioptrics* . . . I feel obliged to reply" (AT, vol. I, pp. 486–87). The result was a bitter controversy, which was eventually eased when Mydorge acted as an intermediary and effected their reconciliation.

In 1654 Fermat entered into correspondence with Pascal on problems of probability and games of chance, the results of which were extended and published by **Christiaan Huygens** in his 1657 *De Ratiociniis in Ludo Aleae*. Number theory was Fermat's principal passion in mathematics, but he was unsuccessful in generating interest for the subject among other mathematicians. Such luminaries as Huygens and Pascal paid little attention to it and ignored Fermat's requests to join him in the attempt to solve number-theoretic problems. Among his many noteworthy results was the famous "last theorem"—the conjecture that the equation $x^n + y^n = z^n$ has no integral solutions for n>2. Fermat asserted this in the margin of his copy of the *Arithmetica* by the Greek mathematician Diophantus, but offered no proof, claiming the margin was too small. A definitive proof of the result was not found until 1994.

Despite his contributions to the advancement of mathematics, Fermat's efforts did not gain the wide audience Descartes had found. In part this is because he published very little, but it is also due to his persistent use of the symbolism and manner of exposition derived from Viète, which had largely been superseded by Cartesian notation.

FERRIER, JEAN (1614–74). A French **Jesuit** who was a **theology** professor in Toulouse and later confessor to **Louis XIV.** Ferrier was a vocal critic of **Jansenism** and, later, of the new Cartesian philosophy. His opposition to Cartesianism is evident in his report to Louis XIV in 1671 that a Cartesian tract on **transubstantiation** written by **Robert Desgabets** is "heretical and very pernicious."

FIRE. *See* ELEMENT.

FONSECA, PEDRO DA (1528–99). Fonseca was a Portuguese **Jesuit** philosopher and theologian who joined the Society of Jesus at Coimbra, and spent some time at the then-new University of Evora. From 1555 to 1561 he was professor at the Colégio das Artes at Coimbra, where he conceived the idea of a *Cursus Conimbricensis,* a uniform series of textbooks that would make up the collegiate curriculum, the realization of which was then delegated to Manuel Gois (see **Conimbricenses**). After another teaching stint at Evora, he participated in the redaction of the Jesuits' *Ratio studiorum* in Rome. He wrote a series of **Aristotelian**

commentaries: *Institutionum dialecticarum* (1564); *Isagoge philo-sophica* (1591); and his important, posthumously published *Commentariorum in libros metaphysicarum* (1615).

FORCE. The term "force" (Latin *vis*) can be defined as that which imparts **motion** to a **body**. Despite this seemingly clear and obvious definition, the doctrine of forces was a contested part of 17th-century **physics**. Controversies over the **nature** of force fall into two groups: those over the ontological or metaphysical status of forces and those concerning the appropriate measure or quantification of forces.

At the level of ontology, the concept of force became problematic because it is difficult to reconcile the **mechanist** dismissal of "occult" powers in bodies with the notion that there is an active **principle** of change intrinsic to bodies and responsible for their motion. The difficulty is most evident in Descartes's principle that **extension** is the essence of body. Cartesian physics holds that all physical phenomena can be explained purely in terms of extension and its **modes**, so it rules out the possibility that bodies might possess intrinsic dynamic principles such as forces. Instead, Cartesian bodies are entirely passive and lack anything recognizable as an active force. Descartes saw this as a virtue of his system, and he prided himself on "having deduced the causes of the phenomena of nature from principles, which I judge to be quite evident, and which are known to everyone and admitted by all, namely the shape, magnitude, position, and motion of particles of matter" (AT, vol. VIIIA, p. 314). Descartes does speak of a force being imparted to a body, and of a "striving" (*conatus*) in bodies to move in a certain direction (for instance in *Principles of Philosophy*, art. 55–60). However, this talk of forces and active striving in bodies is to be understood to mean "merely that bodies are positioned and pushed into motion in such a way that they will in fact travel in that direction, if they are not impeded by some other cause" (AT, vol. VIIIA, p. 108).

This way of dealing with forces ultimately requires Descartes to replace talk about forces with talk about the laws of motion, which themselves are ultimately based on the fact that **God** imparts a fixed "**quantity** of motion" to the world and conserves it. To say that a ball rebounds from a collision with a wall because of a force that repels it is, in the final Cartesian analysis, to say that God's conservation of the quantity of motion requires that the motion of the ball toward the wall be followed by a motion away from it, in accordance with the **conservation principle**. Many later thinkers, notably **Gottfried Wilhelm Leibniz** and **Isaac Newton** argued that the essence of body requires more than simply extension, and they sought to establish a science of dynamics that recognizes the reality of forces as active principles intrinsic to bodies.

The issue of how to measure forces led to significant confusion and controversy in the foundations of physics. Descartes's principle of the conservation of total quantity of motion leads naturally to the idea that a force should be measured by the product of a body's size (or mass) by the speed with which it moves, irrespective of the direction of motion. Others proposed that the directed quantity of velocity (as opposed to speed) must be taken into account, and suggested mv, or the product of mass and velocity, as the appropriate measure. Leibniz put forward mv^2 (which he called "living force") as the proper measure of forces. In his *Principia* Newton defined a force as the product of mass and acceleration (ma), which eventually became the universally accepted account of forces.

FORM, SUBSTANTIAL. In **Aristotelian metaphysics**, a material **substance** is said to be a composite of two "incomplete substances," **matter** and **form**. The matter of a thing is the underlying substrate that persists through all its changes; the form is that which changes. That much is found in Aristotle's *Physics*. **Scholastics** distinguished between "substantial" and "accidental" form. The substantial form of a thing is that which, when joined with its matter, "gives it being" as a substance. Change in substantial form amounts to the destruction of the thing and the generation of a new thing from its matter. For Aristotelians, substantial change, **death** for example, is quite different from mere accidental changes like getting warmer or becoming angry. The substantial form of a thing determines its kind: Socrates is human by virtue of his form. It is also the unifying principle of the powers of a thing. Socrates can think and **will**; he can see and hear; he can nourish himself and grow. That all those powers are joined in one thing is to be explained by referring them to a single cause: his form.

The necessity of distinguishing substantial from accidental form was argued on both physical and metaphysical grounds. Cartesian physics, for which the specific character of a material substance is nothing but its **shape** and size—that is, mere accidental forms in Aristotelian physics—rejected that **distinction**. The production of **fire**, for example, by the combustion of wood is not the generation of a new substance following upon the destruction of the old; it is simply the fragmentation of the relatively coarse particles of wood into the very fine, quickly moving particles we call "fire" (*The World*, chap. 2; AT, vol. XI, pp. 7–10). Descartes takes for granted the absence of any distinction between substantial and accidental form in **natural philosophy**, and devotes little effort to arguing against it. In the "Origin of Forms and

Qualities," **Robert Boyle** argues at length against the distinction between substantial and accidental form, refuting the standard arguments offered by Aristotelians on its behalf. On the other hand, what Descartes in the *Principles* calls the "principal attribute" of a substance (see **categories** and **extension**) does fulfill some of the functions that in Aristotelian metaphysics are fulfilled by form.

FOUCHER, SIMON (1644–96). An honorary canon at Sainte Chapelle in Dijon who defended a probabilistic form of "Academic skepticism" against central elements of Cartesianism. Foucher's skepticism is expressed in his 1675 *Critique* of the first volume of the *Recherche de la vérité* of **Nicolas Malebranche**, attacking in particular what he took to be Malebranche's dogmatic insistence on **substance dualism** and on the correspondence of objects to our ideas. **Robert Desgabets** defended both dualism and correspondence in a 1675 *Critique* of Foucher, and Foucher responded in his 1679 *Nouvelle dissertations sur la recherche de la vérité*. Foucher also was a critic of Malebranche's **occasionalism** as well as the "pre-established harmony" of **Gottfried Wilhelm Leibniz**. Foucher nonetheless shared with Leibniz a dislike of Cartesian dogmatism, and the two engaged in a friendly correspondence that lasted from 1676 to 1695.

FREEDOM/INDIFFERENCE. During the time Descartes was writing his mature philosophical works, there was a dispute among Catholic intellectuals over whether our freedom of action involves an "indifference" that allows our **will** to act otherwise than it does act. The **Jesuits** insisted that the admission of such an indifference is needed to ward off the **Calvinist** doctrine of predestination, whereas the **Jansenists** charged that this admission compromises the **Augustinian** doctrine that meritorious action follows from **God**'s irresistible grace.

In this dispute, Descartes favored different sides at different times. In his Fourth Meditation, for instance, he insisted that an "indifference" that involves a balance of reasons belongs only to the "lowest grade" of human freedom, and that our will is most free when it is led to embrace the true and the good either by **clear and distinct** perception or by divine grace (AT, vol. VII, pp. 57–58). Indeed in 1640, just prior to the publication of the *Meditations*, Descartes wrote to **Marin Mersenne** that his account of freedom agrees perfectly with the account found in an anti-Jesuit tract written by the **Sorbonne Oratorian Guillaume Gibieuf** (AT, vol. III, p. 359).

In the 1644 *Principles*, however, Descartes referred explicitly to the "freedom and indifference" within us involved in our "undetermined" action (AT, vol. VIIIA, p. 20). We can explain this shift from the view in the *Meditations* in terms of Descartes's remark in a 1645 letter, most likely to the Jesuit **Denis Mesland**, that one can identify indifference not only with a balance of reasons, but also with "a positive faculty of determining oneself to one or the other of two contraries, that is to say, to pursue or avoid." Descartes concluded there that our free action always involves such a power, since "absolutely speaking" we can do the contrary of what we freely do, even in the case of clear and distinct perception (grace is not mentioned here) (AT, vol. IV, p. 173). In a related letter, again presumably to Mesland, Descartes wrote that his account of free will seems to be in accord with the account found in an anti-Jansenist tract written by the Jesuit Denis Petau. **Antoine Arnauld**, who normally was a staunch supporter of Descartes, nonetheless was prompted by passages such as these to complain that Descartes's letters "are full of **Pelagianism**." As we have seen, however, a Jesuit-friendly account of freedom can be found not only in Descartes's correspondence, but also in his *Principles*. Moreover, such an account is arguably present in his final work, the 1649 *Passions of the Soul*. In this text, Descartes claimed that God has determined certain matters "to be dependent on our free will" (AT, vol. XI, p. 438), and that our free will "renders us in a certain way like God by making us masters of ourselves" (AT, vol. XI, p. 445).

Though Arnauld represents the main Cartesian opposition to the more positive view of indifference in Descartes, there were other Cartesians who were more favorable to it. In particular, both **Nicolas Malebranche** and **Pierre-Sylvain Régis** insisted that our freedom involves a power to act otherwise. To be sure, both Malebranche and Régis rejected the view that we have an indifference that involves a balance of reasons. For both, our action must be guided by perceptions that incline us to act in a certain way. But both also held that we have the power to resist such inclinations. In Malebranche's case, the challenge was to reconcile such a claim with his **occasionalism**. In Régis's case, the view that we have the power to determine our own modifications is offered as part of a comprehensive alternative to Malebranche's occasionalism.

FREE WILL. *See* FREEDOM/INDIFFERENCE; WILL.

FROMONDUS, LIBERTUS (1587–1653). Professor of philosophy and theology at the University in Louvain. Fromondus (Libert Froidmond or Fromont) was born in Haccourt sur Meuse, near Liège. His early education under the **Jesuits** was in ancient languages (primarily Greek and Hebrew) with an emphasis on Scriptural interpretation and theology, but he was also well read in **natural philosophy** and **mathemat-**

ics. He studied philosophy and languages at the Collège de Faucon in Louvain from 1604 to 1609, when he left to teach philosophy at the abbey Saint-Michel in Anvers. He returned to Louvain in 1609, where he taught rhetoric (1609–14) and then philosophy (1614–28) while pursuing scientific interests that led to the publication of several astronomical treatises. These include his 1619 *Dissertatio de cometa anni 1618* ("Dissertation on the comet of 1618") and the *Meterologicum libri VI* ("Six Books of Meterology") of 1627. In the 1620s he resumed his studies in theology under **Cornelius Jansenius** (with whom he would remain closely associated) and obtained a doctorate in theology in 1628. When Jansenius was appointed bishop of Ypres in 1636, Fromondus assumed his chair as professor of Sacred Scripture. During his fatal illness in 1638, Jansenius entrusted the manuscript of his *Augustinus* to Fromondus, who arranged for its publication in 1640.

Fromondus published numerous theological works in defense of Jansenism, but he is best remembered for his writings on astronomy and mathematics. His *Ant-Aristarchus* of 1631 was an important attack on **Copernicanism**, and his *Labrynthius, sive De compositione continui* ("The Labyrinth, or On the Composition of the Continuum") was a defense of **Aristotle** and attack on **atomism**, which was frequently praised by **Gottfried Wilhelm Leibniz**. Descartes respected Fromondus, although he thought him too attached to **Aristotelianism**. Fromondus replied to Descartes's *Discourse on Method* with a series of objections against what he saw as an overreliance on atomistic and **mechanical** principles in the Cartesian philosophy. The objections touch on such topics as **animal** sensation, physiology, the **nature** of **light**, and the proper account of sensible **qualities**. In a letter of October 3, 1637, forwarded to Fromondus by way of his student **Vopiscus Plemp**, Descartes replied at length to these criticisms (AT, vol. I, pp. 401–31). His attitude toward his critic nevertheless remained cordial. In a March 1638 letter to **Christiaan Huygens**, Descartes explained that his disagreement with Fromondus was "conducted like a chess game: we remained good friends after the match was over, and now we send each other nothing but compliments" (AT, vol. II, p. 660).

– G –

GADROYS, CLAUDE (1642–78). One of the earliest and more avid followers of Descartes. His chief claim to fame rests on his attempt to extend Cartesian principles to astrology in *Discours sur les influences des astres selon les principes de M. Descartes* (1671). This may seem an odd endeavor, but Descartes does invite his followers to use his account of magnetic phenomena as a model to explain "all the most admirable effects on earth": "the particles composed of the first element in the pores of terrestrial bodies can not only be the cause of various attractions, such as those in the magnet and in amber, but also of innumerable other most admirable effects" (*Principles* IV, art. 187). In the French version of this article, Descartes elaborates on the "wholly rare and marvelous effects" that can be explained: "how the wounds of a dead man can be made to bleed when his murderer approaches; how to excite the imagination of those asleep, or even of those awake, and impart to them thoughts that warn them of things to come at a distance, by having them feel the great pains or great joys of a close friend, the evil intents of an assassin, and similar things." Gadroys conceives of similar explanations for astrologic influences, for the occult actions of the stars on human inclinations, passions, temperament, illnesses, and fate.

In his second work, *Le Système du monde selon les trois hypothèses* (1675), Gadroys discusses the three main cosmological hypotheses, Ptolemaic, Copernican, and Tychonic. He rejects the Ptolemaic as the least simple of them, with its excess of eccentrics and epicycles, and as completely contrary to the appearances, given the phases of Venus and Mercury (pp. 124–25). He grants that the Tychonic does not have the difficulties of the Ptolemaic, but rejects it anyway, following Descartes, for the reason that "although Tycho invented his system simply to attribute no motion to the earth, still, he attributes more motion to it than does Copernicus" (p. 129; cf. Descartes, *Principles* III, art. 15–19). Gadroys accepts the Copernican hypothesis and argues for it, in the remainder of his work, by demonstrating its compatibility with Cartesian cosmology, upon which he expounds in great detail.

GALILEI, GALILEO (1564–1642). Italian natural philosopher and mathematician, one of the most important contributors to early modern science. His early education was probably in music, under the tutelage of his father Vincenzo (1520–91), a professional musician and noted musical theorist. Galileo began his formal education in the Faculty of Arts at the University of Pisa in the autumn of 1580. Relatively little is known about the details of his university education, but it is evident that he was exposed to the Aristotelian natural philosophy as interpreted by 16th-century scholastics. By the time he left Pisa in 1585 (without taking a degree), Galileo had developed an antipathy toward the Aristotelian-scholastic natural philosophy and a skill in mathematics that would characterize much of his later scientific career.

Galileo's first original work was a small 1586 treatise on the hydrostatic balance entitled *La bilancetta*, which circulated in manuscript. At approximately the same time he showed the extent of his mathematical sophistication by circulating a sequence of theorems on the centers of **gravity** for various solids of revolution, demonstrated in accordance with the Archimedean method of exhaustion. By the late 1580s Galileo had discovered the isochronous properties of the pendulum, a phenomenon he connected to the harmonic properties of strings: just as the tone of a plucked string remains constant even as the amplitude of the vibrations decreases, so the period of a pendulum remains constant as the amplitude of its excursions from perpendicular decreases. Although he lacked a **geometrical demonstration** of the property of isochronism, his investigations into the relationship of frequency and tone seem to have convinced him that a mathematical **analysis** of natural motions, backed by experimental evidence, would form the basis for a new natural philosophy.

In 1589 Galileo retuned to the University of Pisa to assume the chair of mathematics, a position he retained until 1592. During this period he undertook the attempt to reformulate the accepted Aristotelian account of natural **motion**, as evidenced by a manuscript *De motu* in which he began to work out the principles that became fundamental to his **mechanics**. In opposition to the Aristotelian notion that bodies descend with a speed proportional to their weight, Galileo proposed in *De motu* that in free fall bodies descend with a characteristic uniform speed proportional to their specific gravity. Experiments disconfirmed this theory, and over the next two decades he refined his experiments and reformulated his theories. In the end he arrived at the famous law of free fall which states that (in a **vacuum**) all bodies are uniformly accelerated at the same rate, and that the distance fallen is proportional to the square of the elapsed time. A key tool employed by Galileo in his research on free fall was the inclined plane, which allowed him to study the speed acquired by a descending ball. Observing that a ball moved spontaneously only when it rolled down an incline, and that given an impulse to move up the plane it would spontaneously decelerate, Galileo inferred that a ball placed on a horizontal plane would be indifferent to motion and rest—an insight which led him to formulate an early version of the law of **inertia**.

In 1592 Galileo accepted the chair of mathematics at the University of Padua, where his research into the laws of motion continued. By the mid-1590s he had become convinced of the plausibility of **Copernican** astronomy, whose doctrine of a moving **earth** required further refinement of the concept of motion while also encouraging the search for more accurate astronomical data. In 1609, upon hearing of a device invented in the Netherlands that could make distant objects appear nearer, Galileo set to work replicating and improving it; the result was a telescope with which he made detailed observations of the moon, the satellites of Jupiter, and the phases of Venus. His *Siderius Nuncius (Siderial Messenger)* of 1610 related his observations and argued against the Aristotelian doctrine of a fundamental **distinction** between the incorruptible celestial realm and the terrestrial world of change and decay. He proposed that the laws of motion and **principles** of material things were the same for the Earth and the heavens, and suggested that the observational evidence favored the Copernican system. The challenge to traditional natural philosophy posed by these discoveries led **Christopher Clavius** and other astronomers to question the reliability of telescopic observations, but by the end of 1610 Clavius and other mathematicians of the **Collegio Romano** had confirmed the existence of the satellites of Jupiter and had seen the phases of Venus. In April 1611, during Galileo's visit to Rome, Clavius certified the phenomena revealed by the telescope as genuine.

Galileo was appointed principal mathematician at the University of Pisa and accorded the title of philosopher and mathematician to the Grand Duke of Tuscany (Cosimo II de'Medici, who was duly impressed by Galileo's naming of the satellites of Jupiter for the house of Medici). His astronomical observations continued, resulting in the discovery of sunspots in 1611. A dispute with the **Jesuit** Christoph Scheiner (1573–1650) on the **nature** of sunspots resulted in the 1613 publication of his *Letters on Sunspots*. Public controversy with a member of the Society of Jesus and his support of theologically controversial Copernican astronomy did not help Galileo's reputation with conservative forces in the Catholic Church, and in 1615 he was denounced to the Holy Office. This prompted Galileo to summarize his views on the relationship between theology and natural philosophy in a *Letter to Grand Duchess Christina*, which was circulated widely at the time but was first published (in the Netherlands) in 1636. One recipient of the circulating letter was Robert Cardinal Bellarmine (1542–1621), an influential Jesuit member of the Holy Office. He replied that Copernicanism was an acceptable hypothesis but admonished Galileo against interpreting it in a manner contrary to Scripture or received theology. Copernican teachings were formally condemned in March 1616, and Galileo ceased his advocacy for the new astronomical system.

In the autumn of 1618 the appearance of three comets led to a debate over the nature of comets between Galileo and the Jesuit Orazio Grassi (1592–1654), professor of mathematics at the Collegio Romano, who attempted to account for them without using Copernican assumptions. Galileo's 1623 *Il Saggiatore (The Assayer)* was the resulting polemical piece, which he dedicated to his friend Maffeo Cardinal Barberini (1568–1644) who had recently been elected pope and taken the name Urban VIII. The work was well received in Rome, and Galileo held out hope that the Church would modify its condemnation of Copernican astronomy.

Through the late 1620s Galileo was revising an earlier unpublished treatise on the tides, adding a wealth of astronomical and mechanical material. He cast it in the form of a dialogue, initially intending to publish it under the title *Dialogue on the Ebb and Flow of the Tides*, but later changing the title to *Dialogue on the Two Chief World Systems, Ptolemaic and Copernican*. It was published in early 1632. To Galileo's surprise, the *Dialogue* was condemned as heretical; early in 1633 Galileo was found guilty of vehement suspicion of heresy, forced to recant, and sentenced to imprisonment at the pleasure of the Inquisition. Late in that year Galileo was allowed to retire to his villa in Arcetri near Florence, where he would remain under house arrest for the remainder of his life. Although plagued by health problems in his final years, Galileo continued his research in mathematics and natural philosophy. The principal result of these final years was his *Discourses on Two New Sciences*, published in the Netherlands in 1638 and containing a sequence of dialogues that set out the most systematic and complete statement of Galileo's mechanics.

It is largely through the agency of **Marin Mersenne** that Galileo's work became known outside Italy. In 1634 Mersenne published a French translation of Galileo's 1602 lectures on mechanics under the title *Les Méchaniques de Galilée*, and in 1639 he published a translation of Galileo's *Discourse*. Descartes was familiar with Galileo's contributions, in large part because of Mersenne's efforts, but he found much to criticize. While praising him for his emphasis on mathematics and his commitment to mechanistic explanations of natural phenomena, Descartes criticized Galileo's attention to particular cases and the digressions that intrude in his dialogues. In a letter to Mersenne from October 11, 1638, Descartes complained that Galileo "continually makes digressions and does not stop to explain any single matter, which shows that he has not examined things in order and that he has only sought the explanations of certain particular effects without having considered the first causes of nature, and thus that he has built without a foundation" (AT, vol. II, p. 380).

The condemnation of Galileo had a significant influence on Descartes. When he found out about it in November of 1633, he withdrew *The World* from publication, explaining to Mersenne that the motion of the Earth was demonstrated so evidently that "if it is false, all the foundations of my philosophy are likewise false," with the result that Copernicanism "is so connected to all the parts of my treatise, that I don't know how to remove it without making all the rest defective" (AT, vol. I, p. 271). By the time his natural philosophy was made public in the

Principles of Philosophy, Descartes formulated his astronomical doctrines against a background of a relativistic definition of motion as "the transference of one part of matter or of one body from the neighborhood of those bodies that immediately touch it and are regarded as being at rest, and into the neighborhood of others" (AT, vol. VIIIa, p. 53). This removed the difficulty of a moving Earth, since the definition permits it to be regarded as at rest when considered with respect to immediately surrounding bodies.

GASSENDI, PIERRE (1592–1655). Gassendi was a Catholic priest who, in humanistic tradition, attempted a revival of the philosophy of the **atomist** Epicurus. He began his publishing career in 1624 with an ambitious denunciation of **scholasticism**, *Exercitationes paradoxicae adversus Aristoteleos*, which he intended to consist of seven books. However, prodded by **Marin Mersenne** to abandon this initial project, he published only the first book, though he also completed the second, and started his Christian rehabilitation of Epicurus (circa 1626). Gassendi's work on Epicurus appeared as *De vita et moribus Epicuri* (1647), *Animadversiones in decimum librum Diogenis Laertii* (1649), and *Syntagma philosophicum*, published posthumously in his *Opera omnia* (1658). He wrote the *Fifth Set of Objections* to Descartes's *Meditations* and published it with Descartes's replies and his additional lengthy rebuttals as *Disquisitio metaphysica* (1644). Late in life he was appointed to the chair of mathematics at the Collège Royal.

There were many aspects of Epicurean philosophy that were inconsistent with Christianity, not the least of which was the claim that atoms, the components of the physical universe, are eternal and uncreated. Gassendi amended this seemingly heretical doctrine, claiming the "correction" to be similar to those necessitated by **Aristotle's** own view of matter. Instead, atoms are created **substances** each endowed with their own **motion** at creation. The motion is sustained with the concurrence of **God.** Unlike the **divisible,** composite bodies formed by atoms, atoms themselves are completely solid and, therefore, their integrity cannot naturally be compromised. Further, atoms do not have **forms** or **qualities** other than size, shape, and weight or motion, but provide explanation for all physical change as products of these essential qualities. **Rarefaction,** for example, is explained as a relation between **void** and atoms: a body becomes less dense as the void space is increased within its internal dimensions. The particular types of atoms present (that is, their size, shape, weight, and **quantity** of motion) explain the natural processes of any given composite body. With the exception of the human **soul,** atoms required no immaterial principle to describe secondary causes. Like Descartes, Gassendi epitomized the trend of emphasizing material and **efficient causes**, tending to eliminate formal and **final causes**, reducing the latter to the former (in the realm of bodies). In this way Descartes and Gassendi had "**mechanistic**" understandings of science, though they differed significantly in regard to their conceptions of **body**, motion, **space**, and void as well as their epistemological commitments to science.

The debate between Descartes and Gassendi was long and contentious. After the first exchange in the *Fifth Set of Objections and Replies*, Descartes requested that some his friends boil down Gassendi's objections from the *Disquisitio Metaphysica* to a manageable few. Descartes then answered those in a letter he published with the French translation of the *Meditations* (1647). Gassendi had objected to the First Meditation that Descartes was asking something impossible in wanting people to give up all **preconceived opinions**, that in doing so, we would be adopting even more harmful opinions, and that the **method** of universal **doubt** cannot help us discover any **truths**. He had objected to the Second Meditation that the *cogito* presupposes the major premise "Whatever thinks exists" and what **thought** is, both of which are preconceived opinions. Gassendi also argued that thought cannot exist without an object and that we do not know whether thought is corporeal rather than immaterial. Even though we might not find any **extension** in our thought, it does not follow that our thought is not extended; even though we might distinguish in thought between thought and body, the distinction might be false. Gassendi objected to the Third Meditation that Descartes's **proofs for the existence of God** were not convincing. Not everyone is aware of the idea of God within himself and if someone did have that idea, he should comprehend it. It does not follow that God exists from the fact that we know ourselves to be imperfect. Gassendi also objected to the other Meditations that Descartes was guilty of circularity in proving the existence of God by means of notions in us but in saying afterwards that we cannot be certain of anything without prior knowledge that God exists. He further argued that knowledge of God's existence does not help us in acquiring knowledge of the truth of **mathematics** and that God may be a deceiver.

GENEROSITY (*GÉNÉROSITÉ, MAGNANIMITÉ*). Generosity, which is the term Descartes prefers to the older "magnanimity," is not strictly speaking a **passion** but a virtue or habit; it is also the key to all other virtues. It is best described as legitimate self-esteem and composed of three elements: 1) the knowledge that the only thing that really belongs to us is our **freedom**; 2) the realization that the only thing for which we can be blamed or praised is the use we make of that freedom; 3) our firm resolution to use it well, that is, to do whatever we judge to be the best. Generosity is produced by adding esteem to admiration, which is also the reason why it is related to pride (from which it differs only by its object) and opposed to humility and baseness. A generous person is naturally inclined to do great things, without, for that matter, undertaking anything impossible. Since, on the other hand, his highest aim is to do good to other people, he is courteous, polite, and helpful. Finally, he is not given to jealousy and envy, hatred and anger.

Although generosity and virtuous humility (with which it is perfectly compatible) are habits rather than passions, the fact that their vicious counterparts, pride and baseness, are passions, makes it possible for generosity to be reinforced by the same movement and agitation of the animal spirits that characterizes pride. Given the fact, however, that it is a habit, it is not accompanied by much fluctuation in the spirits. Its best foundation is a good family (*bonne naissance*) because nothing contributes more to legitimate self-esteem than that; but it can also be acquired, by reflecting on our free will and on the advantages of being resolute in one's actions. Generosity is a particularly effective remedy against excessive anger because a generous person will realize that his freedom, which he esteems more than anything else, is at risk if he cannot shrug off the offenses of others. A point of particular interest in the recent literature is that generosity is a form of immediate self-awareness, which as such is comparable to the *cogito*. The only difference would be that, whereas the *cogito* informs us of ourselves as a thinking spirit, generosity makes us aware of ourselves as a free agent.

GEOMETRY. Classically, geometry (literally "earth measurement") was regarded as the abstract science whose object is continuous spatial magnitudes and whose method proceeds by deduction from clearly grasped and transparently true first principles such as common notions and definitions. This classification distinguishes geometry from arithmetic on the basis of its object—where geometry considers continuous magnitudes, arithmetic is the deductively organized study of discrete multitudes or numbers. The principal geometers of Greek antiquity, Euclid, Apollonius, and Archimedes, left behind an immense body of geometric results whose level of sophistication was not revisited until the 17th century. In Descartes's day, one of the principal activities of geometric authors was the preparation of editions and commentaries on classical authors, as well as the speculative "restoration" of lost treatises. One consequence of the success of Descartes's program in the *Geometry* was that the classical division between arithmetic and geometry was undermined; Cartesian analytic geometry uses algebraic methods that apply to any quantity, and are not confined to the specific domain of continuous magnitudes. Further, his success in solving and generalizing problems taken from classical geometry meant that future geometric research departed from the tradition of commentary on ancient authors.

Geometry occupies a central position in Descartes's system, not least because he took the geometric method as a model for all knowledge. As he remarked in the *Discourse*, "those long chains of completely simple and easy reasoning that geometers commonly use to arrive at their most difficult demonstrations gave me occasion to imagine that all things that can fall within the scope of human knowledge are interconnected in the same way" (AT, vol. VI, p. 19). Aside from his fundamental contributions to the development of geometry, Descartes also made geometry fundamental to his physics by insisting that the geometric concept of **extension** was the essence of **body**, with the result that all of **natural philosophy** became a branch of applied geometry. As he put it: "I recognize no matter in corporeal things that which the geometers call quantity and take as the object of their **demonstrations**, i.e. quantity that is in every way capable of being divided, shaped, and moved" (*Principles* II, art. 64; AT, vol. VIIA, pp. 78–79).

GEOMETRY (*GÉOMÉTRIE, GEOMETRIA*). When Descartes arrived in the Netherlands in 1628 he took with him what **Isaac Beeckman** called an "Algebra" (*Journal* III, pp. 94–95), which is no doubt an early version of the *Géométrie*, published eventually in 1637 as one of the essays illustrating the **method** of the *Discourse*. But it is only in 1632, after his work on the problem of **Pappus**, that the text seems to have reached a definitive stage—Descartes's claim that "it was composed while the *Meteors* were already being printed" and that part of it was invented only then (AT, vol. I, p. 458) is presumably an exaggeration, even if the idea of adding the *Geometry* came in the very last stage of the project of the *Discourse*. Descartes knew that his *Geometry* would have few readers; indeed, Descartes meant it to be difficult and left it to his readers to find out the exact details. It is for the few friends that could understand it that he ordered six separate copies to be printed. Its difficulty was the reason not only why a friend of Descartes, Godefroot van Haestrecht (1592/93–59), wrote an introduction ("Calcul de M. Descartes," AT, vol. X, pp. 659–80), but also why **Frans van Schooten**, when he prepared a Latin translation (plans of which were made as early as 1639), added notes and commentaries by himself and by **Florimond Debeaune**. By the time the Latin edition was published (August 1649), however, Descartes had lost interest in it: Van Schooten's Latin was not elegant enough and Descartes had not been able to revise the text before it was printed. Still, the portrait of Descartes, which the book contains (engraved by Van Schooten), is the only one of him published during his lifetime. According to Descartes it was, apart from the beard and the cloths, a good likeness. The Latin version was reprinted in two volumes in 1659 and 1661 (the delay of the second volume being caused presumably by the death of van Schooten) and enlarged with commentaries and additional pieces by Johannes Hudde (1628–1704), Henricus van Heuraet (1633–60), and Erasmus Bartholinus (1625–98).

The *Geometry* is divided into three books, the first of which sets out the foundations of his approach and considers problems solvable by the construction of lines and circles. The second book considers the general nature of curves and the solution problems involving curves, most notably the locus problem propounded by Pappus. The third book is a study in the theory of equations, showing how to determine the number of roots in an equation and how to apply these algebraic results to the classification of curves and the solution of geometric problems.

The fundamental insight in Descartes's *Geometry* is contained in its first sentence: "Any problem in geometry can easily be reduced to such terms that a knowledge of the lengths of certain straight lines is sufficient for its construction" (AT, vol. VI, p. 370). Descartes interprets arithmetical operations (addition, subtraction, multiplication, division, and the extraction of roots) as geometric constructions on straight lines that yield other straight lines. Classical authors had interpreted the product of two lines as a surface and the product of three as a solid, with the result that algebraic equations beyond the third degree had no geometrical interpretation. Descartes overcame this limitation by taking all arithmetical or algebraic operations on line segments to yield other line segments. This criterion of "dimensional homogeneity" permits equations of arbitrary degree to be employed in the study of geometric curves. Furthermore, by interpreting a curve as an equation in two unknowns that form the axes of a coordinate system, curves can be represented in a two-dimensional plane and the nature of the curve is expressed as an algebraic relation among geometric magnitudes.

Descartes proposed that a general method of solution for geometric problems could be found by reasoning in a sort of **analysis** that begins by supposing the problem solved and uncovering the algebraic equations that determine this solution. In Descartes's words: "If, then, we wish to solve any problem, we first suppose the solution already to have been effected, and give names to all the lines that seem needful for its construction—those that are unknown as well as those that are known. Then, making no distinction between known and unknown lines, we must unravel the difficulty in any way that shows most naturally the relations between these lines, until we find it possible to express a single quantity in two ways. This will constitute an equation . . .

and we must find as many such equations as we have supposed lines which are unknown" (AT, vol. VI, pp. 372–73). Exploiting this approach led Descartes to the solution of previously unsolved problems and permitted him to generalize results that had previously been stated only for special cases.

Classical geometry distinguished between "plane" problems whose solutions required only compass and rule constructions, "solid" problems relying on curves (such as conic sections) generated by the intersection of solids and planes, and "linear" solutions which employed more complex curves (such as the spiral) generated by compound motions. Classical authors did not consider curves more complex than conic sections to be properly geometric, but Descartes held that this criterion was too restrictive. He held that any curve that could be given a "precise and exact" measure was properly geometrical (as opposed to mechanical), and identified such curves with those that could be described by a regular **motion** or series of motions (AT, vol. VI, p. 390). Descartes even introduced a complex proportional compass (known as the "mesolabe") that generalizes the traditional compass and produces complex curves that satisfy his criterion for geometric constructability. Descartes further assumed that every geometrical curve could be expressed in terms of an equation, and a principal result of the *Geometry* is the classification of curves into types or genres on the basis of their equations. In view of its many contributions, it is no exaggeration to say that the publication of the *Geometry* fundamentally changed the study of **mathematics**.

GEULINCX, ARNOLD (1624–69). Geulincx was born in Antwerp. He studied theology and humanities in **Louvain**, where he became a professor of philosophy in 1646, first as associate, then, in 1652, as *primarius*. At the beginning of 1658, however, for reasons that have as yet to be clarified, he was dismissed from all his academic functions. He fled to Leiden, where he embraced the Calvinist faith and became a protégé of the Leiden professor of theology Abraham Heidanus (1597–1678), a Cartesian. Thanks to his influence, presumably, Geulincx was appointed reader (1662) and then professor (1665) of philosophy in **Leiden**. Meanwhile he graduated in medicine. He died from the plague in 1669. Apart from "Miscellaneous Questions" (*Quaestiones quodlibeticae*, 1650), a treatise on **logic** (*Logica suis fundamentis restituta*, 1662) and the first part of a work on moral philosophy (*Tractatus ethicus*, 1665) most of his works were published posthumously. His *Ethics* in particular enjoyed great popularity and was reprinted several times until 1709. Although modern commentators value his contribution to logic, Geulincx is still a much-neglected philosopher who deserves more attention than he usually gets.

Geulincx became familiar with Cartesian philosophy in Louvain through his teacher Willem Philippi (ca. 1600–65). What he retains from it is the reform of logic and **method** and the **dualism of body** and **mind**, which he interprets in an **occasionalist** way. The foundation of Geulincx's occasionalism is the **principle** that one cannot do what one does not know how to do. Accordingly, since we do not know how our body works, we are not the real subjects of bodily actions; inversely, it is impossible for a body to act on our minds or on other bodies because it would not know how to do this. Still, Geulincx believes that there is a harmony between what happens in the outside world and what is willed or perceived by our minds. The agent responsible for this is **God**, who also imposed on the material world a certain number of laws. Geulincx is original in completing Cartesianism with an ethical theory, despite the fact that, as he puts it, "I am a spectator on this scene, not an actor" (*Tractatus Ethicus* I, ii, 11). According to Geulincx the object of ethics is **virtue**, that is, **love** of God and of right **reason**. Of the four cardinal virtues, diligence, obedience, justice, and humility, which are the immediate expressions of virtue as such, humility, which is the contempt of oneself out of love for God, is the most important one. It entails a certain number of obligations, which are actually formulated as divine commands. We must be ready to die if God calls us; we should not end our life voluntarily; we should take care of our body, etc. Although Geulincx's views bear some resemblance to **Baruch Spinoza's**, especially as regards his tendency to reduce the substantiality of individual bodies and his interest in practical philosophy, this should not be exaggerated. Apart from the fact that Geulincx has a different conception of moral philosophy and of the relation of mind and body, his God is the Christian God.

GIBIEUF, GUILLAUME (ca. 1591–1650). A French theologian who was a member of the **Oratory** and of the **Sorbonne**. Descartes courted Gibieuf as someone who could promote his *Meditations* to other members of the Paris theological faculty. Gibieuf took enough of an interest to correspond with Descartes concerning his work. However, his primary interests were in theological matters, mainly the issue of **freedom of the will**. His main work is *De Libertate Dei et Hominis* (1630), a critique of the **Jesuit** view that indifference is essential to human freedom. The anti-Jesuit **Cornelius Jansenius** approved of Gibieuf's text, as did Descartes, who told **Marin Mersenne** in 1641 that he has said nothing in the *Meditations* "that is not in accord with what is said in his book *De Libertate*" (AT, vol. III, p. 360). However, some of Descartes's later writings seem to be more sympathetic to the Jesuit position that Gibieuf and other critics of Jesuit **theology** condemned as a form of heretical **Pelagianism**.

GILBERT, WILLIAM (1544–1603). English physician and **natural philosopher** best known for his researches into the phenomenon of magnetism, which culminated in the 1600 publication of the treatise *De magnete* ("On the Magnet"). Born to a prosperous merchant family in Colchester, Gilbert entered St. John's College, Cambridge, in 1558, taking the degrees of B.A. in 1561, M.A. in 1564, and M.D. in 1569. He was elected to a fellowship at St. John's in 1569 and held several college offices. Gilbert established a medical practice in London in the early 1570s, becoming a member of the Royal College of Physicians, to whose presidency he was elected in 1600.

Gilbert employed a wide variety of experiments in *De magnete* to test hypotheses about the **nature** of magnetism, and he was emphatic in his rejection of **Aristotelian** accounts of magnetic attraction. He was the first to distinguish clearly between magnetism and static electricity, and he organized *De magnete* in the form of a comprehensive review of what was known about magnetic attraction. A key component in Gilbert's theorizing was the construction of laboratory models of the Earth from lathe-turned lodestones. He performed experiments on these models and then argued by analogy to draw conclusions about the phenomenon of magnetic attraction in the Earth itself. Gilbert's theory of magnetism was strongly influenced by Neoplatonic doctrines. In his animistic scheme of things, magnetism is literally the **soul** of the Earth, and a perfectly spherical lodestone (if aligned with the Earth's poles) would spin on its axis, just as the Earth spins on its axis in 24 hours. This endorsement of a rotating Earth was based in part on the doctrines of **Nicholaus Copernicus**, to which Gilbert added his own arguments from magnetism; he was nevertheless silent on the issue of whether the heliocentric model of the world was to be preferred.

Descartes was certainly familiar with Gilbert's doctrines, but he had little patience for a theory that postulated a Neoplatonic world soul and characterized magnetism as a ubiquitous immaterial cosmic force. In the *Rules for the Direction of the Mind* he casually mentions that "someone may ask me what conclusions are to be drawn about the nature of the magnet simply from the experiments Gilbert claims to have performed, whether they be true or false" (AT, vol. X, p. 431), but he obviously set little store by Gilbert's doctrines. Instead, Descartes sought to explain magnetism **mechanically**. In the fourth part of the *Principles of Philosophy* he attempts this by means of a constantly cir-

Goclenius 121

culating flow of subtle particles from one hemisphere of the Earth to the other (AT, vol. VIIA, pp. 275–314).

GLANVILL, JOSEPH (1636–80). English clergyman and philosopher. Educated at Exeter College and Lincoln College, Oxford, Glanvill was ordained in the Church of England in 1660 and was appointed rector of the Abbey Church at Bath. He had a strong interest in **natural philosophy** and attacked **scholastic** philosophy in *The Vanity of Dogmatizing* (1661). Glanvill conceived the new philosophy as a kind of skepticism, and he popularized among English readers an interpretation of Descartes that characterized his philosophy as an essentially skeptical **method** for **metaphysics** and natural philosophy. His emphasis on the incompleteness of our knowledge of **nature** and the limits of mechanical explanation was congenial to **Henry More**, and the two became close associates. As was also the case with More, Glanvill's early enthusiasm for Descartes turned to disenchantment and he eventually came to regard Cartesianism as an exercise in dogmatic metaphysics that overemphasized the explanatory success of **mechanism** and denied the reality of spirits. His continuing interest in natural philosophy led to his election as a fellow of the Royal Society, and in 1668 he published *Plus Ultra, or the Progress and Advancement of Knowledge since the Days of Aristotle* where he extolled the world of the Society. He became best known for his investigations into witchcraft and demonic possession, which he conducted with More. His 1666 *Philosophical Endeavour towards the Defence of the Being of Witches and Apparitions* was reissued in 1681 by More, who appended to it an extended polemic against Descartes.

GOCLENIUS, RUDOLPH (RUDOLPH GÖKEL, 1547–1628). German professor of **natural philosophy** and **mathematics**, one of the more influential late **scholastics**. Born in Corbach in the principality of Waldeck, Goclenius attended the University of Marburg from 1564 to 1568 and continued his studies at the University of Wittenberg, with his principal academic interest in natural philosophy. He took the degree *magister artis* in 1571 and was appointed to the rectorship of the local school in Corbach. He composed a Latin celebratory poem dedicated to Prince Wilhelm of Hesse, and the success of this venture brought him the post of rector of the school in Kassel in 1575. In 1581 he was appointed to the professorship in physics at the University of Marburg. He remained at the University of Marburg for the rest of his career, serving in various capacities including professor of **logic**, mathematics, and ethics, as well as rector of the university and dean of the faculty of philosophy.

Goclenius enjoyed a reputation as a conciliator in controversies among **theological** and philosophical factions. In keeping with this reputation, his contributions to natural philosophy, mathematics, and logic were eclectic and show a pronounced reluctance to depart from traditional authorities. He upheld the traditional logic of **Aristotle** against the innovations of **Petrus Ramus**, and promoted the scholastic-Aristotelian method in physics. His encyclopedic work *Physicae completae speculum* ("The Mirror of all Physics," 1604) assembles material from mathematics, geography, astronomy, botany, and medicine, as well as precepts taken from logic, **metaphysics**, ethics, and theology. His influential *Lexicon philosophicum* (1613) introduced such terms as "psychology" and "ontology" into the philosophical vocabulary. His posthumously published *Mirabilium naturae liber* ("Book of the Marvels of **Nature**," 1625) contains a detailed investigation into such phenomena as magnetism.

GOD. Descartes characterizes God as "a **substance** that is **infinite**, independent, supremely intelligent, supremely powerful, and which created both me and everything else" (AT VII, p. 45). This account is typical of the "God of the philosophers"—the infinitely powerful, all knowing Creator whose essence can be understood by finite minds, although orthodoxy requires that God cannot be fully comprehended by a finite being. (See **knowledge of God**.) God plays an absolutely indispensable role in Descartes's philosophy, and specifically in his **metaphysics**, epistemology, and **natural philosophy**.

Cartesian metaphysics emphasizes the role of God as creator, not merely of the universe and the finite creatures that inhabit it, but also of the **eternal truths** such as the **common notion** that nothing comes from nothing. This aspect of Descartes's philosophy emphasizes the absolute dependence of things on God, a dependence so complete that even the truths of **logic** and **mathematics** require God's creative act in order to hold true, which means that God could freely have chosen alternatives to such truths. God's causal power extends to self-creation, and Descartes characterizes God as self-caused, or *causa sui*, a doctrine that led to some intense exchanges with **Antoine Arnauld** in the fourth set of *Objections and Replies* (AT, vol. VII, pp. 235–46). A further aspect of God's creative power is that divine concurrence is necessary to preserve things in existence. The result is that (as Descartes puts it in Meditation III), there is only a conceptual distinction between creation and preservation, and therefore God's sustaining of the world is equivalent to his **continuous** re-creation of it (AT, vol. VII, p. 49).

Descartes held that the **demonstration** of God's existence was a matter of the first importance for philosophy (AT, vol. VII, p. 1), and the *Meditations* pursue two different strategies for demonstrating God's existence. The first (explored in the Third Meditation) begins with the idea of God and reasons that an idea with so much **objective reality** cannot have been caused by anything less perfect and powerful than God himself. Thus, since the mind of a finite individual meditating on the idea of God has insufficient power to have produced such a perfect idea, it must arise from some source outside the meditator's mind; and since such a source cannot have less reality and perfection than God, there must be a God who answers in all respects to the idea of God. (See **cosmological argument.**) The second strategy (worked out in the Fifth Meditation) argues that existence belongs conceptually to the very essence of God. Since God is by definition the supremely perfect being, and existence is a perfection, it follows that God's existence is a necessary consequence of his essence. (See **ontological argument.**) Descartes regarded these demonstrations of God as more certain than those of mathematics, and concluded that an **atheist** mathematician would find himself in the self-contradictory position of denying a truth that is far more certain than any mathematical theorem (AT, vol. VII, p. 141).

Cartesian epistemology is impossible without a God, since the "truth rule" that **clear and distinct perceptions** must be true is guaranteed only by the existence of a benevolent, nondeceiving God. If God were to permit us to be mistaken even about those things we seem to grasp most clearly, then there would be no sure way for us to make a **judgment** and avoid **error.** But such deceit is inconsistent with the perfection of God. This leads to the conclusion that God's nondeceiving **nature** guarantees that those things I clearly and distinctly conceive must be true. As a consequence, I know with certainty that I will not fall into error, provided that I confine my judgments to those things clearly and distinctly perceived.

The place of God in Descartes's natural philosophy is not only as creator of the world, but also as the ultimate source of the laws of **motion** that govern the material world. God's immutability guarantees that the **conservation principle** holds, and this is the foundation of the laws of motion. In fact, Descartes holds that God is the "first and general" cause of motion (AT, vol. VIIIA, p. 61). This emphasis on God's causal role makes it difficult for Descartes's natural philosophy to avoid **occasionalism,** since the God who creates and sustains the world, continuously re-creating it in accordance with immutable laws of motion, would seem to be the only causal agent.

Pierre-Sylvain Régis and **Nicolas Malebranche** offered different developments of Descartes's account of the role of God in natural philosophy. Malebranche was the primary proponent of the occasionalist thesis that God is the only real cause of effects in the material world.

Such a thesis is connected to Descartes's claim in the *Principles* that God is the primary cause who conserves the total quantity of motion by continuing to create the material world in the same way from moment to moment. However, Descartes himself suggested that God's causation of motion involves his "concurrence" with the action of bodily causes. In line with this suggestion, Régis claimed that changes in motion derive directly not from God's action but rather from a created nature that provides the ground for the **laws** of motion.

Descartes was concerned to restrict his claims about God for the most part to what is revealed by **reason**. He thereby attempted to avoid disputes about **theological** matters that depend on **faith**. Even so, his later followers became entangled in theological disputes concerning the relation of human **freedom** to divine grace and the manner in which God brings about **transubstantiation** in the mystery of the Eucharist.

GOD, KNOWLEDGE OF. In the *Meditations*, Descartes claimed that a proof of the existence of a nondeceptive **God** is needed for stable and certain knowledge. The fact that such a proof seems to require such knowledge gave rise to the famous problem of the **Cartesian circle**. However, Descartes countered that his **clear and distinct** perceptions allow him to provide the needed proof. In fact, the *Meditations* included two arguments for the existence of God that drew on different though complementary explications of God's **nature**. (See **cosmological argument** and **ontological argument**.) Both arguments suggest that God possesses an unlimited form of the same sort of substantiality or perfections that creatures possess. Descartes did deny that the term **substance** applies "univocally," or in the same way, to God and creatures (*Principles* I, art. 51), but such a denial is consistent with the standard **Thomistic** view that terms apply to God and creatures "analogically" since God possesses the named perfections primarily and creatures in a derivative way.

However, Descartes's doctrine of God's free creation of the **eternal truths** is in some tension with such a view insofar as it implies that God differs entirely from creatures since they are essentially conditioned by the eternal truths while God is not. Descartes's disciple **Pierre-Sylvain Régis** later emphasized this implication of the eternal truths doctrine since God creates all perfections in creatures *ex nihilo*, the created perfections can bear no relation to God's perfections. Appealing to a position that Thomas and other **scholastics** rejected, Régis concluded that names for perfections could apply to God and creatures only "equivocally." In offering this conclusion, Régis was countering the claim in **Nicolas Malebranche** that perfections in creatures are present "eminently" in God insofar as God has ideas of these perfections that are not distinct from his own substance.

GOUSSET, JACQUES (1635–1704). A **Calvinist** minister and a noted Hebrew scholar. Gousset studied at Saumur, and became a minister at Poiters in 1662, but left France in 1685 when the Edict of Nantes was revoked. He settled in the Netherlands and became minister of the Walloons at Dordrecht. Five years later he gave up the position to occupy the chair of Greek and **Theology** at Groningen, which he held until he died. His principal works concerned the Hebrew language and the interpretation of biblical passages. He also wrote a treatise on whether the Cartesian system of the world should be considered dangerous, *Dissertatio philos. ostendens cartesianum mundi systema non esse . . . periculosum* (1696), and a defense of Descartes's view of the activity of secondary causes against **Nicolas Malebranche's** system of **occasional** causes in *Causarum primae et secundarum realis operatio* (issued posthumously, 1716).

GRAVITY. In **Aristotelian natural philosophy,** heaviness and lightness are **qualities** of bodies derived from the **elements** they are composed of. The elements earth and water are heavy; air and fire are light. Heavy bodies tend to move toward the center of the universe (which is also the center of the Earth); light bodies away from the center. Medieval philosophers, in analyzing the motion of falling bodies, had arrived at a rule equivalent to that still used in elementary physics ($s = \frac{1}{2}gt^2$). **Galileo Galilei** too had presented a derivation of this rule.

In his early collaboration with **Isaac Beeckman,** Descartes also offers a derivation of the rule based on the assumptions that an equal impulse of **motion** is given at each instant to the falling body and that quantity of motion is preserved (see **inertia**). He offered no explanation, however, for the impulse itself. In later work, he argued that the **vortex** surrounding each planet exerts a pressure on every body on that planet, directed toward the center of the planet and proportional, more or less, to the area of the outward-facing surface of the body (*Principles* IV, art. 28). Dense bodies, which have relatively few pores or channels, offer more resistance to vortex particles, and are therefore heavier than more rarefied bodies (*Principles* IV, art. 20).

The explanation of the orbits of the moon around the Earth, and of all the planets around the sun, was quite different. Every planet-sized body is surrounded by a vortex of small particles revolving around it. Their speed is proportional to their distance from the planet. Coarse **matter** in the midst of these vortices is dragged around with them, and settles into an orbit around them in such a way that it is in equilibrium with the vortex particles around it (*Principles* III, art. 140–45).

The tides are explained by yet another **mechanism**. The vortex at whose center is the Earth, and in whose outer layers the Moon revolves, remains constant in diameter. In the region immediately between the Earth and Moon, there is less room for the vortex particles to move. This produces pressure on the atmosphere and oceans of the Earth directly beneath the Moon, and thus a low tide there, and 90 degrees around the Earth's circumference on either side a high tide (*Principles* IV, art. 49).

Although the vortex theory of gravity was defended even into the 1740s (by Bernard de Fontenelle), it was decisively rejected by **Isaac Newton, Christiaan Huygens,** and other physicists well before the end of the 17th century. Explanations based on it were likewise rejected; the Newtonian assumption of a single inverse-square **force** operating between all parts of matter provided a unified explanation of all the phenomena described above, and yielded—as Descartes's theory did not—precise quantitative results. Nevertheless Descartes's theory succeeded in showing how gravity could be accounted for in an isotropic space, thus allowing natural philosophers to abandon the notion that the universe has a *center*—a special place in which heavy bodies congregate.

– H –

HAPPINESS (*FELICITAS, BEATITUDO, BÉATITUDE*). Although in Descartes's early work there is at least one passage in which true happiness (*felicitas*) is said to consist in the contemplation of **truth**, systematic reflection on the subject is almost entirely limited to the correspondence with Princess **Elisabeth** and Queen **Christina**—even if the *Discourse* and the *Passions of the Soul* provide relevant background. According to Descartes we should make a distinction between *bonheur* (good luck) and *béatitude* (blessedness). Good luck does not depend on us but on our environment, whereas beatitude consists in the perfect satisfaction of the **mind** and can be acquired. According to Descartes, three rules help to achieve it: 1) to try and use our own mind to know what we should or should not do; 2) to be resolute in doing whatever **reason** advises us to do; 3) to consider that we have no power over the things we do not possess, and so to avoid **desire** and regret, which are the only obstacles to achieving a perfect satisfaction of mind. This does not mean that we have to give up all desires—the only desires we should avoid are those accompanied with **sadness** and impatience. Nor does it mean that we never should make a mistake—it is enough if our conscience tells us that we have been resolute in doing the things we judged to be the best.

Satisfaction of the mind is not completely independent of the **body**. The **freedom** of the mind and of the **will** that forms the basis of it can be taken away by disease, by **passions**, by temperament, by **imagination**—even if Descartes believes that most of the troubles caused by these can be overcome and that, if they are actually overcome, the satisfaction is even greater. Descartes rejects the Stoic idea that beatitude should consist in the suppression of the passions and tends to agree with Epicurus, who according to him is often misunderstood.

Indeed, pleasure is a real motive. It would be impossible for us to act virtuously if we did not receive some pleasure from it, that is, the feeling of having acquired a perfection. However, if virtue consists in the realization of having acquired a perfection, that perfection should be real and not illusory. Now, of the things that give us pleasure some relate to the mind alone and others to man, that is, to the **union of mind and body**. And since the second are presented to us by the imagination and the passions, they often seem greater than they are, especially before we enjoy them, "which is the source of all life's evil and errors" (to Elisabeth, September 1, 1645, AT, vol. IV, p. 284). Accordingly, pleasure is not itself the highest good. The sovereign good is the exercise of virtue (*exercice de la vertu*), that is, the possession of all those goods that can be acquired by our **free will**, whereas the highest pleasure, that is, the complete satisfaction of the mind, is the result of enjoying the highest good. The role of reason is to examine the value of all the goods that seem to depend on our own. Accordingly, we should not see the passions as a source of knowledge of what is actually good but try and suspend our **judgment** until the emotion calms down. Instead we should try and control them by reason, and that is possible only if we carefully examine them. Thus, the **enumeration** and **analysis** of the passions forms an essential part of the pursuit of happiness, if only because it can teach us how almost all of them can give us **joy** one way or another, if they are well regulated.

All this must of course be distinguished from supernatural beatitude, which pertains to **faith** rather than philosophy. And although Descartes generally leaves questions like these to **theologians**, still, there are a few things he says about this condition of eternal happiness, which directly confronts us with a different sovereign good, namely, **God**. In a letter to **Jean de Silhon** of March or April 1648 he confirms what apparently had already been suggested by his correspondent, namely, that in the state of eternal happiness we have an **intuitive** knowledge of God, which he sees as an "illumination of the mind, by which it sees in the light of God whatever God pleases to reveal to him through a direct impression of the divine clarity on our **intellect**" (AT, vol. V, p. 136). It means that the intellect is no longer an agent but a passive recipient of the luminous rays of the Godhead, whereas, of course, all natural knowledge of God in this life is discursive.

HARVEY, WILLIAM (1578–1657). English physician and anatomist, famed for his discovery of the **circulation of blood.** Harvey was born in Folkestone, Kent, and received his early education at the King's School in Canterbury. He entered Caius College, Cambridge, in 1593, studying philosophy and taking the degree of B.A. in 1597. He traveled to Padua in 1600 to undertake the study of medicine and was awarded the degree of M.D. in 1602. Upon his return to England he was given license to practice medicine in 1603 by the Royal College of Physicians, to which he was elected as a fellow in 1607. Harvey was a very active member of the College and held a variety of offices, and from 1615 until 1645 he regularly delivered lectures at the College. In 1618 he was appointed as a physician to the court of James I. He maintained his association with the court with an appointment as personal physician to Charles I at his accession in 1625, and even accompanied the king on the battlefield in 1642 during the English Civil War. He remained a committed royalist during the Protectorate of Cromwell and the abolition of the monarchy, although his political opinions appear not to have put him in danger. His practice in London flourished and his reputation as a physician grew significantly during the last decade of his life.

In 1618 Harvey discovered that the blood circulates in animals, including humans, but he published the result only in 1628 in the treatise *De motu cordis et sanguinis in animalibus* ("On the motion of the heart and blood in animals"). His discovery fundamentally changed anatomy and physiology but was quite controversial when first proposed. The source of controversy was the fact that Harvey's account contradicted the accepted doctrine (derived from the second-century Greek medical writer Galen) that the **heart** and arterial system were not connected to the liver and venous system. Harvey's publication of his research initially cost him much of his reputation as a physician—patients abandoned his medical practice, numerous books attacked his doctrine, and he was denounced as a crank. In the course of time his theories became the dominant view, and by the early 1650s his doctrine was firmly established. For all his status as an innovator in anatomy and physiology, Harvey was a dedicated **Aristotelian** who dismissed the innovations of the "new philosophy" as ill-conceived speculations. He regarded his own doctrines as the result of anatomical investigation in the style of

Aristotle, and he had little patience for the claims of **mechanistic** philosophy in the style of Descartes.

Descartes endorsed the theory of the circulation of the blood, devoting much of the fifth section of the *Discourse on Method* to an account of animal physiology that emphasizes the heart's role as a pump that circulates blood (AT, vol. VI, pp. 46–55). He even mentions Harvey with approval as "an English physician who must be praised for having broken the ice on this subject" (AT, vol. VI, p. 50). However, Descartes's model of the circulatory system departs from Harvey's in several respects. Descartes held that the heat of the heart instantaneously heats the blood and causes it to expand, which in turn makes the heart to beat and pushes the blood through the arteries; Harvey rejected this account on the grounds that fermentation could not be instantaneous and concluded that the heart must have an internal motive principle that causes it to contract intermittently. Further, Descartes held that blood is composed of **particles** of many different shapes that were filtered through various sievelike structures in the glands to produce different bodily fluids; in contrast, Harvey regarded blood as a uniform substance lacking corpuscular composition and he dismissed the notion that filtering a fluid could cause it to change its **nature.**

HATE. For Descartes, hate is one of the six primitive **passions** or **emotions** of the soul. It is directly opposed to **love.** Love incites the soul to "join in will with objects that appear agreeable to it." Hate "incites the soul to wish to be separated from the objects that present themselves to it as harmful" (AT, vol. XI, p. 387). It thus inclines the **will,** when directed toward the same object, to an act contrary to that which results from love. Hate is never harmless to the soul; even when justified, it is always accompanied by sadness, because in anything real, even something harmful to us, there is some goodness. Just as love is one link in a causal chain leading from pleasure to **joy** to love to an inclination to join oneself in will with the thing loved, so too hate follows upon **pain** and sadness.

Horror, indignation, and anger are species of hate. Horror (or aversion) arises from the perception of something ugly, as delight from the beautiful. Indignation is the hatred of those who commit evil, and is, oddly enough, often accompanied by wonder, because (Descartes thinks) we are surprised by the occurrence of evil. It is more often found in those who pretend to virtue than in those who are genuinely virtuous, because the virtuous person reserves his anger for matters of importance. Anger is aversion in cases where the evil in question is directed toward us. It gives rise to the **desire** for revenge, a desire "incomparably more violent" than the desires that arise from indignation or favor (AT, vol. XI, p. 477). **Generosity** is the best remedy against the excesses of anger; in the generous person anger is mitigated by the knowledge that there are few true goods of which one can be deprived, and that in giving free rein to anger one renounces control of the will.

HEART. Of all bodily organs the heart is according to Descartes the most important for the performance of the vital functions. Contrary to many of his contemporaries, **William Harvey** in particular, Descartes did not see the heart as a muscle (although the access to the heart is governed by a muscle), but as some sort of furnace, whose main significance is that it is warmer than the rest of the body. It contains a "fire without light," which is so hot that the blood that enters it is immediately heated. It expands, breaks its way out of the heart into the lungs, where it is cooled down, returns to the heart, where it is heated again, acquires new force and starts its journey through the body (see **blood, circulation of**). A fire without light is generally produced by mixing different types of bodies or liquids, that is, by some sort of fermentation. This is also the explanation adopted for the heart, although it is not absolutely clear what are the liquids or bodies involved, nor where exactly the fermentation takes place. The explanation given of the bodily movements involved in the **passions** suggests that it is the blood itself that entertains the heat in the heart, so the heat in the heart could be produced, either by mixing venous and arterial blood or by inequalities in the venous blood. That could make Descartes's explanation circular (for it could mean that the heart is heated by the blood and not the blood by the heart).

Descartes rejects the idea that the heart is the place where the passions are felt even if he admits that the heart is the organ most affected by the passions. The passions are actually felt by the **mind** in the brain, albeit "as in the heart," just as other pains are felt "as in the foot." A signal is transmitted to the brain from the heart by a small nerve, where it is perceived by the **soul**, which accordingly "to feel the passions in the heart has no more to be in the heart than it has to be in the heaven to see the stars" (*Passions* I, art. 33, AT, vol. XI, p. 354). Embryologically the heart is the oldest organ, being formed by a fermentation caused by the mixing of male and female semen, which are heterogeneous.

HEEREBOORD, ADRIAAN (1613–61). Adriaan Heereboord (or Heereboort) was born in Leiden. He also studied philosophy and **theology** in **Leiden** and, in 1640, was appointed professor "extraordinary" (that is, reader or associate professor) in **logic**. In 1642 Heereboord was appointed deputy dean of the "Statencollege" (a theological college for bursars of the States of Holland), the dean being **Jacobus Revius** (1586–1658). The main task of the deputy dean was to train theologians in philosophy. From 1644 on he was full professor in philosophy, teaching logic, ethics, and politics. Heereboord was not an easy man nor did he have an easy life. The sordid details of his married life, all having to do with a tenacious drinking problem, were spelled out in several pamphlets by his brothers-in-law, Jan (1622–60) and Pieter de la Court (1618–85), also known as writers on political theory; in the end a permanent separation from his wife could not be prevented. Although from the beginning of his professional career Heereboord had been critical of **Aristotelianism** (by which he meant the slavish following of Aristotle), he was rather eclectic in his preference for modern philosophers, where his heroes were **Francis Bacon, Petrus Ramus, Pierre Gassendi,** Claudius Berigardus, and indeed Descartes. The appointment of Adam Steuart or Stuart (1591–1654), a very traditional philosopher of Scottish origin, as professor of philosophy (with precedence over Heereboord), as well as his own antagonistic relation with Revius, may have caused Heereboord to defend Descartes more openly and more exclusively than he would have done otherwise.

In any case, what one finds in his works and disputations is a provocative defense of isolated ideas and propositions (such as *"cogito, ergo sum* is the first certainty of philosophy" or "doubt is the beginning of a philosophy that cannot be doubted") rather than a systematic rethinking of the Cartesian project as a whole. This lack of commitment is also suggested by the fact that he edited or reedited several more traditional works, such as a textbook on logic by Franco Burgersdijk (1590–1635) and a perfectly orthodox and traditional *Metaphysica* by the Franeker professor of theology Johannes Maccovius (1588–1644). His own works are mostly collections of disputations but there is also a **physics** in which he contrasts typically Aristotelian propositions and definitions with those of others (**Henricus Regius,** for example, or Berigardus), without giving his own opinion, for that matter. The general impression one gets from reading his works therefore remains one of eclecticism.

HOBBES, THOMAS (1588–1679). An English philosopher best known for his political theory, but also closely involved with developments in 17th-century philosophy, including **natural philosophy** and **metaphysics.** Proponent of a strict materialistic ontology that equates **body** with **substance,** Hobbes endorsed the **mechanistic** principle that all phenomena of the world arise through the **motion** and impact of material bodies.

Educated at Oxford and taking a bachelor's degree in 1608, Hobbes entered immediately into the service of the Cavendish family (earls and later dukes of Devonshire), in whose employ he would remain (with a few years of interruption) until his death. As tutor to the son of the Earl of Devonshire in 1614–15, Hobbes made his first journey to the Continent and was introduced to the "new philosophy" that was displacing the **Aristotelianism** he had studied at Oxford. Hobbes's connections with the Cavendish family facilitated his being employed as a secretary by **Francis Bacon** (probably in the 1620s, although the exact date is difficult to determine). According to Hobbes's own report, a chance encounter with the **geometry** of Euclid while on a second journey to the Continent in 1629–30 impressed upon him the power and certainty of its **deductive method** and inspired him to develop a philosophical system *more geometrico*.

During the 1630s Hobbes pursued his scientific and philosophical interests and was active in the intellectual circle centered on **William Cavendish** (nephew of the earl of Devonshire) who was earl, later marquess and duke of Newcastle. In 1634 Hobbes embarked on a third tour of the Continent, this time as tutor to the third earl of Devonshire. During this two-year sojourn Hobbes was introduced (through the agency of Newcastle and his brother **Sir Charles Cavendish**) to the network of scientific and philosophical correspondents around **Marin Mersenne,** including Descartes, **Kenelm Digby, Gilles Personne de Roberval, Claude Mydorge,** and **Pierre Gassendi.** Hobbes also met **Galileo Galilei** during this stay in Europe, where legend has it that they discussed the prospects for presenting moral and political philosophy in the form of a deductive system. By the time of his return to England in 1636, Hobbes was committed to a philosophical system that rejected Aristotelianism and sought to replace it with a mechanical philosophy that took motion as its ultimate explanatory concept.

One of Hobbes's principal interests in the 1630s was the theory of **light** and vision. This resulted in a manuscript treatise on **optics** that took the form of a running critique of Descartes's *Dioptrics*. The theories of both men are, in fact, quite close, particularly in the shared assumption that perception is caused by a diversity of motions in the sensory apparatus having no intrinsic similarities to perceived phenomenal **qualities.** Through the agency of Mersenne (who would later publish a version of Hobbes's optics in his 1644 *Universæ Geometriæ mixtæque Synopsis*), Hobbes entered into a correspondence on topics in optics and **physics** with Descartes in 1640–41. This quickly became an acrimonious exchange of charges, including allegations of plagiarism (AT, vol. III, pp. 287–92, 300–18, 321–26, 341–48). Mersenne disregarded Descartes's expressed desire "to have nothing to do with that Englishman"

(AT, vol. III, p. 320) and gathered from Hobbes the third set of *Objections* to the *Meditations*. These drew notably brief and dismissive replies from Descartes, who was appalled at Hobbes's thoroughgoing materialism.

Concern with the course of political events in England interrupted Hobbes's research in philosophy and prompted him to compose a manuscript treatise, *The Elements of Law*. This work purported to derive the necessity of absolute sovereignty from first principles that included a purely mechanistic account of human psychology and physiology. Fearing Parliamentary retribution for his adamantly pro-Royalist doctrines, Hobbes returned to France in late 1640, where he remained for more than a decade, and worked out the details of his philosophical system. Hobbes envisaged a tripartite system of treatises—*De Corpore*, *De Homine*, and *De Cive*—that would begin with the metaphysics of body, proceed to the nature of man, and conclude with a theory of the commonwealth. He published them out of order: the second in 1642, the third in 1647, while the first did not see print until 1655.

With the defeat of the Royalist cause in the English Civil War and the execution of Charles I, Hobbes's thoughts again turned to politics. He composed his masterpiece *Leviathan* in 1650, recasting his earlier arguments for absolute sovereign power and including a statement of his materialist metaphysics along with a number of inflammatory anticlerical passages. *Leviathan* was published in 1651 and made Hobbes's life in Paris difficult by angering both the exiled court of Charles II (with its implication that a subject's submission to the victorious Parliamentary party was both lawful and rational) and the French clergy (who found Hobbes's anti-Catholic diatribes intolerable). Fearing once again for his safety, Hobbes abandoned France for England at the end of 1651.

Hobbes returned to England with a substantial reputation as a *savant*. However, he soon found himself engaged in a number of controversies—one with John Bramhall over free will, one with John Wallis over failed efforts to square the circle, and one with Robert Boyle over questions of pneumatics and scientific methodology. These controversies occupied much of Hobbes's later life, and their result (particularly in the controversies with Wallis and Boyle) was a general diminution of his philosophical and scientific reputation, although his standing as a political philosopher remained unaffected.

HUET, PIERRE-DANIEL (1630–1721). A native of Caen who was a noted literary scholar and linguist and, later, bishop. Huet accompanied Samuel Borchart to the court of Queen Christina of Sweden in 1652, just two years after Descartes's death there. He returned to Caen soon thereafter to work on an edition of Origen's commentaries. In 1662 he helped to found an academy of science in Caen. Huet was appointed *sous-précepteur* to the dauphin (under the *précepteur* Jacques Bossuet) in 1670, and was elected to the Académie française in 1674. He was named Abbé d'Aunay in 1680, and then was nominated Bishop of Soissons in 1685. The papal bulls for this position were withheld due to political disputes between **Louis XIV** and Innocent XI, but when named Bishop of Avranches in 1689, he was able to assume this position in 1692. He reigned this bishopric and assumed the title of Abbé de Fontenay in 1699, and retired soon thereafter to the Paris house of the **Jesuits**, which held his huge personal library (now at the Bibliothèque Nationale).

Huet reported in his *Mémoirs* (1718) that he was initially a partisan of the new Cartesian philosophy, but that he turned against it once he realized that it lacked secure foundations. This turn is connected to his disgust with the negative view of literary and historical study, including an attack on his old friend Borchart, in the *Recherche de la vérité* of **Nicolas Malebranche**. Huet subsequently became increasingly critical of the Cartesian project of using natural **reason** alone to provide a-historical foundations for knowledge. As Abbé d'Aunay, Huet began work on his critique of Descartes in the *Censura philosophiae cartesianae* (1690). The skeptical arguments in this work are directed against a Cartesian reason that operates independent of **faith**, and are complemented by the position in Huet's *Alnetanae quaestiones concordia rationis et fidei* (1690) that reason requires the guidance of faith and the Catholic tradition. The *Censura* became perhaps the most widely read critique of Cartesianism in early modern Europe, and it drew a response from **Pierre-Sylvain Régis** and other Cartesians. Inspired by the work of **Gabriel Daniel**, Huet also published anonymously the *Nouveaux Mémoires pour servir à l'histoire du cartésianisme* (1692), a satirical account of an interview with a Descartes who had escaped death in Sweden.

HUMAN BEING. *See* UNION OF MIND AND BODY.

HUYGENS, CONSTANTIJN (1596–1678) AND CHRISTIAAN (1629–95). When Constantijn Huygens was born, his godfathers were the Council of Brabant, Count Justin of Nassau (an illegitimate son of William of Orange), and the City of Breda. The important position of his father, who after having been secretary to William of Orange was one of the four secretaries of the State Council, almost predestined Constantijn to play a role in the official life of the country. His private education (in part by his own father) was very broad. Thus he not only learned several foreign languages (Latin, Greek, French, Italian, English), but he was also initiated in music, the arts, and the sciences. He studied law in Leiden. In 1618 he visited London with Sir Dudley Carleton, the English ambassador in The Hague, and profited from the occasion, not only to improve his English, but also to know English artists and musicians. In 1620 he was secretary of a Dutch embassy to Venice. In 1621 he was secretary of an official delegation to England to obtain the support of the English against Spain; he returned to England several times. He met several English scientists and philosophers, **Francis Bacon** among others, and more particularly knew Cornelis Drebbel (1572–1633), a Dutch **alchemist** and inventor (of a microscope, thermometers and thermostats, a *perpetuum mobile*, a submarine, etc.) living in London, who experimented with machines for grinding lenses (lenses usually were still made by hand with a spinning top).

In 1628 Huygens gave up diplomacy and became secretary of the stadtholder, Frederick-Henry of Orange. This gave him no formal power of any kind but made him immensely influential. Moreover, a position such as his was good for many emoluments. After the death of Frederick-Henry (1648) his son William II (1626–50) took him over, but Constantijn's relations with him were not as good as with his father. During the stadtholderless period (1650–72) Huygens did not play any official role but in many ways exerted himself on behalf of the Orange family. Thus he was sent to France to negotiate with the French government when **Louis XIV** took the principality and town of Orange (1660). When William III acceded to power in 1672, Huygens obtained an honorary function and his son Constantijn (1628–97) was appointed secretary.

Nowadays Huygens is best known as a poet (having written hundreds of poems, not only in Dutch, but also in Latin and French) and, to a lesser extent, as a composer—a volume of songs, *Pathodia sacra et profana*, was published in Paris in 1648. But he had also a great interest in art and architecture (he built a house in The Hague and a small castle close to The Hague), as well as in science, and entertained a voluminous correspondence (more than 8,000 letters have been preserved) with people all over the world. Huygens may have heard about Descartes for the first time in 1629 but he probably did not meet him before the spring of 1632 when he mentions him in a letter to Jacob Golius. From the beginning Huygens, who had a great interest in optical problems, was interested in Descartes's plan of building a machine for grinding lenses (see *Dioptrics*) and promised him his support. By 1633 their relations seem to be on a firm footing. In the spring of 1635 Descartes discusses his *Dioptrics* with Huygens and from that date there is a regular **correspondence**, both sides of which are almost completely preserved. At first it concentrates on lens grinding, but later Huygens is closely involved in the preparation of the *Discourse* (1637). He stimulates Descartes, proposes a publisher, corrects the proofs together with his wife, and undoubtedly exerts his influence for obtaining a Dutch printing license. When in 1641 Descartes prepares the *Meditations*, he provides special messengers for the delivery of manuscript and proofs. Inversely, Descartes values Huygens's judgment and generally follows his advice. In the Utrecht crisis Huygens supports Descartes even if his role is behind the scenes.

Although Huygens is one of the most important figures in Descartes's biography and Huygens undoubtedly valued Descartes's genius, there is no evidence at all that he was influenced by Descartes's ideas. At the very moment that Descartes was working on his hyperbolic lenses, Huygens encouraged Martinus Hortensius (1605–39) to go on with circular lenses. And when his children were tutored in physics he instructed their governor that they should learn this discipline, not from Descartes's *Principles*, but from a perfectly traditional textbook on physics by the Dutch philosopher Franco Burgersdijck (1590–1635). Johan Stampioen (1610–53), someone Descartes saw as a windbag, tutored his sons in mathematics, but this was may have been because Stampioen also tutored William II. Finally, in his autobiography, he devotes barely one line to his friendship with Descartes, who by then was a very famous philosopher.

Of Huygens's four sons, Constantijn (1628–97), Lodewijk (1631–99), Christiaan (1629–95), and Philips (1633–57), Christiaan is now undoubtedly the best known. He proved to be a mathematical genius, even as a child: according to a letter of his father Descartes would have referred to him as "someone of his own blood" (to Princess Elisabeth, 31 December 1653, *Briefwisseling*, vol. 5, p. 193). From 1645 he studied law and mathematics (under Frans van Schooten) in Leiden, together with his brother Constantijn. In 1646 his father brought him into contact with Marin Mersenne, with whom the young boy exchanged a few letters in which he criticized Galileo Galilei and Mersenne himself. Although his general outlook in physics was "Cartesian" he also criticized Descartes, especially his laws of collision and impact. Huygens traveled to Paris in 1660, and to London, where in 1661 he was appointed member of the Royal Society. In 1662 Louis XIV gave him a pension and in 1665 he was appointed to the Royal Academy of Sciences in Paris. From then on he lived mainly in Paris, where he had an apartment in the Royal Library. Christiaan was weak and sickly all his life. He was also a profoundly melancholic man, who for long periods was unable to do any work. His first published work concerned the quadrature of circles, hyperbolas, and ellipses (1651). His work on Saturn was published in 1659. In 1673 he published his *Horologium os-cillatorium* and in 1690 his *Traité de la lumière*.

– I –

IDEAS. So central were ideas to philosophy in the 17th century that the *Port-Royal Logic* could declare at the head of its first chapter: "Some words are so clear that they cannot be explained by other words, for none are more clear or more simple. 'Idea' is such a word. All that can be done to avoid mistakes in using such a word is to indicate the incorrect interpretations of which it is susceptible." Traditionally, the term in its modern sense is attributed to Descartes. Descartes himself gives this impression when he tells **Thomas Hobbes** "I used the word 'idea' because it was the standard philosophical term used to refer to the forms of perception belonging to the divine mind, even though we recognize that **God** does not possess any corporeal **imagination**. And besides, there was not any more appropriate term at my disposal" (AT, vol. VII, p. 181). Descartes borrowed a term used to refer to God's ideas (the post-**Augustinian** heir of the Platonic or neo-Platonic "Idea"), and, as he remarked elsewhere, used it more generally for "everything which is in our **mind** when we conceive something, no matter how we conceive it" (AT, vol. III, p. 393).

Ideas, for Descartes, are "as it were images of things," mental acts that represent something. By calling on the ideas in God's mind as his source Descartes set ideas free from their link to sensation. In taking this path Descartes seems to have canceled out the major context of the traditional doctrine of ideas: the context of archetype or model, where the idea informs its imitations, and gives them, or their "images," such reality as they have. Traditionally, ideas are identified with **forms** or species: they have power through a certain agency; they are "efficacious," unlike particular things, which are relatively inert. It is ideas that, primarily through God's **thought**, make things what they are. Analogously, though of course in a lesser degree, an artist's **mind** can produce a copy of a reality, itself in turn informed by the divine patterns, the ideas, in God's mind. Cartesian ideas, patterned after God's pure cogitations, are entertained by minds. They are psychological units such as the ones **mathematicians** use in thinking through problems, thinking of thousand-sided figures as easily as of triangles and pentagons, which they could, but need not, imagine. Ideas as concepts, whether formal or objective, are the units by which Descartes can free pure mind from its **scholastic** bonds to sense. Descartes made a new start in philosophy with his "idea," but he shaped this new conception by using readily available meanings of the term and purifying them of much of their habitual connotations.

IDEAS, INNATE. In the Third Meditation, Descartes examined his ideas and divided them into three kinds: innate, adventitious (that is, coming from the outside), and factitious (or produced by him). He then considered his idea of **God.** He decided that it did not derive externally from the senses and he did not produce it. Thus, his only option was that this idea was innate in him, just as his idea of self (*cogito*) was. Descartes defended this line of reasoning, in his *Replies to Objections*, against the objections of **Thomas Hobbes, Pierre Gassendi,** and others. The criticism that elicited the most interesting response, however, occurred when Descartes responded to his erstwhile supporter **Henricus Regius,** in *Notes Against a Program (Notae in Programma).*

Regius's broadsheet included the following three anti-Cartesian propositions: "The **mind** has no need of innate ideas, or notions, or axioms, but of itself the faculty of thinking suffices for performing its own acts. Therefore all **common notions,** engraved on the mind, owe their origin to the observation of things or to tradition. In fact the very idea of God implanted in the mind is the outcome of divine revelation, or tradition, or the observation of things" (AT, vol. VIII-2, p. 345). Descartes called Regius's dissent in the first proposition merely verbal, because, as he said, he had not asserted that "the mind required innate ideas that were in some way different from its faculty of thinking." Descartes defined ideas as innate "in the same sense we say that in some families generosity is innate, in others certain diseases like gout or stones," that is, the families "are born with a certain disposition or propensity for contracting them" (AT, vol. VIII-2, p. 358). He denied Regius's second statement, arguing that "no ideas of things, in the form in which we envisage them by **thought** are presented to us by the senses." Descartes's possibly radical account was that "nothing reaches our mind from external objects through the sense organs beyond certain corporeal motions. . . . But even these **motions** and the shapes arising from them are not conceived of by us exactly as they occur in the sense organs. . . . Hence it follows that the ideas of the motions and shapes are themselves innate in us. So much the more must the ideas of **pain, color,** sound and the like be innate, so that our mind may, on the occasion of certain corporeal motions, represent these ideas to itself, for they have no likeness to the corporeal motions" (AT, vol. VIII-2, p. 359). Descartes replied to the third proposition by distinguishing between proximate, primary causes and remote, accidental causes: "Tradition or observation is a remote cause, inviting us to give attention to the idea we can have of God, and to present it vividly to our thought.

But no one can maintain that this is the proximate and **efficient cause,** other than the person who thinks that we can understand nothing about God, except that he is called God" (AT, vol. VIII-2, p. 360).

IMAGES. *See* IDEAS.

IMAGINATION. Toward the start of the Sixth Meditation, Descartes held that the distinction between imagination and pure **intellect** is revealed by the fact that he cannot distinctly imagine a chiliagon, or thousand-sided figure, though he can demonstrate that this figure has certain properties (AT, vol. VII, p. 72). He then hypothesized that this **distinction** is due to the fact that imagination involves an "inspection" of a bodily image, whereas pure intellect involves the mind's inspection of one of its own **ideas.** Though he dismissed this explanation as merely probable, Descartes did suggest that imagination depends on the **body** in a manner that distinguishes it from pure intellect. The suggestion is that both this faculty and the faculty of **sensation** require the **soul-body union.** That suggestion is confirmed in Descartes's physiological works. In the *Treatise on Man,* for example, the "man-machine" is credited with a purely corporeal faculty of recomposing images impressed upon the ventricles of the brain. **Animals** too may have an imagination of this sort. Descartes thereby manages to maintain agreement with **Aristotelian** theories according to which imagination belongs to the "sensitive" part of the soul, a part we share with animals, while eliminating much of the complexity of Aristotelian discussions of the internal senses. The distinction between imagination and intellect, on the other hand, though in keeping with standard claims that the intellect has no bodily organ, departs from accounts according to which the so-called "active" intellect, in certain of its operations, draws upon "species" stored in the brain.

Descartes generally indicated a preference for **clear and distinct** intellectual ideas over confused images in the search for **truth.** Indeed, in the Second Meditation he emphasized that the knowledge of the piece of wax as something **extended,** flexible, and mutable goes beyond what can be understood through the imagination (AT, vol. VII, p. 30). The limitations of imagination, because it has a corporeal instrument, derive from those of body; in the *Treatise on Man,* Descartes compares the storage of images in the brain to the punching of holes in cheesecloth: only so many images can be stored before they begin to impinge upon one another—hence their "confusion." Nonetheless, Descartes wrote to Princess **Elisabeth** of Bohemia that though bodily qualities such as extension, shape, and **motion** can be known "by the intellect alone," they are known better by "the intellect aided by the imagination" (AT, vol. III, p. 691). There is an anticipation of this view in Descartes's first work, the *Rules for the Direction of the Mind*, which includes the proposal that problems concerning extension should be "pictured in the imagination entirely by means of bare figures" (AT, vol. XI, p. 438). Thus, even though knowledge of body cannot derive from the faculty of imagination alone, the suggestion in these texts is that we arrive at such knowledge most readily through use of this faculty.

IMMORTALITY. The first edition of the *Meditations* bears the subtitle "in which is demonstrated the **existence of God** and the immortality of **the soul.**" In the dedicatory letter to the **Sorbonne**, moreover, Descartes emphasized the call of the Lateran Council (in 1513) for Christian philosophers to seek to prove by natural **reason** that the soul does not die with the **body** (AT, vol. VII, p. 3). However, he warned in the synopsis of the *Meditations* that he did not produce a proof of the immortality of the soul since this depends "on an account of the whole of **physics**" (AT, vol. VII, p. 14), and in particular on his view of both the indestructibility of bodily **substance** "considered in general" and the difference between individual human bodies and souls. In response to a point raised in the *Second Set of Objections*, moreover, Descartes conceded that he cannot prove by natural reason alone that God does not limit the duration of the soul since this depends on his **free will** and absolute power (AT, vol. VII, p. 108f). These qualifications help to explain why the second edition of the *Meditations* promises in its subtitle only a demonstration "of the distinction between the human soul and the body." Yet Descartes consistently maintained that his **dualism** supports the belief in immortality insofar as it shows that the soul is a substance that is really distinct from and thus can exist apart without the body.

INDEFINITE. Descartes distinguished between the **infinite** and indefinite in a manner similar to **Aristotle's** distinction between actual and potential infinities. In Aristotelian parlance, an actual infinity is a completed whole, while a potential infinity is unending and never complete. So, in Aristotle's view, a line segment is potentially divisible to infinity, in the sense that the process can always be continued, but it cannot be actually divided to infinity, since the completion of such a division process would compose the continuum out of dimensionless points. In the *Principles*, Descartes announces, "in all those things in which, according to some way of considering them, we discover no limits, we will not affirm that they are infinite, but will regard them as indefinite" (AT, vol. VIIIA, p. 15). Only **God** is truly infinite in this sense, as Descartes explained in a 1649 letter to **Henry More**: "It is only God that I positively understand to be infinite, while in the case of other things, such as the **extension** of the world or the number of parts into which **matter** is divisible, I confess I do not know whether they are absolutely infinite; I only know that I know no end to them, and so looking at them from my own point of view, I say they are indefinite" (AT, vol. V, p. 274).

INDIFFERENCE. *See* FREEDOM/INDIFFERENCE.

INDUCTION. *See* ENUMERATION.

INERTIA. Stated generally, inertia is the tendency of a **body** to remain in whatever state it is in at a given time, or the inability of a material body to change its state spontaneously. More specifically, the famous first law of **motion** in **Isaac Newton's** *Principia* asserts that a body in uniform rectilinear **motion** will remain in motion, and a body at rest will remain at rest unless acted upon by an external force. Newton was not the first to formulate an inertial principle. Descartes formulates his first law of **nature** in the *Principles of Philosophy* as the claim that "each and every thing, in so far as it can, always continues in the same state; and thus what is once in motion always continues to move" (AT, vol. VIIIA, p. 62). This is an immediate consequence of the **conservation principle** that "God is the primary cause of motion, and always conserves the same quantity of motion in the universe" (AT, vol. VIIIA, p. 61). Descartes reasons that only God can be understood as the "first and general" cause of motion in the world, so the conservation of "quantity of motion" follows from the nature of God. Further, God's constancy requires not only that the universe contain the same quantity of motion from instant to instant, but also that a body, whether in motion or at rest, will not spontaneously change its state. The inertial principle therefore appears as a consequence of divine immutability. Other thinkers, notably **Galileo Galilei** and **Thomas Hobbes**, proposed similar inertial principles, and all were united in rejecting the **Aristotelian** doctrine that terrestrial bodies in motion tend naturally toward rest.

INFINITE. A traditional epistemological and methodological tenet is that the finite human **mind** is incapable of reasoning about anything infinite. Notorious paradoxes of infinite **divisibility** or the problem of composition of the continuum underwrite the principle that our reasoning should be confined to the case of finite things. Especially in **mathematics**, the notion of infinite magnitudes has long been taken to be the source of error, confusion, and downright contradiction. It is therefore somewhat surprising that Descartes should make the **idea** of the infinite a centerpiece of his epistemology, as he does in the Third Meditation. Descartes's proof of the **existence of God** and his accompanying move from the awareness of the thinking self (gained by the *cogito*) to secure knowledge of the external world proceed by way of the idea of an infinitely perfect God. Notwithstanding the linguistic fact that the term *infinite* is expressed as the negation of the finite, Descartes takes the idea of the infinite as a simple positive idea that is maximally **clear and distinct**: "I should not think that I perceive the idea of the infinite, not by means of a true idea, but only by negation of the finite" (AT, vol. VII, p. 45). In Descartes's view, the idea of the infinite is conceptually prior to the finite, and we actually understand the finite in terms of the negation of the infinite. More importantly, the idea of the infinite cannot have been constructed from experience—we grasp the concept of an infinitely perfect God and see that it cannot be generated by continually increasing the idea of some perfection. Such an idea would at best be of something **indefinite**, rather than infinite: "I judge God to be actually infinite, so that nothing can be added to his perfection" (AT, vol. VII, p. 47).

There remains the difficulty of explaining how a finite mind can have a clear concept of the infinite, and how to avoid the traditional paradoxes of the infinite. Descartes held that the human mind could not have complete or adequate knowledge of the infinite, but that finite humans can come to understand that it exists and clearly grasp at least some of its properties. Speaking of the idea of God, Descartes argues: "Nor is it an objection that I do not comprehend the infinite. . . . For the **nature** of the infinite is such that it is not comprehended by a being such as I, who am finite. It is sufficient that I understand this very point and judge that all those things that I clearly perceive and that I know to contain some perfection—and perhaps even countless other things of which I am ignorant—are either formally or eminently contained in God" (AT, vol. VII, p. 46). The paradoxes of the infinite arise, not in the case of God, but in the attempt to reason about the indefinite as if it were a completed whole. Yet if we keep the **distinction** between indefinite and infinite in mind, such paradoxes will be avoided.

INTELLECT. Sometimes Descartes spoke of the intellect as the mental faculty of perception in general that is distinct from the faculty of **will**, and sometimes he spoke of it as a particular faculty of perception distinct from the perceptual faculties of **sensation** and **imagination**. In the first sense, the intellect is what contributes the **ideas** that, when combined with volitional acts of assent or dissent, yield **judgments** that are capable of **truth** or falsity. The second sense of intellect—sometimes called "pure intellect"—is required to distinguish perceptions that the mind possesses apart from the **body** from perceptions that the mind can possess only in virtue of its **union** with a body. Descartes indicated that it is the faculty of pure intellect that best reveals the real distinction between mind and body, since it is this faculty that shows most clearly that mind can exist without the body. **Nicolas Malebranche** later endorsed the claim in Descartes that we have a pure intellect that can operate independently of the body, whereas **Robert Desgabets** and **Pierre-Sylvain Régis** rejected the existence in us of pure intellect on the grounds that the temporality that infuses all of our **thoughts** can exist only if such thoughts are united with bodily motion. *See also* DUALISM.

INTUITION (*INTUITUS, CONNAISSANCE INTUITIVE***).** According to the *Rules for the Direction of the Mind* intuition is, next to **deduction**, one of the two fundamental ways of knowing things. Accordingly, the aim of the **method** is to teach how to use intuition and how to find deductions. Other things are not required and would in fact make it more difficult for us to know something. Descartes defines intuition as "the concept of a pure and attentive **mind** which is so easy and so distinct that there can be left no doubt about the thing we understand, or, what is actually the same thing, the concept, free from **doubt**, of a pure and attentive mind, which is born only from the light of **reason** and is more certain than deduction because it is more simple" (*Rules* III, AT, vol. X, p. 368). Although in at least one passage Descartes seems to identify intuition with experience, and although in later parts of the *Rules* Descartes also envisages intuitions of sense perceptions and **images**, he explicitly denies that intuition can be our trust in the senses (which is fluctuating) or a **judgment** of the **imagination** (which is deceptive).

Descartes is conscious of the novelty of this definition; indeed **scholastic** philosophers had reserved intuition for sense perceptions. So intuition seems to be characterized by the fact that it is proper to the **intellect** (even if the object is given in the imagination), that it takes away all doubt, that it is simple and that it is easy, but that to have an intuition we should have a "pure and attentive mind." Thus, according to Descartes, everybody can have the intuition that he exists, that he thinks, that a triangle is terminated only by three lines, and so forth. But it can also have a more complex object. Thus, for example, to know that $2 + 2$ is the same as $3 + 1$ all we need is an intuition of $2 + 2 = 4$ and of $3 + 1 = 4$. So if we do have clear intuitions of those, we necessarily see what follows from it, namely that $2 + 2 = 3 + 1$. The only specific difference between intuition and deduction is that deduction relies on **memory**, whereas intuition is a matter of direct apprehension.

Accordingly there are many problems that some people can solve by intuition, whereas others would use deduction. This much is clear: first **principles** are always the object of an intuition, whereas remote conclusions are always the object of a deduction. In any case, the essence of **method** is that we should try and reduce a problem to things of which we can have an intuition and then try and see what can be deduced from it, that is, determine the relation between what is known (by intuition) and what is, as yet, not known.

There are no specific rules for intuition, except that whatever is intuited is more or less simple and that, as we concentrate, we become perspicacious (just as for deduction we must be sagacious). This can be trained: "Artisans who are exercised in minute works and have accustomed themselves direct their eyes to single points, acquire by training the capacity to perfectly distinguish even the smallest and subtlest objects; and in the same way those who avoid to distract their **thought** by many different objects but always occupy themselves with the simplest things that are also the most easy to consider, become perspicacious" (*Rules* IX, AT, vol. X, pp. 400–01).

In Descartes's later work the term intuition (intuition of the mind) seems to be replaced by that of natural light, sometimes in the same opposition to demonstration as intuition to deduction. Thus, for example, it is clear by the natural light that if I doubt I must exist, that a **cause** must have at least as much reality as its effect. It teaches me that, to the extent that a false thought represents something that does not exist, it must come from nothing, that is, that it is in me only insofar as something is lacking to my **nature**; that there is no difference between creation and conservation; that deceptiveness depends on a defect; that the determination of the **will** is preceded by knowledge of the intellect; that whatever exists by its own force exists always; that no more than one sovereign being can be independent of everything else; that a thing that knows there is something more perfect than itself cannot be the cause of itself; and numerous other things. Natural light requires a lot of attention, which can be distracted by the perception of the senses, by which it can be obscured and blinded. Inversely, to the extent that natural light "sees" anything at all it must be true.

Even so, Descartes continues to speak, in accordance with tradition, of a certain type of knowledge as being intuitive, that is, not based on inference. Thus, for example, in a letter to an unknown correspondent Descartes claims that by meditating on the first things I certainly know, namely, that I think, that I am, that I am a **soul**, that is, a being that can exist independently from the **body** and whose essence it is to think, I acquire a "very certain and, if I may say so, intuitive knowledge of intellectual nature in general" (AT, vol. I, p. 353). Similarly, in a letter to

Jean de Silhon of March 1648 he claims that the difference between the knowledge of God we have now and the one we will have in beatitude is that the second will be "intuitive." Intuitive knowledge is "an illumination of the mind by which it sees in the light of God whatever it pleases God to reveal to it by a direct impression of the Divine clarity on our intellect, which in such a case is not seen as an agent but as something receiving the rays of Divinity," whereas in this life all natural knowledge we may have of God proceeds by reasoning (AT, vol. V, pp. 136–37).

– J –

JANSENISM. *See* JANSENIUS, CORNELIUS (1585–1638).

JANSENIUS, CORNELIUS (1585–1638). A member of the Theology Faculty at the **University of Louvain** and later the bishop of Ypres, Jansenius is known primarily for his posthumously published *Augustinus* (1640). In this work, Jansenius offered an Augustinianism that claimed to find in **Augustine** a view that emphasizes the depth of human sin and the irresistibility of divine grace. In France **Antoine Arnauld** and other individuals associated with the convent of Port-Royal were concerned to defend this view against the **Jesuit** charge that it gives aid and comfort to the **Calvinists**. The counter was that the Jesuit view is in line with a heretical **Pelagianism**.

The French First Minister Cardinal Mazarin sided with the Jesuits, and pressure from him brought about the 1653 condemnation of five propositions drawn from Jansenius's text by Pope Innocent X. In response to the claim of Arnauld and others that this text does not endorse these propositions, Pope Alexander VII declared in 1656 that they are in fact to be found in the *Augustinus* in their condemned sense. Arnauld rejoined by distinguishing between matters of **faith** (*droit*), on which the pope's word is authoritative, and matters of fact (*fait*), on which the pope has no special authority.

The great 19th-century historian of Cartesianism, Francisque Bouillier, has claimed that there is "a natural alliance of the doctrine of Jansenius with that of Descartes." This association of Jansenism with Cartesianism goes back to the 17th century, as indicated by the remark in **Gabriel Daniel**'s 1690 *Voiage du Monde* that "there are very few Jansenists who are not Cartesians." This association was no doubt due in large part to Arnauld, who was a powerful defender both of Descartes and of Jansenius. Yet Daniel's comment belies the fact that there was significant opposition among Jansenists to the Cartesian reliance on human **reason**. Moreover, even Arnauld complained at one point that Descartes's views on **free will** were Pelagian. The relations between Jansenism and Cartesianism are thus less straightforward than Bouillier's thesis suggests.

JESUITS. Jesuits are members of the Society of Jesus, a Catholic religious order founded by Saint Ignatius of Loyola that was officially recognized in 1540. Though the Society was primarily a missionary order, it also established schools throughout Europe. It was in fact a Jesuit school, **La Flèche**, where Descartes received his education. Descartes made disparaging remarks concerning his training there in the 1637 *Discourse on Method,* but around the same time he recommended La Flèche to a correspondent as a model school. Moreover, Descartes had a continuing interest in making his philosophical views acceptable to the Jesuits. Thus, he sent copies of his *Discourse* to his old teachers at La Flèche for comment, and later engaged in a friendly correspondence with another Jesuit instructor there, **Denis Mesland.** Some of Descartes's Jesuit contemporaries were critical of his system, particularly **Pierre Bourdin,** who sent Descartes an incomplete set of objections that focuses on the use of the **method** of **doubt** in the *Meditations.* Though this set of objections was not intended for publication, Descartes added responses to these objections and included both in the second edition of the *Meditations* as the *Seventh Set of Objections with Replies.* He also included a letter to Bourdin's superior, Jacques Dinet, in which he complained about how badly he had been treated. Even so, Descartes was soon reconciled with Bourdin, and he maintained cordial relations with the Jesuits until his death in 1650.

Even before Descartes's death, the Jesuits were the primary opponents of **Jansenist** theology. However, it is only after Descartes's death that this opposition to Jansenism was combined with an opposition to Cartesian modifications to **scholastic philosophy**. The Jesuit concern to defend scholasticism culminated in a 1706 order from the General of the Jesuits prohibiting a set of propositions drawn from the work of Descartes and his followers, especially **Nicolas Malebranche.** While the Jesuits were politically powerful in France during the second half of the 17th century, however, their influence increasingly waned throughout the 18th century. Ultimately, scandals involving this order led to its banishment from France in 1762 and its suppression by papal decree in 1773.

JOY/SADNESS. According to Descartes, joy is caused by the consideration of a present good or at least of something the **soul** believes to be good, its opposite being sadness. Next to admiration, **love, hatred, de-**

sire, and sadness, it is one of the six primitive **passions,** out of which all other passions are composed. It is defined as "a pleasant **emotion** of the soul, which is the enjoyment it has of the good the impressions of the brain present to it as its own" (*Passions* II, art. 69, AT, vol. XI, p. 380). In fact it is the only way in which the soul can enjoy a good; if the soul does not have that emotion one might as well say that it does not have that good. Its outward manifestation is an equal pulse, which however is quicker than usual, although less strong than in love, and a pleasant warmth, not only in the breast but all over the body, sometimes to the point of causing a little blush or, in extreme cases, a cataleptic state (*pâmoison*), which is close to death. This is caused by the fact that all the openings of the **heart** open widely, so the **blood circulates** freely throughout the body. Moreover the spirits will be very subtle and homogeneous and, as a result, reinforce the impressions in the brain that give the soul its merry and tranquil **thoughts.** As in all passions this is the result of early conditioning. When we started life the blood that was in our veins was sufficient to entertain the fire in the heart. This caused the soul to experience joy. But whenever the soul is in a joyful mood it causes the body to do the same as it did the first time, namely, to open the orifices of the heart and cause the blood and the spirits to flow freely.

Sadness, on the other hand, is in every aspect the contrary of joy. It springs from the consideration of something bad or evil; it is defined as an unpleasant languor, which manifests itself by a slow and weak pulse, a sensation of anguish around the heart and a feeling of cold throughout the body, sometimes also by paleness but sometimes by a blush or by trembling. This is caused by the fact that if a person is sad the openings of the heart contract and the circulation of the blood slows down. Since, on the other hand, the channels between the stomach and the intestines and between the intestines and the liver remain open, there is no loss of appetite. Again the explanation is in early youth, when hunger was the most menacing condition we could experience: the symptoms of sadness are those of a hungry person. That is also the reason why they involve a health risk: when the body is hungry the spleen releases some of the coarser blood particles it contains.

Given the fact that these are harder to "burn" than the pure particles usually contained in the veins, they cause the heart to beat irregularly and to cause a fever, especially if it is accompanied by **hatred.** Given the general purpose of the passions, namely, to prepare the body for the good or bad things it may expect to happen, joy and sadness are even more fundamental than any of the other passions. The soul is warned of the things that damage the body by **pain,** which causes sadness, then it develops hatred of what caused the pain and finally has the desire to get rid of it. Similarly the soul is warned of something good for the body by a pleasant tickling (*chatouillement*), which excites joy, then conceives love for whatever causes it and finally forms the **desire** to keep or acquire it. Indeed, from that point of view sadness may be even more fundamental than joy because it actually protects the body against danger. That does not mean that they are invariably good, especially because things may seem good or bad and actually be bad or good. But even if we study those passions in themselves it is clear that the physiological condition that accompanies sadness is very damaging for the body, certainly in the long run. All things being equal, joy and love are better than sadness and hatred, even if sadness and hatred are necessary as a first reaction to remove the cause of pain. Both joy and sadness as passions should be distinguished from intellectual joy and intellectual sadness which are caused by the soul to itself, even if, as long as the soul is united with the body, it is almost inevitable that the body is also pleasantly moved by an intellectual joy.

JUDGMENT (*JUGEMENT, JUDICIUM*). Before the *Meditations* (1641), Descartes does not articulate a precise theory of judgment. Presumably, it was developed only in the context of his theory of **error**, which in turn became necessary because Descartes had to show that there is no incompatibility between error and **God's** inability to deceive us. Given the fact that in themselves **ideas** are not false it is only judgments that may be called true or false. Now, according to Descartes, a judgment consists of two elements: 1) an idea or set of ideas; 2) an act of the **will** or volition. Accordingly, a judgment (and consequently an error) is properly an act of the will or volition, for which we are fully responsible—indeed the main point of Descartes's theory of error is to prove that God cannot be held responsible for any of our erroneous judgments. Inversely, a **prejudice** becomes something like a blind impulse, which can be stopped only by an act of the will. From that point of view, systematic doubt, which in fact is nothing but a suspension of judgment, is also an exercise of the will. This voluntarist conception of judgment allows Descartes also to accommodate two types of judgments, which are held to be true (or in any case acceptable) despite the fact that they are not based on **clear and distinct ideas**: 1) the judgments that are part of **faith**; 2) practical judgments based, either on authority, or on the senses, the bodily **sensations**, and the **passions**. In such cases the will (in the case of faith determined by Divine grace) overrules so to speak the obscurity of the ideas involved, so that we do judge a thing to be true or probable. This consequently means that we can except those judgments from systematic doubt.

The problem of Descartes's theory of judgment, on the other hand, is that he must also assume that there are some judgments we are not free to deny, such as *cogito ergo sum* and the **proofs of the existence of God**. To solve that problem Descartes makes a distinction between **indifference** and (true) **freedom**. To be free it is not necessary to have an equal choice between two alternatives (which would be indifference); on the contrary, the more I am inclined to choose the one rather than the other, either because I evidently know that it is good and true, or because **God** disposes my **thought**, the more free I am in choosing and adopting it. Accordingly, neither natural knowledge (if it is based on clear and distinct ideas) nor divine grace diminish my freedom; indeed, they enhance and fortify it. On that point therefore human freedom is completely different from the freedom of God.

In Descartes's earlier work, judgment tends to be ascribed to the **intellect** or indeed, if it is not true but uncertain, to the **imagination**, but in the later parts of the *Rules for the Direction of the Mind* there may be an early version of the theory of the *Meditations* in connection with the theory of simple **natures**, which according to Descartes cannot contain any falsity. To understand this we must, according to Descartes, make a distinction between the faculty of the intellect by which it intuits and knows things and the faculty by which it makes judgments by affirming or denying. Accordingly, it can happen that we falsely believe that we do not know the things we really and truly know, namely, if we believe that, apart from the things we clearly intuit, there is something hidden. Although this theory makes use of the same distinction between what is given to the **mind** (what in the *Meditations* Descartes calls an idea) and the act by which what is given is affirmed to be true (which he later calls volition), it seems to be the intellect that makes the judgment.

– K –

KEPLER, JOHANNES (1571–1630). Astronomer and mathematician best known for his discovery of three laws of planetary **motion**. Born in Weil der Stadt, in the Duchy of Würtemburg, Kepler was educated at Lutheran seminaries in Adelberg and Maulbronn, enrolling at the University of Tübingen in 1589. Kepler's exceptional intellectual abilities were apparent from an early age, and his family intended a church career for him. He indulged his strong scientific interests at the university and greatly admired the astronomy professor Michael Maestlin, who publicly taught the Ptolemaic scheme while privately endorsing **Copernicanism**. Kepler himself defended Copernican astronomy in a public debate. Because Luther himself had mocked the Copernican scheme and quoted scripture to refute it, Kepler's defense of Copernicanism, together with his reservations about the Augsburg confession, precluded the church career for which he had prepared.

Instead, Kepler was offered a professorship of astronomy in the Austrian city of Graz, where he went in 1594. One of the duties of his professorship was to make astrological predictions. Notwithstanding a pronounced skepticism about astrology, Kepler successfully predicted a cold winter and an invasion by the Turks, prognostications that won him a salary increase and powerful patrons. His first important work was the 1596 *Mysterium Cosmographicum* ("Cosmographic Mystery") in which he accounted for the numbers, sizes, and distances of planetary orbits by inscribing them within and circumscribing them about the corresponding spheres in the five Platonic regular solids. Using the idea of a rationally ordered but fundamentally mysterious cosmos as a starting point, Kepler conceived a general plan for reforming astronomy, **optics**, and music on the model of a quasi-theological vision of divine harmony and order.

In 1598 the ruling Hapsburg family closed the Protestant educational institutions in the Austrian provinces, and although Kepler was permitted to stay in Graz, he was compelled to leave in 1600. Moving to Prague, Kepler became an assistant to the great Danish astronomer Tycho Brahe, who served the emperor Rudolph II as the imperial astronomer. Brahe demanded that Kepler write a book attacking the (recently deceased) astronomer Nicholas Ramerius Ursus, a former imperial mathematician with whom Tycho had quarreled for years; the result was *Apologia pro Tychone contra Ursum* ("A Defense of Tycho against Ursus"), which remained unpublished in Kepler's lifetime but contains important methodological arguments. On Tycho's death in 1601, Kepler succeeded him as imperial mathematician and undertook an ambitious program of publication in astronomy and optics. The most important of these publications was the 1609 *Astronomia nova* ("New Astronomy"), which substituted physical reasoning for the geometrical models of all previous astronomical theories and propounded the first two of Kepler's three laws of planetary orbit: that planetary orbits are elliptical, with the sun at one focus of the ellipse, and that the orbital radius of each planet sweeps out equal areas in equal times. In April 1610 Kepler received a copy of the *Siderius Nuncius* ("Starry Messenger") in which **Galileo Galilei** described the results of his recent telescopic observations. Kepler was astounded by these discoveries and wrote a letter to Galileo that he then published under the title *Dissertatio cum Nuncio Siderio* ("Conversation with the Starry Messenger").

Kepler's continuing interest in optics led to another influential publication from this period, the 1611 treatise *Diotrica* ("Dioptrics").

After the forced abdication and subsequent death of Rudolph II in 1612, Kepler was appointed mathematician to the states of Upper Austria in Linz, where he remained for the next 14 years. His 1615 *Nova stereometria doliorum vinariorum* ("New Means of Measuring Wine Casks") was a significant contribution to pure and applied **mathematics**; it presents a means of calculating volumes by the use of techniques that became part of the infinitesimal calculus. The culmination of his harmonic approach to cosmology appeared in his 1619 *Harmonices Mundi* ("Harmonies of the World") and stated his third law of planetary motion: the squares of the planets' sidereal periods are proportional to the cubes of the semimajor axes of the ellipses of their orbits. In 1621 Kepler published a vastly revised edition of the *Mysterium cosmographicum*. His final major project was a collection of astronomical tables, the *Tabulae Rudolphinae* ("Rudolphine Tables") of 1627, which remained the standard work on the subject for decades. Kepler left Linz to enter the service of the Czech Duke Albrecht von Wallenstein in 1628, relocating to Sagan in Silesia. His death in 1630 in the city of Regensburg was the result of a fever contracted while traveling to Linz to settle unresolved business matters.

Descartes was familiar with Kepler's contributions to astronomy, **geometry**, and optics but made little explicit reference to him. One amusing exception to this rule is Descartes's reference to the 1611 treatise *De nive sexangula* ("On the Six-Cornered Snowflake"), which he mentioned to **Marin Mersenne** in a letter from March 1630 in the course of commenting on the mild winter in Holland, which saw neither snow nor frost (AT, vol. I, p. 127). When **Jean de Beaugrand** accused Descartes of taking fundamental ideas in geometric optics from Kepler, he denied that he had seen anything of substance in his *Dioptrica*, but declared Kepler his "first master in optics" and his predecessor who had known the most about the subject (AT, vol. II, p. 86).

KNOWLEDGE. *See* CERTAINTY; INTUITION.

– L –

LA FLÈCHE, COLLEGE OF. The **Jesuit** Collège Henry IV, the school Descartes attended (ca. 1607–15), was founded in 1604 at La Flèche in Anjou. The student population of La Flèche was diverse, geographically and culturally. The college accepted boys from all corners of France and from all walks of life. During Descartes's days, its boarders numbered approximately 100, and it taught, in addition, about 1,200 external, or day, students. Like all other Jesuit schools at the time, the curriculum at La Flèche consisted of four or five years of humanities, that is, French, Latin, and Greek language and literature, a year of rhetoric, plus three years of the collegiate curriculum: ethics and logic, mathematics and physics, and metaphysics.

In the *Discourse on Method* Descartes represented himself as dissatisfied with the education he was given at La Flèche: "in my college days I discovered that nothing can be imagined which is too strange or incredible to have been said by some philosopher" (AT, vol. VI, p. 16). However, he seemed more favorably disposed toward the college in his correspondence. There Descartes asserted: "it is extremely useful to have studied the whole philosophy curriculum in the manner it is taught in Jesuit institutions," and, to give his teachers their due, "there is no place on earth where philosophy is better taught than at La Flèche" (AT, vol. II, p. 378). Descartes praised the academic rigor of its teaching, its discipline, and its social ethos.

LA FORGE, LOUIS DE (1632–ca. 1666). La Forge was a French physician who became an enthusiastic Cartesian. He worked on the 1664 edition of Descartes's *Treatise on Man*, providing it with extensive annotations and illustrations (the latter in collaboration with Gérard van Gutschoven). His main publication was *Traitté de l'esprit de l'homme* (1666). It is an important statement of **occasionalism**, the metaphysical doctrine of causation that became dominant with the later Cartesians. La Forge extended the Cartesian program by discussing in detail the **mind** and its **union** with the **body.**

LA GRANGE, JEAN-BAPTISTE DE (ca. 1641–post-1680). De la Grange joined the **Oratory** in 1660. He taught philosophy at Montbrison and Mans and **theology** at Troyes. He left the Oratory in 1680 to become curé of Chatres, near Paris. De la Grange wrote a very critical two-volume treatise against the new philosophy, *Les principes de la philosophie contre les nouveaux philosophes, Descartes, Rohault, Régius, Gassendi, le p. Maignan, etc.* (1675–79). In this work, he acknowledged the widespread appeal of Cartesian philosophy, but he obviously also wished to caution against that appeal.

One of the primary targets of de la Grange's attack was an unnamed opponent who had just published such views as "some things are known directly through themselves and others are known only through consciousness or inner sensation. . . . As for corporeal things, they are not intelligible by themselves, and thus we can see them only in **God**" (*Les principes de la philosophie*, p. 78). **Nicolas Malebranche,** of course, was the philosopher who presented and defended the claim that we see all things in God, together with the radical **occasionalism** that denies causal efficacy to finite things, including **minds**; Malebranche had entered the Oratory in 1660 and had just published the first volume of his *Recherche de la vérité*. Thus, for de la Grange, Descartes looms as the corrupter of orthodoxy who can even seduce members of the Oratory. De la Grange continued with his refutation of the views of his unnamed opponent; he also wrote critical discussions of Cartesian views on such topics as the possibility of plural worlds, **animal** rationality, the accidents of the **Eucharist**, the **nature** of **place**, the **infinity** of the world, the possibility of the **void**, and the **motion of the Earth.**

LA MOTHE LE VAYER, FRANÇOIS DE (1588–1672). La Mothe Le Vayer trained and practiced as a lawyer in Paris. He became a member of the Académie Française (1638) and teacher to the Duke of Orléans (1647) and **Louis XIV** (1652). He belonged to the circle of writers called *libertins*, or freethinkers, known for their relativism. His first work, *Dialogues faites à l'imitation des anciens*, was published in 1630, with false title pages, under a pseudonym, and reissued in two volumes with additions in 1631. It contained much material thought shocking for its time. Like **Pierre Charron** before him, La Mothe argued that, of the main schools of philosophy, skepticism is the most compatible with Christianity, despite its method of displaying the uncertainty of received opinion. What is more, it is best situated to accommodate the diversity of religious belief and observance from ancients to moderns. Among the issues also considered by Descartes, La Mothe reflected on whether **theology** is a demonstrative science. He considered arguments for **the existence of God** and doubted their effectiveness against **atheists.**

LAMY, BERNARD (1640–1715). Oratorian philosopher. Lamy taught humanities and philosophy and studied **theology** at various **Oratorian** colleges (1661–75). He was teaching at the **College of Angers** in 1673 when he got into trouble for his Cartesian ideas. In 1671 **Louis XIV** had banned the teaching of the new philosophy from French colleges. Because of this, censors examined Lamy's lectures and objected to 10 propositions they identified as Cartesian. They objected to Lamy's definition of **extension** as the essence of **body** and to his rejection of **substantial forms**, which, they said, did not allow for an explanation of the **Eucharist.** They ridiculed Lamy's endorsement of the *cogito*, his assertion that children think in their mother's womb, and his thought that sensations such as **pain** are experienced in the **soul**, not in the body. They also objected to Lamy's opinions that **God** is the principal cause of **motion**, that the **quantity** of motion is **conserved**, and that the only kind of movement is local motion. As a result, Lamy was expelled from Angers in 1675. In 1676 he was sent to the seminary in Grenoble, where he was given a chair in theology. He was in Paris from 1686 to 1689 and afterwards in Rouen, where he stayed for the rest of his life. Lamy is best known for two pedagogical books, *L'art de parler* (1675), a manual of rhetoric which was often reprinted, and *Entretiens sur les sciences* (1683), a collection of essays that discuss the proper way of teaching a variety of subjects to young students.

In *Entretiens sur les sciences*, Lamy showed himself to be a Cartesian, but limited his approbation of Descartes. He discussed, for example, the air pump and the experimental knowledge derived from it, knowledge he said that went beyond what Descartes understood. He also claimed that Descartes gave incorrect explanations of various phenomena because of his lack of experiments. However, he credited him with having opened the path of **mechanism**; as he said, unless they can explain it mechanically, people no longer believe that something is known. Lamy praised Descartes for his account of **mind** and the **union of mind and body** as the philosopher who has spoken the best about the mind and who has distinguished with the greatest clarity its functions from those of the **machine** of the body. According to Lamy, before Descartes nobody had shown as clearly the relation of man to God.

LANGUAGE. From his earliest works Descartes was fascinated by the phenomenon of language, not primarily as a subject of study but as a model for our relation to the external world. In his view perceptions are not pictures but signs: "If words, which signify nothing except by convention, suffice to make us think of things to which they bear no resemblance, then why could **nature** not also have established some sign which would make us have the sensation of **light**, even if the sign contained nothing in itself which is similar to this sensation?" (*The World*, AT, vol. XI, p. 4). But the problem of language also interests Descartes because of its bearing on the question of **animal souls**. Is it really likely that animals have no mind or soul if "animals express their feelings and passions by their kind of language and use signs to show their anger, their fears, their love, their pains, their regret for having done evil"? (**Alphonse Pollot** to Descartes, February 1638, AT, vol. I, p. 514). But according to Descartes "one must not confuse speech with the natural movements which express the **passions** and which can be imitated by machines as well as by animals; nor should we think, like some of the Ancients, that the beasts speak, although we do not understand their language" (*Discourse* V, AT, vol. VI, p. 58). In fact, the "natural language" by which animals and men express their feelings and passions is not indicative of mind or consciousness. The language spoken by humans, however, is based on conventions. Conventional language, on the other hand, is one of the signs by which humans can be distinguished from animals or **automata**.

But language is also a source of obscurity and error. In many learned disputes "the problem is one of words" (*Rules* XIII, AT, vol. X, p. 433). Not only are most of the problems of traditional philosophy nothing but verbal disputes; words can also be used to conceal ignorance. Given the fact that, "when we store the concepts in our **memory**, we always simultaneously store the corresponding words . . . the thoughts of almost all people are more concerned with words than with things; and as a result people very often give their assent to words they do not understand, thinking they once understood them, or that they got them from others who did understand them correctly" (*Principles* I, art. 74, AT, vol. VIIIA, pp. 37–38).

Finally, Descartes deals with the issue of a universal language in reaction to an unidentified project about it (to **Marin Mersenne**, 20 November 1629, AT, vol. I, pp. 76–82). Each language consists of two elements, meaning and grammar, and according to Descartes it is not impossible but impractical to construct a universal language because such a language would have to be learned on the basis of a natural language, which inevitably produces differences in (and difficulties of) pronunciation. Still, the project could be the basis for a new system of written signs, but most people would find even that too much trouble. In what is visibly a second thought, however, Descartes introduces the notion of a system of signs analogous to that of the symbols and numbers of arithmetic. We have a system of natural numbers and rules for combining and manipulating them, because we have an orderly and hierarchical system of numerical concepts, so, if we could devise an orderly system of all **thoughts**, we would also have the means of creating a universal system of signs, in which we can express and produce every possible thought. Accordingly, a universal language should be based not only on true philosophy, but also on an exact **enumeration** of the simple **ideas** of the **imagination**. In the end Descartes sees this as a utopian project.

LAWS OF NATURE (*LOIS DE LA NATURE, LEGES NATURAE*). Descartes first uses the expression "laws of nature" (which until far into the 17th century will keep a normative connotation) in a letter to **Marin Mersenne** of April 15, 1630, in which he reacts to "an evil book," in which, possibly, it was claimed that **God** is subject to the laws of **logic** (see **atheism**). According to Descartes, however, it is blasphemous to believe that **eternal truths** are independent of God. On the contrary

"God has established them as laws in nature, just as a king establishes laws in his realm." Moreover, we can understand those laws simply by considering them, that is, they are evidently true. And finally, they are all, Descartes claims, "inborn in our **minds**" just as a king would print his law in the hearts of his subjects.

An objection considered by Descartes was that, in that case, God could change those "eternal truths." And, indeed, he could if his **will** could change. However, God's power is incomprehensible. Accordingly, we may assume that God can do whatever we understand, but that there are many other things he could also do which we do not understand. Indeed, it would be a great temerity to believe that our **imagination** has as much **extension** as his power. That this has something to do with the laws of nature or what we would call the laws of **physics** is clear only by the fact that Descartes tells Mersenne that in two weeks he will put this in his physics (at the time he was writing *The World*). Usually, however, eternal truths are either demonstrated **mathematical** truths (like the Pythagorean theorem) or general **axioms** (like "the whole cannot be smaller than the sum of its parts" or "two contrary propositions cannot be true at the same time"). "Laws of Nature" or "Laws of God" on the other hand were generally understood to be prescriptive, normative laws (such as "thou shalt not kill"), which according to many people were inscribed in the **heart**. Finally, we do not know whether this was the idea of laws of nature that actually did find its way to Descartes's physics—indeed, Descartes asks Mersenne to publicize this opinion (without naming him), "so I can know the objections one could make against them."

In any case, "laws of nature" do appear in Descartes's physics. The first time is in the context of Descartes's "fable" that God creates a new world without using more than **matter (indefinite** three-dimensional extension) and local motion. In this fable several ideas from the letter to Mersenne can be discerned: 1) God can create whatever we can imagine; 2) it is much easier to ascribe limits to our **thoughts** than to the works of God, which can be seen as the equivalent of the **idea** that God can do many things which we do not understand; 3) there are laws of nature because God cannot change. Still, the "laws God has imposed on nature" (*World* VII, AT, vol. XI, p. 36) do not seem to be arbitrary at all once we suppose that God created matter and local motion. For "nature" is "matter itself insofar as I consider it with all the **qualities** I have attributed to it together, under the condition that God continues to preserve it in the way he created it." But it cannot be denied that in nature there is also change, which, given God's immutability cannot be attributed to him but must be attributed to nature. Finally, the rules according to which these changes occur are called laws of nature, which Descartes also calls the secondary and particular causes of the various motions we see in separate bodies. Accordingly, with respect to the eternity of the laws of nature, the point of God's immutability is not to make them as eternal as God himself but to prevent him from interfering with matter and **motion** as they were once created, that is, their **quantity** and their inherent laws.

However, God's immutability also intervenes on a lower level, namely, that of the laws themselves, which according to the *Principles* can be known on the basis of God's immutability. The first law is that "every particular part of matter continues to be in the same state as long as a meeting with other parts does not force it to change it" (*World* VII, AT, vol. XI, p. 38; *Principles* II, art. 37, AT, vol. VIII-A, pp. 62–63); the second law that in a collision between two bodies no (material) body can lose anything but the exact quantity of motion which the other acquires and vice versa; and the third law that, if a body moves, it tends to continue its movement in a straight line. The second law in particular (in the *Principles*, the third law) is the basis for more specific laws of collision and perhaps also for the laws of statics. In sum Descartes thinks of "laws of nature" not as empirical laws or as formulas concerning a constant relation between two or more variables, but rather as fundamental laws that are constitutive of nature.

LE BOSSU, RENÉ (ca. 1635–80). A French Genévofain about whom Mme de Sévigné remarked in 1676 that he is "**Jansenist**, that is to say, Cartesian." Le Bossu was a proponent of the strategy of "Aristotelianizing" Cartesianism, or perhaps "Cartesianizing" **Aristotle**, in order to render Descartes's views more acceptable to proponents of **scholastic philosophy**. As he saw the situation, Aristotle had been teaching beginners, and so started with what was obvious to everyone, the sensible things around us, for example, and asked what they were made of. Descartes, at a more advanced stage of science, considered the **matter** common to everything, which is extended **substance**, and every particular is given a form by the way that general matter is shaped. Their principles are therefore not so opposite to one another. This strategy is reflected in Le Bossu's *Parallèle des principes de la physique d'Aristotle et de celle de René Des Cartes* (1674), which emphasizes the compatibility of **Jacques Rohault's** brand of Cartesian physics with Aristotelian **categories**. The strategy contrasts with the view of Cartesians such as **Antoine Arnauld** and **Nicolas Malebranche** that Descartes offered a Platonic form of philosophy similar to that found in the work of **Augustine**.

LE GRAND, ANTOINE (?–1699). Le Grand joined the Franciscans at Douai, where he was born and educated, and where he taught philosophy. He was sent by the order as a kind of missionary to England. There he divided his time between his studies and administrative duties. He wrote a popular version of Descartes's philosophy in the form of a **scholastic** textbook. He first published it as *Philosophia veterum e mente Renati Descartes, more scholastica breviter digesta* (1671) and expanded and republished it as *Institutio philosophia, secundum principia Renati Descartes, nova methodo adornata et explicata ad usum juventutis academicae* (1672). It was then translated into English and published as *Entire Body of Philosophy according to the Principles of the famous Renate Descartes* (1694). The English edition presents itself as the 17th-century equivalent of a coffee-table book, illustrated "with more than an hundred sculptures [that is, engravings]," and "Endeavoured to be so done, that it may be of Use and Delight to the Ingenious of Both Sexes."

Le Grand's tactic in the book was to produce a Cartesian philosophy that could be used in the schools, accepting scholastic terminology, but interpreting it in a Cartesian fashion. For example, Le Grand used the scholastic talk of prime **matter** and **substantial form** in his account of matter. According to Le Grand, the **Aristotelians'** prime matter is nothing but an inadequate conception of a **body**, as it may be conceived by us without any shape, hardness, softness, color, or any other modifications, and only as extended, consisting of three dimensions. Four propositions agreed upon by both Cartesians and Aristotelians follow from this: 1) Prime matter is without form, because the notion of extension is abstracted from all modification belonging to the essence of a body. 2) The matter of all things is the same. 3) Matter is capable of all forms. 4) A body as such, or prime matter, is incapable of being generated or corrupted. This results in a truly Cartesian Aristotle.

LEIBNIZ, GOTTFRIED WILHELM (1646–1716). Leibniz attended the Universities of Leipzig (1661–66) and Altdorf (1666–67), graduating with advanced degrees in law and in philosophy. He refused an academic position, preferring instead to become a courtier. He entered the service of the Elector of Mainz and, in 1672, he was sent on diplomatic business to Paris, where he immersed himself in Descartes's philosophy. Leibniz returned to Germany in 1676; for the rest of his life, he served as counselor, mining engineer, head librarian, and historian to the court of Hanover. He is usually considered as one of the three principal Continental Rationalists, along with Descartes and **Baruch Spinoza**. This designation, however, represents very little of Leibniz's multifaceted philosophical personality. There is little of Descartes's philosophy that Leibniz did not criticize, from the *cogito* as first principle of knowledge, to God's veracity as the criterion of truth, to God's existence being derived from the idea we have of him, to God's creation of the eternal truths, and so forth.

Leibniz's positive doctrines also reveal his opposition to Descartes's various positions. For example, in the "Discourse on Metaphysics," Leibniz develops the notion of an individual substance so as to distinguish the actions of God from those of creatures. The nature of an individual substance is to have a notion so complete to allow us to deduce from it all the predicates of the subject to which this notion is attributed. Several of Leibniz's metaphysical doctrines follow from this. Two substances cannot resemble each other completely and differ only in number. A substance can begin only by creation and end only by annihilation. Every substance is like a complete world and like a mirror of the whole universe, expressing, however confusedly, everything that happens in the universe, whether past, present, or future. As further consequences of his view of substance, Leibniz argues against Descartes that extension cannot constitute the essence of any substance. He rehabilitates the scholastic substantial forms as the essence of extended substances. He also distinguishes between certainty and necessity: The truth of each event, however certain, is nevertheless contingent, being based on the free will of God, whose choice always has its reasons, which incline without necessitating. And he further argues for the thesis that everything that happens to a substance is a consequence of its idea or of its being, and that nothing determines it, except God alone. Thus he rejects Descartes's views of human freedom and error.

LEIDEN, UNIVERSITY OF. The University of Leiden, founded in 1575, allegedly as a reward for the heroic defense of the city during the Spanish siege of 1574, was the first university on the territory of the new republic. After a hesitant start it soon developed into an internationally famous institution, renowned for the quality of its humanistic studies, its rich collection of oriental and classical manuscripts, and its "Dutch" school of mathematics, destined primarily for the education of military engineers and providing lessons in advanced mathematics.

Descartes's first contacts with Leiden University date from June 27, 1630, when he matriculated as a student in mathematics. The reason presumably was that Jacob Golius (1596–1667), the professor of oriental languages and mathematics, had brought with him from the Levant an Arabic version of Apollonius of Perga (ca. 262–ca. 190 BC), containing three missing books (V–VII) of his work on conic sections. The discovery of these texts caused a great stir among mathematicians throughout Europe and was also of great importance to Descartes's op-

tics. This short stay laid the foundation for Descartes's friendship with Golius, and, possibly, other Leiden personalities such as Abraham Heidanus (1597–1678), who later became professor of theology.

It is not until 1644, however, that there are any signs of Descartes's philosophy being discussed among professors and students. **Adriaan Heereboord** in particular submitted Cartesian propositions for disputation, albeit in an eclectic spirit. Since he was also deputy dean of the Statencollege (a theological college for bursars of the States of Holland), whose dean was the orthodox theologian and poet **Jacobus Revius**, this led to serious difficulties that, however, became public only in 1647. In that year Revius started a series of disputations in which he wanted to discuss the whole of Descartes's philosophy to test it against orthodox criteria. In fact, no more than five disputations were organized, because the university administration (the "Curatores," recruited among the States of Holland) prevented its continuation. In those disputations Revius attacks the Cartesian **method** of **doubt**, which he finds impious, and the Cartesian **idea** that **God** is his own cause, which he finds contrary to God's majesty. God's essence being inscrutable, it is blasphemous, according to Revius, to apply the category of causality to God. Blasphemy was also the word used by another Leiden professor of divinity, Jacobus Trigland (1652–1705), who blamed Descartes for entertaining the idea that God could be a deceiver.

When Descartes heard of these events in the spring of 1647 he wrote a long and violent letter to the *Curatores*. But to Descartes's exasperation, their only reaction was a decree that forbade professors and students to use Descartes's name or to discuss his theories in public lessons and disputations. Although Descartes's irritation was understandable, the decree was not an attempt to intervene in philosophical debate. For one thing, public lessons were only a small part of academic routine—advanced courses were given in the form of private lessons at the home of the professor. It also remained possible to take up the problem of magnetism, for example, and to discuss Descartes's theory as one among other solutions of that problem. In fact, the only thing really impossible was to make the philosophy of Descartes as such the subject of a public lesson or disputation—which was precisely what Revius wanted.

But the decree did not stop all trouble. Toward the end of the year 1647 a violent quarrel broke out during a disputation of the **Aristotelian** Adam Steuart, who attacked Descartes's idea that God is the cause of himself (attributing it to a "newfangled philosopher"). Cartesian students challenged him either to withdraw his thesis or to name the philosopher who held this idea. In December Revius published a book against Descartes's *Discourse* called *Methodi cartesianae consideratio* *theologica* ("A Theological Consideration of Descartes's Method"). Descartes responded to both incidents at the end of his *Notes Against a Program*, which was published at the beginning of 1648. Both Revius and Steuart countered by publishing new pamphlets. Heereboord also reacted by publishing an open letter to the *Curatores*, in which he provides a general picture of the situation. In reaction to all this the *Curatores* issued another decree (February 1648), forbidding all teaching of metaphysics, whether Cartesian or Aristotelian—a decree displeasing not only to Heereboord, who loved metaphysical discussions, but also to the theologians, who believed that theology requires a metaphysical framework.

However, the Curators were determined to root out the problem not by taking sides with one or the other, but by strictly separating the Faculties of Philosophy and Theology. In practical terms, however, this amounted not only to emancipating philosophy from its propaedeutic role, but also to promoting a non-scholastic type of theology, so in actuality the administration did favor particular trends: Cartesianism in philosophy (as long as it limited itself to physical problems), and Coccejanism (so called after its founder Johannes Coccejus) in theology (which, although certainly orthodox, rejected the formalism of Voetian theology). That is probably also the reason why the measures taken by the administration were not entirely successful and had to be confirmed several times, especially in 1656. In 1656 the continuing discussion over the theological consequences of **Copernicanism**, which all over the republic became the hallmark of Cartesian philosophy, even led to a unique intervention by the States of Holland, which explicitly stated that "the freedom to philosophize" should not undermine theology. Cartesians were free to do physics but should leave all theological problems, including that of reconciling heliocentrism with Scripture, to the Theological Faculty. Meanwhile, the Curators went on appointing Cartesians: **Johannes de Raey** in 1651; **Arnold Geulincx** in 1662; Theodor Craanen (1620–90); Burchard de Volder (1643–1709) in 1670; and Christoph Wittich in 1672. As a result, serious incidents continued to occur.

The publication of **Lodewijk Meyer's** *Philosophy the interpreter of Scripture* (1666) and later **Baruch Spinoza's** *Theologico-political treatise* (1670) and *Posthumous works* (1677) caused new tensions, culminating, in January 1676, with the official condemnation of 20 propositions. Although many of the condemned propositions were Coccejan and some simply Spinozist (20. "Philosophy is the interpreter of Scripture"), many had a Cartesian ring: 6. "In matters of faith clear and distinct perceptions are a norm and measure of **truth**." 12. "[The world] is infinitely extended, so it is impossible that there be more than one world." 13. "The human **soul** is no more than a **thought** and without it man could nonetheless live and be moved." 15. "The human will is truly **free** and undetermined and as infinite with regard to its objects as the will of God." 16. "God can deceive us if he wants." 17. "We have a faculty by which we can prevent **error**; error however is only in the will." 18. "All things, even God's existence, must be doubted in such a way that they are taken to be false." 19. "Men have an adequate idea of God." The Cartesians published a reaction in which the 20 theses were extensively discussed mainly to show that they could be reduced to a misunderstanding of Cartesian or Coccejan positions. Heidanus, who took the responsibility, was immediately dismissed. But even this draconic measure did not stop the spread of Cartesian ideas; indeed, that was stopped not under the influence of any external pressure, but by the rise of **Newtonian** ideas, first introduced on the continent by de Volder. Indeed, it could be argued that the foundation in 1675 of the "physical theatre," which was actually a laboratory of physics, and the introduction of experimental courses not only diverted the attention of the public from metaphysical controversies, but also prepared the eventual demise of Cartesianism. In fact, the very restrictions under which Cartesians worked stimulated them to find new and original ways of doing philosophy.

LE VALOIS, LOUIS (1639–1700). A French **Jesuit** from Caen, about whom little is known beyond the fact that he wrote the *Sentimens de M. Descartes . . . opposez à la doctrine de l'Eglise et conformes aux erreurs de Calvin sur le sujet de l'Eucharistie* (1680) under the pseudonym Louis de la Ville. In this work, Le Valois repeated the charge of **Calvinism** that had been directed a decade earlier against the Cartesian account of **transubstantiation** in the work of **Robert Desgabets**. However, his critique is distinctive in extending this charge to **Pierre Gassendi** and the Gassendists. This feature of the *Sentimens* explains why it received responses not only from Cartesians such as **Nicolas Malebranche** and **Antoine Arnauld**, but also from the Gassendist **François Bernier**. The controversy stirred up by the publication of Le Valois's text not only made it impossible for **Pierre-Sylvain Régis** to continue his public conferences on Cartesianism in Paris, but also delayed for 10 years the publication of his *Système de philosophie*. This work also led Louis-Paul du Vaucel to warn his fellow Jansenist Arnauld, in an unpublished "Observations sur Descartes" (1680), of the dangers of associating **Jansenism** too closely with a discredited Cartesianism.

LIGHT. Descartes devoted a great deal of effort to explaining the **nature** and behavior of light. Among the first triumphs of the new physics was a derivation, contemporary with Willebrord Snell's, of the law of refraction (1620s; a version of it was published in the *Dioptrics* in 1637). Though the details of his theory of light vary from one work to another, one basic idea persists: light consists of pressure exerted by particles of the second or first element (*Principles* III, art. 55, 78, IV, art. 28). It results from the centrifugal force each such particle exerts according to the second law of motion. That pressure is created by the vortices around each major heavenly body, and is directed outward from the center of that body. It is probably stronger in the plane of rotation of the vortex (the equator) than at the poles.

Descartes insisted—indeed he made it an irrepudiable tenet in a 1634 letter to Isaac Beeckman—that light is transmitted instantaneously. The 1676 determination by Ole Christensen Rømer, using observations of the satellites of Jupiter, that the speed of light is finite, was thus a serious problem. It seems not to have been dealt with by later Cartesians (see Samuel Clarke's notes to Jacques Rohault's *Physica*, pp. 180, 186).

The importance of Descartes's theory, however inadequate, was that it explained mechanistically some of the phenomena for which Aristotelian philosophy had supposed qualities (notably, light and color) distinct from the modes of extension.

LOGIC. Logic is the theory of inference, and in the tradition following Aristotle the subject was primarily concerned with the codification of valid forms of inference based on the form of the syllogism. Descartes would have learned the traditional logic of Aristotle at La Flèche, but he held the subject in little regard. In the *Discourse on Method* he remarks that "in the case of logic, its syllogisms and the greater part of its other lessons serve rather to explain to someone else the things one already knows," and complains that, "although it contains, in effect, very true and good precepts, nevertheless there are so many others, mixed up with them, which are either harmful or superfluous, that it is almost as hard to separate the one from the other as to draw a Diana or a Minerva from a block of marble" (AT, vol. VI, p. 17). *See also* DEDUCTION; DEMONSTRATION.

LOUIS XIV (1638–1715). The self-proclaimed Sun King (*Le Roi Soleil*), who ruled France with the help of the First Minister Cardinal Marazin until the death of the latter in 1661, and who subsequently broke with tradition by ruling without a first minister until his death in 1715. Louis issued two decrees directed against Cartesianism, both of which concerned the University of Paris. The first decree, issued in 1671, enjoined university officials to enforce statutes prohibiting the teaching of anti-**Aristotelian** philosophy in order to prevent the airing of views that "could bring some confusion in the explanation of our mysteries." This decree most likely was prompted not by the 1662 condemnation of Descartes in the **University of Louvain**, but rather the growing popularity of Cartesianism in France due primarily to the private conferences of the **natural philosopher Jacques Rohault**. This decree also was immediately preceded by the anonymous publication of the *Considérations sur l'état présent* of the French Cartesian **Robert Desgabets**, which Louis's confessor **Jean Ferrier** condemned for denying the Catholic doctrine of **transubstantiation**. The condemnation of this work may well explain the reference in Louis's decree to the confusion certain views bring to the explanation of the mysteries. In any event, the 1671 decree was invoked in various campaigns against Cartesians and Cartesianism in the 1670s at provincial colleges in **Angers** and Caen.

Louis's second decree, issued in 1691, was a formulary signed by the Paris faculty of philosophy condemning the teaching of 11 propositions. The first three of these propositions concern a **method of doubt** in Descartes that questions even the existence and veracity of **God**, whereas the last four propositions concern various claims that impugn the necessity of absolute **freedom** for our responsibility for sin. The fact that the last set of propositions was drawn from official condemnations of the views of **Cornelius Jansenius** reveals an attempt in the formulary to link Cartesian philosophy to Jansenist theology.

Louis did not allow for unrestrained teaching of Cartesianism in the French universities and religious orders. However, he did allow his son, the dauphin, to be instructed in the fundamentals of Cartesianism by his tutors, one of whom included the Cartesian **Gérauld de Cordemoy**. Moreover, Louis did not take the option open to him of preventing the appointment of Cartesians **Nicolas Malebranche** and **Pierre-Sylvain Régis** to the Paris Académie des Sciences. Thus, one cannot speak of an unqualified opposition to Cartesianism on his part.

LOUVAIN, UNIVERSITY OF. A leading intellectual center of Catholic thought in the Spanish Netherlands (now Belgium). This institution is connected to Cartesianism principally through the 1662 condemnation of five theses from Descartes by its Faculty of **Theology**. These theses all concern aspects of Descartes's metaphysical physics and cosmology. In particular, the theologians condemned Descartes's denial of **substantial forms** other than the human **soul**, his denial of the **real qualities** purportedly required by the Catholic doctrine of the **Eucharist**, his assertion that **extension** is the "essential attribute" of **body**, his claim that the extension of the world is unbounded, and his rejection of the possibility of a plurality of worlds. The papal nuncio, Jérôme de

Vecchi, pushed for the condemnation in order to counter the popularity of the new Cartesian philosophy among the members of the Faculties of the Arts and Medicine at Louvain. There is some evidence that Vecchi also was involved in the 1663 decision of members of the Roman curia to place a selection of Descartes's writings on the *Index librorum prohibitorum*. These writings were still present in the final edition of the *Index* published in 1948.

LOVE (*AMOR, AMOUR*). Together with admiration, joy, sadness and desire, love and hatred are the fundamental or "primitive" **passions** for Descartes (*Passions* II, art. 69, AT, vol. XI, p. 380). Love is defined as "an **emotion** of the **soul** caused by the movement of the spirits, which incites it to readily join the objects that seem suitable to it" (*Passions* II, art. 79, AT, vol. XI, p. 387). Hatred, on the other hand, is "an emotion caused by the spirits, which incites the soul to want to be separated from the objects which present themselves to it as being damaging" (*Passions* II, art. 79, AT, vol. XI, p. 387). The definitions are not without their own difficulties because it seems difficult to distinguish love from **desire**, which almost invariably accompanies it. But the object of desire is in the future, whereas the object of love is the union with (or, in the case of hatred, the separation from) a particular being. Physically love (provided it is not accompanied by other passions) is characterized by an equal heartbeat, a sweet warmth in the breast, and a quick digestion, "which is the reason why this passion is good for health" (*Passions* II, art. 97, AT, vol. XI, p. 402). This is caused by a widening of the entrance to the **heart**, which allows the newly made blood to pass quickly into it, without remaining in the liver. Given the fact that this produces not only blood of a good and equal quality but also **animal spirits** that are quick and strong, this helps the mind to concentrate on the idea of the loved object. As in all passions the connection between love and its physical manifestations goes back to a form of conditioning in early youth, based on our first experience of being fed; for most people this was the first occurrence of a state they wished to retain and the reason why the same physiological phenomena come back whenever we wish to retain a certain condition.

In a letter to **Pierre-Hector Chanut** of February 1, 1647, Descartes completes this account by making a further distinction between passionate love (the type of love discussed so far) and intellectual (or rational) love. This is produced "when our soul perceives some good, whether present or absent, which it judges to be suitable for it, and wants to be united with that good." Thus we can desire or enjoy science without having the bodily experiences that usually accompany love, joy, and desire. Accordingly, intellectual love could be in the soul even if it is not united with the body, although, as long as we are in fact united with the **body**, some form of passionate love usually accompanies intellectual love. A separate case is the love of **God**. The difference between God and us is so great that it is almost impossible to see us as forming a whole of which God and we are parts. Still, if we think of God as a **mind**, we may come to think of our own mind as some sort of emanation of God, without identifying ourselves with him or giving ourselves the **idea** that we could be gods. Indeed, the contemplation of **nature** gives us such an elevated idea of God's infinity and almightiness that our greatest desire is that God's will be done.

LOYOLA, IGNATIUS. *See* JESUITS.

LUYNES, LOUIS-CHARLES D'ALBERT, DUKE OF (1620–90). Louis-Charles d'Albert came from a noble family, whose Italian origins (originally they were called Alberti), go back to the 12th century. In 1639 he became Pair de France ("peer of the realm"). As a military officer he distinguished himself during the defense of Camp, near Arras, when the Spaniards attacked it on April 2, 1640, as well as on several other occasions. On September 23, 1641, he married Marie-Louise Séguier. She died on September 13, 1651, after giving birth to nine children, five of whom did not survive infancy. By papal dispensation he remarried in 1661, taking as his wife Anne de Rohan, a close cousin (his mother was a Rohan). She died in 1684, after giving birth to seven other children. His third marriage was with Marguerite d'Aligre, dowager of Charles-Bonaventure Marquis de Manneville. Luynes died in Paris on October 10, 1690. His son Charles-Honoré, born in 1646 out of his first marriage, became known as Duc de Chevreuse and was a famous military hero.

According to **Adrien Baillet**, Descartes knew of Luynes's translation of the *Meditations* only in 1644, when it was already finished. Apparently, it had been undertaken by the young duke "to exercise his style on a great subject, without having in mind the service he brought to the public" (AT, vol. IV, p. 193). Descartes took it with him from Paris to Bretagne in the summer of 1644 and used this opportunity to correct the text in a few places. Although **Claude Clerselier** also made a translation, which moreover included the *Objections and Replies*, Descartes preferred the translation of the Duc de Luynes for the *Meditations* as such, undoubtedly also because of the high position of the translator. Nothing is known of any direct contacts between Descartes and Luynes, nor is it known in what way and by whom Descartes was informed of the existence of his translation.

– M –

MACHINE. *See* MECHANICS; AUTOMATON.

MALEBRANCHE, NICOLAS (1638–1715). A French **Oratorian** who was concerned to offer a synthesis of the views of his philosophical heroes, **Augustine** and Descartes. In 1660 Malebranche left his theological studies at the **Sorbonne** due to his dislike of **scholastic philosophy**, and entered the Oratory to be trained in the more Augustinian approach to **theology** prevalent there. He was judged by his teachers to be "mediocre," but nonetheless was ordained as a priest in 1664.

A decisive event in Malebranche's intellectual life was his discovery in 1666 of a posthumous edition of Descartes's *Treatise on Man* in a Paris bookstall. Malebranche's biographer, Yves André, reported that he was so ecstatic in reading this dry physiological text that he experienced violent palpitations of the heart that obliged him to set the book aside at intervals. While André did not indicate why Malebranche was so moved, one can speculate that he discovered in Descartes's text an alternative to a stagnant scholastic account of the natural world.

Malebranche subsequently devoted himself to a decade-long study of the Cartesian approach to **mathematics and natural philosophy**. The fruit of this study was his *Recherche de la vérité* (1674–75), which concerns the principal sources of human **error** and the **method** for avoiding these errors and finding the **truth**. This book takes over from Descartes the claim that the senses mislead us concerning the **nature** of reality and that the **intellect** reveals a **dualism** that distinguishes between **mind** as thinking **substance** and **body** as extended substance. However, the *Recherche* also includes two doctrines that reflect Malebranche's Augustinian emphasis on our dependence on **God**. The first is the doctrine that we intellectually comprehend bodies by means of **eternal ideas** in God, while the second is the doctrine that God is the only real **cause** and that creatures merely provide the occasion for his action. This work was amended and corrected in several subsequent editions, but the text itself was never thoroughly reworked. The result is that the sixth and last edition, published in 1712, resembles something of a palimpsest.

The first edition of the *Recherche* drew an immediate response from **Simon Foucher**, a self-proclaimed "academic skeptic" whose *Critique de la recherche de la vérité* (1674) attacks the Cartesian assumption that ideas in us can represent objects external to us. **Robert Desgabets** wrote a *Critique* of Foucher's text that defends this assumption by invoking the principle that all ideas correspond to their objects. For his part, Malebranche responded that both Foucher and Desgabets failed to see that his *Recherche* rejects this assumption insofar as it places representative ideas in God rather than in us.

Malebranche further defended controversial features of the *Recherche* in a set of "Eclaircissements" that were first appended to this work in 1678 and that, like the *Recherche* itself, underwent significant revision in later editions. In the last of the initial set of clarifications, Malebranche introduced the claim that God acts for the most part through "general volitions" and acts through "particular volitions" only in the exceptional case of **miracles**. Even though **Antoine Arnauld** objected that such a claim conflicts with the Scriptural position that God attends to the particular details of creation, Malebranche nonetheless published a defense of his position in the *Traité de la nature et de la grâce* (1680). Though Arnauld had initially approved of the *Recherche*, the publication of the *Traité* led him to compose a critique of Malebranche's theory of ideas in this text. This critique in the *Vraies et fausses idées* (1683) triggered a decade-long debate that was one of the major intellectual events of the day. This increasingly bitter debate concerned not only the philosophical issue of the nature of ideas, but also theological issues concerning divine providence that had initially triggered Arnauld's opposition to Malebranche.

In 1693 Malebranche responded to the criticisms of the *Recherche* in the 1690 *Système de philosophie* of **Pierre-Sylvain Régis**. In his text Régis defended the view, which Arnauld had offered a decade earlier, that the ideas that represent objects are simply modifications of our own **soul**. Malebranche and Régis were admitted together to the Paris Académie des Sciences in 1699. Malebranche's admission was based primarily on his critique of Descartes's laws of **motion**. This critique was shaped by Malebranche's correspondence with **Gottfried Wilhelm Leibniz** on this issue during the 1680s.

MATERIAL FALSITY. In the Third Meditation, Descartes introduced the possibility that his **idea** of cold may be materially false insofar as it "represents what is not a thing as a thing" (AT, vol. VII, p. 43–44). He had in mind here the possibility that cold is merely the privation of the **quality** of heat, and thus is not the "thing" or quality that the idea represents it to be. This sort of falsity of falsity is called "material" since it derives from the idea itself rather than, as in the case of "formal" falsity, from a **judgment** concerning the idea. Descartes defended his use of the notion of material falsity by noting that this same notion is present in the work of **Francisco Suárez**. Suárez did indeed speak of a kind of material falsity that derives from an apprehension of a concept that is prior to any judgment involved in composition and division. However, **Antoine Ar-**

nauld objected that no idea can be materially false since no idea can fail to represent what it does in fact represent (AT, vol. VII, p. 207). In response, Descartes explained the material falsity of an idea by emphasizing not so much the fact that that idea represents a privation as a quality, but more the fact that the idea is obscure and confused (AT, vol. VII, pp. 234–35). The exchange with Arnauld may have prompted Descartes to drop the notion of material falsity, which is not present in his later writings. *See also* CLARITY AND DISTINCTNESS; ERROR.

MATHEMATICS. Mathematics was traditionally characterized as the science of **quantity**, with the development of mathematical theories as **demonstrations** from clear definitions and **common notions** serving as a model of all sciences. Descartes was one of many to regard mathematics as a paradigm of the employment of **reason**; as he explained in his conversation with **Frans Burman**, mathematics "accustoms the **mind** to the recognition of **truth**, because it is in mathematics that examples of correct reasoning are to be found, which you will find nowhere else. Consequently, the man who has once accustomed his mind to mathematical reasoning will also have a mind well equipped for investigating other truths, since reasoning is everywhere the same" (AT, vol. V, p. 177). Although he held mathematical **method** in very high esteem, Descartes regarded the truths of **metaphysics** as much more important than those of mathematics. Thus, in the *Rules for the Direction of the Mind* he could dismiss the "pointless problems with which arithmeticians and geometers are inclined to while away their time," while praising the methodological structure of mathematics as "a more powerful instrument of knowledge than any other with which human beings are endowed" (AT, vol. X, pp. 373, 374).

Descartes's extraordinary skill in mathematics was evident from an early age, and during the 1620s he devoted himself to the study of mathematics and developed the main results that he would later publish in his *Geometry*. Descartes departed from the traditional approach to mathematics with his reliance on **algebra** in the solution of geometric problems. By construing arithmetical operations such as addition or the extraction of roots as applied to line segments and generating other line segments, Descartes assumed a strong thesis on the unity of arithmetical and geometric magnitudes. This undermined the traditional distinction between arithmetic and **geometry**, but Descartes saw nothing particularly arithmetical about the operation of addition, or anything uniquely geometrical about the extraction of roots. His resulting fusion of algebra and geometry treats algebra as a science of magnitude in general, and the specifically geometric content of a problem is removed (and the problem made more intelligible), when it is represented as a relation among various abstract magnitudes.

By the time the *Geometry* was published, Descartes had largely abandoned the pure mathematics whose problems he dismissed as trifles. He nevertheless thought that mathematics was the key to developing a body of knowledge that could both explain the phenomena of the world and resist skeptical doubts. In a letter from July 1638, Descartes asks **Marin Mersenne** to explain to **Girard Desargues** that his decision to abandon the study of pure geometry means that "I have resolved to give up only abstract geometry, that is to say, the investigation of problems which serve only as mental exercises; and I have done this in order to have more time to cultivate another sort of geometry, where the problems have to do with the explanation of natural phenomena. For if he cares to think about what I wrote about salt, snow, the rainbow, etc. he will see that my entire **physics** is nothing but geometry" (AT, vol. V, p. 268). This identification of physics with geometry is underwritten by Descartes's insistence that the essence of **body** is **extension**, which makes the object of physics identical to that of geometry. Thus, in addition to disregarding the classical distinction between the two branches of mathematics (geometry and arithmetic), Descartes also undermined the traditional distinction between pure and applied mathematics.

MATHESIS UNIVERSALIS. Literally, "universal **mathematics**," the expression appears in the *Rules for the Direction of the Mind,* at rules four and 14. There has been some scholarly controversy about the relationship between this universal mathematics and the **method** Descartes sets out in the *Discourse on Method.* Some scholars identify the two, others hold that *mathesis universalis* is more strictly mathematical and indicates Descartes's **algebra** or analytic **geometry,** and some see it as denoting a vague and never fully realized project for a universal science of order and measure. The grand idea of a universal method was hardly original with Descartes, and characterization of such a method as *mathesis universalis* can be found in 16th-century Italian authors concerned with method and mathematics. In the *Rules,* Descartes characterizes *mathesis universalis* as a "venerable term with a well established meaning," that denotes a highly general study of order and measure which serves as the foundation for all other sciences that admit a mathematical formulation (AT, vol. X, p. 378).

MATTER. *See* BODY; EXTENSION.

MECHANICS. Literally the study of machines, the science of mechanics was widely studied in the 16th and 17th centuries, with attention focused on the pseudo-Aristotelian work *Mechanica* and the Archimedean treatise *On the Equilibrium of Planes*. Machines were considered devices that brought about effects which **nature** would not, if left to itself. The Archimedean water screw, for instance, moves water upward out of a stream, a **motion** contrary to its natural tendency to flow downhill. Of course, a machine uses natural materials such as wood, metal, and rope to achieve its effects, so machines ultimately can be explained in terms of the properties inherent in material bodies, but classical and renaissance authors saw a fundamental distinction between artificial mechanical devices and the ordinary workings of nature.

Descartes's philosophy considers the whole of the material world as a gigantic machine, and as he explains at the end of Part IV of the *Principles*, he does not "recognize any difference between artifacts and natural bodies except that the operations of artifacts are for the most part performed by mechanisms large enough to be easily perceivable by the senses," while effects produced by natural means "almost always depend on structures so minute that they completely elude our senses" (AT, vol. VIIIA, p. 326). Thus, in the Cartesian scheme, there is no fundamental difference between mechanical and natural phenomena—the whole world is to be understood in terms of the principles of mechanics, namely the size, figure, and motion of material bodies that act on one another by impact.

There is, however, an interesting ambiguity concerning the role of mechanics in Descartes's philosophy. On the one hand, mechanics is a science that develops out of physics, which in turn depends on the principles of true **metaphysics**. As Descartes puts it in his famous analogy of the tree of knowledge: "The whole of philosophy is like a tree. The roots are metaphysics, the trunk is **physics**, and the branches emerging from this trunk are all the other sciences, which may be reduced to the three principal ones, namely medicine, mechanics, and morals" (AT, vol. IXB, p. 14). This makes mechanics a special case of physics or an application of physics to particular problems. Yet Descartes also characterizes the **laws of nature** as just the laws of mechanics, as he does in the *Discourse on Method* when he speaks of "the laws of mechanics, which are the same as those of nature" (AT, vol. VI, p. 54). It is this conception of mechanics as a foundation for the true physics that led Descartes to declare in an April 1639 letter that his "entire physics is nothing but mechanics" (AT, vol. II, p. 542). These two conceptions of the place of mechanics can be reconciled by understanding that Descartes sees mechanical **principles** as fundamental to all of physics (which accounts for the foundational role of mechanical concepts), while the traditional notion of mechanics as concerned with artificial machines is a special case of the general thesis that nature accomplishes all its effects through the motion and impact of material bodies.

MECHANISM. The mechanist thesis is that the phenomena of the natural world arise from the **motion** and impact of material **bodies**, so that the physical world can be understood as a giant machine. In mechanistic parlance, qualities such as **color**, heat, odor, or weight arise from the motions and collisions of material bodies and the interaction of these bodies with the human sensory apparatus (which itself is understood as a mechanical system). One of the recurring themes in 17th-century **natural philosophy** is the replacement of **Aristotelian** and **scholastic** models of the world by mechanistic theories. Such diverse figures as Descartes, **Francis Bacon**, **Galileo Galilei**, **Thomas Hobbes**, **Pierre Gassendi**, and **Walter Charleton** all championed the mechanist thesis to one degree or another, recommending it as superior to the apparatus of **substantial forms** and other nonmechanical principles that are found in the "philosophy of the Schools." *See also* ATOMISM; MECHANICS.

MEDITATIONS ON FIRST PHILOSOPHY (MEDITATIONES DE PRIMA PHILOSOPHIA, MÉDITATIONS MÉTAPHYSIQUES). According to Descartes's own testimony he spent the first nine months of his stay in the Netherlands working on **metaphysics**, planning also to write something on it—which however he would not have published, preferring to wait and see what people would say of his **physics**. That there had been earlier plans and essays emerges not only from the testimony of **Adrien Baillet,** but also from a letter to **Guillaume Gibieuf** of July 18, 1629, in which he reminds him of his promise to revise a work by Descartes, which, given Gibieuf's interests, can hardly be anything but a work in **theology** or metaphysics. Again, Descartes asks his correspondent to wait: the work will not be ready for two or three years. In any case, this "small metaphysical treatise" apparently was not finished (to **Mersenne**, November 25, 1630, AT, vol. I, p. 182). All we positively know about it is that it was in Latin, that it contained two major points: 1) the existence of God; 2) the existence of our **souls**, when separated from our **bodies**, and that it was more elaborate than the metaphysical part of the *Discourse*. In any case, Descartes admits that the proof of the existence of God in the *Discourse* could have been more convincing if he had included a discussion on the uncertainty of the **senses** and the **imagination** as he had done in his earlier essay.

Although Descartes devoted a few pages to metaphysics in the *Discourse* and thought of including some of the older material in a new Latin edition of the *Discourse* (which he ultimately did not), he started seriously to consider a new presentation only in 1639. It would be no more than five or six leaves (which may be anything between 40 and 60 printed pages) and contain "a good part of metaphysics." It was Descartes's intention to have printed only 20 or 30 copies of them and to send them to the best theologians in France in order to see what they thought of it before publication. Before giving it to a Leiden printer, Descartes sent a copy to **Henricus Regius**, but even in July printing had not yet started. Moreover, Descartes hesitated about his original plan and decided to have the book approved by some theologians and, if possible, by the **Sorbonne**, before publication. But since he could not travel to France he left everything to Marin Mersenne, suggesting that it be given only to "three or four" trusted theologians, especially Gibieuf, after which the book could be dedicated to the Sorbonne "so as to ask them to be my protectors in the cause of God" (to Mersenne, September 30, 1640, AT, vol. III, pp. 183–85); a further motive for the dedication was to facilitate the acceptance of his physics.

In any case, the book was to be printed in France, under the supervision of Mersenne, who received the manuscript in November 1640. At that point there was already one set of objections and replies, those by **Johannes Caterus**. Mersenne immediately started to organize further *Objections and Replies*—somewhat to Descartes's annoyance who believed that one should take one's time to study his work. Meanwhile other things had to be added: the dedicatory letter to the Sorbonne and an "argument of my Metaphysics," which was to be the "Synopsis," necessary so that something on the **immortality** of the soul be inserted.

Apart from the *Replies* to the *Objections* Descartes also dealt, more or less continuously, with Mersenne's remarks and accordingly changed a few formulations in the original manuscript. Printing finally began in the early summer of 1641, the printed sheets being sent by Mersenne to Descartes, sometimes with **Constantijn Huygens** as an intermediary. On August 1 the *Meditations* were submitted to the Sorbonne for approval. The next day Descartes formally ceded (probably because of Mersenne) to Michel Soly, the printer, the *privilège*, which was owned by him. The printing was completed on August 28. Although it is by no means clear that the *Meditations* obtained the approval of the Sorbonne, the book was, according to the title page, printed "with the approval of the learned." While Mersenne asked Soly to send a hundred copies to the Netherlands, these never arrived. In fact, the only extant copies were two copies sent directly to Huygens.

Descartes himself complained that he had no copy at all and decided to have a new edition printed in Amsterdam by Lodewijk Elzevier. This also allowed him to restore the piece on the **Eucharist** in his *Replies* to the *Fourth Set of Objections*, which Mersenne had thought better to suppress. Elzevier worked efficiently, for in January 1642 he had almost achieved the printing. Now it was Descartes who caused the delay, not only because he wanted to include the *Seventh Set of Objections and Replies*, but also because he wanted the proofs to be sent from Amsterdam to Endegeest, where he lived. The *Seventh Objections* became part of a second volume, together with a *Letter to Father Dinet*, provincial of the **Jesuits** in the Île de France, in which Descartes complained, not only of the Jesuit Father **Pierre Bourdin**, but also of **Gysbertus Voetius**, who, according to Descartes had misused his position to extort a negative judgment on Descartes's philosophy from the **University of Utrecht**. The whole became available in May 1642. Apart from restoring the piece on the Eucharist and adding the *Seventh Set of Objections and Replies* and the *Letter to Dinet*, Descartes changed the title, which now, more modestly, claimed that the book contained a proof of the distinction of body and soul (whereas the first edition had boasted that there would be a proof of the immortality of the soul).

The **Duc de Luynes** made a French translation of the *Meditations*, apparently independently from Descartes, who seems to have first heard about it in the summer of 1644, when he made a journey to France. **Claude Clerselier**, too, took the trouble of translating not only the *Meditations*, but also the *Objections and Replies*. Descartes preferred the translation of the *Meditations* by the young duke, flattered no doubt by the attention of this high courtier. He accepted Clerselier's translation of the *Objections and Replies*. Descartes revised both translations, except those of the *Fifth Set of Objections and Replies* (Descartes was still angry at **Pierre Gassendi** for having published a separate edition with a rejoinder), the *Seventh Set of Objections and Replies*, and the *Letter to Father Dinet*, and published the whole of it in 1647 in Paris.

MEMORY. In his early physiological writings, Descartes described memory as a purely corporeal faculty. In particular, the *Treatise on Man* includes the claim that this faculty operates by the retention of corporeal impressions in the "common sense," that is, the **pineal gland** (AT, vol. XI, p. 176). At one point, Descartes characterized these impressions as "not unlike the folds in paper that remain in this paper once it has been folded" (AT, vol. III, p. 20).

This account provided the basis for a later critique in the work of the anti-Cartesian **Simon Foucher**, and the Cartesian **Robert Desgabets**, of the view of the Cartesian **Nicolas Malebranche** that we have a "pure intellect" that operates independently of the brain. The objection in Foucher and Desgabets was that since memory is based in the brain, we would have no ability to remember purely intellectual thoughts that leave no trace there.

In response, Malebranche suggested the position, found also in Descartes's later writings, that we have an "intellectual memory" that does not require any imprint on the brain but depends only on the immaterial mind. Whereas both Descartes and Malebranche held that human and animals alike have corporeal memory, they agreed that humans alone have intellectual memory.

The topic of memory is relevant not only to Descartes's account of mental and bodily faculties, but also to his views in epistemology. In response to the problem of the **Cartesian circle**, Descartes emphasized the distinction between **clear and distinct** perceptions to which one is actually attending and clear and distinct perceptions that one merely remembers having considered in the past. Trust in the latter perceptions is said to require a proof of the existence of a nondeceptive **God**. The point here is not that such a God guarantees the reliability of our memory, but that the proof of his existence removes any support for the suspicion that our faculties may systematically deceive us.

MERSENNE, MARIN (1588–1648). The name of Marin Mersenne has been indelibly, and to a degree unfortunately, associated with that of Descartes since the late 17th century, when **Adrien Baillet**, Descartes's biographer, referred to him as "l'homme de Descartes" ("Descartes's man"). Mersenne, born eight years before Descartes, preceded him at La Flèche (the two probably did not meet there), and in the 1620s had already established himself in his role as the one-man academy of Paris. His **correspondence** helped communicate results and questions to the leading natural philosophers of Europe; it provides an invaluable record of the pursuit of knowledge not only in the natural sciences, but also in biblical criticism and music in the first half of the 17th century. When Descartes came to Paris in the 1620s, Mersenne, who had then already published the *Quæstiones celeberrimæ in Genesim* (1623) and several works directed against skeptics and "**atheists**," was among those who aided the brilliant young mathematician and philosopher to begin making his name in scientific circles. From then until the end of Mersenne's life, Mersenne regularly sent Descartes letters containing questions, primarily physical, that Descartes, though he occasionally complained about them, usually tried to answer. Those answers sometimes contain the germ of doctrines Descartes would develop more fully elsewhere. The doctrine of the creation of the **eternal truths** is one notable instance: it first appears in letters to Mersenne—apparently in answer to theological queries—in 1630. Sometimes, on the other hand, they are the only source we have for Descartes's views on various matters. Descartes's response to the condemnation of **Galileo Galilei**, for example, and his only detailed response to any published work of Galileo's, appear in letters of the 1630s. Like his letters to **Princess Elisabeth**, Descartes's letters to Mersenne (many of them published by **Claude Clerselier**) provide us with drafts and projects for his published works that we would otherwise lack.

Mersenne's most significant effort on Descartes's behalf was the circulation of the *Meditations* in manuscript to would-be objectors; all the *Objections* save the first and last sets were written at his instigation (and the *Second* and *Sixth* were authored partly by him). That Descartes relied on Mersenne to solicit objections to his work is an indication of a trust, if not an intimacy, that Descartes reposed in very few others. It was to Mersenne also that Descartes in the early 1640s described the project that became the *Principles*, a project begun as a kind of commentary on the *Summa philosophica quadripartita* of **Eustachius a Sancto Paulo.**

Mersenne was a dedicated experimenter, a tireless popularizer of the new science (especially Galileo's), and a significant contributor to **natural philosophy**. We can credit his curiosity with bringing before Descartes empirical questions he might otherwise have failed to consider. Mersenne's *Harmonie Universelle* (1636), in addition to being an encyclopedia of music and music theory, includes results in **mechanics** and acoustics; other major works, like the *Quæstiones*, are likewise compendia whose contents exceed their ostensible subject matter. Mersenne, like **Pierre Gassendi, Henry More**, and to some extent **Gottfried Wilhelm Leibniz**, favored what one might call an open, curious, bottom-up science, in contrast to the more single-minded, top-down science of Descartes.

MESLAND, DENIS (1615–72). A French **Jesuit** and teacher at Descartes's old school at **La Flèche**. Mesland was one of the few Jesuits to receive Descartes's *Meditations* enthusiastically, going so far as to work up a summary of this text that would be suitable for use in the schools (see AT, vol. IV, p. 122). Descartes's correspondence with him is important because he addressed most directly there the **theologically** sensitive topics of the **nature** of human **freedom** and of **transubstantiation**. On the first topic, Descartes claimed in a 1644 letter that there is only "a verbal difference" between Mesland's position and his own since he admits that our free action involves "a real and positive power to determine" that action (AT, vol. IV, p. 116). In showing sympathy for the Jesuit position here, Descartes in effect was backing off his earlier endorsement of the critique of the Jesuit account of **indifference** in the work of the **Oratorian Guillaume Gibieuf**. In this same letter, Descartes also noted that he could see no great difference between his views and what the Jesuit Denis Petau wrote in a recently published critique of the account of freedom in **Cornelius Jansenius**. The issue of transubstantiation was also an important one vis-à-vis Descartes's relation to the Jesuits. Already in 1638 he had boasted to a Jesuit correspondent that his philosophy provides the means for defending this doctrine against the objections of the **Calvinists** (AT, vol. II, p. 564). However, his correspondence with Mesland is the only place where he offered a detailed account of transubstantiation. Even here, Descartes requested that Mesland not publicly attribute the account to him. Despite Descartes's repeated attempts to win his endorsement, Mesland never seems to have accepted this account. After the end of his correspondence with Mesland, Descartes refrained from promoting the account of transubstantiation that he offered there. Thus, when **Antoine Arnauld** pressed him on this particular issue in 1648 **correspondence**, Descartes answered with silence.

A footnote in the original Adam and Tannery edition of Descartes's works suggests that Mesland was "consigned to Canada" in 1646 as punishment for his association with Descartes (AT, vol. IV, p. 345n). However, Mesland was assigned first to Martinique and then to Santa Fe (now Bogotá) in Nouvelle-Grenade (now Colombia). Moreover, the evidence suggests that he requested the assignment in order to carry out his plan of "converting the savages" (see AT, vol. IV, 345). This mission deprived Descartes of not only a trusted friend, but also of a potentially valuable religious ally.

METAPHYSICS. In the preface to the French translation of the *Principles*, Descartes compares "the whole of philosophy" to "a tree," with the roots representing metaphysics, the trunk **physics**, and the branches the three principal sciences of medicine, **mechanics**, and morals (AT VIIIA, p. 14). Elsewhere in the preface he contrasts the **principles** of "immaterial or metaphysical things" with those of "corporeal or physical things" (p. 10). Here there is a suggestion of the **scholastic** contrast between metaphysics as the study of immaterial objects such as **God**, **angels** and human **intellects**, and **natural philosophy** as the study of material objects. However, Descartes's tree analogy also indicates that metaphysics provides foundations for the account in physics of **bodies** **in motion**. This explains why he insisted, against his wayward disciple **Henricus Regius**, that the study of metaphysics must precede the study of natural philosophy, including physics. Descartes thereby departed from the scholastic tradition that started with a study of objects of the senses in natural philosophy and then proceeded by **abstraction** to a consideration of immaterial objects in metaphysics.

Despite Descartes's explicit expression of a concern to offer a new metaphysics, some commentators have claimed recently that in fact he did not provide a metaphysics in the sense—prominent among the **Scotists** and explicit in the work of **Francisco Suárez**—of a science of "being *qua* being." The argument here is that Descartes's account of the creation of the **eternal truths** implies that there is no concept of being that applies univocally or even analogically to God and creatures. Though Descartes himself is not clear on this matter, later Cartesians such as **Pierre-Sylvain Régis** took the Cartesian view of the eternal truths to reveal that terms apply to God and creatures only equivocally. Even so, a portion of Régis's *Système de philosophie* is devoted to metaphysics defined as the study both of "intelligent substances separated from matter" and of principles common to all of the sciences. **Johannes Clauberg** provided a version of Cartesian metaphysics that conforms more to the Suárezian definition of it as a science of being *qua* being. Later thinkers such as **Baruch Spinoza** and **Nicolas Malebranche** also offered metaphysical systems that, while inspired by Descartes, nonetheless deviated significantly from Cartesian orthodoxy.

METEORS (*MÉTÉORS, METEORA*). Most of the *Météors*, which forms the second of the three essays published together with the *Discourse* (the other two being *Dioptrics* and *Geometry*), was presumably written in the summer of 1629, after Descartes had obtained from **Henricus Reneri** a description of the parhelia (or false suns) observed that spring in Tivoli, near Rome. This caused Descartes to abandon his work and venture his own explanation, which however he felt could be done only on the basis of a general theory of all sublunary phenomena, collectively called *meteora*. According to a letter to **Marin Mersenne** of the autumn of 1629 these would be the object of a small treatise. Although before long Descartes seems to enlarge this project so as to turn this treatise into a general work on **physics**, it is likely that the two projects became separated again.

In November 1635 Descartes decided to include the work, which by that time must have been completed, in the project of the *Discourse*, which so far consisted only of the *Dioptrics* and a short introduction. The thought of including it must have been especially attractive because meteorology was generally taught as an introduction to physics (mostly on the basis of **Aristotle's** *Meteora*). It also fit Reneri's didactic program, which concentrated on ordinary natural phenomena everybody could observe.

The range of subjects treated in Descartes's *Meteors* is rather exactly described in a letter to Mersenne of March 1636: "I deal mainly with the **nature** of salt, the causes of wind and thunder, the figures of snow, the **colors** of the rainbow (where I also try to show generally what is the nature of each color), and the crowns, or halos, and suns or parhelia as those that were seen in Rome, some six or seven years ago" (AT, vol. I, p. 340). Of these phenomena only those connected with snow, halos, and rainbows are mentioned in the correspondence prior to the publication of the *Meteors* in 1637. It seems that Descartes was first satisfied with his explanation of the rainbow; halos retained his attention until 1635; in March 1630 he complained that the Dutch winter was so mild that he had been unable to observe snow crystals. In October 1636 he still hoped for some snow so as to enable **Frans van Schooten**, who made the engravings, to have an exact picture. It is the only work in which Descartes explicitly deals with the explanation of particular **qualities**. Thus he refers at various times to his explanation of the qualities of salt as an example of the way in which the qualities we perceive can be explained by the form and movement of the **particles** composing that substance. Many of the explanations of the *Meteors* became part of the Fourth Book of the *Principles*. The *Meteors* was criticized in particular by **Libertus Fromondus**, who was himself the author of *Meteorologica* (1627). Like the *Dioptrics* and the *Discourse* the book on meteors was translated into Latin by Étienne de Courcelles.

METHOD (*METHODUS, MÉTHODE*). Descartes was one of many 17th-century thinkers to be obsessed with the idea of a method, i.e., with a procedure for arranging inquiry so as to attain knowledge. Although method (from the Greek *methodos*, which means road or path) is one of the key concepts of Descartes's philosophy it is also very elusive. Descartes's first, and fairly general, point about method is that there should be a set of "reliable rules which are easy to apply and of such a **nature** that if one follows them exactly, one will never take to be true what is actually false or fruitlessly expend one's mental efforts, but will gradually and steadily increase one's knowledge until one arrives at a true understanding of everything within one's capacity" (*Rules* IV, AT, vol. X, p. 372). So one should not go about at random, starting with difficult problems, but proceed "methodically," that is, in a deliberate and orderly way, starting with the problems one can solve and, after learning from their solution, continue to more difficult problems. Descartes's second point is that all humans are naturally able to distinguish **truth** from falsehood: "the power of judging well and distinguishing the true from the false (which is what we properly call good sense or **reason**) is naturally equal in all men" (*Discourse* I, AT, vol.

VI, pp. 1–2). So method is not primarily concerned with criteria of truth but with problems of order and hierarchy: Once the material is digested and presented in an orderly way nobody will have any problem with recognizing (by means of an **intuition**) as true and certain whatever is in fact true. Descartes's third point is that method (as method of solving problems) is always the same, given the fact that "the sciences as a whole are nothing other than human wisdom, which always remains one and the same, however different the subjects to which it is applied, it being no more altered by them than sunlight is by the variety of the things it shines on" (*Regulae* I, AT, vol. XI, p. 360). So whether the problem we are dealing with is one of **mathematics**, or **physics**, or one of moral philosophy, the way to deal with it is the same. Finally, Descartes believes there is no intermediate between true and false—if something is not true and known to be true one may as well do as if it is entirely false.

The polemical thrust of this is sufficiently clear. As far as theoretical truth is concerned Descartes rejects: 1) the category of "probability" (the idea that there is a good chance that something is true because it is claimed to be true by an authority); 2) the idea that science (or wisdom) is the result of the dialectical confrontation of **ideas** (which even if it does not allow us to know the truth makes it possible to eliminate what is certainly false); 3) the idea that science is a cumulative process rather than a finite number of truths, which, in principle at least, can be known by a single mind. In fact, science (or wisdom) is a system of hierarchically ordered insights (*Regulae* V, AT, vol. XI, pp. 379–80). But the suggestion that the relation between those insights is "deductive" (in the sense that one idea logically implies the other) is wrong. Descartes's point is rather that if we establish our truths in the right order the discovery of the first truth facilitates the discovery of the next. The meaning of the idea that *cogito ergo sum* is the first truth is not that all other truths can be deduced from it but that by establishing it we learn that, if we want further truths, we must concentrate on the contents of our **mind**. The actual process of science on the other hand, as it emerges from the first half of the *Rules for the Direction of the Mind* consists of three stages: 1) to reduce a problem to its more simple constituents, that is, to identify the problems that should be solved first; 2) to "see" (by means of an intuition) some simple truth as well as the truths that "follow" immediately (by means of **deduction**); and 3) to institute an adequate **enumeration** in order to ensure that our solution is general (or to establish the extent to which it can be applied).

But on a practical level this picture seems to be much too simple. For method may also mean that we see how a problem is a particular version of a more general problem (for example, how an arithmetical or a **geometrical** problem can be reduced to a problem of **algebra**). So method can also mean that we concentrate on particular aspects of a problem or a phenomenon, namely, those we can understand clearly and distinctly. If we are dealing with the world of phenomena this may also mean that we reduce phenomena to a mathematical or a **mechanical** representation. In **optics**, for example, we do not ask for the essence of **light** but simply represent light as a straight line or visualize **refraction** by imagining a ball thrown against a wall; and in physiology we see the body as a **machine**, that is, we try to find a mechanical equivalent for each vital function. In general physics, on the other hand, we start with the clear and distinct ideas of **extension** and local **motion** and see what comes from it if nothing interferes, thus creating a general and theoretical framework we call nature. Seen in this way method may seem to be nothing more than a systematic search for theoretical models, that is, for clear and distinct representations of the things we want to understand.

A different concern, however, becomes visible, particularly in the second half of Descartes's philosophical career, namely, that an explanation must also be certain, that is, that we must have the certainty that our model not only is intrinsically **clear and distinct** (that our ideal of rationality is in fact rational), but also that the model really pictures the world (that the world actually *is* matter in motion, that our **body** actually *is* a machine, etc). Something of that concern already manifests itself in the four "rules of the method" that are given in the *Discourse*: 1) "Never to accept anything as true if I did not have evident knowledge of its truth; that is, carefully to avoid precipitate conclusions and preconceptions, and to include nothing more in my judgments than what presented itself to my mind so clearly and so distinctly that I had no occasion to doubt it." 2) "To divide each of the difficulties I examined into as many parts as possible and as may be required in order to resolve them better." 3) "To direct my **thoughts** in an orderly manner by beginning with the simplest and most easily known objects in order to ascend little by little, step by step, to knowledge of the most complex, and by supposing some order even among objects that have no natural order of precedence." 4) "Throughout to make enumerations so complete and reviews so comprehensive that I could be sure of leaving nothing out" (*Discourse* II, AT, vol. VI, pp. 18–19). Although most of this reads as a summary of the earlier views, the emphasis shifts to the certainty and indubitability of ideas—the meaning of "clear and distinct" actually seems to be indubitable.

This program is carried out in the *Meditations*, where Descartes first tests ideas (classes of ideas) on their ability to be resistant to **doubt** (finding that even the clear and distinct ideas of mathematics can be doubted under the hypothesis of an evil genius), then discovers the certainty of the *cogito* and of God as an unshaken foundation of knowledge and finally reestablishes the certainty of clear and distinct ideas by showing that God cannot deceive us. This also results in a new order of the sciences, which, as Descartes claims in the preface to the French translation to the *Principles*, can be seen as a tree, whose roots are formed by metaphysics, the trunk by physics, and the branches by the applied sciences: medicine, mechanics, and morals (AT, vol. IXB, p. 14). Again, this suggests a deductive order, whereas in fact there seems to be, not so much a subordination, as a coordination of primitive concepts—mind, matter, and their union—each of which forms the basis of a particular type of science—metaphysics, physics, and practical philosophy respectively—rather than an overall system that displays a deductive order: "all human science consists in making a clear distinction between those notions and attributing to each of them only the things that belong to them" (to Elisabeth, May 21, 1643, AT, vol. III, p. 665).

MEYER, LODEWIJK (1638-81). Lodewijk Meyer (or Meijer) was born in Amsterdam, the son of a Lutheran family. After medical studies in Leiden, where he graduated in 1660, he apparently never settled in a practice but returned to Amsterdam, where he played an important role in the cultural and literary life of the city (he was one of the directors of the theater). Apart from his role as an editor of Baruch Spinoza's works (he edited Spinoza's "geometrical" version of Descartes's *Principles* and was one of the editors of Spinoza's *Posthumous Works*), his main claim to fame, other than a Dutch dictionary, is his book on philosophy as an interpreter of Scripture (*Philosophia S. Scripturae Interpres*, 1666), which caused much controversy. In his book Meyer develops the claim that all interpretation is impossible or in any case uncertain because the author is free to connect any idea with any word. Still, if a particular book contains the truth and nothing but the truth, like Holy Scripture, we could use our knowledge of truth as a means to interpret that work. Moreover, Descartes's method, which consists in linking truth and certainty, makes it possible to know the truth with certainty. Accordingly, we can use the philosophy of Descartes to test any interpretation of Scripture.

That Meyer meant his book as a provocation becomes particularly clear in the "epilogue" where he shows that theology (knowledge as the result of an interpretation of Scripture) is impossible in any case. For not only can we interpret a text only to the extent that we already have the relevant ideas (so no interpretation will give us ideas we did not yet have), knowledge is the fruit of a reflection on ideas anyway (so interpretation as such never amounts to knowledge). Meyer also explicitly undermines the Reformed principle that Scripture is absolutely clear and that to interpret Scripture we need nothing but Scripture—indeed he shows not only that "clear" is always a relative term (something is clear for this or that), but also that if truth is claimed for a text it is impossible to understand it without making an appeal to natural reason. Finally, he undermines the delicate compromise worked out by Cartesian theologians like Christoph Wittich by refuting their claim that theology and philosophy deal with two different types of truth that can be known independently from each other.

MIND. Descartes took mind (Latin *mens*, French *esprit*) to be "thinking substance." He argued that this substance is distinct from **body**, or "extended substance." This understanding contrasts with the **Aristotelian** account of the **soul** (Latin *anima*, Greek *psukhe*) in the work of the **scholastics**, in which the soul is the **principle** not only of the intellectual powers of humans, but also of the sensitive powers that humans share with **animals** and the vegetative powers that humans and animals share with all living things. There was a consensus among the scholastics that all souls are "substantially united" to the bodies they vivify but that human souls are also immaterial and incorruptible since they have intellectual powers that—unlike the powers of vegetation and sensation—do not require bodily organs for their operation. Descartes claimed that he could explain vegetative and sensitive powers of bodies entirely in terms of **extension** and its modifications. It was only the **thought** revealed by reflection on the self in the *cogito* that required a principle distinct from extension. Even so, he did concede to the scholastics that the human soul is united with its body to form a "single thing." Moreover, he agreed with the scholastics that the human **intellect** can operate independently of the body. However, he insisted that **sensations** are not alterations of bodily sense organs, as the scholastics held, but rather modes of thought that can exist only in a thinking thing, albeit a thinking thing united to a body. *See also* DUALISM; IMAGINATION; IMMORTALITY; UNION OF MIND AND BODY; WILL.

MIND AND BODY. *See* DUALISM.

MIND-BODY UNION. *See* UNION OF MIND AND BODY.

MIRACLES. A traditional view in Christian **theology** is that **God** has the power to bring about effects in **nature** that go beyond the powers he has given to creatures (e.g., changing water into wine). In early modern thought, such a view was transformed into the position that God can produce effects that do not follow from **laws of nature**. Descartes insisted that the laws of **motion** follow directly from God's immutability. However, his reluctance to discuss theological matters explains his lack of an account of God's responsibility for deviations from those laws. Among the later Cartesians, the most radical view concerning miracles was held by **Baruch Spinoza**, who argued in his *Tractatus Theologico-Politicus* against the possibility of any miraculous deviations from natural laws. Most other Cartesians openly accepted the possibility of the miraculous, though they gave different accounts of its nature. The French Cartesian **Nicolas Malebranche** defended the **occasionalist** view that God produces natural effects through "general volitions," but that he occasionally produces miraculous effects through "particular volitions." Malebranche's Cartesian critic **Antoine Arnauld** protested that God governs everything by means of particular volitions, and that miracles are merely those events that derive from particular volitions that are not lawlike. Subsequent to this dispute between Malebranche and Arnauld, the French Cartesian **Pierre-Sylvain Régis** proposed in his 1704 *Usage de la raison et de la foy* that the "order of nature," which we understand through **reason**, is wholly distinct from the "order of grace," which we understand through **faith**. Régis held that though everything is governed by laws in the order of nature, miraculous exceptions to these laws are possible in the order of grace.

MODE. Aristotelian metaphysics draws a fundamental distinction between **substance** and mode, with substances being independently existing particulars and modes being dependent entities that must "inhere" in a substance. On this view, the individual Socrates is a substance, but his properties of being bald, snub-nosed, or wise are modes that cannot exist without a substance in which they inhere. Thus conceived, modes are qualifications of substances, or determinate ways in which a substance can exist. Descartes took over the terminology of substance and mode, but interpreted it in a very different manner than his predecessors. Material substances, or **bodies**, are simply **extension**, and the only modes of bodies are the various **shapes** and **motions** that extended things can exemplify—all other properties such as **color** or temperature are to be accounted for in terms of these modes of extension. Likewise, **minds** are essentially thinking substances, and the modes of mind are simply the **thoughts** that can be present in a mind.

MONTAIGNE, MICHEL DE (1533–92). Montaigne was a skeptic and essayist. He studied law at Bordeaux, becoming counselor to the Parlement of Bordeaux. His interest in skepticism began in 1576 after reading Sextus Empiricus. He published two books of *Essais* in 1580, a third book in 1588 along with additions to the first two books, and final additions (posthumously) in 1595. Descartes must have read the *Essais* early on, perhaps before leaving college. His initial writings and the *Discourse on Method* are full of allusions to Montaigne's themes. However, the only explicit reference to Montaigne by Descartes is a criticism of his views on **animals**, especially the view that there is more difference between individual men than between men and animals. Descartes countered: "there has never been found any beast so perfect that it used some sign to make other animals understand something that had no relation at all to its **passions**. And there is no man so imperfect that he does not do this" (AT, vol. IV, p. 575).

MORE, HENRY (1614–87). English philosopher, one of the central figures in the movement now known as the Cambridge Platonists. Born in Grantham, Lincolnshire, More's early education was at Eton College and he entered Christ's College, Cambridge, in 1631. After taking the M.A. in 1639 More was elected to a fellowship in 1641 and spent the rest of his life as a fellow and tutor at Christ's College. More's philosophy was deeply influenced by his **theological** views, which stressed the role of **reason** in matters of religion. He also embraced a fundamentally Platonistic epistemology, holding that the rational **soul** could apprehend **truth** by virtue of its innate capacities to grasp reality.

His earliest writings were philosophical poems celebrating Platonic themes, but a developing interest in contemporary science led More to seek connections between the new **natural philosophy** and Platonism. His 1646 poem *Democritus Platonissans* portrays Descartes as an **atomist** whose philosophy incorporates fundamental insights from Plato. Recognizing that the Aristotelian natural philosophy had fallen into disrepute among the learned, More proclaimed the virtues of the Cartesian philosophy, and particularly Descartes's natural philosophy, even to the point of teaching it to his students at Cambridge and advocating its incorporation into the university curriculum generally. Although More was convinced that Descartes's system offered the most satisfactory explanation of most phenomena in the physical world he was interested in keeping **mechanism** in its place because he was convinced that a full account of the world must make recourse to active "spiritual" principles that go beyond mere mechanism.

In 1648 More entered into **correspondence** with Descartes, announcing in his first letter that "all the masters of the secrets of **nature** who have ever been or are now appear as mere dwarves or pygmies in comparison with you," and celebrating the "Cartesian light" that had dispelled the darkness of earlier philosophy (AT, vol. V, p. 237). For all his manifest enthusiasm for the Cartesian system, More hoped to persuade Descartes that on particular points it required modification, and his four letters to Descartes contain several trenchant observations and objections. The most important of these was his objection that **extension** cannot constitute the essence of corporeal **substance**, but should also be attributed to incorporeal substances. More proposed that the true distinction between soul and **body** lies in the fact that spiritual substances are penetrable but indivisible, while body is impenetrable but **divisible**. In More's view, this explains how **God** acts on the created universe, as well as accounting for **mind-body** interaction. More also contested other of Descartes's **principles**, including his rejection of the **vacuum**, his account of the communication of **motion**, his denial of **animal** souls, and his rejection of **final causes**.

More failed to persuade Descartes on these points of disagreement and eventually adopted a hostile attitude toward Cartesian **metaphysics**. He accepted the general outlines of the mechanical philosophy, but condemned Descartes as a nullibist, or one who denies that spiritual substances have spatial location and is therefore incapable of explaining how they can act in the world. More's repudiation of Cartesianism is developed in greatest detail in his 1671 *Enchiridion Metaphysicum*, where he caricatures Descartes as a dogmatist who steadfastly refuses to modify his natural philosophy even in the face of phenomena his system fails to account for.

MORIN, JEAN-BAPTISTE (1583–1656). Morin was a French physician and astrologer, a professor of **mathematics** at the Collège de France (1629–56). Early on he undertook a trip to Hungary and Transylvania to inspect the mines located there. On the basis of his experiences, he wrote a short treatise, *Nova Mundi sublunaris anatomia* (1619), in which he argued for a new theory of the earth's anatomy, dividing it into three regions, not unlike the three regions into which **Aristotelian natural philosophy** divided the air. In 1623 he published *Astrologicarum domorum cabala detecta*, an argument for the 12 houses of the Zodiac fashioned largely on Cabalistic and numerological grounds; he also made a name for himself with a correct astrological prediction of a former patron's fall from power and influence. In late 1624 he distributed a pamphlet defending Aristotle against the theses of **Etienne de Clave** and his fellow **atomists** and **alchemists**. He was also on Aristotle's side when he attacked **Galileo Galilei**'s opinion on the **motion of the earth** (*De Telluris motu*, 1631). This required Morin to publish additional defenses of the immobility of the earth (*Responsio pro Telluris quiete*, 1634). He became involved in further polemics when he published his solution to the problem of determining longitude, a solution rejected by a commission composed of Etienne Pascal, **Claude Mydorge, Jean de Beaugrand**, and others. He also wrote circulars attacking **Pierre Gassendi's** atomism. His main work was *Astrologia Gallica* (1661), though he was also known for a short treatise on **God**, *Quod Deus sit* (1635), republished in an expanded version (*De vera cognitione Dei*, 1655). *Quod Deus sit* consisted of a **proof for the existence of God** given in a geometric presentation, using definitions, axioms, and theorems.

Descartes knew Morin through his works on the immobility of the Earth and determination of longitude. The two exchanged letters early on. Descartes also sent a copy of his *Discourse on Method* to Morin. This precipitated another exchange of letters. Morin sent some criticisms to Descartes about astronomy and his theory of **light**. Descartes replied and Morin replied as well, but Descartes cut off the exchange, seeing little profit in continuing the discussion. Descartes also read *Quod Deus sit* when **Marin Mersenne** sent it to him for his opinion. The project of establishing God's existence using the kind of self-evident reasoning characteristic of **geometry** clearly appealed to Descartes, but he indicated his disappointment with Morin's work in a letter to Mersenne written shortly before the publication of the *Meditations*: "Mr. Morin's main fault is that he always discusses the **infinite** as if he had completely mastered it and could comprehend its properties. This is an almost universal fault I have tried carefully to avoid. I have never written about the infinite except to submit myself to it and not to determine what it is or is not. . . . Right up to the end, everything he says is very far from the geometrical self-evidence and **certainty** he seemed to promise at the beginning" (AT, vol. III, pp. 293–94).

MOTION. Motion (*motus*) is, in the vocabulary of **Aristotelian** philosophy, the general term for change, especially natural change. Motion so understood can occur in four of the Aristotelian **categories: substance, quantity, quality,** and **place.** To these correspond four kinds of motion: generation (and corruption), augmentation (and diminution), alteration, and locomotion. Generation is the production of new substances (not *ex nihilo*, but from an underlying **matter**). Augmentation (which was, in the case of living things, carefully distinguished from mere *accretion* of parts) is increase of **quantity** or size. Alteration is the replacement of a quality by another contrary to it: heating, for example, is the replacement of coldness by hotness (or of a lower by a higher degree of heat). Local motion is change of place in the Aristotelian sense—the removal of a body from those immediately surrounding it, the inward surface of which defines the place of a **body.**

Descartes, like many natural philosophers in his time, rejected all but local motion. But Descartes's definition of motion is not that of classical **mechanics.** Instead it retains many features of the Aristotelian.

In particular he defines motion in terms of a relation of a body to those contiguous with it: the relation of "separation" or "rupture." Motion is "a translation of one part of matter, or one body, from the vicinity of those bodies that immediately touch it and are regarded as being at rest, to the vicinity of others" (*Principles* II, art. 25). At every instant a body in motion shares its boundary with other bodies; at every instant it ceases to do with some and begins to do so with others.

Motion is thus *reciprocal*, because separation is a symmetric relation: if I separate from you, then you separate from me. But it is not clear that for Descartes motion is *relative* in the sense of classical mechanics. On the contrary, his laws of motion assign a special role to "rest"—the condition under which two parts of matter share a common boundary for some period of time, and are thus effectively *one* part. From the standpoint of classical mechanics that is an anomaly, as **Christiann Huygens** and **Isaac Newton** would argue, and it is not surprising that Descartes's "rules of collision" (*Principles* II, art. 46–52) yield results at variance with experience.

MYDORGE, CLAUDE (1585–1647). A French mathematician known principally for his work in the theory of conic sections, but also a contributor to **optics** and astronomy. Born into a wealthy family and trained for a career in law, Mydorge pursued his mathematical interests while also holding the position of *conseiller* at Chatelet and later the appointment as treasurer of the generalité of Amiens. The modest demands of these governmental appointments left ample time for scientific research, and Mydorge was active in the Parisian intellectual scene. He was appointed by Cardinal Richelieu in 1635 (along with Etienne Pascal, **Jean de Beaugrand**, and Pierre Hérigone) to a committee charged with evaluating **Jean-Baptiste Morin's** claimed solution to the problem of determining longitude by lunar observation. The result was a five-year dispute between Morin and the committee, which deemed the method impractical.

Mydorge befriended Descartes in 1625 and remained a close associate throughout his life, even spending large sums to procure lenses (in whose design he had assisted) for Descartes's optical research. Mydorge's 1631 *Prodromi Catopticorum et Dioptricorum sive Conicorum . . . libri duo* employed a relatively sophisticated treatment of conic sections applied to problems in optics and pure **mathematics**. Descartes mentioned it with some curiosity and concern for his own mathematical reputation with the remark that "they say M. Mydorge has put a solution to the problem of **Pappus** in his *Conics*; but those who, like me, have examined it a bit more closely, cannot easily be persuaded of this" (AT, vol. III, p. 256). It was left to Descartes to solve the Pappus problem in his *Geometry*, but the expanded 1639 version of Mydorge's treatise on conic sections was a standard source for mathematicians through the 18th century. His 1630 *Examen du Livre des Récreations Mathématiques* was a popular success, with several subsequent authors basing their collections of mathematical puzzles and diversions on it.

Always a faithful friend of Descartes, Mydorge served as an intermediary between him and **Pierre de Fermat** when the latter criticized the *Dioptrics* in 1637. In the ensuing mathematical dispute, Mydorge tried to play the role of peacemaker and eventually reconciled them. He also defended Descartes against the **Jesuits** and succeeded in keeping some propositions in Cartesian **natural philosophy** from being condemned. Mydorge was one of few who could disagree with Descartes without provoking a hostile reaction—as witnessed by Descartes's remark to **Marin Mersenne** that their difference of opinion in matters of vision was the result of their following "different principles," but he hoped that Mydorge would accept his view because "he has a mind too good not to come over to the side of truth" (AT, vol. I, p. 501).

– N –

NATURAL LIGHT. *See* DOUBT; INTUITION.

NATURAL PHILOSOPHY. In the early modern period, philosophy was not distinguished as sharply from the empirical sciences as it is today. In the **Aristotelian** tradition, natural philosophy included the study not only of local **motion**, but also of the generation and corruption of living things and even of theological issues relevant to an account of the material world. Descartes inherited this broader notion of natural philosophy, but sometimes suggested that it needs to be revised in two important ways. First, he tried at times to purge natural philosophy of the study of topics that belong to the domain of **theology** (but see **transubstantiation**). Second, he sometimes spoke as if natural philosophy is reducible to physics and physics, in turn, to **mathematics**. This departure from Aristotelian orthodoxy is explained by Descartes's view that all material change is due to local motion and that matter itself is identical to **extension**. However, in an interview with **Frans Burman** he was reported as holding that though the object of mathematics is a "true and real entity," the object of physics is a real being that is "something specifically existing" (AT, vol. V, p. 160). In the preface to the French translation of the *Principles*, moreover, Descartes indicated that natural philosophy includes not only physics, but also the three sciences that derive from physics, namely, medicine, **mechanics**, and morals.

NATURE. In the Sixth Meditation, Descartes held that "nature considered in its general aspect" is nothing other than "**God** himself or the ordered system of created things established by God" (AT, vol. VII, p. 80). In speaking of created things, he further distinguished in this text between nature defined in terms of certain purposes, which is merely a "label that depends on my thought" and that is "quite extraneous to the things to which it is applied," and nature defined in terms of **laws** of nature, which is "really to be found in the things themselves." Thus, a badly made clock runs contrary to nature understood in the first sense, but is perfectly in accord with nature understood in the second sense (AT, vol. VII, pp. 84–85). Here, Descartes was rejecting the **Aristotelian** view that the natures of material objects are determined by the teleological ends that derive from the **forms** of those objects. In his view, such natures were to be explicated rather in entirely **mechanistic** terms.

In the early *The World*, Descartes also noted that he used the term nature to denote not "some goddess or other sort of imaginary power," but rather "**matter** itself, insofar as I am considering it taken together with all the **qualities** I have attributed to it, and under the condition that God continues to conserve it in the same way that he has created it" (AT, vol. XI, p. 37). The suggestion here seems to be that God brings about effects in the material world by means of his continual **conservation** of matter. However, Descartes showed some sympathy for the Aristotelian view that God produces such effects by means of his concurrence with actions in secondary **causes** that are determined by their natures. In contrast, **Nicolas Malebranche** protested that the view that bodies have causal powers deriving from their natures constitutes "the most dangerous error of the philosophy of the ancients." The error is dangerous since it attributes to creatures a power that should be reserved for God alone. Malebranche offered the **occasionalist** alternative that bodily events serve merely as passive "occasional causes" that prompt God to produce effects by means of his efficacious will.

NEWTON, ISAAC (1642–1727). Newton was the foremost mathematician-scientist of the late 17th century. He attended Trinity College, Cambridge, 1661–64, receiving his B.A. in 1665. In 1669 he succeeded Isaac Barrow as Lucasian Professor of Mathematics at Cambridge. He was elected to the Royal Society in 1672 and became its President in 1703. He was knighted in 1705.

Newton's initial interest was in **mathematics**, which he taught himself in 1664, in part by reading Descartes's *Geometry*; he then undertook intensive mathematical research in 1665–66, culminating in an unpublished treatise on the calculus. His exposure to **mechanical** philosophy also dates from this period: he read the works of Descartes, **Pierre Gassendi**, and **Robert Boyle**, and composed a notebook, *Quaestiones quaedam philosophicae* (1664) dealing with issues such as **motion**, **gravity, and light**. Newton became a critic of Descartes's **natural philosophy**. His principal work, *Principia mathematica philosophiae naturalis* ("Mathematical Principles of Natural Philosophy," 1687, an expansion of his unpublished 1684 treatise *De motu*), can be considered as an argument against Descartes's cosmology, namely, that the Cartesian **vortices** of *Principles*, Part III, cannot account for **Johannes Kepler's** three laws of astronomy.

In the *Principia*, Newton proposed his law of universal gravitation, in accordance with which every **body** attracts every other body with a **force** directly proportional to the masses and inversely proportional to the square of the distances. In this way, he offered an explanation for why the planets move about the sun in the particular path they follow, according to Kepler's laws. But, for mechanists such as **Gottfried Wilhelm Leibniz**, Newton's explanation was not sufficient. Leibniz thought that an account of what causes the gravitational pull between the sun and Earth was also needed; and for the account to be intelligible, he believed that it should be given in terms of the communication of motion from one body to another body by collision. He attempted a Cartesian-style mechanical explanation of the phenomena, that is, a vortex theory of planetary motion, the planets being carried around the sun in a huge whirlpool of subtle matter, using two vortices to account for the astronomical observations upon which Newton based his theory.

NOËL, ETIENNE (1581–1659). A French **Jesuit** and teacher of philosophy and **theology** at Descartes's old school at **La Flèche**. Noël taught at La Flèche when Descartes was a student and, 20 years later, he was the rector of La Flèche to whom Descartes sent copies of the *Discourse on Method*. He published some physical treatises in which he deviated from strict **Aristotelianism** and he disputed the conclusions of **Blaise Pascal's** experiments concerning the void.

NOTES AGAINST A PROGRAM (NOTAE IN PROGRAMMA QUODDAM). The *Notes Against a Program* must be explained against the background of Descartes's relation with **Henricus Regius**. Regius, who had earned his **Utrecht** chair in medicine by giving very successful private lessons in philosophy, thought of publishing his views as early as 1641. Descartes, who was obviously less keen on having someone publish ideas he considered his own, dissuaded him from doing so. But by

1645, after Descartes had published the *Meditations* (1641) and the *Principles* (1644), Regius wanted to publish a book, called *Foundations of Physics* (*Fundamenta physices*, 1646), containing a synthesis of his philosophical views. When he submitted the manuscript to Descartes, Descartes was particularly unhappy with the last chapter, which contains not only ideas on the relation between **body** and **mind** (the nature of which Regius finds uncertain), but also a few remarks on **innate ideas** (which he denies) and the **knowledge of God** (whose **idea** he derives from the idea we have of human perfection). Descartes urged his friend to withdraw the book or at least to suppress a few passages (which Regius did eventually). For Descartes this was not enough. He publicly dissociated himself from his former friend in the preface to the French edition of the *Principles* (1647), even to the point of accusing him of plagiarism.

That in turn seems to have been the reason why one of Regius's students, Petrus Wassenaer (d. 1680), undoubtedly with the cooperation of Regius himself, submitted for disputation a series of corollaries to the last chapter of Regius's book, including those Regius had suppressed at the request of Descartes. The rector of the university canceled the disputation with the added reason that it was dedicated to a Remonstrant minister. Wassenaer and Regius then took the unusual step of having the corollaries printed as a broadsheet (a *programma*) and it is in that form that they reached Descartes. Descartes replied to them in a detailed fashion, insisting on the dangerous implications of these views, but he was in doubt whether he should publish his response. Others took the trouble—presumably **Adriaan Heereboord**, who added a preface of his own in which he dealt with his adversaries, the theologian **Jacobus Revius** and the philosopher Adam Steuart (1591–1654); it was published at the beginning of 1648. Although the *Notae* do not break new ground, they are interesting in that they contain a clear formulation of Descartes's views on innate ideas, the relation between **reason** and **faith**, and a reaffirmation of mind-body **dualism**.

– O –

OBJECTIONS AND REPLIES (OBJECTIONES ET RESPONSIONES, OBJECTIONS ET RÉPONSES). Although in a general way Descartes was not fond of discussion, if only because "the very fact that someone braces himself to attack the truth makes him less suited to perceive it" (*Second Replies*, AT, vol. VII, p. 157), he was not averse from it as long as he could control it. Thus he invites the readers of the *Discourse* "to take the trouble of sending their objections to the publisher," promising a reply, "so that readers can see both sides together and decide the truth all the more easily" (*Discourse* VI, AT, vol. VI, p. 75; see **Correspondence**). But originally the *Objections and Replies* added to the *Meditations* had a different purpose, namely, to obtain a certificate of religious orthodoxy. Descartes wanted to submit the text of the *Meditations* to the 20 or 30 best theologians in France to see what they thought of it. Later **Marin Mersenne** was instructed to submit it to "three or four" trusted theologians only. Their approval would be enough to dedicate the book to the **Sorbonne**, "in order to ask them to be my protectors in the cause of God" (September 30, 1640, AT, vol. III, pp. 183–85). To start the ball rolling the Dutch priest **Johannes Caterus** was persuaded to write the *First Objections*, which together with Descartes's replies and the manuscript of the *Meditations* were sent to France to be circulated among possible objectors; Descartes left it to Mersenne to organize this, telling him that he would be "glad if people make as many objections as possible and the strongest they can find" (January 28, 1641, AT, vol. III, p. 297).

But Mersenne also seems to have shown the manuscript to philosophers and suggested that they too could submit objections. Mersenne himself is likely the author of the *Second Set of Objections*, although he tells Descartes they are written by "various theologians" (to Mersenne, December 24, 1640, AT, vol. III, p. 265). They cover a wide range of issues, such as the **Cartesian circle** and the **immortality** of the **soul**, and contain a request (possibly inspired by **Jean-Baptiste Morin**) to reformulate the contents of the *Meditations* in a Euclidean manner (AT, vol. VII, p. 28). **Thomas Hobbes** wrote the *Third Set of Objections*, **Antoine Arnauld** the *Fourth*, and **Pierre Gassendi** the *Fifth*.

Hobbes and Gassendi reject Descartes's **dualism** as well as his conception of **reason**, insisting instead on the empirical basis of all our **ideas** and the dependence of the **mind** from the **body**. They also have little sympathy with Cartesian **doubt**, which they find exaggerated and at best a reheated version of old skeptical arguments; with the *cogito*, which they claim could as well be replaced by "I walk, therefore I am"; with the proof of the **existence of God**; etc. Descartes had little patience with these arguments and sometimes the tone of his replies was sharp and personal. He was much more satisfied with the objections of Arnauld, which he found "the best of all" because Arnauld had grasped the sense of the matter better than anyone. And, indeed, Arnauld concentrates on some of the main themes: the idea of God, relation of mind and body, Cartesian circle. He also raises the question of the **Eucharist**, which he claims requires a more traditional doctrine of substance and accidents. It gave Descartes the opportunity to present his own argument, much of which, for that matter, Mersenne found it wise to suppress. (It was restored in the Amsterdam edition of the *Meditations*.)

Mersenne also compiled the *Sixth Objections*, which in the Paris edition are the last. He added an "appendix" containing the argument of "a group of philosophers and geometers," which concentrates on three questions: 1) How can I be certain that I have a clear idea of the **soul**? 2) How do I know that this idea is wholly different from any other thing? 3) How do I know that this idea contains nothing of a corporeal **nature**? Descartes deplored the fact that there were no **Jesuits** among the contributors, feeling that their approval would carry much weight. Eventually a Jesuit, **Pierre Bourdin**, whom Descartes disliked for his criticism of the *Dioptrics*, sent a voluminous packet of objections. Descartes received them in January 1642, when Elzevier was already printing the second edition of the *Meditations*. They were printed, with Descartes's replies, in a second volume, as a kind of appendix. Since the printer was slow to complete the volume Descartes also added a letter to the provincial of the Jesuits in the Île de France, Father Jacques Dinet, in which he complains of Bourdin's methods and suggests that the order should dissociate from him. Although of unequal quality, the *Objections and Replies* are an important philosophical document; it often clarifies points that remain implicit or obscure in the *Meditations*. Eventually, the *Objections and Replies* were translated by **Claude Clerselier** and, together with the translation of the *Meditations* by the **Duc de Luynes**, published in Paris in 1647.

OBJECTIVE REALITY. *See* COSMOLOGICAL ARGUMENT.

OCCASIONALISM. In its strongest form, occasionalism is the position that **God** is the only true causal agent. This position is often portrayed in the textbooks as a response to the problem of **mind-body** interaction bequeathed to modern philosophy by Descartes. The problem is how two **substances** as distinct as mind and body are for Descartes can be understood to interact. The purported occasionalist solution is to appeal to God as a sort of *Deus ex machina* in order to explain the correspondence of mental and bodily states.

An initial problem with this common story is that occasionalism has a history that predates Descartes, extended back at least to the 11th-century Islamic theologian Algazali. In Algazali, moreover, the emphasis was not on the issue of mind-body interaction, but rather on the absolute power of God. This sort of emphasis was countered by Thomas Aquinas (see **Thomism**) and most of the later **scholastics**, who insisted that it is more consistent with God's goodness that he govern natural events by means of his concurrence with the action of creatures.

Some of Descartes's language is suggestive of scholastic concurrentism. However, he also spoke at times of "occasional" connections between mental and bodily events. Later Cartesians such as **Louis de la Forge** applied this same terminology to the case of connections among bodily states, and they indicated more explicitly than Descartes ever did that occasionalist relations among bodies are to be contrasted with true causal relations deriving from the exercise of power. In particular, La Forge drew on Descartes's own account of the **laws** of **motion** to conclude that changes in motion derive not from the bodies themselves but rather from God's creation and **conservation** of the material world.

The Cartesian **Nicolas Malebranche** borrowed the Cartesian argument that emphasizes the **nature** of divine conservation. However, he went beyond La Forge and other earlier Cartesian occasionalists by arguing that since true causal relations require necessary connections, and since such connections can obtain only between the volitions of an omnipotent being and their upshots, God, as the sole omnipotent being, is the only one who can be a true **cause**. Malebranche claimed that given this argument, there is no longer any force to the old scholastic position that God concurs with the actions of creatures. He also urged that scholastic concurrentism is best discarded since it favors the idolatrous conclusion in **Aristotle** that divine power is diffused throughout nature over the pious conclusion in **Augustine** that all creatures depend entirely on God.

ONTOLOGICAL ARGUMENT. Following Immanuel Kant, we refer to an argument for the existence of **God** as ontological when the existence of God is inferred from concepts alone, and **cosmological** when it is derived from experience. Saint Anselm of Canterbury's argument for the existence of God is typically considered the paradigm ontological argument and Saint Thomas Aquinas's Five Ways the standard model for cosmological arguments (see **Thomism**). Anselm asserts that, as soon as one understands God as that than which nothing greater can be conceived, one sees that God exists, not merely in our **mind**, but also in reality, because to conceive of that than which nothing greater can be conceived in our mind but not in reality would not be to conceive that than which nothing greater can be conceived (*Proslogion*, chap. 2). Aquinas rejected Anselm's argument in part because, according to him, we do not know the essence of God, therefore the proposition that God exists is not self-evident to us and we can deny that God is that than which nothing greater can be conceived. Aquinas proposed instead some arguments from effects such as from the existence of motion, efficient causation, possibility and necessity, gradation in things, and the governance of the world (*Summa theologiae*, I, q. 2, art. 1-2). **John**

Duns Scotus, who produced a hybrid argument, both cosmological and ontological, claimed that Anselm's argument "can be colored," that is, it should be adjusted as follows: "God is that which, having been thought without contradiction, a greater cannot be thought without contradiction" (*Opus Oxoniense*, I, dist. ii, q. 1 and 2).

Descartes would not have used the terminology of ontological and cosmological, but refers to his argument in the Fifth Meditation, which is similar to Anselm's, as an *a priori* proof and his arguments in the Third Meditation as *a posteriori*. Descartes's *a posteriori* arguments resemble Aquinas's proofs, with the principal difference being that, because of hyperbolic **doubt,** they cannot make use of the existence of the world, but are based simply on the existence of the self.

In the Fifth Meditation Descartes claims that "existence can no more be separated from God's essence than its having three angles equal to two right angles can be separated from the essence of a triangle, or than that the idea of a valley can be separated from the idea of a mountain. Thus it is no less contradictory to think of God (that is, a supremely perfect being) lacking existence (that is, lacking some perfection), than it is to think of a mountain without a valley" (AT, vol. VII, p. 66). Many of Descartes's contemporaries rejected this claim. Some of them, like **Johannes Caterus,** revived the kind of reasoning Aquinas used against Anselm. **Pierre Gassendi** claimed that ontological arguments improperly treat existence as a perfection, asserting in his *Fifth Set of Objections* to Descartes's *Meditations*: "you place existence among the divine perfections but do not place it among the perfections of a triangle or a mountain, though it could be said that in its own way it is just as much a perfection of each of these things. In fact, however, existence is not a perfection either in God or in anything else; it is that without which no perfections can be present" (AT, vol. VII, p. 323).

Still, the ontological argument was broadly accepted by Descartes's successors, such as **Baruch Spinoza** and **Gottfried Wilhelm Leibniz.** Leibniz knows and rejects Gassendi's objection that existence is not to be counted among the perfections. His defense of the ontological argument looks something like a revival of Scotus's "coloring" of Anselm's argument. He thinks that the proof Descartes gives is imperfect because we sometimes think about impossible things—for example, squaring the circle or the **motion** having the greatest speed—and even draw consequences about what would happen if they were given. These are grounds for being careful about the idea of the greatest of all beings, whether it might not contain a contradiction. We can understand the **nature** of motion and speed and what it is to be greatest, and not understand whether all those notions are compatible, whether there is a way of joining them and making them into an idea of the greatest speed of which motion is capable. Similarly, we can know what being is and what it is to be the greatest and most perfect, nevertheless not know whether there is not a hidden contradiction in joining all that together, that is, whether such a being is possible. Therefore, to prove that God exists, we would have to prove first that he is possible. Leibniz claims that he has such a proof: God's nature contains all simple forms taken absolutely and simple forms are compatible among themselves; God is therefore possible.

OPTICS. *See* DIOPTRICS.

ORATORIANS/ORATORY. A French religious society founded in 1611 by **Pierre de Bérulle.** By 1629, when Bérulle died, the Oratory maintained 44 flourishing houses. It also had established more than a dozen colleges, even though it did not set education as primary goal for itself.

French education during the first half of the 17th century, whether by seculars or regulars, was fairly similar. Students took four or five years of humanities (French, Latin, and Greek language and literature) succeeded by a year of rhetoric and the collegiate curriculum, that is, two years of philosophy. The latter was an **Aristotelian**-based program of **logic, ethics, physics,** and **metaphysics.** Oratorians followed the general pattern, differing somewhat from the **Jesuits** by conducting their teaching primarily in French. And they seem to have added courses in history and geography as early as the 1640s. In philosophy, like everyone else, they taught a broadly Aristotelian set of courses. Perhaps because of Bérulle's propensity for Platonic thought, the Oratory's Aristotelianism was slightly different from that of the Jesuits. The Jesuits officially leaned toward **Thomism,** though in practice they mixed their Thomism with other kinds of **scholastic** thought, especially **Scotism.** Given the textbooks published by two early Oratorians, William Chalmers and Jacques Fournenc, Oratorian teaching seems to have been more eclectic. Chalmers (or Camerarius, 1596–1678) published texts in logic and ethics, "following the thoughts of the Subtle Doctor," that is, **John Duns Scotus;** Fournenc (1609–69) published a synopsis of Aristotle's doctrine "with various explanations and illustrations from the thoughts of Plato." The Oratorians' propensity for "Platonism" seems to have made them ripe for accepting Cartesian philosophy during the second half of the 17th century. This led a noted Cartesian scholar to assert that "Of all the teaching orders, the one who embraced the new philosophy (Cartesianism) with the most zeal was the Oratory, and of all the Oratorian colleges none was more attached to Cartesianism than the College of **Angers.**" *See also* DUHAMEL, JEAN-BAPTISTE; GIBIEUF, GUILLAUME; LAMY, BERNARD.

ORDER. *See* METHOD.

– P –

PAIN (*DOLOR, DOULEUR*). For Descartes, pain is a feeling of the **soul** caused by the organs of touch, one of the external senses, which in no way resembles the bodily process corresponding to it, let alone the object that causes it. On a physiological level the difference with pleasure is one of degree: a pleasurable **sensation**, caused by stimulating a nerve, changes into pain if the pressure on the nerve becomes stronger. Indeed, "we may sometimes suffer pains with joy and receive titillating sensations that displease us" (*Passions* II, art. 94, AT, vol. XI, p. 399). The fact that the sensation of pain does not picture the object (nor the bodily process) turns it into the prototype of all sensation and perception. Indeed, pain is not in the **body**, but only in the **mind** or the understanding. Like hunger and thirst, however, and like the **passions**, pain has pragmatic significance: the feeling of pain "first produces in the soul the passion of sadness, then hatred of what causes pain, and finally the desire to get rid of it" (*Passions* II, art. 137, AT, vol. XI, p. 430; cf. *Meditations* VI, AT, vol. VII, p. 88). Accordingly, pain is a secondary response, situated between the purely physical process of bodily interaction and a **judgment**. Despite the fact, therefore, that "obscure judgments" usually made in relation to pain (for example, that the pain is "in our foot") are erroneous and based on the prejudices of childhood, they help us to survive in a hostile environment: "the proper purpose of sensory perceptions given by **nature** is simply to inform the mind of what is beneficial or harmful for the composite of which the mind is a part and to that extent they are sufficiently clear and distinct" (Meditation VI, AT, vol. VII, p. 83). Accordingly, **God** cannot be blamed for giving us pain and other sensations even if on a more theoretical level they are intrinsically false.

PAPPUS OF ALEXANDRIA (fl. 320 AD). The last of the great geometers of Greek antiquity. Pappus's *Mathematical Collection* incorporates a wide range of mathematical writings and was in many cases the sole means of transmission of ancient results to later ages. The *Collection* consisted of eight books, of which the first and large parts of the second are lost. Pappus's other writings include commentaries on Ptolemy's *Almagest* and Euclid's *Elements*, as well as works on astronomy and harmonics. The *Collection* gives a systematic treatment of the most significant works of classical Greek geometry, with commentary, suggested alterations, and original results. The work was evidently intended as a guide for a general education in mathematics, supplementing the original works on which it comments. One of the most influential parts of the *Collection* is the methodological preface to the seventh book, where Pappus sets out his account of the distinction between analysis and synthesis, as well as the distinction between linear, planar, and solid problems (i.e., problems solvable purely by constructions with compass and straightedge, problems requiring the section of a cone, and the remaining complex problems requiring curves too irregular to be constructed by such means).

Descartes was very familiar with Pappus's *Collection*, and he regarded the famous "line locus" problem from the seventh book as the true test of his *Geometry*. The first two cases of the general problem involve three and four lines and had been solved by ancient authors before Pappus. These can be stated as follows: given three lines, find the locus of points for which the product of the distances from two lines is the square of the distance of the third; given four lines, find the locus of points for which the product of the distances from any two lines is the product of the distance of the other two. The generalized version of the problem can then be stated thus: given any number of lines, find the locus of points p such that the lengths of the lines drawn from p to meet the given lines at a fixed angle satisfy the condition that the product of first m lines bears a constant ratio to the product of the remaining m lines (if the number of given lines is even) or the condition that the product of first m lines bears a constant ratio to the product of the remaining $m - 1$ lines (if the number of given lines is odd). Pappus left the problem unsolved for the case of more than four lines, but Descartes provided a solution for the general problem (AT, vol. VI, pp. 380–87). The key to Descartes's success in solving the problem is the representation of the sought locus as a curve defined in terms of equations in two unknowns x and y, which represent two of the intersecting lines that determine the locus. Working "analytically" from the assumption that the desired curve has been constructed, Descartes then used algebraic techniques to solve the equations defining the curve and thereby determine the construction of the line locus, regardless of how many lines are involved.

PARIS, UNIVERSITY OF. *See* SORBONNE.

PARTICLES. Cartesian physics tends to explain the sensible phenomena of nature by forming hypotheses about the shape, size, and characteristic motion of parts of matter (identified by Descartes with extension), parts that are typically too small for us to discern by our senses. Water, for example, consists of fine, smooth, spindle-shaped particles or "corpuscles" (*Meteors* I, AT, vol. VI, p. 233). When the **subtle matter** between those particles moves quickly, it separates and flexes them, so that they slide easily past one another like eels, and the mass of water particles becomes liquid and feels wet. When, on the other hand, the subtle matter moves more slowly, and lacks the force to separate the particles of water, they tend to fall together and join in a confused mass. Thus Descartes explains how water becomes ice and vice versa. Hypotheses about corpuscles can be supported only *a posteriori*, by inference from the supposed effects of this or that configuration; in his more optimistic moments, however, Descartes hoped, like certain physicists today, to derive all the varieties of particle, and to explain thereby all the phenomena of nature, *a priori* from the nature of matter and the supposition that **God** endowed matter with a certain **quantity** of motion according to laws demonstrable from the divine attribute of immutability.

Corpuscularianism, which did have precedents in certain parts of **Aristotelian natural philosophy** (e.g., in commentaries on Aristotle's *Generation and Corruption*) and in **atomism**, proved to be very successful in the 17th century; it was popularized by Cartesians like **Nicolas Malebranche, Pierre-Sylvain Régis**, and **Jacques Rohault**, as well as by followers of **Pierre Gassendi** like **Walter Charleton** and **François Bernier**. That genuine explanations of natural phenomena should be based on hypotheses about corpuscles and their motions, and not on the "forms and qualities" of the **scholastics**, was accepted by all except the most conservative proponents of Aristotelianism.

PASCAL, BLAISE (1623–62). French mathematician, natural philosopher, and theologian. Born at Clermont-Ferrand, Blaise Pascal was the son of Etienne Pascal, a wealthy advocate at the court of Clermont whose eclectic scientific interests brought him into contact with Parisian natural philosophers and mathematicians. Pascal's mother died in 1626 and in 1632 Etienne moved the family to Paris. Etienne had unorthodox views on education and supervised the education of his children at home. Legend has it that Blaise was forbidden to study **mathematics** before the age of 15 and all mathematics texts were removed from the house. This ban on mathematics is supposed to have piqued Pascal's curiosity and inspired him to begin teaching himself the subject at the age of 12. When Etienne discovered that his son had independently proved that the sum of the angles of a triangle are two right angles, he relented and allowed Blaise a copy of Euclid. Whatever the particulars of his mathematical education, Pascal quickly showed himself to be a prodigy, and at the age of 14 he started to accompany his father to the regular meetings supervised by **Marin Mersenne** at the Minim convent in Paris, where subjects in mathematics and philosophy were discussed by Mersenne's many associates. Through Mersenne Pascal came into contact with the mathematicians **Girard Desargues, Gilles Personne de Roberval, Claude Mydorge,** and **Jean de Beaugrand**. Pascal was particularly impressed with the projective **geometry** of Desargues, and at the age of 16 established a reputation for himself among Parisian mathematicians by presenting a collection of theorems in projective geometry to Mersenne's group.

In December 1639 Etienne Pascal was appointed as a tax collector for Upper Normandy; to take up the position he relocated his family to Rouen, shortly after the February 1640 publication of Blaise's *Traité des sections coniques* ("Treatise on Conic Sections"). To assist his father with his work collecting taxes, Pascal invented one of the first digital calculators. The device, called a Pascaline, allows the addition or subtraction of two numbers of up to six digits. Pascal developed it over the course of three years from 1642–45 and put it into production, but demand was so negligible that only about 50 units were ever produced. In 1646 Etienne Pascal injured his leg and during his recuperation was looked after by two brothers by the name of Deschamps from a **Jansenist** community outside Rouen. They had a profound effect on the young Pascal and won him over to Jansenism.

In the same year Pascal had learned from Mersenne of Evangelista Torricelli's experiments with the mercury barometer, and with his friend Pierre Petit he undertook a series of experiments on atmospheric pressure and the possibility of a **void**. The successful replication of Torricelli's results, together with some new experimental evidence led to his 1647 pamphlet *Expériences nouvelles touchant le vide* ("New Experiments Concerning the Void").

Always a man of poor health, Pascal returned to Paris early in 1647 on the advice of doctors to seek medical care. He resumed his close contacts with Parisian natural philosophers and mathematicians, with most of his work directed toward problems in hydrostatics and pneumatics. He interpreted the Torricellian barometer as giving evidence for the reality of the void—when a vertical glass tube, closed at the top but open at the bottom, is filled with mercury, inverted, and placed in a dish containing mercury, the column drops partially down the tube, leaving a space at the top. Pascal took this "Torricellian space" to be empty of "all matter known in **nature** and which falls under the senses" (*Expériences nouvelles touchant le vide*, Abrégé of part II, proposition 8). This interpretation of the experiment obviously lent support to the possibility of genuinely empty **space**.

Descartes visited Pascal in September 1647 and discussed the issue of the void at some length in the company of Roberval and others. There were two somewhat acrimonious meetings, an account of which is preserved in a letter from Pascal's sister Jacqueline (AT, vol. V, pp. 72–73). Because he regarded the void as metaphysically impossible, Descartes postulated that "subtle matter" filled the open space at the top of the mercury tube, and in a letter to **Christiaan Huygens** in December 1647 Descartes spoke condescendingly of Pascal as a young man who it seems "has a bit too much vacuum in his head, and is too rash [*se haste beaucoup*]" (AT, vol. V, p. 653). In 1648 Pascal arranged for an experiment designed to show that the height of the mercury column was determined by atmospheric pressure. He had his brother-in-law, Florin Périer, carry a Torricellian barometer up the Puy-de-Dôme Mountain near Clermont. As Pascal had predicted, the mercury column dropped as the device was moved further up the mountainside. Descartes may have given Pascal the idea for this experiment. In a letter to Mersenne in December 1647 (some eight months before the actual experiment) Descartes says "I told M. Pascal to do an experiment to see whether mercury would rise as high when it was at the top of a mountain as when it was at the bottom; I do not know if he has done so" (AT, vol. V, p. 99). In a letter to Pierre de Carcavi nearly a year after the experiment Descartes declared "it was I who had asked him to try the experiment two years ago, and I had assured him of its success, since it agrees completely with my **principles**" (AT, vol. V, p. 391).

Pascal continued to pursue his scientific researches through the early 1650s, composing treatises on hydrostatics and the theory of equilibria, as well as pursuing investigations in pure mathematics. In 1654 he entered into correspondence with **Pierre de Fermat** on questions in the theory of probability. This resulted in fundamental results that are now regarded as the foundation of the subject. However, Pascal's interests had by this time shifted decisively toward **theology**; his father's death in 1651 seems to have prompted considerable soul-searching on Pascal's part and he began to look upon scientific inquiries as unworthy exercises in pride and ambition. During the night of November 23, 1654, his doubts were settled by a sort of vision. His Jansenist fervor was redoubled by the experience and he subsequently practiced a severe asceticism, renounced learning, and traded the world of scientific and mathematical research for the theological matters discussed at Port-Royal, the center of Parisian Jansenism. In 1656 he undertook the public defense of Jansenism against the **Jesuits** by publishing a collection of *Lettres provincales* ("Provincial Letters"). The occasion of the letters was the refusal by the curé of Saint Sulpice to absolve the Duc de Liancourt, a friend of Port Royal. **Antoine Arnauld,** the leader of French Jansenists, wrote two letters on the matter that were censured by the **Sorbonne.** Seeking to appeal to the public, Arnauld submitted a pamphlet on the case to his friends at Port-Royal, but they found it overly dry and theological. He then said to Pascal: "You, who are young, must do something." The next day (January 23, 1656) Pascal brought out the first of 19 letters criticizing Jesuit doctrines and practices, with the full collection being published the next year and condemned as heretical in 1660.

Pascal's most famous work is the *Pensées* ("Thoughts"), a collection of aphorisms devoted to Christian apologetics. It remained unfinished at his death, but a partial edition of the surviving manuscript was published by Port-Royal in 1670. The most celebrated part of the *Pensées* is the "wager" argument, which makes a prudential (as opposed to evidential) argument for belief in **God**: the cost of belief is small, the potential benefit of everlasting life is incalculably great, while the potential loss involved in disbelief is also incalculably great; thus, regardless of the likelihood of God's existence, it makes sense to believe.

In 1658 Pascal briefly resumed mathematical research. Lying awake at night unable to sleep for pain, he considered the properties of the cycloid (the curve generated by the motion of a point on the periphery of a circle as it rolls across a plane). He solved the problem of determining the area and the center of gravity of any segment of the curve, as well as finding the volume and surface area of its solid of revolution. In an uncharacteristic display of pride in his achievements, he publicly posed these as a set of challenge problems, promising a prize for the best solution and naming Roberval as one of the judges. His death at the age of 39 deprived the French intellectual world of one of its most creative and original minds.

PASSIONS. Descartes's most explicit and detailed discussion of the passions is, of course, in the *Passions of the Soul* (1649). There he starts from a somewhat verbal definition that relies on the literal meaning of the word passion. "Passion" comes from the Latin *pati*, that is, "to suffer," "to undergo (passively)." A passion represents the passive side of a process of interaction between an agent and a patient: "whatever happens or occurs is called by philosophers a passion with respect to the subject to which it happens and an action with respect to that which makes it happen, so even though the patient and the agent are often quite different, the action and the passion are always one and the same thing, which goes by those two names because of the two different subjects to which it can be referred" (*Passions* I, art. 1, AT, vol. XI, p. 328). Now given the fact that the agent working immediately on the

soul is the **body** to which it is intimately connected, one must presume that whatever is a passion in the soul is an action of the body. More particularly the passions can be defined as "perceptions or feelings, or emotions of the soul particularly referred to the soul, which are caused, entertained and reinforced by some movement of the [animal] spirits" (*Passions* I, art. 27, AT, vol. XI, p. 349). They are "perceptions" in the sense that they are not autonomous actions of the soul (like volitions). What distinguishes them from other perceptions such as **thoughts** or **ideas** is that, being conditioned by the close **union of body and mind**, they are intrinsically obscure and confused. They are "referred to the soul" to distinguish them from sensations of external objects (like smells) as well as from bodily **sensations** (like hunger). And they are caused, entertained, and reinforced by the **animal spirits** to distinguish them from acts of the **will**, which originate in the soul itself (*Passions* I, art. 29, AT, vol. XI, p. 350). So one could say that a passion is the immediate perception of a bodily process which refers neither to the body nor to the external world, but to the soul, and on which the soul has no immediate influence.

Descartes's essential point with respect to the passions is that they can be brought under control, not simply by the will (which has no direct influence on this type of bodily process), but only by contrary passions. This is possible in turn because by giving myself a thought I can cause myself to have a particular passion. So if I am subject to a passion A all I have to do to get rid of A is to produce in myself a thought which I know causes me to have a passion B contrary to A. The fact that insofar as they are physical phenomena passions mainly affect the **circulation** and the quality of the **blood** explains why passions can cause all sorts of diseases. Thus Descartes claims: "the most common cause of a slow fever is sadness" (to **Elisabeth**, May 18, 1645, AT, vol. IV, p. 201); sadness corresponds to an abnormal condition of the body caused by coarse blood particles coming from the spleen, which, although they "burn" less quickly, produce a greater heat.

But the same **mechanism** makes it possible to cure almost every disease. If sadness causes fever all one has to do to get rid of fever is to give oneself thoughts connected with **joy**. Insofar as the passions are physiological processes they are, initially at least, "good." They are part of the system of purely natural reactions by which an **automaton** either reacts to a threatening situation (sadness, anger, **hatred**, etc.), or tries to persevere in a salutary condition (joy, **love**, etc.); indeed, seen in this way the passions are also found in **animals**. But whereas in animals good and bad correspond to what is good and bad with respect to the survival of the organism, in humans good and bad correspond to what is good and bad with respect to a psychophysical whole. Accordingly, it is

not only what is actually good or bad for our body but also what we believe to be good or bad for us that causes us to have the passions of joy
and sadness. Accordingly, the bodily substrate of a passion can be prolonged beyond what is good physically—hence fevers and diseases and
hence also the need to control passions such as hatred, envy, etc. Descartes's theory of the passions was among the most influential Cartesian
theories of the 17th century, with ramifications into moral and political
philosophy, theory of action, aesthetics, and even epistemology.

**PASSIONS OF THE SOUL (*PASSIONS DE L'AME, PASSIONES
ANIMAE*).** Although Descartes already summarily dealt with the **passions** in his *Treatise on Man* and, very briefly, in his correspondence
with **Henricus Regius**, his correspondence with **Princess Elisabeth**
provided an excellent opportunity to revert to the subject. A more precise occasion seems to have been a request of Elisabeth to Descartes for
an exact definition of the passions—something that, according to Descartes, is possible only on the basis of a thorough examination of them.
At that point Descartes, apparently, has already tried to provide an explanation of each of the passions in particular, but in attempting to do
this he found it difficult to make an **enumeration**, that is, a systematic
classification, of the passions. Although this turns out to take much
time, a first version of the work is finished at the beginning of 1646 and
sent to Elisabeth with a request for commentary. In this early version
the physiological part seems to have been less detailed than in the definitive version, partly because Elisabeth already knew Descartes's
"Treatise on Animals" (that is, what we know as the *Treatise on Man*),
and partly because, to provide an exact picture, Descartes wants a full
explanation of the formation of all bodily parts, which as yet cannot be
given. At that time Descartes has no plans to publish this new work,
being disappointed about the small number of people who are interested
in his work. Still, in 1647, Descartes sends to **Pierre-Hector Chanut**
not only several letters in which he has examined the passions, but also
"a small treatise on the passions," to be communicated to **Queen Christina** (November 20, 1647, AT, vol. V, p. 87). From a letter to Elisabeth
it emerges that this made it necessary for Descartes to make a neat copy
of the work, of which he has kept only "a confused draft" (November
20, 1647, AT, vol. V, p. 91). But, apparently, **Claude Clerselier**, too,
receives a copy and sends back comments. The definitive text is written
only at the beginning of 1649. Descartes tells Clerselier in April 1649
that the book will consist of three parts: the first on the passions in general and on the relation of **body** and **mind**, the second on the six
"primitive passions," and the third on all the other passions (April 23,
1649, AT, vol. V, p. 354). The friend who asked Descartes to send his

treatise to Queen Christina (Chanut) is already preparing its publication with a "preface in his own style" (June 1649, AT, vol. V, p. 363).

The book was finally published in November 1649, when Descartes was already in Sweden. The preface consists of a correspondence between Descartes and someone who is not identified—on the basis of Descartes's letter of June 1649 it could be presumed that it is Chanut. At Descartes's request, copies were offered to people in high places like the chancellor, the advocate general, the **Duc de Luynes**, etc. A Latin translation by Henri Desmarets (1629–1725), the son of the Groningen theologian Samuel Desmarets or Maresius (1599–1673), was published in 1650. It is not known whether Descartes revised the text.

PELAGIUS (fl. 409–18) AND PELAGIANISM. An English theologian, Pelagius was excommunicated in 417 due to pressure exerted by **Augustine**. A primary reason for this action was Pelagius's denial of original sin. Augustine also objected to the claim (later called "Semi-Pelagian") that salvation does not depend wholly on grace, but also requires an act of **free will** on the part of the agent.

Reformers such as **John Calvin** and Martin Luther later insisted on the hard-line Augustinian position. In reaction, the **Jesuits** emphasized the necessity of free choice for salvation. In 17th-century France, the followers of **Cornelius Jansenius** were at the forefront of the Catholic opposition to the Jesuits. Among the opponents was **Guillaume Gibieuf**, a theologian at the **Sorbonne** who Descartes attempted to recruit as a supporter. Descartes even wrote in 1640 that his view that **indifference** is not essential for human **freedom** is in accord with the position in an anti-Jesuit tract of Gibieuf. In later correspondence with the Jesuit **Denis Mesland**, however, Descartes endorsed the Jesuit position that free action requires the exercise of a "real and positive power to determine oneself." He further claimed that his views are "not very different" from those in a work of the Jesuit Denis Petau that was directed against Jansenius (AT, vol. IV, p. 116f). These remarks no doubt prompted the uncharacteristically critical remark of **Antoine Arnauld** that Descartes's letters are "full of Pelagianism" and that his views on theological matters are not to be trusted.

PELL, JOHN (1611–85). English mathematician, best known for his contributions to **algebra**. Educated at Cambridge (taking a B.A. in 1638 and an M.A in 1630), Pell became a schoolmaster and **mathematics** teacher at several English schools. In 1643 he was appointed to the chair of mathematics at the Atheneum Illustre in Amsterdam where his lectures on the ancient Greek mathematician Diophantus of Alexandria won him a reputation as a skilled **algebraist**.

In 1646 Pell accepted the appointment as professor of mathematics at the college of Breda recently founded by the Prince of Orange. He retained this post until 1652 when he returned to England and was appointed by Oliver Cromwell to a post teaching mathematics in London. From 1654 to 1658 he was an ambassador of the Commonwealth in Zurich, another appointment he received from Cromwell. He returned to England shortly before Cromwell's death in 1658. At the Restoration in 1660 Pell's previous connection to Cromwell might have hindered his career prospects, but some obscure services rendered to the Royalist cause during the Protectorate earned him the reward of preferment in the Church of England. The vicarage he obtained in 1661 was his means of support for the remainder of his life.

Despite his reputation, Pell published relatively little. His 1638 *Idea of Mathematics* is an elementary work extolling the intellectual virtues of the subject and proposing a plan for its promotion, while his 1647 *Controversia de vera mensura circuli* is a refutation of the circle-squaring efforts of Christian Severin Longborg (Longomontanus). In support of this latter work, Pell solicited the judgment of noted European mathematicians on the soundness of his refutation. Descartes supplied a favorable judgment of Pell's efforts (AT, vol. V, pp. 342–43), which Pell then published. Pell also contributed significantly to Johannes Rahn's 1659 *Teutsche Algebra*, which contains a study of the equation $y^2 = ax^2 + 1$, where a is a nonsquare integer; this has come to be known as "Pell's equation." His extensive correspondence with **Sir Charles Cavendish** from the 1640s is an important source of information about Descartes, **Thomas Hobbes**, and other members of the circle connected with **Marin Mersenne**.

PHYSICS. *See* NATURAL PHILOSOPHY.

PICOT, CLAUDE (1601–68). Picot was born in Moulin, the eldest son of a tax officer. Although in his early years he seems to have frequented libertine circles he became an ecclesiastic and was appointed prior of the Abby of Le Rouvre. Together with two libertine friends, Jacques Vallée Desbarreaux and the Abbé de Touchelaye, Picot visited Descartes in the Netherlands in 1641. Descartes and Picot became close friends. Picot remained when the other two returned to France. He familiarized himself with Descartes's **metaphysics**, which Descartes suggests led to his "conversion" (to **Mersenne**, March 18, 1641, AT, vol. III, p. 340), and temporarily settled in Utrecht to be introduced to Descartes's **mathematics**. When Picot returned to France in the second half of 1642 Descartes and he started a **correspondence**, most of which is now known only through the abstracts and short quotations by **Adrien**

Baillet. They show that Picot often assisted Descartes in financial matters. Almost immediately after the publication of the *Principles* Picot started work on a French translation, which was published in 1647.

PINEAL GLAND. This gland, also known as the *conarion*, is located in the seat of the brain near the brain stem. Descartes took the pineal gland to be in **animals** and humans the primary mediator between the senses and the motor nerves; in humans it is also the site at which the **mind** is most closely joined with the **body**. In making this claim Descartes differs not only from **Aristotle**, for whom the **heart** is the seat of the **soul**, but from Galen and other medical authors who ascribed that function to the vermiform epiphysis of the cerebellum or the anterior ventricles of the brain (Avicenna and his followers).

Descartes's grounds for his claim were in part anatomical (it seemed that the pineal gland was the meeting place of nerves coming from the sense organs) and in part functional (the pineal gland, unlike other parts of the brain, is not divided into symmetrical halves; it can play the role of uniting the two images issuing from the eyes and thus account for binocular vision). Even in the 1640s doubts about the role of the pineal gland were voiced by philosophers like Christophe de Villiers and **Kenelm Digby**. By the 1660s Descartes's claims had been, in many philosophers' view, decisively refuted by the observations of Thomas Willis and other anatomists.

PLACE. *See* SPACE.

PLEMP, VOPISCUS FORTUNATUS (1601–71). Born in Amsterdam on December 23, 1601, the son of a Roman Catholic Amsterdam family (given his first names presumably as the surviving half of a twin) Plemp (Plempius) studied philosophy in **Louvain** and medicine in **Leiden**, Padua, and Bologna, where he took his degree in 1624. After his return he practiced in Amsterdam. In 1633 he was appointed professor of medicine in Louvain, where he was four times rector of the university. From a declared adversary of **William Harvey** he became a follower in the second edition of his *Fundamenta medicinae* (1644). His translation of Avicenna (*Canon Medicinae*, 1658) testifies to his admiration for the classical tradition in medicine and his knowledge of oriental languages.

According to Plemp's own testimony he often visited Descartes when he lived in Amsterdam (1629–32) and also went to see him in Santpoort (1639–40). After the publication of the *Discourse* he distributed copies among his colleagues in Louvain and collected the reactions of **Libertus Fromondus**, professor of philosophy, and the Jesuit Ciermans (1602–48), a professor of mathematics. Plemp's own reaction concentrates on the **circulation of the blood**, which he rejects for empirical reasons. Throughout their exchange the tone remains polite and respectful. This changes after Plemp partly published abstracts from his **correspondence** with Descartes, in his *De Fundamentis medicinae* (1638), apparently without asking Descartes, or sending him a copy. It was **Henricus Regius** who not only drew Descartes's attention to this fact, but also publicly and in rather strong words denounced it in one of his disputations, accusing Plemp of mutilating Descartes's words. After Descartes used similar qualifications in a letter to **Joannes van Beverwijck** (to be published in the latter's *Epistolicae quaestiones*, 1644), and put at Beverwijck's disposal the entire correspondence, Plemp did the same in the second edition of his own work (1644).

POISSON, NICOLAS-JOSEPH (1637–1710). Poisson studied at the **Sorbonne**, joined the **Oratorians** in 1660, and became a priest in 1663. His first publication (1668) was an edition and French translation, with introduction and commentary, of Descartes's *Compendium of Music* and lengthy letter to **Constantijn Huygens** known as *Traité de la méchanique*. In 1671 he published *Commentaire ou Remarques sur la méthode de M. Descartes, où l'on établit plusieurs principes généraux nécessaires pour entendre toutes ses oeuvres*; the study was intended as the first of a series of commentaries on all of Descartes's works. Poisson was also urged by many to write a biography of Descartes. But the growing controversy over Descartes's philosophy induced him to abandon these projects and to return to ecclesiastical matters. The difficulty in defending Cartesian philosophy is well illustrated by the final page of Poisson's *Commentaire*. There, in the "Avis de l'auteur," Poisson wrote that it is evident that he does not always agree with Descartes. But, he added, because of requirements placed on him by his superiors, he needed to assert that he does not claim to defend anything that the Catholic Church or even the smallest university has condemned.

POLLOT, ALPHONSE (ca. 1602–68). After the death of their father, an Italian Protestant, Alphonse Pollot (also Pollotti or Pallotti) and his brother Giambattista were sent to the Netherlands to serve in the States' army. At the siege of Bois-le-Duc (1629) Alphonse lost his right arm, but that did not prevent him from pursuing his military career. In 1641 he was appointed to the court of the stadtholder, Frederick-Henry, who valued him so much that from time to time he sent him on diplomatic missions. He spent his last years in Geneva. Pollot's first contacts with Descartes date from the summer of 1637. Given that Pollot was a friend of **Constantijn Huygens**, André Rivet, and **Henricus Reneri**, any of these may have introduced him to Descartes. Pollot was a gifted mathematician. His skills in that field were highly appreciated by Descartes, who gave him one of the six separately printed copies of his *Geometry*, intended to the few who would understand it. Pollot's good relations in court circles were of great use to Descartes during the crises on his philosophy at the Universities of Utrecht and Leiden. Pollot not only advised Descartes on the way he should react, but also mediated interventions by the stadtholder and the French ambassador. He also introduced Descartes to Princess Elisabeth. Descartes's letters to Pollot were published in the 19th century after copies made at the end of the 17th century for the famous theologian Jean Alphone Turrettini (1671–1716), who was a grandson of one of Pollot's sisters. Although of great importance for the knowledge of Descartes's life, they rarely touch on philosophical problems.

POURCHOT, EDMOND (1651–1734). An influential professor of philosophy who was one of the first to introduce Cartesianism at the University of Paris. Pourchot was first led to Cartesianism by **Antoine Arnauld**, who served as tutor for his nephew. In 1677 Pourchot was named professor of philosophy in the Collège des Grassins at the University of Paris. His popular courses incorporated Cartesian concepts and views into the format common in the teaching of **scholastic** philosophy. Pourchot's course involved several innovations, including the placement of **metaphysics** before **physics**, the introduction of a section on **geometry**, and the emphasis on the detailed study of **mechanistic** physics. In 1690 Pourchot moved to the new Paris Collège de Quatre-Nations, and the following year **Louis XIV** ordered the Paris Faculty of Philosophy to sign a formulary condemning various Cartesian and **Jansenist** propositions. There is little doubt that Pourchot was a primary target of the formulary. However, he escaped any direct condemnation, and his fidelity to the formulary, as well as his interest in the new Cartesian philosophy, are evident in his lecture notes, which were first published in 1695 with the title, *Institutio philosophica ad faciliorum veterum ac recentiorum philosophorum lectionem comparata.* In 1720, as an administrator at the University of Paris, Pourchot initiated a reform of the university curriculum that included the introduction of a study of Descartes's *Meditations* as an illustration of "the wondrous doctrine of Plato." Pourchot therefore was able to witness the transition at the University of Paris from the view of Descartes as an unacceptable anti-**Aristotelian** to a view of him as a valuable Platonist.

PRECONCEIVED OPINIONS. The primary target of Cartesian **doubt** and revision is our *præjudicia* or preconceived opinions. At the outset of the *Meditations*, the meditator notes "how many false things, in my early years, I took for true" (AT, vol. VII, p. 17). Certain opinions are acquired by the **soul** almost as soon as it is joined with the **body**. The *Principles* offer the fullest account of their genesis. When it was first joined with body, the soul was so bound up with it that it could "devote itself to no other thoughts than those by which it sensed those things that affected the body" (AT, vol. VIIIA, p. 35). It judged them according to the vividness with which they affected the senses and their importance to the conservation of the body. Hence, among other things, it failed to distinguish qualities like **shape** and **motion**, that really exist in bodies, from qualities like **color** and smell that don't; it came to believe that where nothing can be sensed there really is nothing, that the Earth is flat and immobile, and so forth. Not surprisingly many of these preconceived opinions coincide with the **Aristotelian** opinions Descartes was attempting to refute: the philosophy of the Schools is an insufficiently critical systematization of common sense. In its early moments with the body the soul felt also a great enjoyment and love of the body and whatever nourishes it, and was thus strongly disposed to maintain whatever beliefs it then acquired. Those tenacious beliefs can be relinquished, even when recognized to be false, only by strenuous effort. It is for that reason, among others, that Descartes recommends in the *Meditations* that the meditator should persist obstinately in doubting his former opinions, and impress upon himself the **truths** he has learned.

PREJUDICE. *See* PRECONCEIVED OPINIONS.

PRINCIPLE. In his correspondence, Descartes distinguishes two senses of principle, the chief one being that it is something whose existence is better known to us than the existence of other things, such that it allows us to know other things. He dismisses the **scholastic** view of **truths** like "it is impossible for something to be and not to be at the same time" as principles: "they do not make known the existence of anything, but only confirm its truth once something is known" (AT, vol. IV, p. 444). Cartesians such as **Jacques Du Roure** followed Descartes in this, asserting: "principles are known self-evidently and serve to make other things known" (*La physique*, p. 4), and again: "Principle of knowledge in the sciences must satisfy two conditions. 1. It must be evident or manifest . . . 2. It must render other things evident or manifest" (*Abrégé de philosophie*, Metaphysique, art. 89).

The way Descartes uses the term allows him to refer to the *cogito* as the first principle of knowledge. Scholastics, following **Aristotle** (*Posterior Analytics* 73b 26-30), would think, in contrast, that the first principle of knowledge, or science, properly speaking, must be a "commensurate **universal**," a proposition whose predicate belongs essentially to every instance of its subject. Thus the *cogito* would not fit the scholastic model for pure scientific knowledge at all, being neither universal nor necessary, but singular and contingent.

PRINCIPLES OF PHILOSOPHY (*PRINCIPIA PHILOSOPHIAE, PRINCIPES DE LA PHILOSOPHIE*). The origin of the *Principles of Philosophy* (1644) goes back to the end of 1640, when Descartes conceived the idea of a book containing a full exposition of his philosophy: "My plan is to write a series of theses which will constitute a complete textbook of my philosophy. I will not waste any words but simply put down all my conclusions with the true premises from which I derive them." It is his intention "to have printed in the same volume a textbook of traditional philosophy," with notes by himself in which he discusses not only his own ideas on the subject, but also those of others. The book would end with a general comparison of the two philosophies (to **Mersenne**, November 11, 1640, AT, vol. III, p. 233). The philosopher chosen for comparison is **Eustachius a Sancto Paulo**, who is also mentioned in an earlier letter as an author who could save Descartes "the time to read their huge tomes" (to Mersenne, September 30, 1640, AT, vol. III, p. 185). Accordingly, the original plan is to a certain extent polemical not only because Descartes now explicitly compares his own philosophy with traditional philosophy (whereas until then he was satisfied to present his own theories), but also because he wants to refute "the slander of those who fail to understand my **principles** and are trying to persuade the world that I have views far removed from the **truth**" (to Mersenne, December 1640, AT, vol. III, p. 258). Supplementary aims are that this will be a form in which Descartes's philosophy can easily be taught and that it may be a reason to postpone a definitive judgment on Descartes's philosophy for the **Jesuits**.

Descartes started almost immediately. A planned journey to France was cancelled; he postponed experiments. All the time the Jesuits were very much on Descartes's mind. Although in a letter to the Jesuit **Etienne Charlet**, a distant cousin, Descartes first refers to this project as one undertaken by a friend, in a letter to Marin Mersenne which he intends to be shown to Jesuits he refers to it as a "Philosophy" he is working on, "in which I admit there will be much that is different from what they teach in their schools, but which is written without any wish to contradict others and only out of love for truth" (December 22, 1641, AT, vol. III, p. 465). And in the *Letter to Father Dinet* (1642) he announces it as his next publication, which moreover will be written in a "style more suited to the current practice in the Schools," dealing "with each topic in turn, in short articles" (AT, vol. VII, p. 577). By that time the idea of presenting new and traditional ideas side by side seems to be dropped, possibly because Eustachius died in the meanwhile but certainly also because by now Descartes is convinced that traditional philosophy is "so utterly and clearly destroyed by the establishment of mine that no refutation is wanted" (to Mersenne, December 22, 1641, AT, vol. III, p. 470). In February 1643 Descartes announces that his book will be printed that summer. Actually, the work is completed only at the beginning of 1644. Although printing is well on its way in May, the figures (by **Frans van Schooten**) cause some delay. It is in that stage too that Descartes definitively settles for the title of *Principles of Philosophy*—earlier he called it his Physics or his Philosophy and even his *Summa philosophiae* (to Huygens, January 31, 1642, AT, vol. III, p. 782). Urgent business in France made it necessary for Descartes to leave the Netherlands when the book was still being printed. Together with a Latin translation of the *Discourse* and the *Essays* (*Specimina philosophiae*, 1644), the *Principia* were published in June while Descartes was in France, visiting his relatives in Brittany. A French translation, due to the Abbé Picot, which on some important points deviates from the Latin original, was published in Paris in 1647.

In the 17th century the *Principles* was often seen as Descartes's main work, its only rival being the *Passions of the Soul* (1649), which was hugely popular outside academic circles. Many Dutch professors lectured on the *Principles*, often combining it with the three first parts of the *Discourse*. Although the original model was traditional (treating of the principles of knowledge, principles of **physics**, celestial physics, and terrestrial physics successively), it was the first textbook on physics in the modern sense of the word—physics being understood as the theory of nonliving bodies. In a sense this was an accident, caused by the fact that Descartes did not have the time to do the necessary experiments.

– Q –

QUALITIES, REAL. Also called real accidents, these constitute a special category in **scholastic** philosophy distinct from the traditional **Aristotelian** categories of **substance** and **mode**. Introduced by the scholastic **Francisco Suárez**, this category includes beings that are distinct from substances insofar as they do not naturally subsist by themselves, but that are distinct from modes insofar as they can miraculously subsist by themselves (this is also why such qualities are called "real"). Descartes protested that the very notion of a non-substantial being that can subsist on its own is incoherent, since anything that can so subsist counts as a substance. He further concluded that, in the case of **body**, all that can be said to exist is quantified substance and its modes.

This conclusion in Descartes was controversial in the early modern period primarily because it was seen to conflict with the Tridentine doctrine that in the Eucharist the "species" of the bread and wine remain after **transubstantiation**. Following Suárez, scholastics identified these species with real qualities that miraculously subsist apart from the substance of the elements. In his *Fourth Set of Objections* to the *Meditations*, **Antoine Arnauld** emphasized that this scholastic position provides the main basis for **theological** opposition to Descartes's system. In response, Descartes protested that official Church declarations do not require the belief in real accidents, and that the persistence of the species can be accounted for in terms of the persistence of the **surfaces** or boundaries that contain bodies. He noted that this understanding of species is allowed by his system since the surfaces are only modes. In the original version of his response to Arnauld, Descartes added the charge that the scholastic appeal to real qualities is contrary to Church doctrine since it suggests that there is in fact something substantial in the **elements** that remains after consecration. Descartes's editor **Marin Mersenne** excised this charge from the 1641 Paris edition of the *Meditations* out of fear that it would compromise the attempt to win the approval of the **Sorbonne**. However, Descartes reinserted the excised portion into the 1642 edition of this text, published in Amsterdam.

QUANTITY. The classical understanding of quantity defined it as anything capable of greater or less. Thus, lengths, angles, and times are all quantities because they can be increased or diminished. There is a further fundamental distinction between **continuous** quantities (known as magnitudes) and discrete quantities (or multitudes). The former are the **infinitely divisible** objects of **geometry** while the latter are studied in arithmetic. Descartes held that quantity could only be conceptually distinct from a thing having that quantity, so that there are no self-subsistent **abstract** quantities over and above a number of measured quantity. As he put the matter in the second part of the *Principles*, "There is no real distinction between quantity and extended substance, but only a distinction in our **thought**, like that between number and the thing which is numbered" (AT, vol. VIIIA, p. 44).

– R –

RACONIS, CHARLES FRANÇOIS D'ABRA DE (ca. 1580–1646). De Raconis taught philosophy at the Parisian colleges of des Grassins and du Plessis (from circa 1610 on) and held a chair in theology in the Collège de Navarre, Paris, in 1616. He published a philosophy textbook, *Summa Totius Philosophiae* (1617, with many editions variously titled until 1651). He became bishop of Lavaur in 1637. Descartes read de Raconis's *Summa* in the 1640s when he was seeking a widely read summary of scholastic philosophy with which he could compare his philosophy.

RAEY, JOHANNES DE (1622–1702). There is little we know of Johannes de Raey (or Raei) before he is mentioned as a student of **Henricus Regius** in one of Descartes's letters. Without graduating he moved to **Leiden** in 1647, where he took degrees in philosophy and medicine and settled as a highly successful private teacher in philosophy. Despite the fact that he was an outspoken Cartesian, Leiden University gave him an extraordinary professorship in philosophy in 1651, stipulating that he should lecture on **Aristotle's** *Problems*. In fact he taught Cartesian natural philosophy, allegedly with the aim of showing that there is fundamental agreement between Aristotle (as opposed to the Aristotelians) and Descartes. This is also the theme of his first book, a compilation of disputations called *Clavis philosophiae naturalis, sive Introductio Aristoelico-cartesiana in contemplationem naturae* ("A Key to Natural Philosophy, being an Aristotelico-Cartesian Introduction to the Contemplation of Nature," 1654). The use of the expression "contemplation of **nature**" indicates a second theme, which would become more and more important, namely, the idea that philosophy is pure contemplation and has nothing to do either with practical problems or with the disciplines taught in the "Higher Faculties" (theology, medicine, and law). Accordingly, De Raey emancipates philosophy from its propaedeutic role in the academic curriculum (it is no longer an introduction to theology, medicine, and law), but at the cost of philosophy's practical relevance. In 1669 conflicts with his Leiden colleagues led De Raey to accept an appointment at the Athèneum Illustre of Amsterdam, where this theme was further developed, especially against **Baruch Spinoza** and his friends.

This culminated with a theory of **language**, which he developed in his last work, *Cogitata de interpretatione* ("Thoughts on Interpretation," 1691). According to this theory the meaning of a word is an **idea**. But there are two types of ideas: the **clear and distinct** ideas of science, which are **innate**, and the obscure and confused ideas of experience, which the **mind** acquires in cooperation with the **body**. These two systems of ideas are separate and accordingly form the basis of two separate linguistic systems: the **language** of science (virtually the language of **mathematics**), which refers to the clear and distinct ideas we find in ourselves, and ordinary language (or any form of language that is parasitical on daily language), which refers to the ideas of the senses. Since, on the other hand, practical problems are formulated in daily language, it is impossible that philosophy, which is the domain of the language of science, can contribute anything to their solution. More particularly, philosophy cannot contribute anything to theology, given the fact that the text of theology, Holy Scripture, was written in ordinary language. Although in his best moments De Raey seems to anticipate some of the problems Immanuel Kant (1722–1802) would still be grappling with, there is a lot of confusion, especially in his later work. More specifically, he cannot solve the problem of how to relate **physics** to the "real" world, that is, the world we experience with the senses.

RAMUS, PETRUS (PIERRE DE LA RAMÉE, 1515–72). Philosopher, rhetorician, and the most eminent logician of his day. Born in Cuts in Picardy, Ramus enrolled at the Collège de Navarre in Paris, receiving the *magister artis* in 1536. He defended the thesis entitled *Quaecumque ab Aristotele dicta sunt, commentitia sunt* ("Everything taught by **Aristotle** is a fabrication"), a topic showing the extreme novelty of his views on philosophy and method. He taught a reformed version of Aristotelian **syllogistic logic** at the Collège du Mans, in Paris, and at the Collège de l'Ave Maria, where he worked with Audomarus Talaeus (Omer Talon). Talaeus, under Ramus's influence, reformed Ciceronean rhetoric upon the principles applied by Ramus to the rearrangement of Aristotle's works on logic. As part of his project for the reform of Aristotelian logic, Ramus published *Dialecticae partitiones* ("The Parts of Dialectic") and *Aristotelicae animadversiones* ("Aristotelian Thoughts"), both in 1543. These works so provoked the orthodox Aristotelian philosophers at the University of Paris that they induced Francis I in 1544 to suppress them and forbid him to teach. After a public disputation on the matter, Ramus was denounced as "rash, arrogant and impudent." Through the influence of Cardinal Charles de Lorraine, Henry II lifted the ban against Ramus in 1547, and in 1551 he was appointed regius professor of philosophy and eloquence at the Collège de France. In 1562 he converted to Protestantism; mounting persecution from his academic and ecclesiastical enemies marked the last years of his life. Hired assassins murdered him two days after the outbreak of the Massacre of Saint Bartholomew's Day in August 1572.

Ramus identified logic with dialectic, neglecting the traditional role that logic played as a **method** of inquiry. Instead, he emphasized the view that logic is a method of disputation, its two parts being invention, the process of discovering proofs in support of a thesis, and disputation, which taught how the material of invention should be arranged. Ramus's logic had enormous vogue in Europe during the 16th and 17th centuries.

RAREFACTION AND CONDENSATION. Certain fluids, notably air, appear to be capable of occupying larger or smaller volumes without the addition or subtraction of **matter**. Certain kinds of stuff, iron for example, weigh more per unit volume than do other kinds like wood. **Atomists** explained these phenomena by supposing that empty **space** can be more or less completely filled by matter; density is then the proportion of occupied space. Philosophers who denied the existence of empty space had to find another explanation. Some **Aristotelians** followed Ægidius Romanus and other medievals who held that the same quantity of matter can occupy different volumes in space. Others held that the density of a body is determined by the number and size of the pores or interstitial spaces it contains. Those spaces are filled with particles of air or **subtle matter**, and do not contribute to the heaviness of the body. Descartes, who denies even the possibility of empty space, adopts the second sort of explanation (*Principles* II, art. 5–7, AT, VIIIA, pp. 42–44), holding that "no more intelligible explanation can be given" than his. Experimental evidence on behalf of the **vacuum** (see **extension**) undermined Descartes's denial of its possibility, and thus also his explanation of rarefaction and condensation.

REAL ACCIDENTS. *See* QUALITIES, REAL; SUBSTANCE.

REASON. Descartes identifies reason with "good sense" or "the power of judging well and distinguishing the true from the false" (*Discourse on Method* I; AT, vol. VI, pp. 1–2). This account is broadly consistent with the **Aristotelian** model of reason as a discursive faculty that enables the **mind** to draw inferences and to distinguish reality from appearance. When applied properly, that is, when restricted to drawing conclusions on the basis of **clear and distinct** perceptions, reason is infallible: it cannot arrive at a false conclusion. This complete reliability of reason is ultimately underwritten by the benevolence of **God**, since it would be inconsistent with the divine **nature** to deceive people when they restrict their use of reason to clear and distinct **ideas**. The faculty of reason is also wholly present in every person—the differences in intellectual attainment among people are due to their greater or lesser exercise of reason, but the faculty itself "remains one and the same" in all persons (*Rules for the Direction of the Mind*, Rule 1; AT, vol. X, p. 360). Another important feature of the capacity to reason is that it distinguishes humans from **animals**. According to Descartes, the inability of brute animals to use **language** shows "not only that the beasts have less reason than humans, but that they have no reason at all" (*Discourse on Method*, Part V; AT, vol. VI, p. 58).

REFRACTION. *See* OPTICS.

RÉGIS, PIERRE-SYLVAIN (1632–1707). French natural philosopher and a prominent promoter of Cartesianism. Régis was converted to Cartesianism in the late 1650s by the famous Paris conferences of the Cartesian natural philosopher **Jacques Rohault**. He was sent as a Cartesian missionary to Toulouse during the 1660s, and he lectured with great success both there and, in the 1670s, in Montpellier. He returned to Paris in 1680 to revive Rohault's conferences (Rohault having died in 1672), but the conferences were suspended due to controversies surrounding the Cartesian account of **transubstantiation**, which the Jesuit **Louis Le Valois** had criticized as **Calvinist** in a pseudonymous work that same year. These controversies also led to Régis's failure to receive permission to publish his grand *Système de philosophie*, a work that was not published until 1690. The section of this text on **metaphysics** takes over **Robert Desgabets's** interpretation of Descartes's doctrine concerning the creation of the **eternal truths**, and also endorses Desgabets's view that **ideas** of **substances** require real external objects and that our temporal **thought** requires a union with **motion**.

In the early 1690s Régis published Cartesian responses to the critiques of Descartes in the work of the skeptic **Pierre-Daniel Huet** and the scholastic **Jean Duhamel**. The focus here was primarily on Descartes's views concerning the *cogito* and the **method of doubt**. In the middle of this decade, he entered into a dispute with the Cartesian **Nicolas Malebranche** and his disciple Henri de Lelevel. Part of this dispute concerned the question of why the moon appears to be larger on the horizon than it is on the meridian. Régis's answer appealed to the distorting effects of the atmosphere, while Malebranche and Lelevel emphasized the effect of natural **judgments**. The main issue between these antagonists, though, concerned the view in Malebranche that the ideas we perceive exist in **God**. Régis countered by defending the position, which **Antoine Arnauld** had offered a decade earlier against Malebranche, that our ideas are only modifications of our **mind**.

Régis and Malebranche were admitted together into the Paris Académie des sciences in 1699. Régis's final publication was *L'Usage de la raison et de la foy* (1704), which argues that **faith and reason** do not conflict since reason is infallible only in the realm of **nature** while faith is infallible only in the realm of grace. This work also includes, as an appendix, a response to the first half of the first part of **Baruch Spinoza's** *Ethics.* Two striking features of this response are its concession to Spinoza that divisible bodies are only modes of one indivisible material substance, and its claim that God is not a substance but rather a "supersubstantial" being.

REGIUS, HENRICUS (1598–1679). Henricus de Roy (the Latinized form Regius was used only after he became a professor) was born in Utrecht. His parents died from the plague when he was still a youth and he was brought up by an uncle, who sent him to Franeker and Groningen to study medicine. In his student days Regius traveled extensively (Paris, Montpellier), obtaining his degree at the University of Padua. On his return to the Netherlands he became town physician (in charge of the care for the poor) in Utrecht and later head of the Latin School (secondary education) in Naarden near Amsterdam. Naarden was also the place where the orthodoxy of his beliefs first came under attack: his conflict with the local minister was brought before the Church Council of Amsterdam and ended only by his formally renouncing the incriminated opinions concerning the resurrection of the body. In 1638 he became professor extraordinary (reader) of theoretical medicine and botany at the **University of Utrecht;** in 1639 he became an ordinary professor. The rector of the university, **Gysbertus Voetius,** granted him the right to lecture and dispute on general philosophical questions in 1641, a right that was withdrawn in 1642 after he had been the center of a row over Cartesianism. In 1646 he published a work on **natural philosophy,** *Fundamenta physices* (see below). A new edition, *Philosophia naturalis* (1654; reprinted 1661) has a more systematic structure. Until the publication of Descartes's *Treatise on Man* (in Latin translation in 1662) Regius's works on theoretical and practical medicine were the only Cartesian textbooks in that field.

Before his appointment at the university Regius gave private lectures on philosophy based on his reading of Descartes's *Dioptrics* and *Meteors.* The fact that these were very successful with students may have been one reason for giving him a chair. But the fact that a new chair was created was undoubtedly the result of the skillful machinations of the professor of philosophy, **Henricus Reneri,** a friend of Descartes who was also on very good terms with the first burgomaster of Utrecht, Gysbert van der Hoolck (1598–1680), who governed the university on behalf of the town. This explains why in his first letter to Descartes Regius thanks Descartes profusely.

For Regius the friendship with Descartes was very stimulating. He obviously was aware of the revolutionary character of Descartes's ideas and also sensed the immense advantages medicine could draw from Cartesian **physics**. From the point of view of Descartes, the friendship with Regius was doubly attractive. Not only did he find in Regius an intelligent interlocutor, he also understood that Regius was in a very good position to make propaganda for his ideas. Still, from the beginning there were differences in their orientation and, possibly, their temperament and character, which after some years became fatal for their friendship. First of all, Descartes may have underestimated Regius's ambition. Although Regius was a loyal supporter of Descartes, he presumably did not want to be known as being no more than a follower of Descartes. Moreover, Regius was a professional physician but he was an amateur in philosophy, sometimes confusing and blending ideas of different origin and being altogether much more empirically minded than Descartes. And, finally, as compared to Descartes, Regius was much less sensitive to the religious and theological implications of his position—or, others would say, more naive.

These differences, which occasionally played a role even at the beginning of their friendship, became fully manifest in 1645 when Regius submitted to Descartes the manuscript of what he planned to be his first publication for a larger audience, the *Fundamenta physices*. Descartes's reaction was one of disappointment (he thought that Regius did too little to prove his views) and, when he reached chapter 12 (On Man), his reaction was one of shock, because it showed that on many **metaphysical** issues Regius took a line that was completely different from his: that as far as natural **reason** is concerned the **mind** could be a **mode** of the body as well as a separate **substance**; that the existence of the world is uncertain; that it is impossible to prove the **immortality** of the **soul**; that to think we do not need **innate ideas**; that the presence of an idea of **God** in ourselves is not enough to **prove the existence of God**, etc. In a general way Regius solved these and similar questions by calling in the evidence of Scripture—even if we cannot understand how mind and body are related or cannot certainly know that an external world exists, the authority of Scripture is enough to convince us that the soul does not die with the body and that God created the world. But Descartes also found that Regius's method of presentation was weak. In his view his method could be appropriate for disputations but was unfit for a work that was meant to convince. He urged Regius to suppress certain passages, which Regius did to a certain extent, but was so infuriated by the way Regius reacted to his suggestions that he broke with him.

After the book was finally published in 1646 Descartes complained about it in letters to **Marin Mersenne** and **Princess Elisabeth**, accusing his former friend of plagiarizing as well as being unable to under-stand his ideas, and in the preface to the French version of his *Princi-ples* (1647) dissociated himself from him in rather violent terms. When one of Regius's students, Petrus Wassenaer, reacted by publishing a number of theses from chapter 12 of *Fundamenta physices*, restoring more particularly the passages Regius had suppressed in concession to Descartes, Descartes replied by the *Notes Against a Program* (1648). When Descartes in turn published the *Passions of the Soul* (1649) Regius replied by publishing *De affectibus animi* ("Dissertation on the Passions of the Soul," 1650). Regius also refused all cooperation with **Claude Clerselier** when he started to publish Descartes's **correspon-dence.** More particularly he accused him of providing false versions of the texts of Descartes's letters—to a certain extent that is right, given the fact that Clerselier worked on the draft letters and often combined fragments in a rather unfortunate way. Still, Clerselier seems to have gotten hold of copies of Regius's letters to Descartes. They are quoted, and sometimes summarized, by **Adrien Baillet.** So much is clear, the unfavorable picture of Regius that dominates the literature on Descartes should be corrected. Without being an original thinker Regius's impor-tance for Descartes personally as well as for the diffusion of his ideas has been great.

RENERI, HENRICUS (1593–1639). Reneri was born in Huy (near Liège) and educated in **Louvain** (Collège du Faucon), presumably to become a priest. His conversion to **Calvinism** made this obviously im-possible. He pursued his studies in **Leiden,** where he studied **theology,** but instead of becoming a minister, he earned a living as a private teacher and as a governor in a rich Amsterdam family. In Amsterdam he met Descartes, with whom he became friends and whom he intro-duced to various Dutch personalities, like David le Leu de Wilhem (1588–1658) and **Constantijn Huygens.** When in 1632 he was ap-pointed professor of philosophy and rhetoric at the Illustrious School of Deventer, Descartes followed him to work on his *Treatise on Light.* And when in 1634 Reneri was appointed professor of philosophy in Utrecht, Descartes followed him in 1635. Although there is some evi-dence that Reneri studied Descartes's *Dioptrics* and *Meteors* with his Utrecht students, there is little reason to call him a Cartesian. In fact, his outlook is rather that of an empirically minded **Aristotelian** with little interest in **metaphysics,** if any, who may have learned more from **Francis Bacon** and **Pierre Gassendi** than from Descartes. Still, while keeping Descartes at work, he admired him enormously and seems to have created a Cartesian excitement among Utrecht students. At the oc-casion of his death in 1639 he was commemorated in a funeral oration by his colleague Antonius Aemilius (1589–1660), professor of history. In fact, this became a long eulogy of Descartes, undoubtedly to the surprise of everybody present. For **Gysbertus Voetius** the exaggerated claims made about Descartes's philosophy in Aemilius's speech may have been a reason for tabulating a series of disputations on **atheism**; indeed, in his eyes, the inevitable disappointment caused by those claims could produce skepticism, which is no more than one step to atheism. Apart from a few disputations Reneri did not publish anything.

REVIUS, JACOBUS (1586–1658). Revius (or Reefsen) was born in Deventer in 1586. He studied philosophy and **theology** at the universities of **Leiden**, Franeker, and Saumur. In 1614 he became minister in Deventer. He met Descartes through their common friend **Henricus Reneri**. In 1641 Revius was appointed dean of the Statencollege (a college for theological bursars of the states of Holland) at Leiden University. A great literary talent, writing fluently in Dutch, French, Latin, and Greek, he supervised the official Dutch translation of the Bible (*Statenvertaling*, 1637), in particular the Old Testament. His poems are mostly religious, but they also concern the victories of the Dutch army. Like **Gysbertus Voetius** he believed that theology needs a philosophical framework. It is to that end that he wrote *Suarez repurgatus* (1643), a **Calvinist** commentary on **Francisco Suárez's** *Metaphysical disputations*. Revius may have distrusted Descartes from the time that Descartes lived in Deventer (1632–34). It is Revius to whom Descartes, on being questioned about his faith, said: "I have the religion of my king," and when further questioned, "I have the religion of my wet-nurse."

But his irritation about the new philosophy turned into exasperation when at the Statencollege he had to bear the company of his deputy dean **Adriaan Heereboord**, who was an outspoken Cartesian. After incidentally commenting on the theological implications of Descartes's position in *Suarez repurgatus*, Revius wanted to devote a whole series of disputations to Cartesian philosophy in 1647. Only a few (on Cartesian **doubt** and on the Cartesian **idea of God**) could be held before the administrators (*curatores*) of Leiden University ordered him to stop and issued a decree in which they forbade professors to mention Descartes's name and to discuss his opinions. This did not deter Revius from writing a book on Cartesian **method** (*Methodi cartesianae consideration theologica* 1648), something that was also forbidden, and from publishing several pamphlets. **Johannes Clauberg** and Tobias Andreae wrote against him, and Revius replied each time in books that became more and more voluminous. Christoph Wittich's proposal for reading Scripture in a nonphysical sense also received an answer. Although Revius's criticism does not lack substance and in many ways is even more articulate than Voetius's, it had little influence; Revius is now known only as a poet, even in the Netherlands.

ROBERVAL, GILLES PERSONNE DE (1602–75). A French mathematician and natural philosopher, known for his contributions to infinitesimal **mathematics** and **mechanics**. Little is known about Roberval's early years or his education, but he arrived in Paris in 1628 and became active in **Marin Mersenne's** circle, gaining such a substantial reputation that Mersenne referred to him as "our geometer" in published works relating the investigations of the group. Appointed professor of philosophy at the Collège de Maître Gervais in 1632, Roberval won the triennial competition for the **Ramus** chair of the Collège Royal in 1634, a position he would hold until his death. In 1655 he succeeded to the mathematics chair formerly held by **Pierre Gassendi**, another post he held for the rest of his life. The statutes of the Ramus chair required the incumbent to defend his position every three years in an open competition, with problems set by the incumbent. This contributed to Roberval's reluctance to publish any of his **methods**, and as a result his mathematical results were communicated to contemporaries only in correspondence, and often accompanied by allegations of plagiarism. Indeed, the only works he published in his lifetime were his 1636 *Traité de méchanique* and a 1644 edition and commentary on Aristarchus (*Aristarchii Samii de mundi systemate*). He was elected to the Académie Royale des Sciences in 1666.

Roberval was a persistent critic of Descartes in both mathematics and **natural philosophy**. Descartes's biographer **Adrien Baillet** suggested that his failure to be included among those who received presentation copies of the *Discourse on Method* and *Essays* was the origin of Roberval's antipathy; although this seems somewhat improbable, the relationship between them was certainly marked by hostility. Roberval belittled Descartes's *Geometry* in the course of a controversy that erupted between Descartes and **Pierre de Fermat** in 1637–38, contributing a piece to the dispute in which he defended Fermat's methods and summarized points of obscurity and inadequacies in Cartesian **geometry** and **optics** (AT, vol. II, pp. 103–15). Even a decade later, Descartes would insist that Roberval "and his sort" offered criticisms and amendments to the *Geometry* only because "they are not capable of understanding it" (AT, vol. V, p. 142). In natural philosophy Roberval defended the possibility of a **vacuum** against Descartes's identification of **space** with **body**, critiqued the Cartesian treatment of the **laws** of **motion** and impact, as well as objected to Descartes's account of the center of oscillation of the pendulum.

Roberval's *Traité des indivisibles*—first published in 1693 by the Académie Royale des Sciences—is his most important single work, even though it was unpublished in his lifetime. In this systematic treatise, he found areas of figures and arc lengths of curves by treating **continuous** geometric magnitudes as composed of infinite collections of infinitely small parts. Another technique he employed was to consider curves as traced by a "composition of motions" and then draw tangents or construct arc lengths by analyzing the component motions. His most celebrated application of these methods was to the problem of finding area and tangent to the cycloid—the curve traced by a point on the periphery of a circle as it rolls uniformly across a plane surface. He achieved his results in the mid-1630s and claimed priority for them in a dispute with Evangelista Torricelli, who had undertaken similar investigations and published them. Commenting on Roberval's treatment of the cycloid, Descartes remarked with characteristic venom that "I don't see why he made such a fuss over having found something so easy that anyone who knows even a little geometry could not fail to find it if he went looking for it" (AT, vol. II, p. 135).

ROHAULT, JACQUES (1620–72). The foremost proponent of Cartesian **natural philosophy** in the decades immediately following the death of Descartes, Rohault was best known for his popular 1671 *Traité de physique* ("Treatise on Physics"), which went through numerous editions and remained a standard textbook in Cartesian **natural philosophy** well into the 18th century. Born in Amiens to a moderately prosperous merchant family, Rohault's early education was undertaken at Amiens (probably under the Jesuits), after which he continued his studies at Paris, taking an M.A. degree in 1641. Rohault distinguished himself in **mathematics** and natural philosophy. He established himself as a private tutor in these subjects, in which capacity he tutored the children of several prominent families as well as the dauphin. In the mid-1650s he began to hold weekly lectures at his house in Paris. These "mercredis de Rohault" did much to popularize Cartesian natural philosophy and brought him to the attention of prominent Cartesians. In 1658 he assisted **Claude Clerselier** in publishing a reply to certain criticisms of Descartes's *Dioptrics* advanced by **Pierre de Fermat.** At about the same time he won **Pierre-Sylvain Régis** over to the cause of Cartesianism, and in 1665 Régis accepted Rohault's invitation to serve as a kind of Cartesian missionary by spreading the doctrine in Toulouse through a series of lectures in the style of Rohault.

By the 1660s Rohault had emerged as the arbiter of Cartesian scientific affairs in Paris. In addition to his public lectures and private tutoring on Cartesian natural philosophy he was an active participant in the intellectual circles of leading natural philosophers. In 1667 he organized the ceremonies marking the return of Descartes's remains to Paris from Stockholm. His prominence among Cartesians led to political and theological difficulties in his later years. The increasing hostility to Cartesianism in France in the late 1660s, which culminated in the 1671 decree of **Louis XIV** suppressing anti-**Aristotelian** teachings at the University of Paris, brought Rohault under suspicion of heresy. In his *Entretiens sur la philosophie* ("Conversations on Philosophy"), published in 1671, the same year as the *Traité de physique*, Rohault tried to reconcile Cartesian natural philosophy with Catholic **theology** by insisting on a strict separation of scientific and religious questions. This attempt met with little success, and at the time of his death in December of 1672 leading authorities in Paris still regarded him as a heretic.

Rohault held that the explanations of natural philosophy could only be probable and he sought to overcome the Cartesians' reputation for dogmatism by illustrating Cartesian principles through practical experiments. In his *Traité de physique* he posed as an arbiter between the systems of Descartes and Aristotle, offering Cartesian **corpuscular-mechanical** explanations for experimental phenomena from pneumatics, magnetism, and other branches of natural philosophy. He thereby introduced Cartesian doctrines as more complete elaborations of traditional Aristotelian teachings and undertook to ground them in experimental practice.

Rohault's *Traité de physique* was translated into English by John Clarke and augmented by Samuel Clarke, who had originally annotated and translated the *Traité* into Latin. First published in English in 1697 as *Rohault's System of Natural Philosophy*, it became a standard textbook for generations of English students. As it went through multiple editions, Samuel Clarke increasingly "illustrated" it with "notes taken mostly out of Sr. **Isaac Newton**'s Philosophy." Although Clarke's footnotes often eclipsed the Cartesian text, the work became a monument to the improbable marriage of Cartesian natural philosophy with Newtonian physical theory.

ROSICRUCIANS. A secret brotherhood allegedly founded by Christian Rosencreutz, who it is said, was born in the 14th century and lived for over 100 years. Rosencreutz supposedly traveled in the east, learned magic and cabala, and then returned to Europe to establish the society devoted to the reformation of universal knowledge. Early on Descartes was attracted to the brotherhood and sought out its members. Clearly, the themes of new science that would harmonize all sciences and the dismissal of intellectual authorities such as **Aristotle** and Galen appealed to Descartes. In 1620 Descartes had mentioned his hope for a new harmonious science: "The sciences are now masked. If the masks were taken off, they would appear in all their beauty. Anyone who would see the linkage of the sciences, would not find them any more difficult to retain in the **mind** than a series of numbers" (AT, vol. X, p. 215). Descartes had previously penned the following brief description of a proposed treatise he would write under the pseudonym Polybius the Cosmopolitan: "[It] gives the true way of solving all the difficulties of **mathematical** science; it demonstrates that the human mind cannot achieve anything more with respect to these difficulties. The work is aimed at people who promise to show new miracles in all the sciences, so that it can shake them out of their laziness. . . . The work is offered for a second time to the learned of the world, and particularly to the most celebrated Rosicrucian Brothers in Germany" (AT, vol. X, p. 214). According to Descartes's biographer, **Adrien Baillet**, Descartes was not able to find any member of the society, and thus he decided that the whole thing was a fabrication. *See also* FAULHABER, JOHANNES.

RUBIO, ANTONIO (1548–1615). Rubio entered the **Jesuits** in 1569, received his doctorate in **theology** in Mexico, 1577, and taught philosophy and theology there from 1577 to 1599 (after which he returned to Spain). He published commentaries on many works of **Aristotle** (*Logica*, 1603, *Physica*, 1605, *De anima*, 1611). Descartes remembered him as one of the Jesuit philosophers whose textbooks he read in his youth, along with the **Conimbricenses** and **Franciscus Toletus**.

RULES FOR THE DIRECTION OF THE MIND (REGULAE AD DIRECTIONEM INGENII). The *Rules for the Direction of the Mind* were written somewhere between 1619 and 1625, but never finished. The work should have contained at least 24 rules, each with its own commentary, but that is almost certainly the belated result of a desperate attempt to create unity in what may have been a series of small essays on **methodological** problems. Internal evidence shows that Descartes frequently abandoned the manuscript; there are many inconsistencies in it, especially in the first 10 rules. Despite this, the *Regulae* are among Descartes's most interesting treatises because it is the only one that explicitly deals with the problem of **method** and with universal **mathematics** (*mathesis universalis*). All published and manuscript versions of the text go back to a copy made by Walter von Tschirnhaus after an original in the possession of **Claude Clerselier**. The work was published for the first time in a Dutch translation in 1684, together with a Dutch version of the *Search for Truth*. It was published in a Latin version in 1702 (as part of the *Opuscula posthuma*). Neither goes back to the only other version we know, namely, a copy in the Leibniz Archives.

– S –

SADNESS. *See* JOY/SADNESS.

SCHOLASTICISM/SCHOLASTICS. The philosophy taught in European universities from the 13th through the 17th centuries is typically called "scholasticism." Strictly speaking, there is no unified body of scholastic philosophy, since there is no single set of philosophical **principles** endorsed and taught by all philosophers who have been classified as scholastics. Nevertheless, there are a number of common characteristics that can be found among the philosophers thus classified. These include: engagement with (and broad but not universal acceptance of) **Aristotelian** philosophy, especially as interpreted by St. Thomas Aquinas (ca. 1225–74); a tradition of commentary on the works of Aristotle and subsequent authorities; and an expository style that emphasizes the framing of doctrines in the form of disputations on a series of questions. *See* SCOTISM; THOMISM.

SCHOOCK, MARTINUS (1614–69). Schoock was born in Utrecht. He studied philosophy, literature, and theology in Leiden and Utrecht. In 1636 he was the first to obtain a degree with **Henricus Reneri** at Utrecht University, the subject of his dissertation being the echo. In this text, which he published in an amplified form and to which he added a collection of echo-poems, he still seems to be in favor of new philosophy, even if his style is Humanistic rather than Cartesian. The protection of **Gysbertus Voetius**, however, with whom he often collaborated in his polemics against Catholics and Remonstrants, may have led to a change of mind, although some contemporaries suggest that he never was more than an opportunist. In 1636 he became reader in the humanities in Utrecht. But, when he received a call to the chair of philosophy in Deventer in 1637, Utrecht did little to keep him. In 1641 finally he became professor of philosophy in Groningen.

In 1642 Voetius asked for Schook to protect him by writing against the allegations of Descartes, who in his *Letter to Father Dinet* (1642) accused Voetius of abuse of power. The result, called *Admiranda methodus novae philosophiae Renati Des-Cartes* ("The Admirable Method of the New Philosophy of René Descartes," 1643), is a curious mixture of slander and argument, based partly on disputations Schoock had held in Groningen and partly on material provided by Voetius. In it Schoock depicts Descartes as the propagator of an easy (if not simply lazy) style of philosophizing, which works without books (the first precept of Descartes's **method** being to forget everything one has learned) and discussions, and gives much room to personal feelings and inspirations, to the detriment of **logic** and experience. According to Schoock Descartes claims a lot but does little to prove it; indeed, given Descartes's rejection of experience and logic as well as his professed ignorance of philosophy, this makes his position similar to that of a dreamer or a madman. The book becomes very personal in the last four chapters, where Schoock sets out to prove that Descartes's method leads to madness, skepticism, "enthusiasm" (the usual name for all religious doctrines based on an allegedly individual revelation), and **atheism**. There is even an extended comparison with the atheist **Lucilio Vanini**, burned on the stake in 1619, suggesting that there is not much difference between him and Descartes.

When at the end of 1642 Descartes got hold of the proofs of the first half of Schoock's book (printing was interrupted to allow the printer to take care of another book by Voetius), he immediately set out to write a refutation, which eventually was published as *Epistola ad Voetium* ("Letter to Voetius," 1643), believing that *Admiranda methodus* was actually written by the Utrecht professor of theology. When that proved to be wrong—Voetius is referred to as a revered teacher of the author —he seems to have lost interest. But it is certain that the final version aroused his fury, especially because of the extended parallel with Vanini. In any case, Descartes continued to see Voetius as the author in the sense that he had inspired and condoned Schoock's book, and accused the theologian of atheism for the same reason as he himself had been accused, namely, that he discouraged people from proving the existence of God. However, in the trial before the academic tribunal that followed, Schoock put all the blame on Voetius, which allowed Descartes in turn to reopen the matter in Utrecht. As part of the complicated events that followed, Schoock was several times arrested on the accusation of perjury, but the trial Voetius had started against him came to a dead end, after many years. Schoock continued his career in Groningen, writing, lecturing, and disputing on a great variety of subjects, such as inundations, ecclesiastical goods, turf, cheese, skepticism, and physics. Plagued by debts and by a deserved reputation of alcoholism, he accepted the offer of the elector of Brandenburg to become a professor of history. He left Groningen in the most clandestine way in 1666 and died three years later in Frankfurt on the Oder.

SCHOOTEN, FRANS VAN (ca. 1615–60). Dutch mathematician whose Latin editions of the *Geometry* did much to promote Descartes's mathematics. Van Schooten's father (also named Frans) was a professor of mathematics at the engineering school of the **University of Leiden.** The younger van Schooten enrolled at Leiden University in 1631 and studied mathematics, but there is no indication that he took a degree. He met Descartes in 1637, and through him was introduced to leading mathematicians in the circle of **Marin Mersenne.** In the late 1630s van Schooten traveled to Paris and then London, where he stayed from 1641 to 1643. He returned to Leiden in 1643 serving as assistant to his father, and on his father's death in 1645 he was appointed to his chair. He supplemented his income by tutoring mathematics, and among his pupils were several gifted mathematicians, including Jan de Witt (1625–72) and **Christiaan Huygens.** Van Schooten had become acquainted with the work of **François Viète** during his time in Paris, and he brought copies of several of Viète's manuscripts with him when he returned to Leiden. He published the first collected edition of Viète's works in 1646. His 1649 Latin translation of Descartes's *Geometry* (which contained valuable notes elucidating the original text) continued van Schooten's practice of making important mathematical works more widely available. An enlarged edition of his Latin version of the *Geometry* was issued in two volumes in 1659 and 1661. This edition supplemented Descartes's text with van Schooten's introduction and an expanded commentary, and included appendices by three of his students, Jan de Witt, Johan Hudde (1628–1704), and Hendrik van Heuraet (1633–60). Van Schooten's original contributions to mathematics were modest, but by broadening the reception of the work of Viète and Descartes he exercised a significant influence on the development of 17th-century mathematical thought.

SCOTISM. The doctrine associated with John Duns Scotus and his followers. Scotism can be thought of as a blend of **Aristotelianism** and moderate **Augustinianism.** Unlike the **Thomists,** Scotists held that the proper object of the human **intellect** is being in general and not the "quiddity" of material being, thus displaying a commitment to the doctrine that humans have knowledge of **infinite** being. Scotists also exhibited an attachment to the doctrine of **God's** absolute omnipotence, requiring many propositions thought to infringe too much upon that omnipotence to be rejected or modified. These tendencies entailed a contrast with many Thomist theses. Scotists thought that the concept of being holds univocally (not analogically) between God and creatures; that there is only a formal or modal (not real) **distinction** between essence and existence and **substance** and accidents; that prime matter can subsist independently of **form** by God's omnipotence; that a *haecceity*, or form (not "signate" or quantified matter) is the principle of individuation for bodily creatures; that a **body** can be in two places at the same time; and that humans are a composite of plural forms: rational, sensitive, and vegetative **souls**. Moreover, some Scotists accepted the **ontological** (or *a priori*) **argument** for the existence of God in some fashion, as self-evident to us, and not as Thomists would have it, as merely self-evident in itself.

In the 17th century oppositions between Thomists and Scotists were significant enough that treatises were written detailing the "two great systems of philosophy," Thomism and Scotism; others tried to reconcile the two systems or wrote textbooks following Thomas or following Scotus.

SCOTUS, JOHN DUNS (ca. 1265–1308). See SCOTISM.

SEARCH FOR TRUTH (RECHERCHE DE LA VÉRITÉ). Recherche de la vérité is the title given to a dialogue among three people, Poliander, Epistemon, and Eudoxe, in which Poliander represents the views of a gentleman of good breeding but without any formal education in philosophy, Epistemon the position of a traditional philosopher who has read extensively in philosophical literature, and Eudoxe, the position of a Cartesian, who relies on his own intelligence. The work was left unfinished, and it is not clear when Descartes wrote it. Some place it somewhere at the beginning of Descartes's career and in any case before the *Discourse* (1637), suggesting that it was written for **Constantijn Huygens**, whereas others place it at the end of his career, in the belief that it was written for Queen **Christina**. It could be an experiment in style, but it could also be an imitation of **Galileo Galilei**. What is clear is that the dialogue was written for a nonacademic audience. Its editorial fate was closely connected with that of the *Rules for the Direction of the Mind*. Both were first published in a Dutch translation in 1684 and in both cases the published text goes back to a copy made by Walter von Tschirnhaus (1651–1708) of the autograph in the possession of **Claude Clerselier**. Both were also published in a Latin version in 1701 as part of Descartes's *Opera posthuma*. The important difference is that the *Search for Truth* was written in French and the *Rules* in Latin. However, all we have for the French text of the *Search for Truth* is an incomplete copy in the Leibniz Archives.

SENSATION. Absent **miracles**, external bodies affect the **mind** only by way of interacting with certain organs of the **body** to which that mind is joined. Changes in the mind brought about in this way are sensations.

Aristotelian philosophy assigned sight, hearing, and other sensory powers to a part of the **soul** called the "sensitive" soul, which is found in both humans and **animals**. A red apple, for example, acts on the organ of vision (usually thought to be the crystalline humor of the eye) which transmits species of **color** to the ventricles of the brain and thus to the internal senses of **imagination** and **memory**.

Descartes rejected both the Aristotelian account of sensation and the sensitive soul. On the side of the body, sensation is nothing more than local motion in the organ of sense. Descartes explains these motions and their causes in some detail in the *Treatise on Man*, *Dioptrics*, and *Principles*. On the side of the mind, it is a particular **mode**. The mode whose presence in the mind we call "seeing red" is different from the mode whose presence we call "seeing blue" (as well as from the mode we call "smelling musk"); more than that we cannot say, because the **ideas** of sensible qualities are obscure; we do not understand the basis upon which they differ. Only if we forsake sensible qualities, including those that Aristotelian philosophy supposes to exist in bodies, and restrict ourselves to the **clear and distinct ideas** of **extension** and its modes, can we hope to attain genuine knowledge of the material world.

Nevertheless, as Descartes argues in the Sixth Meditation, it is only by appealing to sensation that we can **demonstrate** the existence of such a world. We understand that sensations arise from a passive power of the mind. They are not caused by the mind itself. Moreover we are incorrigibly persuaded that they are caused by extended things or bodies. **God** would therefore be a deceiver if he caused those sensations himself, or allowed them to be caused by something other than a body. Hence we cannot be in error in holding that the cause of our sensations is our bodies, and thus that such things exist. The Sixth Meditation attempts to extend that guarantee to more detailed claims about the world, thus vindicating the use of the senses in scientific enquiry.

SHAPE. Shape or figure is a **mode** of extended things or **bodies**. Although the shape of an individual body is determined by its **motion** in relation to the bodies contiguous with it, Descartes tends to attribute a more-or-less permanent shape to particles of the coarsest **element**, earth. Oil, for example, consists of slender, branched particles—hence its viscosity. In general the chief means of distinguishing terrestrial stuffs like water, oil, and iron is by way of the shapes of their particles, which determine not only their chemical but also their sensible qualities. **Nicolas Malebranche** usefully distinguishes figure from configuration: a cannonball has a spherical figure; the iron of which it is made consists of particles whose configuration is that of thick branched particles.

SILHON, JEAN DE (1596–1667). A religious apologist and friend and correspondent of Descartes. Silhon's main work, *Les deux vérités*, about the existence of **God** and the **immortality** of the **soul**, was well received when it was printed in 1626. Silhon also published a lengthy treatise, *L'immortalité de l'âme* (1634). Both works prefigure some of Descartes's characteristic theses. In the Second Discourse of the latter work, entitled "That It Is Necessary to Show God Exists before Proving the Immortality of the Soul. Refutation of Pyrrhonism and of the Arguments that Montaigne brings forth to establish it," Silhon argued that the existence of God, supreme cause of our being, unfolds from our knowledge of self, which overthrows the possibility that the senses are deceiving us or that we are dreaming.

SIMPLE NATURES. *See* JUDGMENT.

SORBONNE. Another name for the theology faculty at the University of Paris, not to be confused with the Collège de Sorbonne at the University. Descartes attempted to win the approbation of the **theology** faculty for his *Meditations* by dedicating the work to it. Individuals associated with the Sorbonne such as **Guillaume Gibieuf** and **Antoine Arnauld** were sympathetic to Descartes, and while this body never did formally endorse the *Meditations*, it also refrained from formally condemning it. Despite the best efforts of Arnauld, however, the Sorbonne followed its dean, Claude Morel, in enthusiastically supporting the state-sponsored campaign in the 1670s against the teaching of Cartesianism in the French universities. This support continued into the last decades of the reign of **Louis XIV**, when there were renewed attempts to eliminate Cartesian philosophy from the University of Paris.

SOREL, CHARLES (ca. 1602–74). Sorel was a French writer, best known for satirical histories and novels, such as *La Vraie histoire comique de Francion* (1622, 1633) and *Le Berger extravagant* (1627). He appears to have been one of Descartes's rivals. He wrote some criticism of the essayist **Jean-Louis Guez de Balzac**, to which Descartes replied. He also published *La Science universelle* (1634–41), a work that seems broadly to anticipate Descartes's project in the *Discourse on Method* for a new **method** and universal science. Sorel's science, like Descartes's, was supposed to reply to the claims of the skeptics and to supplant what the dogmatists taught in the schools. In the end, however, it was not as radical as what Descartes proposed, staying closer to **scholastic** thought; it was not especially attuned to the new **mathematics** and it seemingly made more room than Descartes's work for conclusions from **alchemy**, divination, the cabala, and so forth. In one of his later books, *La bibliothèque françoise* (1664, 1667), Sorel recommended to his readers "Descartes's method, his **natural philosophy**, his **metaphysics**, treatise on **passions**, and all his other works" as "masterpieces of subtlety and doctrine that produce admiration in innumerable people."

SOUL. Descartes preferred to use the term **mind** (Latin *mens,* French *esprit*) instead of the more traditional **Aristotelian** term, soul (Latin *anima,* French *âme*). The reason for this preference is indicated in his comment to his critic, **Pierre Gassendi,** that soul is ambiguous insofar as it can refer either to "the **principle** by which we are nourished and grow and accomplish without any thought all the other operations which we have in common with the brutes," or to "the principle in virtue of which we think." Since he focused for the most part on the soul as the principle that serves to distinguish us from other **animals,** Descartes held that "to avoid ambiguity I have, as far as possible, used the term mind for this. For I consider the mind not as part of the soul but as the thinking soul in its entirety" (AT, vol. VII, p. 356).

Even so, some later Cartesians insisted on the importance of the distinction in humans between soul and mind. Thus, **Robert Desgabets** protested that the Cartesian view in **Nicolas Malebranche** that we can understand the **nature** of our soul in terms of thought alone fails to distinguish the "pure mind" of an **angel** from a soul in us with thoughts that "naturally demand to be united with corporeal motions." **Pierre-Sylvain Régis** later adopted Desgabets's alternative position that all human thoughts require a **union** with **motion.** The argument for this position in both Cartesians emphasizes the Aristotelian definition of **time** as the measure of motion. On this argument, time can measure the duration of human **thoughts** only in virtue of the relation these thoughts bear to motion. *See also* DUALISM; IMAGINATION; IMMORTALITY; INTELLECT.

SOUL, IMMORTALITY OF. *See* IMMORTALITY.

SPACE. Descartes's **metaphysics** of space is structured by his definition of **matter** as simply **extension** in three dimensions. This implies that there is only a conceptual **distinction** between matter and the space it occupies: "space or internal place and the corporeal **substance** contained in it are not really distinct; the only difference is in the way we are accustomed to conceive of them" (AT, vol. VIIIA, p. 45). This identification of space and matter also implies the metaphysical impossibility of a **vacuum:** "As for a vacuum as it is understood philosophically, that is a space in which there is absolutely no substance, it is manifest from the fact that there is no difference between the extension of space and the extension of body that there can be no such thing" (AT, vol. VIIIA, p. 49). The common belief in empty space comes about because of our prejudice in favor of the senses. Not seeing any water in a pitcher, we call it empty and imagine that there is literally nothing in it when it is in fact filled with air; and if the air were removed, subtle matter would remain, but in no case could the pitcher contain literally nothing. Indeed, Descartes reasoned that if there were literally nothing in the pitcher, then its sides would be separated by nothing, which is to say that they would be in immediate contact with one another (AT, vol. VIIA, p. 50).

The Cartesian metaphysics of space also rules out the possibility of **atoms**. Being a plenum, space has its every part filled with material bodies whose essence is extension; but anything extended is **divisible**, so material bodies and space itself are filled with **indefinitely** divisible bodies. Space is also indefinite in extent, because the supposition of a finite space implies a limit or bound. But because we can imagine space extending beyond any supposed limit, there can be no end of space itself, which (because essence of **matter** is extension) implies that there is also an indefinite amount of matter contained in the universe. An additional consequence of this theory of space is that there cannot be a plurality of worlds: "even if there were an **infinity** of worlds, they would all have to be composed of the same matter; and thus there cannot be a plurality of worlds but only one; because we clearly conceive that this matter whose **nature** consists only in its being an extended substance, already occupies all the imaginable spaces where any of these other worlds would have to be" (AT, vol. VIIIA, p. 52).

SPINOZA, BARUCH (1632–77). Baruch (Benedictus) Spinoza (or d'Espinosa or de Spinoza) was born in 1632 the son of an Amsterdam family of Spanish ("Portuguese") Jews. Because of his impious doctrines and behavior he was expelled from the Synagogue in 1656. In Amsterdam he frequented libertines as well as heterodox Christians. In 1660 or 1661 he moved to Rijnsburg, a small village close to Leiden, in 1663 to Voorburg, close to The Hague, then, in 1669, to The Hague itself, where he died. The only works of his published during his lifetime are a "geometrical" and abridged version of Descartes's *Principles*, together with an appendix ("Metaphysical Thoughts") concerning general and special **metaphysics**, and a "Theologico-Political Treatise" (*Tractatus theologico-politicus*, 1670), published anonymously. Still, he was famous enough that many foreigners (for example, Henry Oldenburg and **Gottfried Wilhelm Leibniz**) came to visit him. He seems to have been an expert in lens grinding, providing lenses to **Christiaan Huy-**

gens and others. His "Posthumous Works" (*Opera posthuma*, 1677) were published after his death in 1677 and a bit later in Dutch translation as well. Apart from an unfinished "Treatise on the Improvement of the Intellect," the *Opera* also contains an "Ethics" (*Ethica*), generally seen as his main work, his correspondence, and an unfinished "Political Treatise" (*Tractatus politicus*). In the 19th century a "Short Treatise" (*Korte verhandeling*) appeared in manuscript—presumably the Dutch version of a Latin text. Given the alleged Cartesian **nature** of Spinoza's first work and Euclidean form of the *Ethics* he is often seen as a radical Cartesian: someone who, while using strictly Cartesian criteria, has the courage to apply them in areas Descartes avoided (such as morality and religion). But in Spinoza's own time there were also authors (**Pierre Bayle**, for example) who saw Spinozism as no more than a very old system, newly presented. According to this view, Spinoza's Cartesian **method** is strictly irrelevant for its result, which could also be reached without it.

What is clear is that there are many Cartesian theories Spinoza emphatically rejects. Not only has he a different conception of the relation of **God** to the world and of the mind to the **body**; he also rejects the Cartesian theory of **judgment** and the Cartesian theory of **ideas**. On the other hand, it is also clear that Spinoza uses specifically Cartesian concepts (like **substance**), even if he does not arrive at the same conclusions as Descartes. The best practice presumably is to interpret the relation between Spinoza and Descartes (Cartesianism) as dialectical: Spinoza uses and interprets Cartesian concepts in such a way that they can be used against Cartesian metaphysics. But it should be underscored that there is much disagreement about the way Spinoza should be interpreted: as a profoundly religious, albeit pantheist, thinker, or as a naturalist who sees religion at best as an instrument of the sovereign.

Spinoza's philosophy centers on the notion of God, whom he defines as "a substance consisting of infinite attributes, each of which expresses an eternal and infinite essence" (*Ethics* I, def. 6). This entails two types of conclusions. The first, negative: God cannot be the creator of the world, he is not free in the sense that he has freedom of choice; nor can he be seen as a divine lawgiver. The second, positive: God is nature; he coincides with world; he is power, infinite if considered at the level of nature as a whole, finite if seen at the level of finite being. Both results have, of course, extremely important consequences, not only for the theory of man, but also for that of morality, politics, and religion. First, man is part of nature. Spinoza rejects Descartes's idea that the human mind would be a thinking substance. Instead he believes that the human **mind** must be seen as the "idea of an actually existing human body" (*Ethics* II, prop. 13), that is, as the medium in which what is happening to the body is registered. Spinoza also rejects the Cartesian idea that man is a free agent. Instead he generalizes the model Descartes had developed for the **passions** to see the life of consciousness as the causally determined result of the interplay of various mental forces (passions, **imaginations, ideas**). Finally, Spinoza rejects the Cartesian theory of judgment, according to which each judgment consists of a passive and a dynamic element (an idea and a volition), claiming instead not only that in order to be true an idea does not have to be asserted to be true, but also that ideas may develop a certain force and momentum only by being associated with a passion.

Second, Spinoza's rejection of the idea that God could be a lawgiver implies that all authority is of human origin and inversely that the object of all obedience is ultimately a human institution. Naturally, this entails a reinterpretation of other forms of authority usually associated with religion, such as the authority of the Church or the authority of Scripture—indeed, it entails a theory of religion and revelation as the product of human minds. Still, the example of Moses shows how important religion can be in a political context; indeed, at best it provides an extra motive (next to the fear of the sovereign) for preferring the good of the whole (society, the state) to one's own interest, which, moreover, has the immense advantage of giving people the idea that their obedience is free.

Third, the positive determination of God's essence as power—a power not checked by any of the other attributes traditionally given to God, like wisdom, mercifulness, etc.—makes it possible to arrive at a new determination of right. Right is power, that is, the ability to do whatever a being can do in virtue of its own constitution insofar as that is not checked by the power of other beings. In the state of nature, which like **Thomas Hobbes** Spinoza sees as a kind of lower limit to human behavior, power, and accordingly right, is more or less equally divided among the members of the same species: All have the same constitution and all have basically the same power to resist the intrusion of others. But this equal division of power results in chaos and misery, given the fact that it is a law of nature that "nobody rejects what he judges to be good except through hope of a greater good or fear of a greater loss, and that no one endures any evil except to avoid a greater evil or to gain a greater good" (*Theologico-Political Treatise*, chap. 16, ed. Gebhardt, vol. III, pp. 191–92). Spinoza does not explain how the transition to a civil society takes place but describes the resulting situation as a redistribution of power: "The right of the sovereign is nothing but simple natural right, limited by the power, not of every individual, but of the multitude, which is guided as it were by one mind" (*Political Treatise*, chap. 3, §2). So the paradox of the civil society is that it can exist only insofar as "the multitude" subjects itself to a superior power, but that the very fact of subjecting itself collectively creates a force greater than any sovereign. Accordingly, any sovereign is best advised if he does not antagonize the people. A serious interpretive problem is posed by Part V of the *Ethics*, which introduces the notion of an "intellectual love of God." Based on "intuitive knowledge" (or "knowledge of the third kind") this should be sufficiently powerful to become a motive for virtue. The problem is not that that the only motive that is powerful enough to overcome evil is love—the problem is how knowledge of the being described as "God," whose essence is nothing but power, can produce "love."

SUÁREZ, FRANCISCO (1548–1617). Spanish **Jesuit** philosopher and theologian. Suárez entered the Society of Jesus in 1564 and studied law, philosophy, and **theology**. He taught philosophy and theology at various Jesuit colleges, including the **Collegio Romano** and the Colegio das Artes at Coimbra (1571–1616). In 1597 he published his massive *Disputationes metaphysicae*, perhaps the most important work in late **scholastic** thought. He also wrote numerous commentaries on the works of **Aristotle**. Jesuits at the time were required to teach Aristotelian and **Thomist** doctrines ordinarily. However, Suárez generally considered issues in the light of his predecessors and sided with others, John Duns Scotus in particular, almost as frequently as he sided with Thomas Aquinas; he also often took a direction that was his alone. Even when he agreed with Thomas or with Scotus, he modified their doctrines significantly. For example, he accepted Thomas's doctrine of analogical predication between **God** and creatures, but thought that a concept of being can be found which is strictly one. He identified this view as the common opinion that Scotus and all his disciples defended. Moreover, he accepted the **Scotist** view of **matter** existing without **form** by divine power, but, on the question of the plurality of human forms, he sided with Thomas. He argued, against Thomas and with Scotus, that the principle of individuation is a form (though he rejected other parts of Scotus's doctrine). He affirmed against Thomas the existence of a third **distinction** other than real and rational. He disputed the Thomist doctrine of a real distinction between essence and existence (calling it a distinction of **reason** with a basis in things) and between **substance** and accidents (though he rejected the Scotist formal distinction for what he called a modal distinction). Thus, Suárez seems to have been almost as much a Scotist as a Thomist. Descartes was clearly acquainted with the *Metaphysical Disputations*; he referred to Suárez's definition of material falsity and seems to have been influenced by his views on distinctions, especially the distinction of reason.

SUBSTANCE. In the **Aristotelian categories,** existent things are divided into substances and accidents. Aristotelian physics treats corporeal substances as composites of **substantial form** and prime **matter.** Each of these is regarded as a substance in its own right, "incomplete" because it requires the other to exist naturally, but substance nevertheless. Substance is defined in two ways: 1) a substance is a "subject of predication," as Socrates is of baldness or wisdom; 2) a substance is capable of subsisting by itself: Socrates can exist without his baldness and wisdom, but not vice versa.

Descartes made 2) the definition of substance. A substance is "a thing that exists in such a way that it needs no other thing to exist" (*Principles* I, art. 51). If that definition is taken strictly, only **God** is a substance, as **Baruch Spinoza** would later argue. Descartes therefore weakens it: a substance is a thing that requires "only the concurrence of God to exist." **Mind** and **body** are substances in the weaker sense. All other things do require something more than God's concurrence to exist. They are called **modes.** Each mode has a substance upon which it depends. The spherical shape of the Earth, for example, depends on the matter of the Earth, that is, on a certain portion of **extension** whose shape it is. Were the matter to be annihilated, its shape would cease to exist too.

Every substance other than God has, according to Descartes, a unique principal attribute. We find that in all the substances we encounter just two principal attributes are found: **thought** and **extension.** All the other modes of a substance are, with a few minor exceptions like duration and existence, "referred to" its principal attribute. The principal attribute of a substance constitutes its **nature** and essence; in Cartesian **metaphysics,** the principal attribute functions in many of the ways that substantial form does in Aristotelian metaphysics.

SUBSTANTIAL FORM. *See* FORM, SUBSTANTIAL.

SUBTLE MATTER. The term subtle was widely used in medieval and early modern **physics** to denote very small bits of matter. Fire, for example, was said to consist of "subtilized" air. In Cartesian physics, **bodies** come in three sizes which Descartes calls **elements.** "Subtle" denotes **particles** of the first or second kinds (fire and air), neither of which is perceptible as such to the senses. Subtle matter easily passes through the pores with which coarse matter tends to be traversed; Descartes invokes that capacity in explaining phenomena like the **rarefaction and condensation** of air and the transparency of glass. It is also invoked in order to save the Cartesian tenet on the impossibility of a **vacuum** (AT, vol. V, pp. 105, 116; see also **Rohault**, *Physica* I, chap. 12, pp. 59–73).

In Cartesian physiology, the **animal spirits that**, subtilized from the blood, fill up the nerves and the ventricles of the brain are also said to be "subtle." Even though they consist of "earthy" particles, those particles are much finer than the particles of other bodily fluids. In Descartes's world a particle tends to move faster the smaller it is. The animal spirits, therefore, like fire (their physical analogue) are capable of communicating small impulses of motion rapidly over a distance.

SURFACE. Euclid defines a surface as "that which has length and breadth only" (*Elements*, Book I, Definition 5). Thus defined, a surface is a limit or boundary of a solid in the same way a point is the limit of a line or a line a limit of a surface. Descartes accepted this traditional geometric understanding of surfaces, characterizing it as the conception "all mathematicians and philosophers have (or should have) when they distinguish a surface from a **body**" (*Sixth Replies*, AT, vol. VII, p. 433). He nevertheless had no great interest in the purely mathematical content of this definition. Instead, he employed the concept of surface in **natural philosophy** and **theology.** The application to natural philosophy appears in Descartes's definition of the external **place** of a body in terms of its surface. A body's external place, or its location as determined extrinsically by reference to its surroundings, is distinguished from internal place, or the portion of **space** circumscribed by it. As Descartes phrases the **distinction:** "internal place is exactly the same as space; but external place can be understood as the surface immediately surrounding what is in the place."

In commenting on this definition, Descartes stresses that "by 'surface' is not to be understood any part of the surrounding body, but simply the boundary between the surrounding and surrounded bodies, which is nothing more than a **mode**" (AT, vol. VIIIA, p. 48). A more interesting use of the definition of surface is Descartes's reconciliation of his **metaphysics** with the doctrine of **transubstantiation.** As he explains in the *Fourth Replies*, the surface of the communion bread is not a part of the bread, but merely a mode. Nevertheless, it is only the surface that is accessible to the senses; thus, the same surface can contain a very different kind of substance while appearing the same to the senses. The result is that transubstantiation is explained by the bread's having been turned into the body of Christ while its surface retains its original qualitative appearance. Descartes thought very highly of his theory of the Eucharist, remarking that "all these matters are so neatly and correctly explained by my **principles** that I have no reason to fear that anything here might give the slightest offence to orthodox theologians. On the contrary, I am confident that I will receive their thanks for putting forward opinions in physics that are far more in accord with theology than those commonly accepted" (AT, vol. VII, p. 252).

SYLLOGISM. In **Aristotelian logic**, the syllogism is the canonical form of an argument, consisting of two premises and a conclusion. In his *Prior Analytics* Aristotle distinguished between different "moods" and "figures" of syllogistic inference, which depend on the relationship among the predicate terms and quantifiers appearing in the premises. The great majority of medieval and early modern writings on logic were devoted to exposition and commentary on the Aristotelian *corpus*, and a course in Aristotelian syllogism was part of the standard curriculum in universities throughout Europe. Some authors, like **Petrus Ramus**, took a decidedly critical attitude toward the theory of the syllogism, complaining that it simply recapitulated what was already known and could not provide a **method** for the discovery of new **truths**.

Descartes was sympathetic to this sort of criticism, and in the second section of the *Discourse on Method* he repeated a standard complaint that "they serve rather to explain to someone else the things one already knows," or even to "speak without judgment on matters of which one is ignorant, rather than to learn them" (AT, vol. VI, p. 17). This is not to say that Descartes saw no place for the syllogism, since he was prepared to cast his own arguments in syllogistic form when he thought it appropriate, such as in the "Geometrical Appendix" to the Second Replies (AT, vol. VII, pp. 160–70). Nevertheless, he regarded the syllogism as a means of arranging things already known rather than a method of discovering anything new.

SYNTHESIS. *See* ANALYSIS.

– T –

THEOLOGY. In Descartes's time, there was an established distinction between "sacred" or "revealed theology," which concerns Christian mysteries that can be established only through an appeal to the Scriptures, and "natural theology," which concerns **truths** about Christianity that can be established through the use of natural **reason**. Protestants tended to emphasize the subordination of reason to the Scriptures in matters of **faith**, and so did not give a prominent place to natural theology. Though there also was a skeptical tradition in Catholic thought, the Catholic Church tended to allow for reason to play a more prominent role in theology. Descartes drew attention to this fact in the letter dedicating his *Meditations* to the Sorbonne. There he noted that the 1513 session of the Lateran Council condemned followers of Averroes who took Aristotle to show that personal immortality cannot be established by natural reason alone, and enjoined Christian philosophers to refute their arguments (AT, vol. VII, p. 3).

For the most part, Descartes attempted to steer clear of issues in sacred theology on the grounds that he was not competent to defend particular interpretations of Scripture or Church doctrine. However, he also insisted on the consistency of his philosophical system with the results of Catholic sacred theology, as when he noted in a 1637 letter that "the opinions that seemed to me most true in physics, when considering natural causes, have always been those which agree best of all with the mysteries of religion" (AT, vol. I, pp. 455–56). In a later letter to Marin Mersenne, Descartes held that critics who deny the theological purity of his views "confound Aristotle with the Bible and abuse the authority of the Church in order to vent their passions" (AT, vol. III, p. 349). One way in which Descartes attempted to respond to such critics was by arguing that his views are more compatible than the views of the Aristotelians with what the Church teaches about transubstantiation.

THIRTY YEARS' WAR. This war began in 1618 as a religious civil war in Bohemia and ended as a European-wide conflict that was settled in 1648 by the Treaty of Westphalia. The initial dispute was between Ferdinand II, Emperor of Bohemia, who had the support of Prince Maximillian of Bavaria and his Catholic League, and his Protestant opponents in Bohemia and the German Protestant princes allied with them. In its later stages, however, the war became a proxy for the struggle between two Catholic powers: Spain, which sided with Ferdinand, and France, which sided with the Protestant forces. In 1635, after France had openly intervened on the side of the Protestants, the Louvain theologian Cornelius Jansenius wrote a pamphlet, *Mars Gallicus*, that criticized the anti-Catholic policies of the French First Minister Cardinal Richelieu. This pamphlet foreshadowed the later theologico-political battles in France over Jansenius and Jansenism.

In 1619, after finishing his schooling at La Flèche, Descartes decided to join the army of the Catholic Maximillian, which at this early point was supported by France. While en route to his military service, he was detained in a small stove-heated room near Ulm. Descartes's biographer Adrien Baillet reported that it was there, in November 1619, that Descartes had a series of three dreams that gave rise to the project of showing that all of knowledge is interconnected. About this time Descartes may also have drafted parts of his *Rules for the Direction of the Mind*.

THOMAS AQUINAS (ca. 1225–74). *See* THOMISM.

THOMISM. The doctrine associated with Saint Thomas Aquinas and his followers, a synthesis of **Aristotelian** philosophy and Christian theology. There was a renaissance in Thomism during the second half of the 16th century. For the duration of the Council of Trent (1545–63), Thomas's *Summa theologiae* was placed next to the Bible, on the same table, to help the council in its deliberations. In 1567 Pope Pius V proclaimed Thomas Doctor of the Church. Ignatius of Loyola, founder of the **Jesuits,** advised the members of his society to follow his doctrines. Thus the philosophy the Jesuits taught Descartes at La Flèche was primarily Thomism.

The modern Catholic Church promoted Thomism as well. It attempted to define Thomism through its essential theses. The first set of theses characterized Thomist **metaphysics.** All beings are composed of potential and actual principles, except **God,** who is pure act, utterly simple, and unlimited. He alone exists independently; other beings are composite and limited. Being is not predicated univocally of God and creatures, and divine being is understood by analogy. There is a real distinction between essence and existence and between **substance** and accidents. Spiritual creatures (such as **angels**) are composed of essence and existence and substance and accident, but not **matter and form.**

The next set of theses treated corporeal beings, then humans more specifically. Corporeal creatures are composite; that is, they are constituted of matter and form, neither of which may exist by itself *(per se)*. They are extended in **space** and subject to quantification; quantified (or *signate*) matter is the principle of individuation. **Bodies** can be in only one place at a time. There are animate and vegetative **souls,** which are destroyed at the dissolution of the composite entity. Human souls are capable of existing apart from their bodies, are created by God, are without parts and so cannot be disintegrated naturally (that is, they are immortal). They are the immediate source of life, existence, and perfection in human bodies, and are so united to the body as to be its single **substantial form.** The two faculties of the human soul, cognition and **volition,** are distinguished from each other, and sensitive knowledge is distinct from intellection. The proper object of the human **intellect,** in its state of **union with a body,** is restricted to "quiddities" (or essences) abstracted from material conditions. Volitions are said to be free.

The last three theses concerned knowledge of God. Divine existence is neither intuited nor demonstrable *a priori*, but it is capable of demonstration *a posteriori*. The simplicity of God entails the identity between his essence and his existence. God is creator and first cause of all things in the universe.

THOUGHT. Descartes distinguished between thought as a "principal attribute" of **mind**, that is, of thinking **substance**, from particular thoughts as modes that depend on that attribute. He also held that though all minds possess the same generic attribute of thought, they nonetheless are distinct since they possess numerically distinct attributes of the same kind. Thought as principal attribute is manifested in various different "faculties" with their own peculiar kind of **mode**. There is an initial distinction between **intellect** as the passive faculty of perception and **will** as the active faculty of volition. The faculty of perception is itself distinguished into the faculties of **sensation** and **imagination**, which rely on the **soul-body union**, and the faculty of "pure intellect," which the mind possesses even apart from its union with the body. Descartes indicated in the Sixth Meditation that pure intellect is the only perceptual faculty that pertains to the "essence" of mind, since it is the only such faculty that the mind cannot lack.

TIME. In Aristotle's *Physics*, time is defined as "the measure of **motion** with respect to before and after," which is **continuous** insofar as the motion it measures is continuous. In correspondence with Descartes, **Antoine Arnauld** appealed to this definition in order to object to Descartes's claim in the Third Meditation that his **mind** has a duration that is divisible into "innumerable parts" (AT, vol. VII, p. 49). Arnauld's objection is that since at this point in the *Meditations* Descartes was doubting the existence of **bodies** in motion, he cannot attribute to his mind a **divisible** temporal duration (AT, vol. V, p. 188f). Descartes responded that Arnauld's objection "rests on the **scholastic** position . . . with which I greatly differ." He noted in particular that even if there were no material world, it would still be the case that there is a successiveness in our **thoughts** that allows us to distinguish the duration of our mind from the eternity of God's existence (AT, vol. V, p. 193). Descartes also indicated that the primary case of duration for us is not that of bodily motion, but rather "the before and after of the successive duration that I detect in my own thought, with which other things coexist" (AT, vol. V, p. 223).

Descartes scholars disagree over the precise import of the view in the Third Meditation that our existence is divisible into parts. Some take this view to suggest that time is a discontinuous quantity composed of durationless instants. These commentators have appealed to this reading in taking Descartes to claim that we grasp the **truth** of the *cogito* in a timeless instant. Others have objected that Descartes was no more sympathetic to temporal **atomism** than he was to atomism in the physical world. For them, instants are merely the boundaries of continuous parts of time. On this reading, our grasp of the *cogito* occurs not in a timeless instant, but rather in a bounded portion of time.

Among Descartes's later followers, **Robert Desgabets** insisted that our thoughts concerning the *cogito* occur in continuous time. Since he also accepted the traditional Aristotelian view that this sort of time is the measure of motion, however, Desgabets further held that the duration of these thoughts is tied to bodily motion. Thus, he rejected Descartes's claim, to which Arnauld also had objected, that we can understand our mind to have a temporal duration even while doubting the existence of the material world.

TOLETUS, FRANCISCUS (1532–96). Spanish **Jesuit** philosopher and theologian. Toletus (Francisco de Toledo) studied in Valencia and Salamanca (under the Dominican philosopher Domingo de Soto). He entered the Society of Jesus in 1558, and taught philosophy then **theology** (1559–69) at the **Collegio Romano**, the Jesuits' main educational institution. He went on several diplomatic missions for the Catholic Church and, in 1593, became a cardinal (the first who was a Jesuit). Toletus published several commentaries on **Aristotle's** works, all of them receiving multiple editions. He also wrote a commentary on **Thomas Aquinas's** *Summa Theologiae* (published posthumously in the 19th century). Descartes remembered him as one of the Jesuit philosophers whose textbooks he read in his youth, along with the **Conimbricenses** and **Antonio Rubio**.

TRANSUBSTANTIATION. A term invented in the 12th century that was used in a 1551 decree from the Council of Trent to express the Catholic doctrine that the sacrament of the Eucharist involves the Real Presence of Christ. On the Tridentine view, the words of consecration bring about the replacement of the **substance** of the bread and wine with the substance of the body and blood of Christ. There were disputes about the **nature** of this replacement between **Thomists**, who held that the substance of the Eucharistic elements is converted into the substance of Christ's body and blood, and **Scotists**, who insisted that the substance of the former is annihilated and replaced by the substance of the latter. However, Catholics were united in their opposition to Protestants who denied the doctrine of transubstantiation altogether. This dispute provides some of the background to the religious wars in late-16th and early-17th-century France between the Catholic majority and the Calvinist minority. In his set of objections to the *Meditations*, Antoine Arnauld raised the issue of the Eucharist as a potential theological objection to Descartes's system. He emphasized not the issue of the transubstantiation, but rather the Tridentine doctrine that the "species" of the Eucharistic elements remain after consecration. In his original response, Descartes included the charge that the **scholastic** identification of these species with **real qualities** verges on heresy. Descartes's editor **Marin Mersenne** excised this passage from the 1641 Paris edition of the *Meditations* out of fear that it would compromise the attempt to win the approval of the **Sorbonne**. However, Descartes reinserted the excised portion into the 1642 edition of this text, which was published in Amsterdam.

Descartes addressed the even more sensitive issue of transubstantiation privately in 1645 **correspondence** with **Denis Mesland**, where he proposed that the Real Presence involves the union of Christ's **soul** with the matter of the Eucharistic elements. After Descartes's death, his literary executor **Claude Clerselier** refrained from publishing this correspondence out of fear that critics of Cartesianism would interpret it as supporting the Calvinist denial of the Real Presence. In 1671, however, **Robert Desgabets** published a pamphlet in which he defended this proposal as offering an intelligible form of Thomistic conversion theory. Critics such as the royal confessor **Jean Ferrier** took the pamphlet rather to support a heretical Calvinist position, and the ensuing controversy helped to bring about a state-sponsored campaign in France to suppress the teaching of Cartesianism in the French universities and religious orders.

TREATISE ON LIGHT OR THE WORLD (*TRAITÉ DE LA LUMIÈRE, LE MONDE*). Descartes's first documented attempt to write a general treatise on **physics** goes back to the winter of 1629–30, after he returned from Franeker to Amsterdam. Especially in its first phase, this project can hardly be distinguished from that of the *Meteors*, which starts in about the same period. But whereas the *Meteors* grow from an attempt to explain a single phenomenon thoroughly, Descartes soon wants to "explain all phenomena of **nature**," that is, write "a complete physics." He already has a plan "for I believe I found a way to present all my thoughts in such a way that they will satisfy some without giving others the opportunity to contradict them" (to **Mersenne**, November 30, 1630, AT, vol. I, p. 70). Whether that is already the definitive plan is not certain strictly speaking but the way in which Descartes refers to it here resembles in any case the way he describes and motivates it when he looks back in the *Discourse*: "Just as painters, who cannot represent in a flat picture all the sides of a solid body choose to enlighten one of the more important while leaving in the shadow all the others and show them only partially, I too, fearing that I could not put into my discourse all the things I had in my mind, I decided to present fully only what I thought of **light**; then to add something on the sun and the fixed stars because almost all light comes from them; on the heavens because they transmit it; on the planets, the comets and the earth because they reflect it; and particularly of all bodies on the earth because they are either colored, or transparent, or luminous, and finally on man who is of all that the spectator" (*Discourse* V, AT, vol. VI, pp. 41–42).

So the new treatise would be organized, not in the fashion of a **scholastic** textbook like the *Principles* will be, but in a quite novel way, namely, around the concept of light. Descartes further adds that, "in order to say more freely what I thought" and to avoid a discussion of alternative explanations and opinions, he decided to leave the actual world to the disputes of the learned and to limit himself to a presentation of what would happen in a new world, that is, "if **God** now created somewhere in the imaginary **spaces** enough **matter** to compose it and if he moved in all sorts of ways and without any order the various parts of that matter, and so create a chaos as confused as the poets can imagine, without giving it any more than his ordinary assistance, leaving it to act according to the laws he has established" (*Discourse* V, AT, vol. VI, p. 42).

In any case, Descartes goes to work immediately even if he has great difficulty in keeping himself at work. On December 18, 1629, he asks Marin Mersenne not to write again: "for one or two months I want to do some serious work; what is written down of my treatise would occupy less than half of this letter and I am deeply ashamed of it" (AT, vol. I, p. 104). In April he admits that he is working slowly but "that does not prevent me from finishing the small treatise I started but I don't wish that others know about it in order for me to be free to denounce it" (to Mersenne, April 15, 1630, AT, vol. I, pp. 137–47). Finally, in July 1633 the treatise is "almost finished" despite the fact that, as Descartes had told Mersenne in an earlier letter, the result is no more than "an abridged version" (*quasi un abrégé*). In fact, correcting and copying the draft cost so much time and trouble that in November 1633 there is a neat copy of only the first half. That is what Descartes is about to offer Mersenne as a New Year's gift when he learns that the Roman Catholic Church officially condemned **Galileo Galilei** for holding the view that the earth moves around the sun. He does not send the text to Mersenne and "suppresses" it and "destroys the work of four years simply to obey the Church" (to Mersenne, February 1634, AT, vol. I, p. 281). Although Descartes continues to work on what would have been the second half of his "Treatise on Light" he completely abandons the first half, which apparently he has given the title "The World" (*Le monde*). It is under that title that the text was shown to a few reliable friends, like Henricus Regius and Constantijn Huygens. Huygens even tries to make Descartes come back on his decision not to publish it, but to no avail. The only concession Descartes is prepared to make is that he includes a summary of *The World* in Part V of the *Discourse*, leaving out whatever relates to the **motion of the earth**.

The World was first published in 1664 after Descartes's death by a certain "D. A." This is generally believed to be Pierre d'Alibert, who in the 1660s was also responsible for bringing Descartes's body to France and reburying it there. **Claude Clerselier** provided a better edition in 1677, together with the *Treatise on Man*. The original manuscript never resurfaced. The work is interesting not only as a stylistic experiment, but also because it is presumably the first time that nature is defined not in terms of a set of phenomena (say, the whole of the world of change), but in terms of what can be conceived clearly and distinctly. Nature is whatever we can understand by means of the **clear and distinct ideas** of **extension** and local **motion**. Accordingly, the "fable" of the "new world" is actually a theoretical model of the universe or, alternatively, a general framework for the science of nature.

TREATISE ON MAN (*TRAITÉ DE L'HOMME; TRACTATUS DE HOMINE*). Already in his original plan of a *Treatise on Light* Descartes presumably foresaw a part on man, but it is not absolutely clear what he had in mind, whether a treatise on **optics** or a treatise on man as a living being. In June 1632 the point seems to be settled in favor of the second alternative: "For a month I have been wondering whether I would describe how the generation of **animals** goes in my world but in the end I decided not to do it because that would take too much time. I finished whatever I wanted to propose concerning inanimate bodies; all I have to do now is to add a few things concerning the **nature** of man" (to **Mersenne**, June 1632, AT, vol. I, pp. 254–55). But in November 1633 it became clear to Descartes that the Roman Catholic Church condemned the ideas of **Galileo Galilei** and that it would be impossible to publish his "Treatise on Light." Accordingly, he separated the two halves, kept the first, finished half for himself but continued to work on the second half, which most of the time he called his "Treatise of Animals" (*Traité des animaux*).

A summary of the treatise (rather a list of the subjects treated in it) was published in 1637 in the *Discourse*. It shows that in its original form it contained a discussion not only of all vital and animal functions,

including the **circulation of the blood,** but also of the difference between animals and men, of the human **soul** and of the **union of body
and mind.** Descartes's main heuristic hypothesis is that, if considered
without a **mind,** man can be seen as an **automaton,** that is, as a self-
regulating **machine;** in other words if we can imagine a mechanical
equivalent for a given biological function, that function is "mechanical." According to a letter to Marin Mersenne of September 23, 1646,
written after the publication of **Henricus Regius's** *Fundamenta
physices* (1646), parts of which were, according to Descartes, stolen
from the manuscript of his unpublished treatise, he had started to work
on it "twelve or thirteen years ago," that is, 1633–34, and continued
until "four or five years ago," that is, in 1641–42, when the paper on
which he had written it had become such a mess that, when he lent it to
"an intimate friend," this person made a neat copy, "which since then
was transcribed by two others, with my permission, but without me su-
pervising or correcting it" (to Mersenne, November 23, 1646, AT, vol.
IV, pp. 566–67). As a result, the finished treatise, as it was eventually
published, reflects an evolution that took almost 10 years.

The work was first published in a Latin translation in 1662. The
editor/translator was Florentius Schuyl (1619–69), who also made most
of the drawings. According to the preface, his text is based on two
copies made after the autograph, one in the possession of Antonie
Studler van Zurck (ca. 1608–66), a Dutch nobleman who was a friend
of Descartes, and the second from **Alphonse Pollot,** whose copy would
be the source of two of the drawings—all other drawings were made
by, or under the direction of Schuyl. For a second edition, published in
1664, he also made use of two other copies, one of which came from
Adriaan Heereboord. Also in 1664 **Claude Clerselier** published a
French version of the text, which according to him is based on the only
authentic manuscript, namely, the one possessed by Descartes himself.
An additional problem is produced by the illustrations. Apparently, the
copy in the possession of Clerselier was not illustrated at all. Eventually
two sets of illustrations were made, one by Gerard van Gutschoven
(1615–68), a professor of philosophy and medicine from **Louvain,** and
the other by **Louis de La Forge,** who also wrote a commentary on Descartes's work. A selection from both was used for the book.

TRUTH. Descartes holds that, in the first instance, truth is a property of
ideas, so that truth and falsity are a matter of an idea's conformity (or
lack of conformity) to an external realm of things. Descartes phrases the
issue by saying that truth is "the conformity of **thought** with its object"
(AT, vol. II, p. 597). This means that it makes sense to speak of true or
false ideas or thoughts, and the truth of a judgment amounts to its being

the affirmation of a true idea. Descartes regarded the concept of truth as something so simple that it was incapable of further explication beyond saying that truth is conformity of an idea to the extra-mental world. To seek anything beyond this verbal definition of truth would require the employment of the very concept being explicated. As he remarked in a letter to **Marin Mersenne**: "we cannot give a definition that helps to know its **nature**" (AT, vol. II, p. 597), since to understand the definition of the concept of truth we would have to know that this was the true explication of its nature. The concept of truth is therefore innate, and serves as part of the ultimate foundation of all knowledge, like the ideas of the self, **God**, or the **infinite**. The question remains how we can ascertain the truth of our ideas, since Descartes's account of truth does not provide a means of discerning which ideas correctly represent an extra-mental world. The Cartesian solution to this difficulty is the so-called "truth rule" in the Fourth Meditation which guarantees that all those ideas we **clearly and distinctly** perceive are true (AT, vol. VII, p. 62).

– U –

UNION OF MIND AND BODY. Descartes holds that the human **mind** and its **body** together form a union. In the philosophical vocabulary of his period, union can be said to hold between any things that form a unity; since things can be said to be one in many ways, there are many sorts of union (**Rudolph Goclenius**, *Lexicon* s.v.). The union between **soul** and body is, according to **Aristotelian** authors, real, physical, and substantial: the soul is the **substantial form** of the body, with which it forms one complete **substance**.

On this question Descartes agrees with the Aristotelians. The soul is comparable to a substantial form insofar as it "gives being" to the body (by unifying its many parts into one thing) and yields a single thing—a human being. The unity of soul and body in the human being is the highest degree of unity that distinct substances can enter into. Our evidence for the union consists in the causal relations between soul and body whose existence we infer with moral **certainty** from experience (*Principles* II, art. 2) and in the influence of the **passions** on the **will**, which produces in us a solicitude for our own body that we do not have for any other (Sixth Meditation).

Descartes's **physics** made substantial forms superfluous, and his analogy therefore unpersuasive. Few subsequent authors accepted the doctrine of union in the version proposed by him. Even **Pierre-Sylvain Régis** treats the relation as one of mutual dependence in action.

UNIVERSALS. A universal is a property or quality that many individuals may share. Thus, in addition to the many red things in the world there is the property of redness, or the **quality** of being red. More abstract properties, such as justice, and abstract mathematical objects such as numbers are also typically taken to be universals. A standard philosophical problem arises concerning the ontological status of universals—do they exist outside of our **thought**, or is their reality purely linguistic or conceptual? Descartes held that universals were merely modes of thought, with no extra-mental reality; as he put it in article 58 of Part I of the *Principles*: "Number and all universals are only modes of thought" (AT, vol. VIIIA, p. 27). Cartesian universals are not an object of the senses, but rather the **intellect**, which arrives at them by a process of **abstraction** from particular cases. This process of abstraction involves the consideration of common features (and differences) among individuals, whose ultimate result is that "five universals are commonly reckoned, namely, genus, species, difference, property, accident" (AT, vol. VIIIA, p. 28).

UTRECHT, UNIVERSITY OF. The University of Utrecht was founded in 1636, after the Universities of **Leiden**, Franeker, and Groningen, which were founded in 1575, 1581, and 1619 respectively, but before the University of Harderwijk, which was founded in 1648. Started as an "illustrious school" (an institution for higher education, which is not allowed to confer academic degrees) in 1634, it had from the beginning a civic character, being governed and funded by the municipal government. Among its first professors were **Henricus Reneri** (philosophy), Antonius Aemilius (history), and **Gysbertus Voetius (theology)**. Although Reneri is often seen as the first Cartesian, it is more correct to describe him as an eclectic. In 1639 at his funeral, however, Aemilius, who pronounced the funeral oration, caused great unease by mixing into his speech a eulogy of Descartes. The terms in which he praised Descartes and his philosophy presumably were a reason for Voetius to include, without naming Descartes for that matter, a few warnings against the exaggerated expectations some people had with respect to certain new philosophies. The disappointment he anticipated could only lead to skepticism, which in turn was the main condition for **atheism**. The first Cartesian to be appointed to the University was in fact **Henricus Regius**, who became a professor "extra ordinem" (today we would probably say "associate professor") in theoretical medicine in 1638.

Although a series of disputations submitted by Regius in the spring of 1641 caused some suspicions, nothing serious happened before December 8, when Regius submitted a series of propositions, one to the effect that man is an accidental being, because **body** as well as **mind** are complete **substances**, and another defending the **Copernican** hypothesis on the **motion of the Earth.**

For the theologians, who became increasingly irritated by Regius's attacks on **Aristotle,** this was obviously the last straw. Voetius, at that point rector of the university and already an authority in Orthodox theology, added to a disputation planned for December 18 a gravamen in which the idea that man is an accidental being is implied to be atheist, or at least to favor atheism; the heliocentric hypothesis is proclaimed to be contrary to biblical evidence; and the rejection of "**substantial forms**" (one of the principal concepts of the Neo-Aristotelian philosophy usually taught in the 17th century) is considered to be dangerous and premature. Further objections, which were detailed in a letter of the theologians to their colleagues of other faculties, were that without Aristotelian philosophy it became impossible to teach theology; that without knowing the technical terms of Aristotelian philosophy, students would not be able to participate in the academic debate; and that students from Utrecht would find it more difficult to obtain a job.

Thanks to the intervention of Gysbertus van der Hoolck, a Utrecht burgomaster, who on behalf of the municipal government was more particularly in charge of matters regarding the university but who also was a personal friend of Descartes, the theologians toned down their intervention but, after the disputation had taken place on December 18, Voetius added a small treatise on "substantial forms," which he submitted for disputation on December 23 and 24. The burgomasters, on the other hand, asked the Senate (the assembly of professors) to write a memorandum on the limits which philosophy teaching would have to respect. Apparently, they hoped to arrive at a strict demarcation between the faculties of theology and philosophy.

While all this was happening, Regius, helped by Descartes, prepared a "Response to Voetius" (*Responsio*), which was published in February. It amounted to a clumsy attempt to turn the tables on Voetius by showing that the greatest threat to traditional theology is the doctrine of substantial forms, rather than the philosophy of Descartes. The result was not only that Regius was relegated to the Faculty of Medicine, but also that the Senate, headed by their rector, Voetius, obtained permission to issue a judgment on the new philosophy, by which they not only dissociated from Regius but also voiced their reservations on the new philosophy. Descartes, on the other hand, took advantage of the delay in the printing of the second edition of the *Meditations* to include a "Letter to Father Dinet," in which he complained about the slow and hesitant reaction of the Jesuit order to his philosophy (Jacques Dinet was provincial of the Jesuits in the Île-de-France) and gave a detailed report on the crisis in Utrecht. More particularly, he accused Voetius, whom he saw as the real author of the judgment, of misusing his position as rector of the university to settle a personal account with Regius. Finally, he included a vitriolic portrait of Voetius as a person of limited intellectual abilities and someone with a quarrelsome **nature**, who by preaching against the rich and the worldly actually undermined the position of the authorities.

Not surprisingly, Voetius did not take this well. He asked **Martinus Schoock** to take his defense, which Schoock did by writing a book that would be known as "The Admirable Method of René Descartes" (*Admiranda methodus*, 1643). Before it was even completely printed Descartes got hold of the first part of the proofs. He wrote a reply in the form of an open letter to Voetius (*Epistola ad Voetium*, 1643, also published in a Dutch translation), which caused new trouble. Indeed, Voetius managed to have the tables turned on Descartes, who was now accused of libel. A lawsuit followed but was stopped after an intervention of the stadtholder. Descartes turned his attention to Schoock in Groningen and, through an intervention of the French ambassador, filed a complaint with the States of Groningen—not only to the upper judicial authority of the province, but also to the highest governors of the University. In his highly ambiguous declaration before the academic tribunal Schoock put all the blame on Voetius: he was the real author of *Admiranda methodus*; all Schoock had done was to give it its final form. But Descartes's attempt to use this outcome for building a new case against Voetius failed. A letter to the Utrecht municipality remained unanswered. A long and formal request to reopen the case, which Descartes sent in two languages (Dutch and French) in 1648 and in which he gave a report of his dealings with Voetius, was filed but did not lead to any action—it was published posthumously in a Latin translation in 1656 and is now known as *Lettre apologétique aux Magistrats d'Utrecht*.

Still, if abstraction is made from the personal feelings of bitterness Descartes may have had about how things developed, it becomes clear that the situation of Cartesian philosophy in Utrecht was not excessively bad. Not only did Regius continue to teach Cartesian ideas in the Medical Faculty; few people outside the Theological Faculty had much sympathy with Voetius. And although Voetius managed to have his two sons, Paulus (1619–67) and Daniel (1630–60), appointed reader in metaphysics, in 1652 the administrators appointed the Cartesian Johannes de Bruyn (1620–75) to the chair of philosophy. Moreover, the vacancy left by the early death of Daniel Voetius in 1660 was filled by Regnerus van Mansvelt, a representative of the new ideas. Finally, in 1663 the administration appointed **Frans Burman** (1628–79), a prominent representative of Coccejan theology who openly sympathized with

Cartesianism, to counterbalance the influence of Voetius. It was only after the political crisis of 1672 (when with the help of the Church and the people William III took power), the occupation by the French troops (which exacted a levy from the town that impoverished it for many years), and the appointment of the very traditional Gerard de Vries as primary professor of philosophy, that reaction set in and that the University of Utrecht became one of the most anti-Cartesian of the Netherlands.

– V –

VACUUM/VOID. In his *Principles of Philosophy*, Descartes emphasized that "the philosophy of Democritus differs from my own just as much as it differs from the standard view of **Aristotle** and others" (AT, vol. VIIIA, p. 325). One aspect of Democritus's **atomism** that he criticized explicitly is the claim that there is a vacuum or void separating corpuscles that itself contains no matter. Somewhat surprisingly, Descartes's critique of the vacuum in the *Principles* is linked to certain points that Aristotle had earlier offered against the void. In his *Physics*, Aristotle appealed to the result that place is simply the boundary of a **body** to show that there cannot be a place that is separate from body. In **scholastic** philosophy, the Aristotelian account of place was complicated somewhat with the introduction of a **distinction** between internal place, or the **space** that a body occupies, and external place, or the external surface that contains a body. In his early *Rules for the Direction of the Mind*, Descartes ridiculed this scholastic distinction. In the later *Principles*, however, he offered a version of it. In particular, Descartes distinguished between the internal place identified with the volume of a particular body, which must move with that body, and the external place identified with a particular **surface** considered in abstraction from any particular body. However, he endorsed the basic Aristotelian point that there cannot be any place or space that is ontologically distinct from body. Thus, there cannot be any place or space without body, that is to say, there can be no vacuum or void.

In 1647, Descartes learned during a visit with the young **Blaise Pascal** in Paris about experiments that involved the creation of a space at the top of a tube of mercury. Whereas Pascal took these experiments to reveal the existence of vacua in **nature**, Descartes insisted that the top of the tube could be filled with "**subtle matter**" that penetrates through pores in the glass. Descartes's physics teacher at **La Flèche**, the **Jesuit Étienne Nöel**, had defended a similar view against Pascal. Since **light** can be transmitted through the supposedly empty space in the top of the tube and this transmission requires an appropriate medium, there must be some such medium in the top of the tube.

VANINI, LUCILIO (1585–1619). Vanini was a churchman who was condemned as an **atheist** and burned at the stake in Toulouse. His two principal works were *Amphitheatrum aeternae Providentiae divino-magicum, christiano-physicum, necnon astrologo-catholicum* (1615) and *De admirandis Naturae Reginae Deaeque mortalium Arcanis* (1616). Descartes referred to Vanini as one of the "innovators," along with **Giordano Bruno** (another philosopher burned at the stake) and **Sebastian Basso**. In 1643 Descartes had to defend himself against the accusation of the **Utrecht** theologian **Gysbertus Voetius** that his philosophy was similar to Vanini's in that both strengthened atheism by merely pretending to dispute it, using weak arguments.

VATIER, ANTOINE (1591–1659). A French **Jesuit** and teacher at La Flèche. Vatier studied philosophy at La Flèche (1615–18, just after Descartes had left) and stayed to teach humanities and **mathematics** (1618–21). He taught philosophy in Paris when Descartes resided there and returned to La Flèche as professor of philosophy and **theology** (1630–32 and 1634–42). Descartes received some letters from Vatier praising the *Discourse on Method*. He was quite pleased by this approbation, mentioning it a number of times. In his letter to **Denis Mesland** Descartes even asked for Vatier's opinion of his explanation of the **Eucharist**.

VIÈTE, FRANÇOIS (1540–1603). French mathematician renowned for his fundamental contributions to the development of **algebraic methods**. Viète was the son of Etienne Viète, a lawyer in Fontenay-le-Comte in western France about 50 kilometers east of the coastal town of La Rochelle. Little is known about his early education, but he trained for a career in law, taking a law degree from the University of Poitiers in 1560. After completing his legal studies, he practiced law in La Rochelle. Viète's religious sympathies were Protestant, and the persecution of Huguenots in Brittany forced him to relocate to Paris in 1570. He survived the Saint Bartholomew's Day Massacre of Protestants in 1572 and even became counselor for the Parlement of Brittany in 1573. The Parlement was based in Rennes, and Viète moved there in 1573, where he remained until returning to Paris in 1580. Viète was appointed as royal privy counselor by Henry III in March 1580 and he was attached to the Parlement in Paris. Although he was never employed as a professional scientist or mathematician, Viète's increasing wealth and the minimal demands of his legal offices left him time to pursue his long-standing mathematical interests. Much of his research focused on questions in cryptology and algebra. He achieved numerous results in these fields, which he began to publish privately in small quantities and circulate among French mathematicians, particularly those in Paris.

In 1584 political events forced Viète to leave Paris; his position as a known Huguenot made him the object of intrigue and he was banished by his political enemies from the court. He moved to the Brittany coast and spent the next five years engaged almost exclusively in mathematical studies. He returned to Paris in 1589 after the accession of Henri IV. By the early 1590s Viète had established a considerable reputation as a mathematician and cryptographer. This reputation increased substantially in 1590 when Viète broke a complex cipher of more than 500 characters in use by King Philip II of Spain, in the course of his war against Huguenot forces in France. When Philip discovered that his French opponents were aware of his military plans, he complained that his enemies must have used black magic to frustrate his campaign against the Huguenots.

Viète published numerous works, often in very small quantities, dealing with algebra, trigonometry, and astronomy. He was one of the first European mathematicians to undertake a systematic study of plane and spherical trigonometric methods, utilizing all six trigonometric functions. Viète has been called the father of modern algebraic notation. His most influential work was his 1591 *In artem analyticem isagoge* ("Introduction to the Analytic Art"), which was the standard work on algebra for decades. His posthumously published *D e aequationum recognitione et emendatione* ("On the Recognition and Emendation of Equations," 1615) presented methods for solving equations of the second, third, and fourth degree.

Despite the centrality of Viète's contributions and the widespread reputation of his works among French mathematicians, Descartes was very reluctant to acknowledge any intellectual debts to him. In defense of the originality of his *Geometry*, Descartes claimed he had "never even seen the cover" of Viète's *In artem analyticem isagoge* and denied ever having studied any of Viète's works (AT, vol. II, p. 524).

VINCENT, JEAN (ca. 1606–ca. 1673). Jean Vincent joined the Doctrinaires around 1625, taught philosophy and became rector of the college at Toulouse, then ultimately provincial of the province (1663–73). Vincent published a conservative textbook, *Cursus philosophicus* (1658-1671), mostly following **Thomist** philosophy. In 1677 he published a critique of Cartesian philosophy, *Discussio peripatetica in qua philosophiae cartesianae principia . . . examinantur*. There he rejected the

method of **doubt**, denied the *cogito*, and opposed **extension** as the essence of **body**. Vincent's arguments were often based on the authority of revelation. For example, he claimed that the Cartesian proposition that the **nature** of body consists only in extension could not be maintained without heresy. His argument was that a conclusion derived from a mystery of the **faith** cannot be denied without error and we know by faith that Christ's body is in the **Eucharist**. Moreover, in the Eucharist, the body of Christ is present entirely in each and every part of every consecrated host: "The body of Christ is found, therefore, integrally and without any division in the least part of the holy sacrament and thus, as a result, indivisibly and without extension" (*Discussio*, p. 39).

VIRTUE. Apart from one passage in *The World*, where Descartes uses *vertu* in a physical sense as the power a **body** has to move itself, virtue is usually taken in a moral sense as the habit of doing the good things that depend on us, that is, on our **free will**. Descartes also calls them habits of the **soul**, which dispose it to certain **thoughts**. In sum, virtue is the "firm and constant resolution to do exactly whatever one judges to be the best and to use all the forces of one's mind to know them" (to **Christina**, November 20, 1647, AT, vol. V, p. 83). Accordingly, it is based on knowledge and **judgment**: "given the fact that our will follows or avoids only those things which our understanding represents as good or bad, to do the good it is enough to judge well, and to do the best we can, that is, to acquire all virtues and at the same time all the other goods one can acquire" (*Discourse* III, AT, vol. VI, p. 28). But this condition is not absolute, given the fact that virtue may spring from a defect or an **error**: "Thus simplicity is often the cause of goodness, fear of devotion, and despair of courage" (*Principles*, Dedicatory letter to **Elisabeth**, AT, vol. VIIIA, p. 2). Whereas virtues based on imperfection are different among themselves and accordingly have different names, "pure" virtues are actually all the same and can be identified with wisdom. "For whoever has a firm and constant will always to use his **reason** as good as he can and to do whatever he judges to be the best is truly wise and as such he is also just, courageous, moderate, and has all the other virtues" (*Principles*, *ibid.*).

Accordingly, the key to all virtue is **generosity**, that is, legitimate self-esteem, which consists partly in the knowledge of our own **freedom** and the realization that we can be praised or blamed only for the use we make of that freedom, partly in the feeling that we are firmly and constantly resolved to make a good use of our freedom, that is, "never to lack the will to do whatever we judge to be the best" (*Passions* III, art. 153, AT, vol. XI, pp. 445–46). Undoubtedly that is also the reason why virtue manifests itself by cheerfulness, tranquility, and a quiet conscience. All this primarily relates to what is called "natural virtue," not to "Christian virtue." The only place where Descartes discusses their relation is in a letter to **Marin Mersenne** of January 1630: "As to your question how the Christian virtues relate to the natural virtues, all I can say is that, just as to straighten a stick which is bent, one does not simply stretch it but bends it the other way, the fact that our nature is too much inclined to vengeance is the reason why God commands us, not only to forgive our enemies but even to do them good" (AT, vol. I, p. 110).

VOETIUS, GYSBERTUS (1589–1676). Voetius was born in Heusden, a garrison town in the Province of Brabant, on the front line between the Dutch and the Spanish Low Countries, as the son of a military officer. He was sent to **Leiden** to study **theology** in 1604 and followed closely, as it developed, the conflict between the two professors of theology, Franciscus Gomarus (1563–1641) and Jacobus Arminius (1560–1609), which eventually would result in the excommunication, through the National Synod of 1619–20, of the Arminians or Remonstrants as they came to be called. Like other orthodox theologians of his generation Voetius believed that the Arminian threat could only be conjured by giving theology a solid basis in **scholastic** philosophy, especially that of **Francisco Suárez**. After his studies he was appointed minister in Heusden and then in Vlijmen (also in Brabant). After the conquest of 's-Hertogenbosch (Bois-le-Duc) by the States' Army in 1629 his mission was to spread **Calvinist** faith among the largely Catholic population—without too much success it should be said: the Protestant community always remained very small. During his period in 's-Hertogenbosch Voetius became involved in a polemic on **faith** and authority, which involved several Catholic theologians of **Louvain**, among them **Cornelius Jansenius**, the founder of the Jansenist movement.

In 1634 he was appointed professor of theology at the Illustrious School (Gymnasium) of **Utrecht**, which in 1636 would acquire the status of a university or academy. Being of a combative and polemical nature he struggled against whatever he saw as deviations from the Word of **God**: Catholicism, Arminanism, and Socinianism, of course, but also Cartesianism and all sorts of local abuses, like the worldly use of ecclesiastical goods. In his eyes Cartesianism was a particularly dangerous aberration not only because it undermines the authority of scholastic philosophy, which he saw as the incarnation of common sense, but also because it voluntarily gives up experience and **logic**, the only two instances that can prevent fallen man from error.

Voetius's favorite literary form was the disputation. These were collected in several huge volumes (*Disputationes theologicae selectae*,

5 vols., 1648–69; *Politica ecclesiastica*, 4 vols., 1663–76). Together they form an impressive body of texts, which for the ultraorthodox wing of Protestant theology are still authoritative. Probably Voetius first heard about Descartes from **Henricus Reneri** but apparently his suspicions were aroused only in 1639, when the professor of history Antonius Aemilius (1589–1660) used his funeral oration for Reneri to deliver a eulogy for Descartes. It may have been a reason for him to read Descartes, of whom no more than the *Discourse* and the *Essays* (*Dioptrics*, *Meteors*, and *Geometry*) had been published, or he may have been willing just to denounce the excessive expectations people apparently had with respect to this unknown French philosopher. Voetius was suspicious of change but he was particularly suspicious of exaggerated knowledge claims. In his view fallen man never fully protects himself from error and evil. Accordingly, the Cartesian promise of a definitive science, which would also be absolutely certain, was in his view bound to fail, which in turn would lead to skepticism and therefore **atheism**. More specific charges against Descartes concerned his **proofs of the existence of God**, which according to Voetius were inconclusive, and his use of the **method** of voluntary **doubt**, which Voetius found sinful. Finally, he believed that **Aristotelian** philosophy, and more specifically the notion of **substantial forms**, was best equipped to accommodate what he called Mosaic physics, that is, the view of the world presupposed in the Book of Genesis.

VOID. *See* VACUUM/VOID.

VOLITION. *See* JUDGMENT.

VORTEX. Each major heavenly body is surrounded by a collection of **particles**. Those particles, which are of either the first or the second Cartesian **element**, revolve rapidly around the body at their center, with speeds that vary according to their distance from the center (*Principles* III, art. 23–25, 53). The vortices of the planets, each of which has its own vortex, are contained in and made to revolve around the sun, by the sun's vortex. Hence (Descartes argues) the earth can be said to be at rest with respect to its own vortex, but in motion with respect to the sun and the other planets. Aside from explaining the motions of the planets, the vortices are also invoked in the explanation of **light**. *See* EARTH, MOTION OF.

– W –

WEIGHT. *See* GRAVITY.

WHITE, THOMAS (1593–1676). Also known as Thomas Blacklo, or by the Latinized names "Albius" and "Vitus," White was a major figure in English Catholicism as well as a contributor to **natural philosophy.** Born in Essex, White was educated on the Continent at the English Colleges of Saint Omer, Valladolid, Douai, and Seville. He was granted a B.D. from the English College at Louvain in 1617 and was ordained priest in the same year under the name Blacklo (Blackloe or Blacklow). He taught **theology** at the college of Douai until 1630, when he was appointed president of the English college in Lisbon. In 1633 he resigned that post and returned to England, where he devoted himself to writing numerous works that involved him in bitter theological controversy. He remained in England until 1642, when political events connected with the English Civil War made life difficult for professed Catholics. He relocated to Paris, where he remained for eight years. In 1650 he was appointed vicepresident and professor of the English College at Douai, remaining there until 1662, when he returned to England.

White was a prolific author of theological tracts, as well as treatises on natural philosophy. In matters of methodology and philosophy he was a dedicated **Aristotelian** who attempted to accommodate new scientific advances within the framework of Aristotelianism; this aspect of his thought is most evident in his 1660 treatise *Religion and Reason*, which attempted to harmonize Christianity and the new science. White was on friendly terms with **Galileo Galilei, Thomas Hobbes,** and **Kenelm Digby;** indeed, much of his Aristotelian natural philosophy was developed in response to their work. His 1642 *De mundo dialogi tres* ("Three Dialogues on the World"), a response to Galileo's *Dialogue on the Two Chief World Systems*, was the object of an extended critique by Thomas Hobbes. White always subordinated scientific thought to theological considerations, an enterprise most fully explored in his 1646 *Institutionum Peripateticarum . . . pars theorica* ("The Theoretical part of the Peripatetic Institutions"), a cosmological treatise influenced by Digby that develops cosmology in the light of religious and moral concerns.

White opposed the **Jesuits** and held theological views similar to those of the **Jansenists.** Several of his opinions were censured by the Inquisition in decrees of 1655 and 1657, and many of his friends and former students publicly disclaimed his principles. His most controversial theological work was the 1653 *De medio animarum statu*

("On the Middle State of Souls"), which included a denial of purgatory. In addition to his unorthodox view on the afterlife, White denied the infallibility of the pope and was accused of theological innovations that undermined the traditional views of sin and redemption. Church authorities also objected to his politico-religious views, especially his teaching in favor of passive obedience to any established government. He eventually withdrew the censured opinions and submitted himself and his writings to the Holy See.

Descartes was aware of White's treatises on natural philosophy, although he makes relatively little mention of them. In a letter to **Marin Mersenne** from January of 1642 Descartes replies to an objection White had raised against his account of evaporation, explaining that the difficulty can be overcome by considering the action of "**subtle matter,**" and adding that "I have heard M. Digby esteem him so highly that I expect to have him on my side" (AT, vol. II, pp. 482–83).

WILL. The will is one of the two faculties of **mind** involved in **judgment**, the other being the faculty of perception, or **intellect**. In the Fourth Meditation Descartes called the will the "faculty of choice or freedom of the will" (AT, vol. VII, p. 56). It is in fact a crucial doctrine for him that we have **freedom** of the will, though he arguably offered different conceptions of this freedom at different times. *See also* THOUGHT.

WORLD, THE. *See TREATISE ON LIGHT OR THE WORLD (TRAITÉ DE LA LUMIÈRE, LE MONDE)*.

Bibliography

Introduction

There are over 3,500 items in G. Sebba's annotated Cartesian bibliography, *Bibliographia Cartesiana: A Critical Guide to the Descartes Literature 1800–1960*. The post-1960 Descartes literature is even more extensive, but students of Descartes will soon have at their disposal the continuation of Sebba; in press right now is: J.-R. Armogathe, V. Carraud, and M. Savini, *Bibliographia cartesiana II*. Henceforth the post-1960 Descartes literature will not have to be pieced together from disparate sources. Given the availability of such massive Cartesian bibliographies, the present bibliography (of approximately 700 items) concentrates on the more important sources. It is divided into four parts: 1) editions of Descartes's works; 2) editions of the works of other, mostly 17th-century thinkers referred to in this *Dictionary*; 3) secondary literature on Descartes; and 4) secondary literature on Cartesians and other relevant 17th-century thinkers.

In this introductory essay, we highlight and comment on some of the more useful (mostly English-language) items from our list. The standard edition of Descartes's works is the 11-volume *Oeuvres de Descartes*, edited by C. Adam and P. Tannery, begun in the 1890s and given a second, expanded edition in the 1970s. "AT," as it is referred to, is an impressive accomplishment; it is especially important because of its editorial apparatus; however, it may be showing its age. At present it can be supplemented in two directions: first by the handy, searchable database edited by A. Gombay et al., *Oeuvres complètes de René Descartes*, and second by the Conte Editore exact reprints of the works of Descartes, which give readers the look and feel of the originals. Better annotations than those in AT will be found in the forthcoming three-volume French-language Pleiades edition of the works of Descartes, the first two volumes edited by J.-M. Beyssade et al. and the third volume of correspondence by J.-R. Armogathe.

The most comprehensive English-language edition of Descartes's works is the two-volume *Philosophical Writings of Descartes*, edited and translated by J. Cottingham, R. Stoothoff, and D. Murdoch, with a third volume of Descartes's correspondence by the same trio and A. Kenny. This collection contains entire translations of Descartes's major works plus selections from his other works and correspondence. One can supplement it with the complete English translations of *Principles of Philosophy* by V. R. Miller and R. P. Miller, *The World* by S. Gaukroger, and *Discourse on Method, Optics, Geometry, and Meteorology* by P. Olscamp. The first two volumes of *Descartes in Seventeenth-Century England*, edited by R. Ariew and D. Garber, provide those works of Descartes translated into English during the 17th century: *Compendium of musick* (1653), *Mechanicks* (1661), *A discourse of a method* (1649), *Six metaphysical meditations with objections* by Thomas Hobbes (1680), and *Passions of the soule* (1650). *Philosophical Essays and Correspondence*, edited by R. Ariew, is a single volume of Descartes's works, chronologically ordered together with some of his correspondence.

There are three new English-language biographies of Descartes: S. Gaukroger, *Descartes: An Intellectual Biography*; G. Rodis-Lewis, *Descartes: His Life and Thought*, and R. Watson, *Cogito, Ergo Sum: The Life of René Descartes*. However, the standard and still indispensable Descartes biography is the 17th-century, two-volume work by Adrien Baillet, *La Vie de M. Descartes*, based on the memoirs of people who had known Descartes personally (Claude Clerselier, Pierre-Hector Chanut, and others); Baillet had access to documents and manuscripts lost long ago. He also issued a single-volume *Abregé de la Vie de Monsieur Des-Cartes*. This volume was translated into English in 1693 (and reprinted in volume 3 of *Descartes in Seventeenth-Century England*). What is important about the one-volume abridgment is that it functions as a second edition of the *Life of Descartes*. There are numerous corrections and tidbits in it not found in the two-volume biography.

As important as his work may be, Baillet was still a historian, writing his history some 40 years after Descartes's death, and his historiography may be questionable. While not quite hagiography, it still needed to turn Descartes's family into a noble family, etc. Moreover, Baillet's history was written for polemic purposes (as part of Jansenist attacks on the Jesuits). We have learned much about Descartes that Baillet did not know. This is where the new biographies might help. In effect, Rodis-Lewis takes it as her task to confront Baillet. She corrects his chronology, his account of Descartes's family history, and his recital of Descartes's travels. More importantly, she shows us that others read his manuscripts quite differently, complaining that Baillet's "translations" of now-lost documents are more like paraphrases. Rodis-Lewis's biography concentrates on the details of Descartes's life and how these details might allow us to understand better the works of a 17th-century Descartes. Gaukroger, in contrast, is more interested in showing us Descartes the scientist-mathematician. He wages war against a recent past that elevates Descartes as the "father of modern philosophy" in opposition to the Descartes who, as he reminds us more than once, is more interested in the fruits of philosophical labor, who thinks that metaphysical questions draw the mind too far away from physical and observable things, and make it unfit to study them. Similarly, Watson's biography, written for a more general audience, rejects what Watson takes to be a French Catholic apologetic tradition, begun by Baillet and continued by Rodis-Lewis (allegedly members of the "Saint Descartes Protection Society") to elevate and ennoble the details of Descartes's life.

As for Descartes's philosophy, one can begin its study with something like G. Hatfield's guidebook to the *Meditations, Descartes and the* Meditations, or J. C. Cottingham's *Cambridge Companion to Descartes*, a collection of commissioned articles on Cartesian topics. Or one can set Descartes's philosophy into its broader context by reading selected chapters of the two-volume *Cambridge History of Seventeenth Century Philosophy*, edited by D. Garber and M. Ayers. (One can also consult as background the essays in the *Cambridge History of Renaissance Philosophy*, edited by C. B. Schmitt, Q. Skinner, and E. Kessler.) J.-L. Marion's studies in Descartes's metaphysics and theology are important; his *On Descartes' Metaphysical Prism: The Constitution and Limits of Onto-theo-logy in Cartesian Thought* has been translated into English and translations of his other works are in preparation. There are valuable studies of Descartes's physics—for example, D. Garber, *Descartes' Metaphysical Physics*, and D. Des Chene, *Physiologia: Philosophy of Nature in Descartes and the Aristotelians*—as well as of Descartes's biological thought—D. Des Chene, *Spirits and Clocks: Machine and Organism in Descartes*, and its predecessor volume, *Life's Form: Late Aristotelian Conceptions of the Soul*. There are also studies of Descartes's ethical thought, such as J. Marshall, *Descartes's Moral Theory*. R. Ariew, in *Descartes and the Last Scholastics*, investigates the relation between Descartes's thought and that of the scholastics; T. M. Lennon compares the philosophies of Descartes and Gassendi in *The Battle of the Gods and Giants: The Legacies of Descartes and Gassendi, 1655–1715*; and T. Verbeek studies the reception of Descartes's philosophy in the Netherlands during Descartes's life, in *Descartes and the Dutch: Early Reactions to Cartesianism (1637–1650)*. The relations between Descartes and the objectors to his *Meditations* are studied by the various contributors to the collection of essays edited by R. Ariew and M. Grene, *Descartes and His Contemporaries: Meditations, Objections and Replies*.

The bibliographical situation with the other relevant 17th-century thinkers is more complex. There are standard editions and a growing number of English translations of the major works of the primary figures, such as Galileo Galilei, Thomas Hobbes, G. W. Leibniz, Nicolas Malebranche, and Baruch Spinoza; there is an increasing number of intellectual biographies of these thinkers and valuable studies of their works. For Galileo, one can mention S. Drake's biography, *Galileo at Work*, and the studies by A. Koyré, *Galileo Studies*, and M. Clavelin, *The Natural Philosophy of Galileo*. *The Cambridge Companion to Galileo*, edited by P. Machamer, can provide a good introduction to Galileo's thought. For Hobbes, one can begin with the various essays in *The Cambridge Companion to Hobbes*, edited by T. Sorell. D. Jesseph supplies a valuable study of Hobbes's mathematics in *Squaring the Circle: The War between Hobbes and Wallis*. For Leibniz, there is E. J. Aiton's *Leibniz: A Biography*, the essays in *The Cambridge Companion to Leibniz*, edited by N. Jolley, and the studies by R. C. Sleigh, *Leibniz and Arnauld: A Commentary on Their Correspondence*, and C. Mercer, *Leibniz's Metaphysics: Its Origins and Development*. One can delve into Malebranche with the assistance of *The Cambridge Companion to Malebranche*, edited by S. Nadler. One can also read Nadler's *Malebranche and Ideas* or T. M. Schmaltz, *Malebranche's Theory of the Soul: A Cartesian Interpretation*. Finally, with Spinoza, one can read Nadler's biography, *Spinoza: A Life*, D. Garrett's collection of essays, *The Cambridge Companion to Spinoza*, or the studies of H. A. Wolfson, *The Philosophy of Spinoza*, A. Donagan, *Spinoza*, and E. M. Curley, *Behind the Geometrical Method: A Reading of Spinoza's Ethics*.

There are few modern editions and even fewer English translations or analyses of the works of the "lesser" 17th-century figures, including most of the Cartesians. One can mention in this category the useful background study of colleges and universities during Descartes's time by L. W. B. Brockliss, *French Higher Education in the Seventeenth and Eighteenth Centuries: A Cultural History*, and the selection of background primary texts, *Descartes' Meditations: Background Source Materials*, edited and translated by R. Ariew, J. Cottingham, and T. Sorell. There are a number of excellent studies of Descartes's influence in the 17th century: for example, R. A. Watson, *The Downfall of Cartesianism 1673–1712* (mostly about Simon Foucher); E. Harth, *Cartesian Women: Versions and Subversions of Rational Discourse in the Old Regime*; D. M. Clarke, *Occult Powers and Hypotheses: Cartesian Natural Philosophy under Louis XIV*; and T. M. Schmaltz, *Radical Cartesianism: The French Reception of Descartes* (primarily about Robert Desgabets and Pierre-Sylvain Régis). Moreover, there are valuable examinations of particular figures and their relations to Descartes—for example, for Marin Mersenne: P. R. Dear, *Mersenne and the Learning of the Schools;* for Pierre Gassendi: L. Joy, *Gassendi the Atomist: Advocate of History in an Age of Science*; for Antoine Arnauld: S. Nadler, *Arnauld and the Cartesian Philosophy of Ideas*; and for Henry More: A. R. Hall, *Henry More and the Scientific Revolution*, and *Henry More: Magic, Religion and Experiment*.

Texts and Editions: Descartes

Descartes, René. *Discours de la methode pour bien conduire sa raison et chercher la verité dans les sciences. Plus La dioptrique. Les meteores. Et La geometrie. Qui sont des essais de cete methode.* Leiden, 1637. (Reprint, Lecce: Conte, 1987.)

————. *Meditationes de prima philosophia, in qua Dei existentia, et animae immortalitas demonstratur.* Paris, 1641.

————. *Meditationes de prima philosophia, In quibus Dei existentia, et animae humanae à corpore distinctio, demonstratur.* Amsterdam, 1642. (Reprint, Lecce: Conte, 1992.)

————. *Principia philosophiae.* Paris, 1644. (Reprint, Lecce: Conte, 1994.)

————. *Specimina Philosophiae.* Amsterdam, 1644. (Reprint, Lecce: Conte, 1998.)

————. *Les principes de la philosophie.* Paris, 1647.

————. *Les méditations métaphysiques de René Descartes touchant la premiere philosophie dans lesquelles l'existence de Dieu, et la distinction réelle entre l'ame et le corps de l'homme, sont demonstrées.* Paris, 1647.

————. *Les passions de l'âme.* Paris, 1649. (Reprint, Lecce: Conte, 1996.)

————. *Passiones Animae,* Amsterdam, 1650. (Reprint, Lecce: Conte, 1997.)

————. *Lettres de Mr Descartes.* Edited by C. Clerselier (3 vols.). Paris, 1657–67.

————. *L'Homme de René Descartes, et un Traité de la Formation du Foetus du mesme Autheur, Avec les Remarques de Louys de la Forge . . . sur le Traitte de l'Homme de René Descartes, et sur les Figures par luy inventées.* Paris, 1664.

————. *L'Homme de René Descartes, et la Formation du Foetus, avec les Remarques de Louis de la Forge. A quoy l'on a ajouté Le Monde, ou Traité de la Lumiere, du mesme Autheur.* Paris, 1677.

————. *Descartes: Correspondence publiée avec une introduction et des notes.* Edited by C. Adam and G. Milhaud (8 vols.). Paris: Alcan and Presses Universitaires de France, 1936–63.

————. *The Geometry of René Descartes: With a Facsimile of the First Edition, 1637.* Translated by D. E. Smith and M. L. Latham. New York: Dover Publications, 1954.

————. *Lettres à Regius et remarques sur l'explication de l'esprit humain.* Edited by G. Rodis-Lewis. Paris: Vrin, 1959.

————. *Oeuvres philosophiques.* Edited by F. Alquié (3 vols.). Paris: Garnier, 1963.

————. *Discours de la méthode. Texte et commentaire par Etienne Gilson*, 4th ed. (Bibliothèque des Textes Philosophiques: Textes et Commentaires). Paris: Vrin, 1967 [first ed. 1925].

————. *Philosophical Letters*. Translated by A. Kenny. Oxford: Oxford University Press, 1970.

————. *Treatise of Man*. Translated by T. S. Hall. Cambridge, Mass.: Harvard University Press, 1972.

————. *Conversation with Burman*. Translated by J. Cottingham. Oxford: Oxford University Press, 1976.

————. *Règles utiles et claires pour la direction de l'esprit en la recherche de la vérité*. Edited and translated by J.-L. Marion. The Hague: Nijhoff, 1977.

————. *L'entretien avec Burman*. Edited by J. M. Beyssade. Paris: Presses Universitaires de France, 1981.

————. *Principles of Philosophy*. Translated by V. R. Miller and R. P. Miller. Dordrecht: Reidel, 1983.

————. *The Philosophical Writings of Descartes*. Edited and translated by J. Cottingham, R. Stoothoff, D. Murdoch, and A. Kenny (3 vols.). Cambridge: Cambridge University Press, 1984–91.

————. *The Passions of the Soul*. Translated by S. Voss. Indianapolis, Ind.: Hackett, 1986.

————. *Abrégé de la musique. Compendium musicae*. Edited and translated by F. de Buzon. Paris: Presses Universitaires de France, 1987.

————. *Oeuvres de Descartes*. Edited by C. Adam and P. Tannery (11 vols.). Paris: Vrin, 1996 [original ed. Paris: Cerf, 1897–1913].

————. *Le Monde, L'Homme*. Edited by A. Bitbol-Hesperies and J.-P. Verdet. Paris: Seuil, 1996.

————. *The World and Other Writings*. Translated by Stephen Gaukroger. Cambridge: Cambridge University Press, 1998.

————. *Meditations and Other Metaphysical Writings*. Edited and translated by D. S. Clarke. London: Penguin, 1998.

————. *Discourse on Method and Related Writings*. Edited and translated by D. S. Clarke. London: Penguin, 1999.

————. *Philosophical Essays and Correspondence*. Edited by R. Ariew. Indianapolis, Ind.: Hackett, 2000.

————. *Écrits physiologiques et médicaux*. Edited by V. Aucante. Paris: Presses Universitaires de France, 2000.

————. *Discourse on Method, Optics, Geometry, and Meteorology*. Translated by P. J. Olscamp. Indianapolis, Ind.: Hackett, 2001.

————. *Oeuvres complètes de René Descartes. Connaught Descartes project*. Edited by André Gombay et al. Charlottesville, Va.: InteLex, 2001. http://pastmasters2000.nlx.com.

Texts and Editions: Other Writers

Abra de Raconis, Charles François d'. *Totius philosophiae, hoc est logicae, moralis, physicae, et metaphysicae.* Paris, 1633 [with numerous other editions].

———. *Tertia pars philosophiae, seu Physica.* Paris, 1651.

Ariew, Roger, John Cottingham, and Tom Sorell, eds. and trans. *Descartes' Meditations: Background Source Materials.* Cambridge: Cambridge University Press, 1998.

Ariew, Roger, and Daniel Garber, eds. *Descartes in Seventeenth-Century England* (10 vols.). Bristol: Thoemmes, 2002.

Aristotle. *The Complete Works of Aristotle.* Edited by J. Barnes (2 vols.). Princeton, N.J.: Princeton University Press, 1984.

Arnauld, Antoine. *Oeuvres de Messire Antoine Arnauld, docteur de la maison et société de Sorbonne* (43 vols.). Paris, 1775–83 [repr. Brussels: Culture et Civilisation, 1965–67].

———. *On True and False Ideas.* Translated by S. Gaukroger. Manchester: Manchester University Press, 1990.

Babin, François. *Journal ou relation fidele de tout ce qui s'est passé dans l'université d'Angers au sujet de la philosophie de Des Carthes en l'execution des ordres du Roy pendant les années 1675, 1676, 1677, et 1678.* Angers, 1679.

Bacon, Francis. *The Works of Francis Bacon.* Edited by J. Spedding, R. L. Ellis, and D. D. Heath (14 vols.). London: Longmans, 1857–74 [repr. Stuttgart: Frommann, 1989].

Basso, Sebastian. *Philosophia naturalis adversus Aristotelem libri XII, in quibus abstrusa veterum physiologia restauratur, et Aristotelis errores solidis rationibus refelluntur.* Geneva, 1621 [2nd ed. Amsterdam, 1649].

Bayle, Pierre. *Projet et fragmens d'un Dictionnaire critique.* Rotterdam, 1692.

———. *Dictionnaire historique et critique.* Rotterdam, 1697 [with numerous other editions].

———. *Oeuvres diverses* (4 vols.). The Hague, 1727 [repr. Hildesheim: Olms, 1964–68].

———. *Historical and Critical Dictionary,* 2nd ed. London, 1734–38 [1st ed. 1710, repr. New York: Garland, 1984].

———, ed. *Recueil de quelques pièces curieuses concernant la philosophie de M. Descartes.* Amsterdam, 1684.

Beeckman, Isaac. *Journal tenu par Isaac Beeckman de 1604 à 1634.* Edited by C. de Waard (4 vols.). The Hague: Nijhoff, 1939–53.

Bernier, François. *Abrégé de la philosophie de Gassendi* (7 vols.). Lyon, 1678 [with numerous other editions].

Bérulle, Pierre de. *Oeuvres complètes.* Edited by J. P. Migne. Paris, 1846.

Bossu, R. le. *Parallèle des principes de la physique d'Aristote et de celle de Descartes.* Paris, 1674 [repr. Paris: Vrin, 1981].

Bourdin, Pierre. *Prima geometriae elementa.* Paris, 1639.

————. *Geometria, nova methodo.* Paris, 1640.

————. *L'introduction à la mathématique, contenant les coignaissances, et pratiques necéssaires à ceux qui commencent d'apprendre les mathématiques. Le tout tiré des élémens d'Euclide rengez et demonstrez d'une façon plus briève, et plus facile que l'ordinaire.* Paris, 1643.

————. *Sol flamma sive tractatus de sole, ut flamma est, eiusque pabulo sol exurens montes, et radios igneos exsufflans Eccles. 43. Aphorismi analogici parvi mundi ad magnum magni ad parvuum.* Paris, 1646.

————. *L'architecture militaire ou l'art de fortifier les places regulières et irregulières.* Paris, 1655.

————. *Le dessein ou la perspective militaire.* Paris, 1655.

————. *Cours de mathématique.* 3rd ed. Paris, 1661.

Boyle, Robert. *The Works of the Honourable Robert Boyle.* Edited by T. Birch (6 vols.). London, 1772 [repr. Hildesheim: Olms, 1965].

Bruno, Giordano. *Opere latine.* Edited by F. Fiorentino et al. Naples and Florence: Morano, 1879–91 [repr. Stuttgart: Frommann, 1969].

————. *Dialoghi italiana.* Edited by G. Gentile and G. Aquilecchia. Florence: Sanson, 1957.

————. *The Expulsion of the Triumphant Beast.* Translated by Arthur D. Imerti. New Brunswick, N.J.: Rutgers University Press, 1964.

————. *Cause, Principle, and Unity.* Translated by J. Lindsay. Westport, Conn.: Greenwood Press, 1976.

Charleton, Walter. *The Darknes of Atheism Dispelled by the Light of Nature.* London, 1652.

————. *Physiologia Epicuro-Gassendo-Charltoniana: Or a fabrick of science natural, upon the hypothesis of atoms, founded by Epicurus, repaired by Petrus Gassendus, augmented by Walter Charleton.* London, 1654 [repr. New York and London: Johnson, 1966].

————. *Epicurus's Morals.* London, 1656.

————. *The Immortality of the Soul.* London, 1657.

————. *A Natural History of the Passions.* London, 1674.

————. *Enquiries into Human Nature.* London, 1680.

Charron, Pierre. *Of Wisdome Three Books.* Translated by S. Lennard. London, 1606.

————. *Oeuvres* (2 vols.). Paris, 1635 [repr. Geneva: Slatkine, 1970].

Chauvin, Stephanus. *Lexicon philosophicum.* 2nd ed. (1st ed.: 1692). Leeuwarden, 1713 [repr. Düsseldorf: Stern-Verlag Janssen & Co., 1967].

Clauberg, Johannes. *Opera omnia philosophica.* Edited by J. T. Schalbruch (2 vols.). Amsterdam, 1691 [repr. Hildesheim: Olms, 1968].

Clave, Etienne de. *Positiones publicae.* Paris, 1624.

————. *Paradoxes ou Traittez Philosophiques.* Paris, 1635.

————. *Nouvelle lumière philosophique.* Paris, 1641.

Clavius, Christopher. *Opera mathematica.* Rome, 1611–12.

Collegium Conimbricense. *In octo libros physicorum Aristotelis.* Coimbra, 1592.

————. *In tres libros de anima Aristotelis.* Coimbra, 1598.

————. *In quatuor libros de coelo, meteorologicos et parva naturalia Aristotelis Stagiritae.* Cologne, 1603.

————. *In universam dialecticam Aristotelis.* Coimbra, 1606.

————. *In libros de generatione et corruptione Aristotelis Stagiritae.* Mainz, 1606.

Cordemoy, Gérauld de. *Les Oeuvres de Feu Monsieur de Cordemoy.* Paris, 1704.

————. *Oeuvres Philosophiques.* Edited by P. Clair and F. Girbal (Le mouvement des idées au XVIIe siècle). Paris: Presses Universitaires de France, 1968.

Cousin, V. *Fragments de philosophie cartésienne.* Paris, 1845 [2nd ed. 1866].

Cureau de la Chambre, Marin. *Nouvelles pensées sur les causes de la lumière, du débordement du Nil et de l'amour d'inclination.* Paris, 1634.

————. *Traité de la connoissance des animaux.* Paris, 1647.

————. *Les caractères des passions.* Paris, 1648.

————. *Nouvelles observations et conjectures sur l'iris.* Paris, 1650.

————. *La lumière.* Paris, 1657.

————. *Les caractères des passions* (vols. I–II). Amsterdam, 1658.

————. *Les charactères des passions, volumes III et IV: haine, douleur.* Paris, 1659.

————. *L'art de connoistre les hommes. Première partie où sont contenus les discours préliminaire.* Paris, 1659.

————. *Les charactères des passions, volume V: larmes, crainte, désespoir.* Paris, 1662.

————. *Le Système de l'âme.* Paris, 1664.

————. *L'art de connoistre les hommes. Partie troisième qui contient la défense de l'extension des parties libres de l'âme.* Paris, 1666.

————. *Discours de l'amitié et de la haine qui se trouvent envers les animaux.* Paris, 1667.

————. *Traité de la connoissance des animaux.* Edited by O. Le Guern. Paris: Fayard, 1989.

Daniel, Gabriel. *Voiage du Monde de Descartes.* Paris, 1690.

————. *Nouvelles difficultés proposées par un péripatéticien à l'auteur du Voyage du monde de Descartes.* Paris, 1693 [repr. Amsterdam: Rodopi, 1970].

————. *Entretiens de Cléandre et d'Eudoxe sur les Lettres provinciales de Pascal.* Cologne and Rouen, 1694.

Desgabets, Robert. *Critique de la critique de la recherche de la vérité.* Paris, 1675.

————. *Oeuvres Philosophiques inédites.* Edited by J. Beaude. Amsterdam: Quadratures, 1983.

Digby, Kenelm. *A conference with a Lady about choyce of religion.* Paris, 1638.

————. *Observations upon Religio Medici.* London, 1643.

————. *Two Treatises. In the one of which the Nature of Bodies; in the other, the Nature of Mans Soule; is looked into: in the way of discovery, of the Immortality of Reasonable Soules.* Paris, 1644 [repr. New York: Garland, 1978].

————. *Observations upon Religio Medici. . . . The second Edition corrected and amended.* London, 1644 [repr. Menston: The Scholar Press, 1973].

————. *Discours fait en une célèbre assemblée . . . touchant la guérison des playes par la poudre de sympathie.* Paris, 1658.

————. *A Late Discourse Made in a Solemne Assembly of Nobles and Learned Men of Montpellier in France . . . Touching the Cure of Wounds by the Powder of Sympathy, with Instructions How to Make the Said Powder, Whereby Many Other Secrets of Nature Are Unfolded.* London, 1658.

Drake, S., and I. E. Drabkin, eds. *Mechanics in Sixteenth-Century Italy. Selections from Tartaglia, Benedetti, Guido Ubaldo, and Galileo* (The University of Wisconsin Publications in Medieval Science). Madison: University of Wisconsin Press, 1969.

Du Hamel, Jean. *Reflexions critiques sur le système cartésien de la philosophie de M. Regis.* Paris, 1692.

————. *Lettre de Monsieur Du Hamel, ancien professeur de philosophie de l'Université de Paris, pour servir de replique à Monsieur Régis.* Paris, 1699.

————. *Philosophia universalis, sive commentarius in universam Aristotelis philosophiam ad usum scholarum comparatam quaedam recentiorum philosophorum ac praesertim Cartesii propositiones damnatae ac prohibitae.* Paris, 1705.

Du Hamel, Jean-Baptiste. *Astronomia physica.* Paris, 1660.

———. *De meteoris et fossilibus libri duo.* Paris, 1660.

———. *De consensu veteris et novae philosophiae.* Paris, 1663.

———. *Philosophia vetus et nova ad usum scholae accomodata.* Paris, 1678.

Dupleix, Scipion. *La curiosité naturelle redigée en questions, selon l'ordre alphabetique.* Paris, 1606.

———. *L'Ethique ou Philosophie morale.* Paris, 1610.

———. *Corps de philosophie, contenant la logique, l'ethique, La physique, et la metaphysique.* Geneva, 1623.

———. *La logique.* Paris: Fayard, 1984.

———. *La physique.* Edited by R. Ariew. Paris: Fayard, 1990.

———. *La métaphysique.* Edited by R. Ariew. Paris: Fayard, 1991.

———. *L'ethique.* Edited by R. Ariew. Paris: Fayard, 1993.

Eustachius a Sancto Paulo. *Summa philosophiae quadripartita, de rebus Dialecticis, Ethicis, Physicis, et Metaphysicis.* Paris, 1609 [with numerous other editions].

———. *Summa theologiae tripartita.* Paris, 1613–16.

Fabri, Honoré. *Tractatus physicus de motu locali, in quo effectus omnes, qui ad impetum, motum naturalem, violentum, et mixtum pertinent, explicantur, et ex principiis physicis demonstrantur.* Edited by P. Mousnier. Lyon, 1646.

———. *Philosophiae tomus primus.* Lyon, 1646.

———. *Physica, id est, scientia rerum corporearum, in decem tractatus distributa.* Lyon, 1669–71.

———. *De plantis et de generatione animalium, de homine.* Lyon, 1666.

Fermat, Pierre de. *Varia opera mathematica.* Toulouse, 1679.

———. *Oeuvres de Fermat.* Edited by C. Henry and P. Tannery (4 vols.) with supplements by C. de Waard (vol. 5). Paris: Gauthier-Villars, 1891–1922.

Fonesca, Pedro da. *Commentarium in metaphysicorum Aristotelis Stagiritae libros tomi quatuor.* Cologne, 1615 [repr. Hildesheim: Olms, 1964].

Galilei, Galileo. *Opere.* Edited by A. Favaro (20 vols.). Florence: Barbera, 1890–1909 [reissued 1965].

———. *The Discoveries and Opinions of Galileo.* Edited by S. Drake. Garden City, N.Y.: Doubleday, 1957.

———. *The Controversy on the Comets of 1618: Galileo Galilei, Horatio Grassi, Mario Guiducci, Johann Kepler.* Translated by S. Drake and C. D. O'Malley. Philadelphia: University of Pennsylvania Press, 1960.

———. *On Motion and On Mechanics.* Translated by I. E. Drabkin and S. Drake. Madison: University of Wisconsin Press, 1960.

———. *Dialogue Concerning the Two Chief World Systems.* Translated by S. Drake. Berkeley: University of California Press, 1967.

————. *Two New Sciences. Including Centers of Gravity and Force of Percussion.* Translated by S. Drake. Madison: University of Wisconsin Press, 1974.

Garasse, François. *La doctrine curieuse des beaux esprits de ce temps ou prétendus tels.* Paris, 1623.

Gassendi, Pierre. *Animadversiones in decimum librum Diogenis Laertii* (3 vols.). Lyon, 1649 [repr. New York: Garland, 1987].

————. *Opera omnia* (6 vols.). Lyon, 1658 [repr. Stuttgart: Frommann, 1964].

————. *Exercitationes Paradoxicae adversus Aristoteleos.* Edited and translated (French) by B. Rochot. Paris: Vrin, 1959.

————. *Disquisitio Metaphysica.* Edited and translated (French) by B. Rochot. Paris: Vrin, 1962.

————. *Selected Works.* Edited and translated by C. B. Brush. New York and London: Johnson Reprint Corporation, 1972.

————. *Pierre Gassendi's Institutio logica (1658).* Edited and translated by H. Jones. Assen: Van Gorcum, 1981.

Geulincx, Arnold. *Opera philosophica.* Edited by J. P. N. Land (3 vols.). The Hague: Nijhoff, 1891–93 [repr. Stuttgart: Frommann, 1965].

Gibieuf, Guillaume. *De libertate Dei et creaturae.* Paris, 1630.

Gilbert, William. *De magnete, magnetisque corporibus, et de magno magnete tellure: Physiologia nova plurimis et argumentis et experimentis demonstrata.* London, 1600 [repr. Berlin: Mayer and Müller, 1892; Brussels: Culture et Civilisation, 1967].

————. *De mondo nostro sublunari nova philosophia.* Amsterdam, 1651 [repr. Amsterdam: Menno Hertzberger, 1965].

————. *De magnete.* Translated by P. F. Mottelay. New York: Dover, 1958.

Glanvill, Joseph. *The Vanity of Dogmatizing; or, Confidence in Opinions.* London, 1661 [repr. Hildesheim: Olms, 1970].

————. *Lux Orientalis.* London, 1662.

————. *Scepsis Scientifica.* London, 1665 [repr. Hildesheim: Olms, 1985].

————. *Philosophical Considerations Touching Witches and Witchcraft.* London, 1666.

————. *Plus Ultra; or, The Progress and Advancement of Knowledge Since the Days of Aristotle.* London, 1668 [repr. Gainesville, Fla.: Scholars Facsimiles and Reprints, 1966].

————. *Essays on Several Important Subjects in Philosophy and Religion.* London, 1676 [repr. New York: Johnson, 1970].

————. *Saducismus triumphatus, or, Full and plain evidence concerning witches and apparitions.* Edited by H. More. London, 1681 [2nd ed. London: 1682].

————. *Two Choice and Useful Treatises: The one Lux Orientalis; or An Enquiry into the Opinion of the Eastern Sages Concerning the Praeexistence of Souls. Being a Key to unlock the Grand Mysteries of Providence. In Relation to Mans Sin and Misery. The other, A Discourse of Truth, By the late Reverend Dr. Rust, Lord Bishop of Dromore in Ireland. With Annotations on them both* [by H. More]. London, 1682 [repr. New York: Garland, 1978].

————. *The Vanity of Dogmatizing.* Edited by S. Medcalf. Sussex: Harvester Press, 1970.

————. *A Discourse concerning the Difficulties of the way to Happiness, whence they arise and how they may be overcome.* London, 1670.

Goclenius, Rudolf. *Problemata logica.* Marburg, 1597 [repr. Frankfurt: Minerva, 1967].

————. *Lexicon philosophicum.* Frankfurt, 1613 [repr. Hildesheim: Olms, 1964].

Heereboord, Adrian. *Parallelismus Aristotelicae et Cartesianae philosophiae naturalis.* Leiden, 1643.

————. *Sermo extemporaneus de recta philosophice disputandi ratione.* Leiden, 1648.

————. *Meletemata philosophica in quibus pleraeque res metaphysicae ventilantur.* Leiden, 1650.

————. *Philosophia rationalis, moralis et naturalis.* Leiden, 1654.

————. *Philosophia naturalis cum . . . novis commentariis partim e nob. D. Cartesio . . . aliisque praestantioribus hujus seculi philosophis petitis, partim ex propria opinione dictatis, explicata.* Leiden, 1663.

Hill, Nicholas. *Philosophia Epicurea, Democritiana, Theophrastica proposita simpliciter, non edocta.* Geneva, 1619.

Hobbes, Thomas. *Opera philosophica quae Latine scripsit omnia.* Edited by W. Molesworth (5 vols.). London, 1839–45 [repr. Darmstadt: Scientia, 1966].

————. *The English Works of Thomas Hobbes of Malmesbury.* Edited by W. Molesworth (11 vols.). London, 1839–45 [repr. Darmstadt: Scientia, 1962].

————. *Man and Citizen.* Edited by B. Gert. Garden City, N.Y.: Doubleday, 1972.

————. *Thomas White's* De mundo *Examined.* Translated by H. W. Jones. London: Bradford University Press in association with Crosby Lockwood Staples, 1976.

————. *De cive, The English Version.* Edited by H. Warrender. Oxford: Oxford University Press, 1983.

————. *Leviathan.* Edited by R. Tuck. Cambridge: Cambridge University Press, 1991.

————. *The Correspondence of Thomas Hobbes.* Edited by N. Malcolm (2 vols.). Oxford: Oxford University Press, 1994.

Huet, Pierre-Daniel. *Censura Philosophiae Cartesianae.* Paris, 1689 [repr. Hildesheim: Olms, 1971].

————. *Nouveaux Mémoires pour servir à l'histoire du cartésianisme.* [n.p.], 1692.

————. *Traité philosophique de la foiblesse de l'esprit humain.* Amsterdam, 1723.

Huygens, Christiaan. *Opuscula postuma.* Leiden, 1703.

————. *Oeuvres complètes.* Edited by D. Bierans de Haan, J. Bosscha, D. J. Kortweg, and J. A. Vollgraff (22 vols.). The Hague: Société Hollandaise des Sciences and Nijhoff, 1888–1950.

————. *Treatise on Light.* Translated by S. P. Thompson. London: Macmillan, 1912.

Ignatius of Loyola. *Exercitia spiritualia* (Monumenta historica Societatis Iesu). Edited by J. Calveras. Rome: Institutum historicum Societatis Iesu, 1969.

————. *The Spiritual Exercises of St. Ignatius Loyola.* Translated by H. Backhouse. London: Hodder and Stoughton, 1989.

Jansenius, Cornelius. *Augustinus* (3 vols.). Louvain, 1640 [repr. Frankfurt: Minerva, 1964].

Kepler, Johannes. *Gesammelte Werke.* Edited by W. von Dyck and M. Caspar (20 vols. to date). Munich: C. H. Beck, 1937–.

Knorr von Rosenroth, Christian, ed. *Kabbala Denudata, seu Doctrina hebraeorum transcendentalis et metaphysica atque theologica* (2 vols.). Sulzbach, 1677.

La Forge, Louis de. *Traitté de l'esprit de l'homme et de ses facultez et fonctions, et de son union avec le corps. Suivant les principes de René Descartes.* Paris, 1666.

————. *Oeuvres Philosophiques.* Edited by P. Clair (Le mouvement des idées au XVIIe siècle). Paris: Presses Universitaires de France, 1974.

La Grange, Jean-Baptiste de. *Les principes de la philosophie contre les nouveaux philosophes, Descartes, Rohault, Régius, Gassendi, le p. Maignan, etc.,* vol. I, *Traité des qualitez,* and vol. II, *Traité des éléments et météores.* Paris, 1675.

La Mothe le Vayer, François de. *Oeuvres* (14 vols.). Dresden, 1756–59.

Lamy, Bernard. *L'art de parler.* Paris, 1675 [2nd ed. Paris, 1676; 3rd ed. Paris, 1688; 4th ed. Amsterdam, 1699 and Paris, 1701].

————. *Entretiens sur les Sciences.* Edited by F. Girbal and P. Clair. Paris: Presses Universitaires de France, 1966.

Le Bossu, René. *Parallele des Principes de la Physique d'Aristote et de celle de René Des Cartes.* Paris, 1674.

Le Grand, Antoine. *Le Sage des Stoiques ou l'Homme sans Passions. Selon les sentiments de Sénèque.* The Hague, 1662.

———. *Les caractères de l'homme sans passions, selon les sentiments de Sénèque.* Paris, 1665.

———. *L'Epicure spirituel, ou l'empire de la volupté sur les vertus.* Paris, 1669.

———. *Institutio philosophiae secundum principia R. Descartes.* London, 1672.

———. *Man without Passion: or the Wise Stoic according to the Sentiments of Seneca.* London, 1675.

———. *Apologia pro R. Des-Cartes contra S. Parkerum.* London, 1679.

———. *An Entire Body of Philosophy According to the Principles of the Famous Renate Des Cartes.* Translated by R. Blome. London, 1694.

Leibniz, Gottfried Wilhelm. *Opera omnia.* Edited by L. Dutens (6 vols.). Geneva, 1768.

———. *Mathematische Schriften.* Edited by C. I. Gerhardt (7 vols.). Berlin and Halle: A. Asher and H. W. Schmidt, 1849–63 [repr. Hildesheim: Olms, 1962].

———. *Die philosophischen Schriften* (7 vols.). Edited by C. I. Gerhardt. Berlin: Weidmannsche Buchhandlung, 1875–90 [repr. Hildesheim: Olms, 1978].

———. *Opuscules et fragments inédits.* Edited by L. Couturat. Paris: Alcan, 1903 [repr. Hildesheim: Olms, 1966].

———. *Sämtliche Schriften und Briefe.* Edited by Deutsche [before 1945, Preussische] Akademie der Wissenschaften. Berlin: Akademie Verlag, 1923–.

———. *Textes inédits d'après les manuscrits de la bibliothèque provinciale de Hanovre.* Edited by G. Grua (2 vols.). Paris: Presses Universitaires de France, 1948.

———. *Theodicy.* Translated by E. M. Huggard. London: Routledge, 1951.

———. *Philosophical Papers and Letters.* Edited and translated by L. E. Loemker. Dordrecht: Reidel, 1969.

———. *New Essays on Human Understanding.* Translated by P. Remnant and J. Bennett. Cambridge: Cambridge University Press, 1981.

———. *Philosophical Essays.* Edited and translated by R. Ariew and D. Garber. Indianapolis, Ind.: Hackett, 1989.

———. *De Summa Rerum: Metaphysical Papers, 1675–1676.* Translated by G. H. R. Parkinson. New Haven, Conn.: Yale University Press, 1992.

———. *The Labyrinth of the Continuum: Writings on the Continuum Problem, 1672–1686.* Translated by T. W. Arthur. New Haven, Conn.: Yale University Press, 2002.

Locke, John. *The Works* (10 vols.). London, 1823 [repr. Darmstadt: Scientia, 1963].

———. *The Correspondence*. Edited by E. S. de Beer (9 vols.). Oxford: Oxford University Press, 1976–92.

Malebranche, Nicolas. *Oeuvres complètes*. Edited by A. Robinet (20 vols.). Paris: Vrin, 1958–84.

———. *La recherche de la vérité*. In: *Œuvres* I. Edited by Geneviève Rodis-Lewis and Germain Malbreil. Paris: Gallimard, 1979. (Bibliothèque de la Pléiade).

———. *The Search after Truth*. Translated by T. M. Lennon and P. J. Olscamp. Columbus: Ohio State University Press, 1980.

———. *Dialogues on Metaphysics*. Translated by W. Doney. New York: Abaris Books, 1980.

———. *Philosophical Selections*. Translated by T. M. Lennon et al. Edited by S. Nadler. Indianapolis, Ind.: Hackett, 1992.

———. *Treatise on Nature and Grace*. Translated by P. Riley. Oxford: Oxford University Press, 1992.

Mersenne, Marin. *Quaestiones celeberimae in Genesim*. Paris, 1623.

———. *L'impiété des déistes, athées et libertins de ce temps, combatue et renversée* (2 vols.). Paris, 1624 [repr. (vol. I) Stuttgart: Frommann, 1975].

———. *La verité des sciences*. Paris, 1625 [repr. Stuttgart: Frommann, 1969].

———. *Questions théologiques; Les méchaniques de Galilée; Les préludes de l'harmonie universelle*. Paris, 1634.

———. *Harmonie universelle contenant la theorie et la pratique de la musique*. Paris, 1636–37.

———. *Cogitata physico-mathematica*. Paris, 1644.

———. *Universae geometriae mixtaeque mathematicae synopsis*. Paris, 1644.

———. *Correspondance du P. Marin Mersenne, religieux minime*. Edited by C. de Waard et al. (17 vols.). Paris: Beauchesne (vol. 1), Presses Universitaires de France (vols. 2–4), CNRS (vols. 5–17), 1932–88.

———. *Questions Inouyes*. Edited by A. Pessel. Paris: Fayard, 1985.

Montaigne, Michel de. *Oeuvres complètes*. Edited by R. Barral and P. Michel. Paris: Seuil, 1967.

———. *Complete Essays*. Translated by D. Frame. Stanford, Calif.: Stanford University Press, 1965.

More, Henry. *Opera omnia* (3 vols.). London, 1975–79.

Morin, Jean-Baptiste. *Refutation des theses erronées*. Paris, 1624.

———. *Astrologia gallica*. The Hague, 1661.

Newton, Isaac. *Philosophiae naturalis principia mathematica*. London, 1687 [2nd ed. London, 1713; 3rd ed. London, 1726].

————. *Opticks*. London, 1704.

————. *Isaaci Newtoni opera quae exstant omnia* (5 vols.). London, 1779–85.

————. *Mathematical Principles of Natural Philosophy*. Translated by A. Motte, revised by F. Cajori. Berkeley: University of California Press, 1934.

————. *Isaac Newton's Papers and Letters on Natural Philosophy and Related Documents*. Cambridge, Mass.: Harvard University Press, 1958.

————. *The Correspondence of Isaac Newton*. Edited by H. W. Turnbull, J. F. Scott, A. R. Hall, and L. Tilling (7 vols.). Cambridge: Cambridge University Press, 1959–77.

————. *Unpublished Scientific Papers of Isaac Newton*. Edited by C. R. Hall and M. B. Hall. Cambridge: Cambridge University Press, 1962.

————. *The Mathematical Papers of Isaac Newton*. Edited by D. T. Whiteside (8 vols.). Cambridge: Cambridge University Press, 1967–81.

————. *Isaac Newton's Philosophia Naturalis Principia Mathematica: The Third Edition with Variant Readings*. Edited by A. Koyré and I. B. Cohen (2 vols.). Cambridge, Mass.: Harvard University Press, 1972.

————. *Papers and Letters on Natural Philosophy*. Edited by I. B. Cohen. 2nd ed. Cambridge, Mass.: Harvard University Press, 1978.

————. *Certain Philosophical Questions: Newton's Trinity Notebook*. Edited by J. E. McGuire and M. Tamny. Cambridge: Cambridge University Press, 1983.

————. *Optical Papers of Isaac Newton*. Edited by A. E. Shapiro. Cambridge: Cambridge University Press, 1984–.

Pappus of Alexandria, *Pappi Alexandrini Collectionis quae Supersunt, E Libris Manu Scriptis Edidit*. (3 vols.). Edited by F. Hultsch. Berlin, 1875 [repr. Amsterdam: Adolf Hakkert, 1965].

Pascal, Blaise. *Oeuvres complètes*. Edited by L. Lafuma. Paris: Editions du Seuil, 1963.

————. *Oeuvres complètes*. Edited by J. Mesnard (4 vols.). Paris: Desclée de Brouwer, 1964–94.

————. *Pensées*. Translated by A. J. Krailsheimer. Harmondsworth, England: Penguin, 1966.

Plemp, Vopiscus Fortunatus. *Ophthalmographia sive tractatio de oculi fabrica*. Amsterdam, 1632 [new ed. Louvain, 1648, 1659].

————. *Fundamenta medicinæ*. Louvain, 1638 [2nd ed. 1644; 3rd ed. 1659].

Poisson, Nicolas-Joseph. *Commentaire ou remarques sur la methode de René Descartes où on établit plusieurs principes generaux, necessaires pour entendre toutes ses Oeuvres.* Vendôme, 1670.

Poulain de la Barre, François. *De l'égalité des deux sexes.* Paris, 1673.

Pourchot, Edmond. *Institutio philosophica.* Paris, 1695.

Raey, Johannes de. *Disputationes physicae ad problemata Aristotelis.* Leiden, 1651–52.

———. *Clavis philosophiae naturalis, seu introductio ad contemplationem naturae Aristotelico-Cartesiana.* Leiden, 1654.

———. *Clavis philosophiae naturalis aristotelico-cartesiana.* Amsterdam, 1677.

Régis, Pierre-Sylvain. *Cours entier de philosophie, ou système général selon les principes de M. Descartes . . . dernière édition augmentée d'un discours sur la Philosophie ancienne & moderne* (3 vols.). Amsterdam, 1691 [repr. New York: Johnson Reprint, 1970].

———. *Système de philosophie contenant la logique, la métaphysique, la physique et la morale* (3 vols.). Paris, 1690.

———. *Réponse aux Reflexions critiques de M. Du Hamel.* Paris, 1692.

———. *L'usage de la raison et de la foi, ou l'accord de la foi et la raison.* Paris, 1704.

Regius, Henricus. *Fundamenta Physices.* Amsterdam, 1646.

———. *Explicatio mentis humana.* Utrecht, 1647.

———. *Brevis explicatio mentis humana sive animae rationalis.* Utrecht, 1648.

———. *De affectibus animi dissertatio.* Utrecht, 1650.

———. *Philosophia naturalis. Editio secunda, priore multo locupletior et emendatior.* Amsterdam, 1654 [2nd edition of Regius 1646].

Renaudot, Théophraste. *A General Collection of Discourses of the Virtuosi of France.* London, 1664.

Revius, J. *Suarez Repurgatus.* Leiden, 1643.

Roberval, Gilles Personne de. *Aristarchi Samii de mundi systemate partibus et motibus eiusdem libellus.* Paris, 1644.

———. "Traité des indivisibles." In *Divers ouvrages de mathematique et de physique. Par Messieurs de l'Academie Royale des Sciences,* 190–245. Paris, 1693.

Rohault, Jacques. *Traité de physique.* Paris, 1671.

———. *Entretiens sur la philosophie.* Paris, 1671.

———. *Oeuvres posthumes de Mr. Rohault.* Edited by C. Clerselier. Paris, 1682.

———. *Physica.* 4th ed. with additions and plates. Latin trans. and notes by Samuel Clarke. London, 1718.

————. *A System of Natural Philosophy, Illustrated with Dr. Samuel Clarkes Notes.* . . . *Done into English by John Clarke* (2 vols.). London, 1723 [repr. New York: Johnson Reprint Co., 1969].

————. *Jacques Rohault: 1618–1672: Bio-bibliographie, avec l'édition critique des Entretiens sur la philosophie.* Edited by P. Clair. Paris: CNRS, 1978.

Rubius, Antonius. *Commentarium in libros Aristotelis De anima.* Lyon, 1620.

————. *In universam Aristotelis Dialecticam.* London, 1641.

Schurman, Anna Maria van. *Amica dissertatio inter Annam Mariam Schurmanniam et Andr. Rivetum de capacitate ingenii muliebris ad scientias.* Paris, 1638.

————. *Dissertatio logica de ingenii muliebris ad doctrinam et meliores litteras aptitudine, cui accedunt epistolae aliquot (Schurmanniae ipsius et Riveti) ejusdem argumenti.* Leiden, 1641.

————. *Nobliss Virginis Annae Mariae à Schurman, Opuscula hebraea, graeca, latina, gallica, prosaica et metrica.* Leiden, 1648.

————. *Euchlepia seu Melioris partis electio.* Altona, 1673.

Sennert, Daniel. *Epitome naturalis scientiae.* Wittenberg, 1618.

————. *Hypomnemata Physica.* Wittenberg, 1636.

————. *Thirteen books of natural philosophy.* London, 1659.

Silhon, Jean de. *Les deux vérités: l'une de Dieu, et de sa providence, l'autre de l'immortalité de l'ame.* Paris, 1624.

————. *De l'immortalité de l'ame.* Paris, 1634.

————. *Les deux vérités: l'une de Dieu, et de sa providence, l'autre de l'immortalité de l'ame.* Edited by J. R. Armogathe. Paris: Fayard, 1991.

Sirmond, Antoine. *Demonstration de l'immortalité de l'ame.* Paris, 1637.

Sorel, Charles. *La science des choses corporelles, premiere partie de la science humaine ou l'on connoit la verité de toutes choses du monde par les forces de la raison et ou l'on treuve la refutation des erreurs de la philosophie vulgaire.* Paris, 1634.

Spinoza, Baruch. *Opera.* Edited by C. Gebhardt (4 vols.). Heidelberg: C. Winter, 1925.

————. *The Correspondence of Spinoza.* Edited and translated by A. Wolf. London: Allen and Unwin, 1928.

————. *Collected Works,* vol. I. Edited and translated by E. M. Curley. Princeton, N.J.: Princeton University Press, 1985.

Suárez, Francisco. *Opera Omnia.* Edited by D. M. André (28 vols.). Paris, 1856–78 [*Disputationes Metaphysicae* (vols. 25–26), repr. Hildesheim: Olms, 1965].

————. *On the Various Kinds of Distinctions.* Translated by C. Vollert. Milwaukee, Wisc.: Marquette University Press, 1947.

————. On formal and universal unity, De unitate formali et universali. Translated by J. F. Ross. Milwaukee, Wisc.: Marquette University Press, 1964.

————. *Suarez on Individuation. Metaphysical Disputation V: Individual Unity and Its Principle.* Edited and translated by J. J. E. Gracia. Milwaukee, Wisc.: Marquette University Press, 1982.

————. *On the Essence of Finite Being, etc.* Translated by N. Wells. Milwaukee, Wisc.: Marquette University Press, 1983.

————. *On Efficient Causality.* Translated by A. J. Freddoso. Notre Dame, Ind.: Notre Dame University Press, 1994.

————. *On Beings of Reason.* Translated by J. P. Doyle. Milwaukee, Wisc.: Marquette University Press, 1995.

————. *On the Formal Cause of Substance.* Translated by J. Kronen. Milwaukee, Wisc.: Marquette University Press, 2000.

Toletus, Franciscus. *Commentaria una cum quaestionibus in octo libros de Physica auscultatione.* Venice, 1573.

————. *Commentaria una cum quaestionibus in tres libros Aristotelis de anima.* Cologne, 1594.

————. *Commentaria una cum quaestionibus universam in Aristotelis Logicam.* Cologne, 1596.

————. *In Summam theologiae S. Thomae Aquinatis enarratio.* Rome: Typis S. Congregationis de Propaganda Fide, 1869–70.

Vanini, Giulio Cesare. *Amphiteatrum aeternae providentiae.* Lyon, 1615.

————. *De admirandis naturae reginae Deaque mortalium arcanis libri IV.* Paris, 1616.

————. *Opera.* Edited by G. Papuli and F. P. Raimondi (4 vols.). Galatina: Congedo, 1990.

Viète, François. *Opera mathematica.* Edited by F. van Schooten. Leiden, 1646 [repr. Hildesheim: Olms, 1970].

Ville, Louis de la [Louis le Valois]. *Sentimens de Monsieur Descartes touchant l'essence et es proprietez du corps opposez à la Doctrine de l'Eglise, et conforme aux erreurs de Calvin sur le sujet de l'Eucharistie.* Caen, 1680.

Vincent, Jean. *Discussio peripatetica in qua philosophiae cartesianae principia.* Toulouse, 1677.

White, Thomas. *De mundo dialogi tres, quibus materia, hoc est, quantitas, numerus, figura, partes, partium qualitas et genera: forma, hoc est, magnorum corporum motus, et motuum intentata hactenus philosophis origo: caussae, hoc est, movens, efficiens, gubernans, caussa finalis, durationis quoque principium et terminus: et tandem definitio, rationibus purè à natura depromptis aperiuntur, concluduntur.* Paris, 1642.

————. *Institutionum peripateticarum ad mentem . . . Kenelmi equitis Digbaei pars theorica.* Lyon, 1646.

————. *An answer to the Lord Faulklands Discourse of infallibility.* Cary, 1651.

————. *Peripateticall Institutions in the way of . . . Sir Kenelm Digby: The theoricall part.* London, 1656.

————. *Euclides physicus, sive de principiis naturae.* London, 1657.

————. *Euclides metaphysicus, sive de principiis sapientiae.* London, 1658.

Works on Descartes

Aiton, E. J. *The Vortex Theory of Planetary Motions.* New York: Neale Watson, 1972.

Allard, Jean-Louis. *Le Mathématisme de Descartes.* Ottawa: Editions de l'Université d'Ottawa, 1963.

Alquié, Ferdinand. *La découverte métaphysique de l'homme.* Paris: Presses Universitaires de France, 1950.

Ariew, Roger. "The Infinite in Descartes' Conversation with Burman." *Archiv für Geschichte der Philosophie* 69 (1987): 140–63.

————. "Descartes and the Tree of Knowledge." *Synthese* 92 (1992): 101–16.

————. "Sur les septièmes réponses." In *Descartes: Objecter et Répondre,* edited by J.-M. Beyssade and J.-L. Marion, 123–40. Paris: Presses Universitaires de France, 1994.

————. "Descartes and the Late Scholastics on the Order of the Sciences." In *Philosophy in the Sixteenth and Seventeenth Centuries: Conversations with Aristotle,* edited by C. Blackwell and S. Kusukawa, 350–64. Aldershot, England: Ashgate, 1999.

————. *Descartes and the Last Scholastics.* Ithaca, N.Y.: Cornell University Press, 1999.

Ariew, Roger, and Marjorie Grene, eds. *Descartes and His Contemporaries: Meditations, Objections and Replies.* Chicago: University of Chicago Press, 1995.

Armogathe, Jean-Robert. *Theologia Cartesiana. L'explication physique de l'Eucharistie chez Descartes et dom Desgabets.* The Hague: Nijhoff, 1977.

————. "L'approbation des *Meditationes* par la faculté de théologie de Paris (1641)." *Bulletin Cartésien XXI, Archives de Philosophie* 57 (1994): 1–3.

Armogathe, Jean-Robert, and Giulia Belgioioso, eds. *Descartes: Principia Philosophiae (1644–1994).* Naples: Vivarium, 1996.

————. *La Biographia Intellettuale di René Descartes attraverso la Correspondance*. Naples: Vivarium, 1999.

Armogathe, Jean-Robert, Vincent Carraud, and Massimiliano Savini. *Bibliographia cartesiana II*. Lecce: Conte, 2003.

Armour, Leslie. "Descartes and Eustachius a Sancto Paulo: Unravelling the Mind-Body Problem." *British Journal for the History of Philosophy* 1 (1993): 3–21.

Atherton, Margaret. "Cartesian Reason and Gendered Reason." In *A Mind of One's Own*, edited by L. M. Antony and C. Witt, 19–34. Boulder, Colo.: Westview, 1993.

Baillet, Adrien. *La Vie de M. Descartes* (2 vols.). Paris, 1691.

————. *Vie de Monsieur Descartes*. Paris: Table Ronde, 1946.

Balz, Albert G. A. *Cartesian Studies*. New York: Columbia University Press, 1951.

Beck, L. J. *The Method of Descartes: A Study of the Regulae*. Oxford: Oxford University Press, 1952.

————. *The Metaphysics of Descartes: A Study of the Meditations*. Oxford: Oxford University Press, 1965.

Belgioioso, Giulia. *La Variata Immagine di Descartes*. Lecce: Edizioni Milella, 1999.

Belgioioso, Giulia, et al., eds. *Descartes: Il metodo e I saggi*. Rome: Istituto della Enciclopedia Italiana, 1990.

Beyssade, Jean-Marie. *La Philosophie première de Descartes*. Paris: Flammarion, 1979.

————. "Création des vérités éternelles et doute métaphysique." *Studia Cartesiana* 2 (1981): 86–105.

————. "La classification cartésienne des passions." *Revue Internationale de Philosophie* 146 (1983): 278–87.

————. "Descartes on the Freedom of the Will." *Graduate Faculty Philosophy Journal* 13 (1988): 81–96.

Beyssade, Jean-Marie, and Jean-Luc Marion, eds. *Descartes: Méditer, objecter, répondre*. Paris: Presses Universitaires de France, 1994.

Blackwell, Richard J. "Descartes' Laws of Motion." *Isis* 57 (1966): 220–34.

Blanchet, Léon. *Les Antécédents historiques du "Je pense, donc je suis."* Paris: Presses Universitaires de France, 1920.

Bordo, Susan. *The Flight to Objectivity: Essays on Cartesianism and Culture*. Albany: State University of New York Press, 1987.

Bos, Erik-Jan. *The Correspondence between Descartes and Henricus Regius*. Utrecht: Zeno, 2002.

Bouillier, Francisque. *Histoire de la philosophie cartésienne*, 3rd ed. (2 vols.). Paris, 1868 [repr. New York: Garland, 1987].

Boutroux, E. *Des vérités éternelles chez Descartes.* Translated (French) by G. Canguilhem. Paris: Alcan, 1927.

Brockliss, L. W. B. "Descartes, Gassendi and the Reception of the Mechanical Philosophy in the French Collèges de Plein Exercice, 1640–1730." *Perspectives on Science* 3 (1995): 450–79.

————. "Aristotle, Descartes, and the New Science: Natural Philosophy at the University of Paris, 1600–1740." *Annals of Science* 38 (1981): 33–69.

Broughton, Janet, and Ruth Mattern. "Reinterpreting Descartes on the Notion of the Union of Mind and Body." *Journal of the History of Philosophy* 16 (1978): 23–32.

Brunschvicg, L. *Descartes et Pascal lecteurs de Montaigne.* Neuchâtel: La Baconnière, 1945.

Buchdahl, Gerd. *Metaphysics and the Philosophy of Science: The Classical Origins, Descartes to Kant.* Oxford: Blackwell, 1969.

Buson, Frédéric de, and Denis Kambouchner. *Le Vocabulaire de Descartes.* Paris: Ellipses, 2002.

Busson, Henri. *La pensée religieuse française de Charron à Pascal.* Paris: Vrin, 1933.

Butler, R. J., ed. *Cartesian Studies.* Oxford: Blackwell, 1972.

Carriero, John. "The First Meditation." *Pacific Philosophical Quarterly* 68 (1987): 222–48.

————. *Descartes and the Autonomy of Human Understanding.* New York: Garland, 1990.

Carter, Richard B. *Descartes' Medical Philosophy: The Organic Solution to the Mind-Body Problem.* Baltimore, Md.: Johns Hopkins University Press, 1983.

Chappell, Vere, and Willis Doney, eds. *Twenty-five Years of Descartes Scholarship 1960–1984: A Bibliography.* New York: Garland, 1987.

Clarke, Desmond M. "Descartes' Critique of Logic." In *Truth, Knowledge and Reality: Inquiries into the Foundations of Seventeenth Century Rationalism* (Studia Leibnitiana, Sonderheft), edited by G. H. R. Parkinson. Stuttgart: Steiner, 1981.

————. *Descartes' Philosophy of Science.* Manchester: Manchester University Press, 1982.

Cole, John R. *The Olympian Dreams and Youthful Rebellion of René Descartes.* Urbana: University of Illinois Press, 1992.

Cossuta, Frederic, ed. *Descartes et l'argumentation philosophique.* Paris: Presses Universitaires de France, 1996.

Costa, M. J. "What Cartesian Ideas Are Not." *Journal of the History of Philosophy* 12 (1983): 53–64.

Cottingham, John C. *Descartes.* Oxford: Blackwell, 1986.

————. *The Rationalists.* Oxford: Oxford University Press, 1988.

------. *A Descartes Dictionary*. Oxford: Blackwell, 1993.
------, ed. *The Cambridge Companion to Descartes*. Cambridge: Cambridge University Press, 1992.
------. *Reason, Will, and Sensation*. Oxford: Oxford University Press, 1994.
Cress, Donald. "Does Descartes' 'Ontological Argument' Stand on Its Own?" *International Studies in Philosophy* 5 (1973): 127–36.
Cronin, T. J. "Eternal Truths in the Thought of Descartes and of His Adversary." *Journal of the History of Ideas* 21 (1960): 553–59.
------. *Objective Being in Descartes and Suarez*. Rome: Analecta Gregoriana, 1966.
Cummins, Phillip, and Guenter Zoeller, eds. *Minds, Ideas and Objects*. Atascadero, Calif.: Ridgeview, 1992.
Curley, E. M. "Descartes on the Creation of the Eternal Truths." *Philosophical Review* 93 (1984): 569–97.
------. *Descartes Against the Skeptics*. Cambridge, Mass.: Harvard University Press, 1978.
Dalbiez, Roland. "Les sources scolastiques de la théorie cartésienne de l'être objectif: A propos du 'Descartes' de M. Gilson." *Revue d'Histoire de la Philosophie* 3 (1929): 464–72.
Derrida, Jacques. "Le Cogito et l'histoire de la folie." In *L'Ecriture et la différence*. Paris: Seuil, 1967.
Des Chene, Dennis. *Physiologia: Philosophy of Nature in Descartes and the Aristotelians*. Ithaca, N.Y.: Cornell University Press, 1995.
------. "Cartesiomania: Early Receptions of Descartes." *Perspectives on Science* 3 (1995): 534–81.
------. *Spirits and Clocks: Machine and Organism in Descartes*. Ithaca, N.Y.: Cornell University Press, 2001.
Dijksterhuis, E. J., et al. *Descartes et le cartésianisme hollandais. Études et documents*. Paris and Amsterdam: Presses Universitaires Françaises and Éditions Françaises d'Amsterdam, 1950.
Doney, Willis, ed. *Descartes: A Collection of Critical Essays*. Garden City, N.Y.: Doubleday, 1967.
Echarri, J. "Uno influjo español desconcido en la formación del sistema cartesiano: dos textos paralelos de Toledo y Descartes sobre el espacio." *El Pensamiento* 6 (1950): 291–332.
Faye, Emmanuel. *Philosophie et perfection de l'homme: De la Renaissance à Descartes*. Paris: Vrin, 1998.
------, ed. *Descartes et la Renaissance*. Paris: Honoré Champion, 1999.
Fowler, C. F. *Descartes on the Human Soul: Philosophy and the Demands of Christian Doctrine*. Dordrecht: Klewer, 1999.
Frankfurt, Harry. "Memory and the Cartesian Circle." *Philosophical Review* 71 (1962): 505–11.

————. "Descartes' Discussion of his Existence in the Second Meditation." *Philosophical Review* 75 (1966): 329–56.

————. *Demons, Dreamers and Madmen: The Defense of Reason in Descartes' Meditations.* Indianapolis, Ind.: Bobbs-Merill, 1970.

————. "Descartes on the Creation of Eternal Truths." *Philosophical Review* 86 (1977): 36–57.

Fuchs, T. *Mechanization of the Heart: Harvey and Descartes.* Translated
by M. Grene. Rochester: University of Rochester Press, 2001.

Gabbey, Alan. "Les trois genres de découverte selon Descartes." In *Actes
du XIIe Congrès International d'Histoire des Sciences, Paris 1968,*
vol. II, 45–49. Paris, 1970.

————. "Descartes' Physics and Descartes' Mechanics: Chicken and Egg?"
In *Essays on the Philosophy and Science of René Descartes,* edited by
Steven Voss, 311–23. Oxford: Oxford University Press, 1998.

Garber, Daniel. *Descartes' Metaphysical Physics.* Chicago: University of
Chicago Press, 1992.

————. "Descartes, the Aristotelians and the Revolution that Did Not
Happen in 1637." *The Monist* 71 (1988): 471–86.

————. *Descartes Embodied: Reading Cartesian Philosophy through
Cartesian Science.* Cambridge: Cambridge University Press, 2001.

————. "Descartes, Mechanics, and the Mechanical Philosophy." In *Mid-
west Studies in Philosophy: Renaissance and Early Modern Philosophy,* vol. 26, edited by Peter French and Howard K. Wettstein,
185–204. Oxford: Blackwell, 2002.

Garber, Daniel, and Michael Ayers, eds. *Cambridge History of Seventeenth-Century Philosophy* (2 vols.). Cambridge: Cambridge University Press, 1997.

Garin, P. *Thèses cartésiennes et thèses thomistes.* Bruges: Desclée de
Brouwer, 1932.

Gaukroger, Stephen. *Cartesian Logic. An Essay on Descartes's Conception of Inference.* Oxford: Oxford University Press, 1989.

————. *Descartes: An Intellectual Biography.* Oxford: Oxford University
Press, 1995.

————. *Descartes' System of Natural Philosophy.* Cambridge: Cambridge
University Press, 2002.

————, ed. *Descartes: Philosophy, Mathematics and Physics.* Sussex:
Harvester Press, 1980.

Gaukroger, Stephen, John Schuster, and John Sutton, eds. *Descartes'
Natural Philosophy.* London: Routlege, 2000.

Gibson, Boyce A. *The Philosophy of Descartes.* London: Methuen, 1932.

Gilson, Étienne. *La liberté chez Descartes et la théologie.* Paris: Alcan,
1913 [repr., Paris: Vrin, 1982].

————. *Études sur le rôle de la pensée médievale dans la formation du système cartésien.* Paris: Vrin, 1930.

Gouhier, Henri. *Essais sur Descartes.* Paris: Vrin, 1937.

————. "Doute méthodique ou négation méthodique?" *Les Etudes Philosophiques* 9 (1954): 135–62.

————. "La crise de la théologie au temps de Descartes." *Revue de Théologie et de Philosophie,* 3e ser. 4 (1954): 45–47.

————. *Les premières pensées de Descartes: Contribution à l'histoire de l'anti-Renaissance (De Pétrarque à Descartes).* Paris: Vrin, 1958.

————. *La pensée métaphysique de Descartes.* Paris: Vrin, 1962 [2nd ed. 1969, 3rd ed. 1978].

————. *La pensée religieuse de Descartes.* 2nd ed. Paris: Vrin, 1972.

————. *Cartésianisme et Augustinisme au XVIIe siècle.* Paris: Vrin, 1978.

Gregory, Tullio. "Dio ingannatore e genio malignio. Nota in margine alla *Meditationes* di Descartes." *Giornale critico della filosofia italiana* 53 (1974): 477–516.

Grene, Marjorie. "Die Einheit des Menschen: Descartes unter den Scholastikern." *Dialectica* 40 (1986): 309–22.

————. *Descartes.* Minneapolis: University of Minnesota Press, 1985.

————. *Descartes among the Scholastics.* Milwaukee, Wisc.: Marquette University Press, 1991.

————. "Animal Mechanism and the Cartesian Vision of Nature." In *Physics, Philosophy, and the Scientific Community,* edited by K. Gavroglu et al., 189–204. Dordrecht: Kluwer, 1995.

Groarke, Leo. "Descartes' First Meditation: Something Old, Something New, Something Borrowed." *Journal of the History of Philosophy* 22 (1984): 281–301.

Grosholz, Emily. *Cartesian Method and the Problem of Reduction.* Oxford: Oxford University Press, 1991.

Gueroult, Martial. *Nouvelles réflexions sur la preuve ontologique.* Paris: Vrin, 1955.

————. *Etudes sur Descartes, Spinoza, Malebranche et Leibniz.* Hildesheim: Georg Olms, 1970.

————. *Descartes' Philosophy Interpreted According to the Order of Reasons.* Translated by R. Ariew et al. (2 vols.). Minneapolis: University of Minnesota Press, 1984.

Hamelin, Octave. *Le système de Descartes.* Paris: Félix Alcan, 1911.

Hannequin, A. "La preuve ontologique de Descartes défendue contre Leibniz." *Revue de métaphysique et de Morale* 4 (1896): 433–58.

Hatfield, Gary. "Force (God) in Descartes' Physics." *Studies in History and Philosophy of Science* 10 (1979): 113–40.

————. "First Philosophy and Natural Philosophy in Descartes." In *Philosophy: Its History and Historiography*, edited by A. J. Holland. Dordrecht: Reidel, 1985.

————. "Science, Certainty, and Descartes." In *PSA 1988*, vol. 2, edited by A. Fine and J. Leplin. East Lansing, Mich.: Philosophy of Science Association, 1989.

————. *Descartes and the* Meditations. London: Routledge, 2003.

Heyd, Michael. "From Rationalist Theology to Cartesian Voluntarism." *Journal of the History of Ideas* 40 (1979): 527–42.

Hintikka, Jaako, and Unto Remes. *The Method of Analysis: Its Geometrical Origin and Its General Significance* (Boston Studies in the Philosophy of Science). Dordrecht: Reidel, 1974.

Hoffman, Paul. "The Unity of Descartes' Man." *Philosophical Review* 95 (1986): 342–49.

————. "Cartesian Passions and Cartesian Dualism." *Pacific Philosophical Quarterly* 71 (1990): 310–32.

Hooker, Michael, ed. *Descartes: Critical and Interpretive Essays*. Baltimore, Md.: Johns Hopkins University Press, 1978.

Jolley, Nicholas. *The Light of the Soul: Theories of Ideas in Leibniz, Malebranche, and Descartes*. Oxford: Oxford University Press, 1990.

Judovitz, Dalia. *Subjectivity and Representation in Descartes: The Origins of Modernity*. Cambridge: Cambridge University Press, 1988.

————. "Vision, Representation and Technology in Descartes." In *Modernity and the Hegemony of Vision,* edited by D. M. Levin. Berkeley: University of California Press, 1993.

Keeling, S. V. *Descartes*. London: Benn, 1934.

Kennington, Richard. "Finitude of Descartes' Evil Genius." *Journal of the History of Ideas* 32 (1971): 441–46.

Kenny, Anthony. *Descartes*. New York: Random House, 1968.

————. "The Cartesian Circle and the Eternal Truths." *Journal of Philosophy* 57 (1970): 685–700.

Koyré, Alexandre. *Essai sur l'idée de Dieu et les preuves de son existence chez Descartes*. Paris: Leroux, 1922.

Krailsheimer, A. J. *Studies in Self-Interest: From Descartes to La Bruyere*. Oxford: Oxford University Press, 1962.

Kraus, Pamela A. "From Universal Mathematics to Universal Method: Descartes's 'Turn' in Rule IV of the Regulae." *Journal of the History of Philosophy* 21 (1983): 159–74.

————. "'Whole Method' The Thematic Unity of Descartes' *Regulae*." *Modern Schoolman* 63 (1986): 83–109.

Lalande, A. "Sur quelques textes de Bacon et de Descartes." *Revue de métaphysique et de morale* 19 (1911): 296–311.

Landucci, S. *La teodicea nell'eta cartesiana*. Naples: Bibliopolis, 1986.

Laporte, J. *Le rationalisme de Descartes.* Paris: Presses Universitaires de France, 1950.

Larmore, Charles. "Descartes' Psychologistic Theory of Assent." *History of Philosophy Quarterly* 1 (1984): 61–74.

Lasswitz, Kurd. *Geschichte der Atomistik vom Mittelalter bis Newton* (2 vols.). Hamburg: L. Voss, 1890.

Lennon, Thomas M. "Occasionalism and the Cartesian Metaphysics of Motion." *Canadian Journal of Philosophy,* supp. 1 (1974): 29–40.

———. "The Inherence Pattern and Descartes' Ideas." *Journal of the History of Philosophy* 12 (1974): 43–52.

———. *The Battle of the Gods and Giants: The Legacies of Descartes and Gassendi, 1655–1715.* Princeton, N.J.: Princeton University Press, 1993.

Lennon, Thomas M., John Nicholas, and John Davis, eds. *Problems of Cartesianism.* Montreal: McGill-Queen's University Press, 1982.

Levi, Anthony. *French Moralists: The Theory of the Passions 1585 to 1649.* Oxford: Oxford University Press, 1964.

Lindeboom, G. A. *Descartes and Medicine.* Amsterdam: Rodopi, 1979.

Loeb, Louis. *From Descartes to Hume.* Ithaca, N.Y.: Cornell University Press, 1981.

Marion, J.-L. "Is the Ontological Argument Ontological?" *Journal of the History of Philosophy* 30 (1992): 201–18.

———. *Sur l'ontologie grise de Descartes.* Paris: Vrin, 1975 [2nd ed. 1981].

———. *Sur la théologie blanche de Descartes.* Paris: Presses Universitaires de France, 1981.

———. *Questions Cartésiennes II.* Paris: Presses Universitaires de France, 1996.

———. *Cartesian Questions.* Chicago: University of Chicago Press, 1999.

———. *On Descartes' Metaphysical Prism: The Constitution and Limits of Onto-theo-logy in Cartesian Thought.* Chicago: University of Chicago Press, 1999.

Marion, Jean-Luc, and Nicolas Grimaldi, eds. *Le Discours et sa méthode.* Paris: Presses Universitaires de France, 1987.

Markie, Peter. *Descartes's Gambit.* Ithaca, N.Y.: Cornell University Press, 1986.

Marlin, Randal. "Cartesian Freedom and the Problem of the Mesland Letters." In *Early Modern Philosophy: Metaphysics, Epistemology, and Politics: Essays in Honour of Robert F. McRae,* edited by G. J. D. Moyal and S. Tweyman. Delmar, N.Y.: Caravan, 1985.

Marshall, John. *Descartes's Moral Theory.* Ithaca, N.Y.: Cornell University Press, 1998.

McLaughlin, Peter. "Descartes on Mind-Body Interaction and the Conservation of Motion." *Philosophical Review* 102 (1993): 155–82.

Menn, Stephen. *Descartes and Augustine.* Cambridge: Cambridge University Press, 1998.

Mesnard, Pierre. *Essai sur la morale de Descartes.* Paris: Boivin, 1936.

Morgan, Vance G. *Foundations of Cartesian Ethics.* New York: Humanities Press, 1994.

Mouy, Paul. *Le développement de la physique cartésienne 1646–1712.* Paris: Vrin, 1934.

Moyal, Georges J. D. "The Unity of Descartes' Conception of Freedom." *International Studies in Philosophy* 19 (1987): 33–51.

Nadler, Steven. "Arnauld, Descartes, and Transubstantiation: Reconciling Cartesian Metaphysics and Real Presence." *Journal of the History of Ideas* 49 (1988): 229–46.

———. "Deduction, Confirmation, and the Laws of Nature in Descartes's *Principia Philosophiae.*" *Journal of the History of Philosophy* 28 (1990): 359–83.

———. "Descartes and Occasional Causation." *British Journal for the History of Philosophy* 2 (1994): 35–54.

———, ed. *Causation in Early Modern Philosophy.* University Park: Pennsylvania State University Press, 1993.

Nuchelmans, G. *Judgment and Proposition: From Descartes to Kant.* Amsterdam: North Holland Publishing, 1983.

Oakley, Francis. *Omnipotence, Covenant and Order: An Excursion in the History of Ideas from Abelard to Leibniz.* Ithaca, N.Y.: Cornell University Press, 1984.

O'Neill, Eileen. "Mind-Body Interaction and Metaphysical Consistency: A Defense of Descartes." *Journal of the History of Philosophy* 25 (1987): 227–45.

Osler, Margaret J. "Eternal Truths and the Laws of Nature: The Theological Foundations of Descartes' Philosophy of Nature." *Journal of the History of Ideas* 46 (1985): 349–62.

———. *Divine Will and the Mechanical Philosophy: Gassendi and Descartes on Contingency and Necessity in the Created World.* Cambridge: Cambridge University Press, 1994.

Otegem, Matthijs van. *A Bibliography of the Works of Descartes.* 2 vols. Utrecht: Zeno, 2002.

Pace, Anna de. "Descartes critico di Descartes: Il concetto di quiete nelle leggi del moto da *Il Mondo* ai *Principi.*" In *Miscellanea secentesca: Saggi su Descartes, Fabri, White.* Milan: Cisalpino-Goliardica, 1987.

Passmore, John. "Descartes, the British Empiricists, and Formal Logic." *Philosophical Review* 62 (1953): 545–53.

Petrik, James M. *Descartes' Theory of the Will*. Durango, Colo.: Hollow-brook, 1992.

Popkin, Richard H. *The History of Skepticism from Erasmus to Spinoza*. Berkeley: University of California Press, 1979.

Prendergast, Thomas L. "Descartes and the Relativity of Motion." *Modern Schoolman* 50 (1972–73): 64–72.

———. "Motion, Action, and Tendency in Descartes' Physics." *Journal of the History of Philosophy* 13 (1975): 453–62.

Prost, J. *Essai sur l'atomisme et l'occasionalisme dans la philosophie cartésienne*. Paris: Paulin, 1907.

Remnant, Peter. "Descartes: Body and Soul." *Canadian Journal of Philosophy* 9 (1979): 377–86.

Renault, Laurence. *Descartes ou la felicité volontaire*. Paris: Presses Universitaires de France, 2000.

Richardson, Robert. "The 'Scandal' of Cartesian Interaction." *Mind* 92 (1982): 20–37.

Rodis-Lewis, Geneviève. *L'individualité selon Descartes*. Paris: Vrin, 1950.

———. *La Morale de Descartes*. Paris: Presses Universitaires de France, 1957.

———. *L'oeuvre de Descartes* (2 vols.). Paris: Vrin, 1971.

———. *Idées et vérités éternelles chez Descartes et ses successeurs*. Paris: Vrin, 1985.

———. "Le dernier fruit de la métaphysique cartésienne: La generosité." *Les études philosophiques* 1 (1987): 43–54.

———. *L'anthropologie cartésienne*. Paris: Presses Universitaires de France, 1990.

———. *Descartes: His Life and Thought*. Ithaca, N.Y.: Cornell University Press, 1995.

———, ed. *Méthode et métaphysique chez Descartes*. New York: Garland, 1987.

Rogers, G. A. J. "Descartes and the Method of English Science." *Annals of Science* 29 (1972): 237–55.

Rorty, Amélie O., ed. *Essays on Descartes' Meditations*. Berkeley: University of California Press, 1986.

Rorty, Richard. *Philosophy and the Mirror of Nature*. Princeton, N.J.: Princeton University Press, 1978.

Rosenfield, Leonora Cohen. *From Beast-Machine to Man-Machine: Animal Soul in French Letters from Descartes to La Mettrie*, 2nd ed. New York: Octagon Books, 1968.

Rozemond, Marleen. *Descartes's Dualism*. Cambridge, Mass.: Harvard University Press, 1998.

Ruler, J. A. van. *The Crisis of Causality, Voetius and Descartes on God,*

Nature and Change. Leiden: Brill, 1995.

Sabra, A. I. *Theories of Light from Descartes to Newton.* Cambridge: Cambridge University Press, 1981 [1st ed., London: Oldbourne, 1967].

Sakellariadis, Spyros. "Descartes's Use of Empirical Data to Test Hypotheses." *Isis* 73 (1982): 68–76.

Schankula, H. A. S. "Locke, Descartes, and the Science of Nature." *Journal of the History of Ideas* 41 (1980): 459–77.

Schmaltz, Tad M. "Platonism and Descartes' View of Immutable Essences." *Archiv für Geschichte der Philosophie* 73 (1991): 129–70.

Schouls, Peter A. *The Imposition of Method: A Study of Locke and Descartes.* Oxford: Oxford University Press, 1980.

———. "Descartes on Innate Ideas, Sensation, and Scholasticism: The Response to Regius." In *Studies in Seventeenth-Century European Philosophy,* edited by M. A. Stewart. Oxford: Clarendon Press, 1997.

Schuster, John A. "Descartes and the Scientific Revolution, 1618–1644: An Interpretation." Ph.D. diss., Princeton University, 1977.

———. "Cartesian Method as Mythic Speech: A Diachronic and Structural Analysis." In *The Politics and Rhetoric of Scientific Method: Historical Studies,* edited by J. A. Schuster and R. R. Yeo. Dordrecht: Reidel, 1986.

Scott, J. F. *The Scientific Work of René Descartes (1596–1650).* London: Taylor and Francis, 1952.

Sebba, G. *Bibliographia Cartesiana: A Critical Guide to the Descartes Literature 1800–1960.* The Hague: Martinus Nijhof, 1964.

Secada, Jorge. "Descartes on Time and Causality." *Philosophical Review* 99 (1990): 45–72.

———. *Cartesian Metaphysics: The Scholastic Origins of Modern Philosophy.* Cambridge: Cambridge University Press, 2000.

Shea, William R. *The Magic of Numbers and Motion: The Scientific Career of René Descartes.* Canton, Mass.: Science History Publications, 1991.

Simon, G. "Les vérités éternelles de Descartes, évidences ontologiques." *Studia Cartesiana* 2 (1981): 124–35.

Sirven, J. *Les années d'apprentissage de Descartes (1596–1628).* Paris: Vrin, 1930 [repr. New York: Garland, 1987].

Smith, Norman Kemp. *Studies in the Cartesian Philosophy.* London: Macmillan, 1902 [repr. New York: Russell and Russell, 1962].

———. *New Studies in the Philosophy of Descartes.* New York: St. Martin's Press, 1952.

Sorell, Tom. *Descartes.* Oxford: Oxford University Press, 1987.

————, ed. *The Rise of Modern Philosophy: The Tension between the New and Traditional Philosophies from Machiavelli to Leibniz.* Oxford: Oxford University Press, 1993.

Sortais, Gaston. "Descartes et la Compagnie de Jésus, menaces et avances (1640–1646)." *Estudios de la Academia literaria del Platal Buenos Aires* 57 (1937): 441–68.

Verbeek, Theo. *La querelle d'Utrecht.* Paris: Les impressions nouvelles, 1988.

————. *Descartes and the Dutch: Early Reactions to Cartesianism (1637–1650)* (Journal of the History of Philosophy Monograph Series). Carbondale: Southern Illinois University Press, 1992.

————. "'Ens per Accidens': Le origini della Querelle di Utrecht." *Giornale critico della filosofia italiana* 71 (1992): 276–88.

————, ed. *Descartes et Regius: Autour de l'Explication de l'esprit.* Amsterdam: Rodopi, 1993.

Voss, Stephen, ed. *Essays on the Philosophy and Science of René Descartes.* Oxford: Oxford University Press, 1993.

Waard, Cornelis de. "Un Entretien avec Descartes en 1634 ou 1635." *Archives internationales d'Histoire des Sciences* 6 (1953): 14–16.

Watson, Richard. *Cogito, Ergo Sum. The Life of René Descartes.* Boston: Godine, 2002.

Weber, Jean-Paul. "La Méthode de Descartes d'après les Regulae." *Archives de Philosophie* 35 (1972): 51–60.

Wells, Norman J. "Descartes' Uncreated Truths." *The New Scholasticism* 56 (1982): 185–99.

————. "Descartes' *Idea* and Its Sources." *American Catholic Philosophical Quarterly* 67 (1993): 513–35.

Williams, Bernard. *Descartes: The Project of Pure Enquiry.* Hassock, Sussex: Harvester, 1978.

————. "Descartes' Use of Scepticism." In *The Sceptical Tradition*, edited by M. Burnyeat. Berkeley: University of California Press, 1983.

Wilson, Margaret. *Descartes* (Arguments of the Philosophers). London: Routledge, 1978.

————. "Descartes on the Representationality of Sensation." In *Central Themes in Early Modern Philosophy*, edited by J. A. Cover and M. Kulstad. Indianapolis, Ind.: Hackett, 1990.

————. "Descartes on the Origin of Sensation." *Philosophical Topics* 19 (1991): 293–323.

Woolhouse, Roger S. *Descartes, Spinoza, Leibniz: The Concept of Substance in Seventeenth-Century Metaphysics.* London: Routledge, 1993.

Yolton, John W. *Perceptual Acquaintance from Descartes to Reid.* Minneapolis: University of Minnesota Press, 1984.

Zarka, Yves-Charles. "La matière et la représentation: L'expérience dans la philosophie naturelle de Descartes." In *Problématique et réception du Discours de la méthode et des Essais,* edited by H. Méchoulan, 81–98. Paris: Vrin, 1988.

Works on Cartesians and Other 17th-Century Figures

Abercrombie, Nigel. *The Origins of Jansenism.* Oxford: Oxford University Press, 1936.
Adams, Robert Merrihew. *Leibniz: Determinist, Theist, Idealist.* Oxford: Oxford University Press, 1994.
Aiton, E. J. *Leibniz: A Biography.* Bristol: Hilger, 1985.
Åkerman, Susanna. "Queen Christina and Messianic Thought." In *Sceptics, Millenarians and Jews,* edited by D. S. Katz and J. Israel. Leiden: Brill, 1990.
———. *Queen Christina of Sweden and Her Circle* (Brill Studies in Intellectual History). Leiden: Brill, 1991.
Allison, Henry E. *Benedict de Spinoza: An Introduction,* revised edition. New Haven, Conn.: Yale University Press, 1987.
Alquié, Ferdinand. *Le cartésianisme de Malebranche.* Paris: Vrin, 1974.
———. *Le rationalisme de Spinoza.* Paris: Presses Universitaires de France, 1981.
Ariew, Roger. "Oratorians and the Teaching of Cartesian Philosophy in Seventeenth-Century France." *History of Universities* 17 (2001–02): 47–80.
Armour, Leslie. "Le cartésianisme au Québec." *Bulletin Cartésien XVI, Archives de Philosophie* 51 (1988): 1–12.
Auger, Léon. *Gilles Personne de Roberval (1602–1675).* Paris: Blanchard, 1962.
Ayers, Michael R. *Locke* (2 vols.). London: Routledge, 1991.
Battail, Jean-François. *L'avocat philosophe Géraud de Cordemoy.* The Hague: Nijhoff, 1973.
Beaude, J. "Cartésianisme et anticartésianisme de Desgabets." *Studia Cartesiana* 1 (1979): 1–24.
Belaval, Yvon. *Leibniz critique de Descartes.* Paris: Gallimard, 1960.
Belgioioso, Giulia. *La variatta immagine di Descartes.* Lecce: Editioni Milella, 1999.
Berkel, Klaas van. *Isaac Beeckman (1588–1637) en de Mechanisering van het Wereldbeeld (with a summary in English).* Amsterdam: Rodopi, 1983.
Blair, Ann. "Tradition and Innovation in Early Modern Natural Philosophy: Jean Bodin and Jean-Cecile Frey." *Perspectives on Science* 2

(1994): 428–54.

Blay, Michel. *La naissance de la mécanique analytique: La science du mouvement au tournant des XVIIe et XVIIIe siècles*. Paris: Presses Universitaires de France, 1992.

Bloch, Olivier René. *La philosophie de Gassendi: Nominalisme, matérialisme et métaphysique* (International Archives of the History of Ideas). The Hague: Nijhoff, 1971.

Boas Hall, Marie. *Robert Boyle on Natural Philosophy: An Essay with Selections from His Writings*. Bloomington: Indiana University Press, 1965.

————. *The Mechanical Philosophy*. New York: Arno Press, 1981.

Boehm, Alfred. "L'Aristotélisme d'Honoré Fabri (1607–1688)." *Revue des sciences religieuses* 39 (1965): 305–60.

Bohatec, Josef. *Die Cartesianische Scholastik in der Philosophie und Theologie der reformierten Dogmatik des 17. Jahrhunderts*. Leipzig: Deichert, 1912 [repr. Hildesheim: Olms, 1966].

Broad, C. D. *Leibniz: An Introduction*. Cambridge: Cambridge University Press, 1975.

Brockliss, L. W. B. *French Higher Education in the Seventeenth and Eighteenth Centuries: A Cultural History*. Oxford: Oxford University Press, 1987.

Brown, Harcourt. *Scientific Organizations in Seventeenth-Century France (1620–1680)*. Baltimore, Md.: Williams and Wilkins, 1934.

Brown, Stuart. *Leibniz* (Philosophers in Context). Minneapolis: University of Minnesota Press, 1984.

Brundell, Barry. *Pierre Gassendi: From Aristotelianism to a New Natural Philosophy*. Dordrecht: Reidel, 1987.

Brush, Craig. *Montaigne and Bayle: Variations on the Theme of Scepticism*. The Hague: Nijhoff, 1966.

Burtt, E. A. *The Metaphysical Foundation of Modern Physical Sciences*. London: Routledge, 1932 [2nd ed. New York: Humanities Press, 1980].

Carraud, V. *Pascal et la philosophie*. Paris: Presses Universitaires de France, 1992.

Clair, Pierre. "Louis de la Forge et les origines de l'occasionalisme." *Recherches sur le XVIIème siècle* 1 (1976): 63–72.

Clarke, Desmond M. "Pierre-Sylvain Régis: A Paradigm of Cartesian Methodology." *Archiv für Geschichte der Philosophie* 62 (1980): 289–310.

————. "Cartesian Science in France, 1660–1700." In *Philosophy, Its History and Historiography*, edited by A. J. Holland. Dordrecht: Reidel, 1985.

————. *Occult Powers and Hypotheses: Cartesian Natural Philosophy under Louis XIV.* Oxford: Oxford University Press, 1989.

Clavelin, Maurice. *The Natural Philosophy of Galileo.* Cambridge, Mass.: MIT Press, 1974.

Cohen, I. Bernard. *The Newtonian Revolution: With Illustrations of the Transformation of Scientific Ideas.* Cambridge: Cambridge University Press, 1980.

————. *The Birth of a New Physics,* rev. ed. New York: W. W. Norton, 1985.

Cope, Jackson. *Joseph Glanvill: Anglican Apologist.* St. Louis, Mo.: Washington University Press, 1956.

Cottingham, John G. "The Intellect, the Will and the Passions: Spinoza's Critique of Descartes." *Journal of the History of Philosophy* 26 (1988): 239–57.

Courtine, J.-F. *Suarez et le système de la métaphysique.* Paris: Presses Universitaires de France, 1990.

Cranston, Maurice. *John Locke: A Biography.* London: Longmans, Green, 1957.

Crapulli, Giovanni. *Mathesis universalis: Genesi di un'idea nel XVI secolo.* Rome: Edizioni dell'Ateneo, 1969.

Crombie, Alistair C. *Medieval and Early Modern Science.* 2nd ed. Garden City, N.Y.: Doubleday, 1959.

Curley, E. M. *Spinoza's Metaphysics: An Essay in Interpretation.* Cambridge, Mass.: Harvard University Press, 1969.

————. *Behind the Geometrical Method: A Reading of Spinoza's Ethics.* Princeton, N.J.: Princeton University Press, 1988.

Curley, E. M., and Pierre-François Moreau, eds. *Spinoza: Issues and Directions.* Leiden: Brill, 1990.

Dainville, François de. *L'éducation des jésuites (XVIe–XVIIIe siècles).* Paris: Les Editions de Minuit, 1978.

Darmon, Albert. *Les corps immatériels: Esprits et images dans l'oeuvre de Marin Cureau de la Chambre (1594–1669).* Paris: Vrin, 1985.

Dear, Peter R. *Mersenne and the Learning of the Schools.* Ithaca, N.Y.: Cornell University Press, 1988.

————. *Discipline and Experience: The Mathematical Way in the Scientific Revolution.* Chicago: University of Chicago Press, 1995.

Della Rocca, Michael. "'If a Body Meet a Body': Descartes on Body-Body Causation." In *New Essays on the Rationalists,* edited by R. J. Gennaro and C. Huenemenn. New York: Oxford, 1999.

Des Chene, Dennis. *Life's Form: Late Aristotelian Conceptions of the Soul.* Ithaca, N.Y.: Cornell University Press, 2000.

Dibon, Paul. *La Philosophie néerlandaise au siècle d'or: Tome I, L'Enseignement philosophique dans les universités a l'époque pré-cartésienne (1575–1650)*. Paris: Elsevier, 1954.

Dijksterhuis, E. J. *The Mechanization of the World Picture*. Translated by C. Dikshoorn. Oxford: Oxford University Press, 1961.

Dobbs, Betty Jo Teeter. *The Foundations of Newton's Alchemy, or "The Hunting of the Greene Lyon."* Cambridge: Cambridge University Press, 1975.

———. *The Janus Faces of Genius: The Role of Alchemy in Newton's Thought*. Cambridge: Cambridge University Press, 1991.

Donagan, Alan. *Spinoza*. Chicago: University of Chicago Press, 1988.

Drake, Stillman. *Galileo at Work*. Chicago: University of Chicago Press, 1978.

Emerton, Norma E. *The Scientific Reinterpretation of Form*. Ithaca, N.Y.: Cornell University Press, 1984.

Farrington, Benjamin. *The Philosophy of Francis Bacon: An Essay on Its Development from 1603 to 1609, with New Translations of Fundamental Texts*. Liverpool: Liverpool University Press, 1964.

Feingold, Mordechai, ed. *Jesuit Science and the Republic of Letters*. Cambridge, Mass.: MIT Press, 2003.

Ferrier, F. *Un oratorien ami de Descartes: Guillaume Gibieuf*. Paris: Vrin, 1978.

Fleitmann, Sabina. *Walter Charleton (1620–1707), "Virtuoso": Leben und Werk*. Frankfurt am Main: Peter Lang, 1986.

Fouke, Daniel C. *The Enthusiastical Concerns of Dr. Henry More: Religious Meaning and the Psychology of Delusion*. Leiden: Brill, 1997.

Funkenstein, Amos. *Theology and the Scientific Imagination from the Middle Ages to the Seventeenth Century*. Princeton, N.J.: Princeton University Press, 1986.

Garrett, Don. *The Cambridge Companion to Spinoza*. Cambridge: Cambridge University Press, 1996.

Gjertsen, Derek. *The Newton Handbook*. London: Routledge, 1986.

Gouhier, Henri. *La vocation de Malebranche*. Paris: Vrin, 1926.

———. *La philosophie de Malebranche et son expérience religieuse*. Paris: Vrin, 1926 [2nd ed. 1947].

———. *Pascal: Commentaires*. Paris: Vrin, 1966 [3rd ed. 1978].

———. *Blaise Pascal: Conversation et Apologétique*. Paris: Vrin, 1986.

Grant, Edward. *Much Ado About Nothing: Theories of Space and Vacuum from the Middle Ages to the Scientific Revolution*. Cambridge: Cambridge University Press, 1981.

Gregory, Tullio. *Scetticismo ed empirismo: Studio su Gassendi*. Bari: Laterza, 1961.

————. "Studi sull'atomismo del seicento. I. Sebastiano Basson." *Giornale critico della filosofia italiana* 43 (1964): 38–65.

————. "Studi sull'atomismo del seicento. II. David van Goorle e Daniel Sennert." *Giornale critico della filosofia italiana* 45 (1966): 44–63.

————. "Studi sull'atomismo del seicento. III. Cudworth e l'atomismo." *Giornale critico della filosofia italiana* 46 (1967): 528–41.

Grene, Marjorie. "Aristotelico-Cartesian Themes in Natural Philosophy: Some Seventeenth-Century Cases." *Perspectives on Science* 1 (1993): 66–87.

Grisard, J. *François Viète, mathématicien de la fin du seizième siècle: Essai bio-bibliographique présenté en vue de l'obtention du doctorat de troisième cycle.* Paris: École Pratique des Hautes Études, VIème section, 1976.

Gueroult, Martial. *Malebranche* (3 vols.). Paris: Aubier, 1955–59.

————. *Leibniz: Dynamique et métaphysique.* Paris: Aubier, 1967.

————. *Spinoza* (2 vols.). Paris: Aubier, 1968–74.

Hall, A. Rupert. *Henry More and the Scientific Revolution.* Cambridge: Cambridge University Press, 1990.

————. *Henry More: Magic, Religion and Experiment* (Blackwell Science Biographies). Oxford: Blackwell, 1990.

Harth, E. *Cartesian Women: Versions and Subversions of Rational Discourse in the Old Regime.* Ithaca, N.Y.: Cornell University Press, 1992.

Heilbron, John L. *Electricity in the 17th and 18th Centuries: A Study of Early Modern Physics.* Berkeley: University of California Press, 1979.

Herivel, John W. *The Background to Newton's Principia.* Oxford: Oxford University Press, 1965.

Heyd, Michael. "From Rationalist Theology to Cartesian Voluntarism." *Journal of the History of Ideas* 40 (1979): 527–42.

————. *Between Orthodoxy and the Enlightenment: Robert Chouet and the Introduction of Cartesian Science in the Academy of Geneva.* The Hague: Martinus Nijhoff, 1982.

Hildesheimer, Françoise. *Le Jansenisme en France au XVIIe et XVIII siècles.* Paris: Publisud, 1991.

Hintikka, Jaako, and Unto Remes. *The Method of Analysis: Its Geometrical Origin and Its General Significance* (Boston Studies in the Philosophy of Science). Dordrecht: Reidel, 1974.

Hoffman, Joseph E. *Frans van Schooten der Jüngere* (Boethius: Texte und Abhandlungen zur Geschichte der exakten Wissenschaften). Wiesbaden, Germany: F. Steiner Verlag, 1962.

Hooykaas, R. *Religion and the Rise of Modern Science.* Edinburgh: Scottish Academic Press, 1972.

Hutton, Sarah, ed. *Henry More.* Dordrecht: Kluwer, 1990.

Jardine, Lisa. *Francis Bacon: Discovery and the Art of Discourse.* Cambridge: Cambridge University Press, 1974.

Jardine, Nicholas. *The Birth of History and Philosophy of Science: Kepler's A Defense of Tycho Against Ursus with Essays on its Provenance and Significance.* Cambridge: Cambridge University Press, 1984.

Jesseph, Douglas M. "Philosophical Theory and Mathematical Practice in the Seventeenth Century." *Studies in History and Philosophy of Science* 20 (1989): 215–44.

———. *Squaring the Circle: The War between Hobbes and Wallis.* Chicago: University of Chicago Press, 1999.

Jolley, Nicholas. *The Cambridge Companion to Leibniz.* Cambridge: Cambridge University Press, 1995.

Jones, Howard. *Pierre Gassendi, 1592–1655: An Intellectual Biography.* Nieuwkoop: De Graaf, 1981.

Joy, Lynn. *Gassendi the Atomist: Advocate of History in an Age of Science* (Ideas in Context). Cambridge: Cambridge University Press, 1987.

Kargon, Robert H. *Atomism in England from Hariot to Newton.* Oxford: Oxford University Press, 1966.

Koyré, Alexandre. *From the Closed World to the Infinite Universe.* New York: Harper, 1957.

———. *Etudes galiléennes,* 2nd ed. Paris: Hermann, 1966.

———. *Newtonian Studies.* Chicago: University of Chicago Press, 1968.

———. *Galileo Studies.* Atlantic Highlands, N.J.: Humanities Press, 1978.

Krailsheimer, A. J. *Pascal.* Oxford: Oxford University Press, 1980.

Kubbinga, H. H. "Les premières théories 'moléculaires': Isaac Beeckman (1620) et Sébastien Basson (1621)." *Revue d'Histoire des Sciences et de leurs applications* 37 (1984): 215–33.

Labrousse, Elisabeth. *Pierre Bayle* (2 vols.). The Hague: Nijhoff, 1963–64.

———. *Bayle* (Past Masters). Oxford: Oxford University Press, 1983.

Larmore, Charles. "Newton's Critique of Cartesian Method." *Graduate Faculty Philosophy Journal* 12 (1987): 81–09.

Lasswitz, Kurd. *Geschichte der Atomistik vom Mittelalter bis Newton* (2 vols.). Hamburg: L. Voss, 1890.

Lattis, James M. *Between Copernicus and Galileo: Christoph Clavius and the Collapse of Ptolemaic Cosmology.* Chicago: University of Chicago Press, 1994.

Lattre, Alain de. *L'Occasionalisme d'Arnold Geulincx: Etude sur la constitution de la doctrine.* Paris: Editions de Minuit, 1967.

Laudan, Laurens. "The Clock Metaphor and Probabilism: The Impact of Descartes on English Methodological Thought, 1650–1665." *Annals of Science* 22 (1966): 73–104.

Lemaire, P. *Le cartésianisme chez les bénédictins: Dom Robert Desgabets, son système, son influence et son école.* Paris: Alcan, 1901.

Lennon, Thomas M. "Jansenism and the *Crise Pyrrhonienne.*" *Journal of the History of Ideas* 38 (1977): 297–306.
———. "The Leibnizian Picture of Descartes." In *Nature Mathematized*, edited by W. R. Shea, 215–26. Dordrecht: Reidel, 1983.
Lennon, Thomas M., and Patricia Ann Easton. *The Cartesian Empiricism of François Bayle*. New York: Garland, 1992.
Lenoble, Robert. *Mersenne ou la naissance du mecanisme*, 2nd ed. Paris: Vrin, 1971 [first published in 1943].
Lukens, David C. *An Aristotelian Response to Galileo: Honoré Fabri, S.J. (1608–1688), on the Causal Analysis of Motion*. Ph.D. diss., University of Toronto, 1979.
Lüthy, Christoph. "Thoughts and Circumstances of Sébastien Basson, Analysis, Micro-History, Questions." *Early Science and Medicine* 2 (1997): 1–73.
Lux, David S. *Patronage and Royal Science in Seventeenth-Century France*. Ithaca, N.Y.: Cornell University Press, 1989.
Machamer, P. *The Cambridge Companion to Galileo*. Cambridge: Cambridge University Press, 1998.
Madden, Edward H., ed. *Theories of Scientific Method: The Renaissance Through the Nineteenth Century*. Seattle: University of Washington Press, 1960.
Maddison, R. E. W. *The Life of the Honourable Robert Boyle, F.R.S.* London: Taylor and Francis, 1969.
Mahoney, Michael S. *The Mathematical Career of Pierre de Fermat*. 2nd rev. ed. Princeton, N.J.: Princeton University Press, 1994 [1st ed., Princeton, 1973].
Malbreil, Germain. "Descartes censuré par Huet." *Revue Philosophique* 3 (1991): 311–28.
Marion, J.-L. "De la création des vérités éternelles au principe de raison suffisante: Remarques sur l'anti-cartésianisme de Spinoza, Malebranche et Leibniz." *XVIIe siècle* 147 (1985): 143–64.
Martin, H.-J. *Livre, Pouvoirs et Société à Paris au XVIIe siècle (1598–1701)* (2 vols.). Geneva: Droz, 1969.
McClaughlin, Trevor. "Censorship and Defenders of the Cartesian Faith in Mid-Seventeenth Century France." *Journal of the History of Ideas* 40 (1979): 563–81.
McCracken, Charles J. "Stages on a Cartesian Road to Immaterialism." *Journal of the History of Philosophy* 24 (1986): 19–40.
McMullin, Ernan, ed. *The Concept of Matter in Modern Philosophy*. Notre Dame, Ind.: University of Notre Dame Press, 1978.
Meinel, Christoph. "Early Seventeenth-Century Atomism: Theory, Epistemology and the Insufficiency of Experiment." *Isis* 79 (1988): 68–103.

———. "Empirical Support for the Corpuscular Theory in the Seventeenth Century." In *Theory and Experiment*, edited by D. Batens and J. P. van Bendegem, 77–92. Dordrecht: Reidel, 1988.

Mercer, Christia. *Leibniz's Metaphysics: Its Origins and Development.* Cambridge: Cambridge University Press, 2001.

Nadler, Steven. "Cartesianism and Port-Royal." *Monist* 71 (1988): 573–84.

———. *Arnauld and the Cartesian Philosophy of Ideas.* Princeton, N.J.: Princeton University Press, 1989.

———. *Malebranche and Ideas.* Oxford: Oxford University Press, 1992.

———. *Spinoza: A Life.* Cambridge: Cambridge University Press, 1999.

———. *The Cambridge Companion to Malebranche.* Cambridge: Cambridge University Press, 2000.

Nielsen, Lauge Olaf. "A 17th-Century Physician on God and Atoms: Sebastian Basso." In *Meaning and Inference in Medieval Philosophy: Studies in Memory of Jan Pinborg*, edited by N. Kretzmann, 297–369. Dordrecht: Kluwer, 1988.

Peltonen, Markku, ed. *The Cambridge Companion to Bacon.* Cambridge: Cambridge University Press, 1996.

Pérez-Ramos, Antonio. *Francis Bacon's Idea of Science and the Maker's Knowledge Tradition.* Oxford: Oxford University Press, 1988.

Pintard, René. *Le Libertinage érudit dans la première moitié du XVIIe siècle.* Paris: Boivin, 1943 [repr. Geneva: Slatkine, 1983].

Plantinga, Alvin, ed. *The Ontological Argument.* London: Macmillan, 1968.

Popkin, Richard H. "The Religious Background of Seventeenth-Century Philosophy." *Journal of the History of Philosophy* 25 (1987): 35–50.

Prost, J. *Essai sur l'atomisme et l'occasionalisme dans la philosophie cartésienne.* Paris: Paulin, 1907.

Radner, Daisie. *Malebranche: A Study of a Cartesian System.* Assen: Van Gorcum, 1978.

Redondi, P. *Galileo Heretic.* Princeton, N.J.: Princeton University Press, 1987.

Rochemonteix, Camille de. *Un collège des Jesuites au XIIe et XIIIe siècle: le collège Henri IV de la Flèche.* Le Mans, 1889.

Rodis-Lewis, Geneviève. *Le problème de l'inconscient et le cartésianisme.* Paris: Presses Universitaires de France, 1950.

———. *Nicolas Malebranche.* Paris: Presses Universitaires de France, 1963.

Rosenfield, Leonora Cohen. "Peripatetic Adversaries of Cartesianism in 17th-Century France." *Review of Religion* 22 (1957): 14–40.

Ross, G. MacDonald. "Occultism and Philosophy in the Seventeenth Century." In *Philosophy, Its History and Historiography*, edited by A. J. Holland. Dordrecht: Reidel, 1985.

Ruestow, Edward G. *Physics at Seventeenth and Eighteenth Century Leiden: Philosophy and the New Science in the University* (International Archives of the History of Ideas, 11). The Hague: Nijhoff, 1973.

Rutherford, D. *Leibniz and the Rational Order of Nature.* Cambridge: Cambridge University Press, 1995.

Sargent, Rose-Mary. *The Diffident Naturalist: Robert Boyle and the Philosophy of Experiment.* Chicago: University of Chicago Press, 1995.

Schmaltz, Tad M. "Descartes and Malebranche on Mind and Mind-Body Union." *Philosophical Review* 101 (1992): 281–325.

———. *Malebranche's Theory of the Soul: A Cartesian Interpretation.* Oxford: Oxford University Press, 1996.

———. "Spinoza on the Vacuum." *Archiv für Geschichte der Philosophie* 81 (1999): 174–205.

———. "What Has Cartesianism to Do with Jansenism?" *Journal of the History of Ideas* 60 (1999): 37–56.

———. "The Disappearance of Analogy in Descartes, Spinoza, and Regis." *Canadian Journal of Philosophy* 30 (2000): 85–114.

———. "The Cartesian Refutation of Idealism." *British Journal for the History of Philosophy* 10 (2002): 1–28.

———. *Radical Cartesianism: The French Reception of Descartes.* Cambridge: Cambridge University Press, 2000.

Schmitt, Charles B. *Aristotle and the Renaissance.* Cambridge, Mass.: Harvard University Press, 1983.

Schmitt, C. B., Q. Skinner, and E. Kessler, eds. *Cambridge History of Renaissance Philosophy.* Cambridge: Cambridge University Press, 1988.

Shapiro, Barbara J. *Probability and Certainty in Seventeenth-Century England; A Study of the Relationships between Natural Science, Religion, History, Law, and Literature.* Princeton, N.J.: Princeton University Press, 1983.

Sleigh, R. C. *Leibniz and Arnauld: A Commentary on Their Correspondence.* New Haven, Conn.: Yale University Press, 1990.

Sorell, Tom, ed. *The Cambridge Companion to Hobbes.* Cambridge: Cambridge University Press, 1996.

Sortais, Gaston. *Le cartésianisme chez les Jésuites français au 17e et 18e siècles* (*Archives de philosophie*, vol. 6, no. 3). Paris: Beauchesne, 1928–29.

Stolpe, Sven. *Christina of Sweden.* New York: Macmillan, 1966.

Sutton, Geoffrey V. *Science for a Polite Society: Gender, Culture, and the Demonstration of Enlightenment.* Boulder, Colo.: Westview Press, 1995.

Taton, René. *Les origines de l'Académie royale des sciences.* Paris: Palais de la Découverte, 1965.

Thijssen-Schoute, C. Louise. *Nederlands Cartesianisme*. Amsterdam: North Holland, 1954.

Vailati, E. *Leibniz and Clarke: A Study of Their Correspondence*. Oxford: Oxford University Press, 1997.

Verbeek, Theo. "Regius's *Fundamenta Physices*." *Journal of the History of Ideas* 55 (1994): 533–51.

———. *Johannes Clauberg (1622–1665) and Cartesian Philosophy in the Seventeenth Century*. Dordrecht: Kluwer, 1999.

———. *Spinoza's Theologico-political Treatise: Exploring the "Will of God."* London: Ashgate, 2003.

Waithe, M. E., ed. *Modern Women Philosophers, 1600–1900* (A History of Women Philosophers). Dordrecht: Kluwer, 1991.

Wallace, William A. *Causality and Scientific Explanation* (2 vols.). Ann Arbor: University of Michigan Press, 1972–74.

———. *Galileo and His Sources: The Heritage of the Collegio Romano in Galileo's Science*. Princeton, N. J.: Princeton University Press, 1984.

Ward, Richard. *The Life of the Learned and Pious Dr. Henry More*. London: Theosophical Society, 1911.

Watson, Richard A. *The Downfall of Cartesianism 1673–1712* (International Archives of the History of Ideas, 2). The Hague: Nijhoff, 1966.

———. *The Breakdown of Cartesian Metaphysics*. Atlantic Highlands, N.J.: Humanities Press, 1987.

Weier, Winfried. "Der Okkasionalismus des Johannes Clauberg und sein Verhältnis zu Descartes, Geulincx, Malebranche." *Studia Cartesiana* 2 (1981): 43–62.

Westfall, Richard S. *The Construction of Modern Science: Mechanisms and Mechanics*. New York: John Wiley, 1971.

———. *Never at Rest, A Biography of Isaac Newton*. Cambridge: Cambridge University Press, 1980.

Whitmore, P. J. S. *The Order of the Minims in Seventeenth-Century France* (International Archives of the History of Ideas). The Hague: Nijhoff, 1967.

Wolfson, Harry A. *The Philosophy of Spinoza* (2 vols.). Cambridge, Mass.: Harvard University Press, 1934.

Yates, Frances. *Giordano Bruno and the Hermetic Tradition*. Chicago: University of Chicago Press, 1964.

About the Authors

Roger Ariew (Ph. D., University of Illinois at Urbana-Champaign) is professor of philosophy at Virginia Polytechnic Institute and State University. He is the author of *Descartes and the Last Scholastics* and the editor, with Marjorie Grene, of *Descartes and His Contemporaries*, and, with Daniel Garber, of the 10-volume reprint collection, *Descartes in Seventeenth-Century England*. He is also the editor and translator of *Descartes: Philosophical Essays and Correspondence*, of *Leibniz: Philosophical Essays*, with Daniel Garber, and, of *Background Source Materials: Descartes' Meditations*, with John Cottingham and Tom Sorell. Ariew's research has been supported by a fellowship from the National Endowment for the Humanities (NEH), an independent federal agency.

Dennis Des Chene (Ph. D., Stanford University) is associate professor of philosophy at Emory University. He is the author of *Physiologia: Philosophy of Nature in Descartes and the Aristotelians*; *Life's Form, Late Aristotelian Conceptions of the Soul*; and *Spirits and Clocks: Machine and Organism in Descartes*.

Douglas M. Jesseph (Ph. D., Princeton University) is professor of philosophy at North Carolina State University. He is the author of *Squaring the Circle: The War between Hobbes and· Wallis* and *Berkeley's Philosophy of Mathematics*. He is the editor and translator of Berkeley's *De Motu* and *The Analyst* and the editor of the forthcoming three-volume *Hobbes's Mathematical Works*.

Tad M. Schmaltz (Ph. D., University of Notre Dame) is associate professor of philosophy at Duke University. He is the author of *Malebranche's Theory of the Soul: A Cartesian Interpretation* and *Radical Cartesianism: The French Reception of Descartes*.

Theo Verbeek (Ph. D., University of Utrecht) is professor of philosophy at the University of Utrecht. He is the author of *La querelle d'Utrecht*; *Descartes and the Dutch: Early Reactions to Cartesianism (1637–1650)*; and *Spinoza's Theologico-political Treatise: Exploring the "Will of God."* He is the editor of *Descartes et Regius: Autour de l'explication de l'esprit* and *Johannes Clauberg (1622–1665) and Cartesian Philosophy in the Seventeenth Century*.

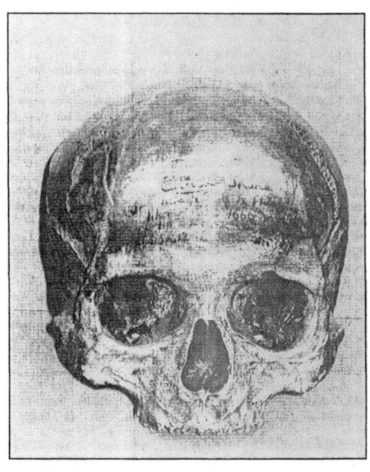

*Skull on display at the Musée de l'Homme, Paris,
alleged to be Descartes's*